RAILROADS IN THE MIDWEST

HEARTLAND HISTORY

Jon K. Lauck

H. ROGER GRANT

RAILROADS IN THE MIDWEST

AN EPIC HISTORY

INDIANA UNIVERSITY PRESS

This book is a publication of

INDIANA UNIVERSITY PRESS
Office of Scholarly Publishing
Herman B Wells Library 350
1320 East 10th Street
Bloomington, Indiana 47405 USA

iupress.org

First Printing 2025

Cataloging information is available from the Library of Congress.

ISBN 978-0-253-07365-5 (hdbk.)
ISBN 978-0-253-07368-6 (pbk.)
ISBN 978-0-253-07367-9 (ebook)
ISBN 978-0-253-07366-2 (web PDF)

For my daughter Julia Dinsmore Grant

A California transplant, but still a midwesterner at heart

PUBLISHER'S NOTE

Indiana University Press was pleased and privileged to work with H. Roger Grant for fifteen years, both as an author and as the coeditor of the Railroads Past and Present series. His enthusiasm and professionalism were evident in all his work.

Sadly, Roger passed away only two days after submitting his final manuscript to the press. The press wishes to thank Carlos Schwantes for agreeing to review the copyediting of Railroads in the Midwest *in Roger's stead.*

CONTENTS

PREFACE

WHERE IS THE MIDWEST? ALTHOUGH THIS QUESTION MIGHT seem easy to answer, debate persists about its precise location. Is it the Corn Belt? Yes and no. If it is, these states include Michigan, Ohio, Indiana, Illinois, Wisconsin, Minnesota, Iowa, Missouri, North Dakota, South Dakota, Nebraska, and Kansas. This is how historian Lewis Atherton defines the region in his classic 1954 book, *Main Street on the Middle Border.* Forty years later geographer John Hudson embraces this same area in his *Making the Corn Belt: A Geographical History of Middle-Western Agriculture.* The US Census Bureau also uses this grouping, deeming these twelve states as one of its four core population divisions. Yet I do not consider the four Great Plains states "midwestern," accepting the arguments made by historian Walter Prescott Webb in his thought-provoking *The Great Plains: A Study in Institutions and Environment,* published in 1931. "The Great Plains environment constitutes a geographic unity whose influences have been so powerful as to put a characteristic mark upon everything that survives within its borders," concludes Webb. Much of this vast region, especially west of the 98th meridian, was once described as the "Great American Desert." Other scholars endorse the eight-state definition, including Andrew Cayton, Walter Havighurst, Howard Odum, Peter Onuf, and John Stover. I used these same states in my book *Twilight Rails: The Final Era of Railroad Building in the Midwest* (University of Minnesota Press, 2010). At times writers have been vague about how they describe this part of the country, failing to provide exact definitions or exact geographic delineations for "American Heartland,"

"Midwest," "Midlands," "Midsection," "Great Plains," or any other label attached to this "flyover" section.

This work focuses on those political entities that stretch west from roughly the Appalachian Mountains to the Missouri River, south to the Ohio River, and north to the Great Lakes. Cincinnati, Cleveland, Detroit, Chicago, Council Bluffs, Milwaukee, Minneapolis–St. Paul, St. Louis, and Kansas City developed into the principal railroad nodes of America's midsection. As with all parts of the nation, the Midwest also has subregions. The lower-tier areas of Ohio, Indiana, and Illinois, for example, possess southern characteristics, but they have not been excluded from this regional railroad study.

The national heartland developed an impressive railroad network. By the 1920s steam roads operating in my geographical definition sported nearly seventy thousand route miles, representing more than 35 percent of the country's rail mileage. This figure consisted of every type of carrier, ranging from tiny shortlines to sprawling trunk roads. In *Rails across the Midlands* (1964), Richard J. Cook commented, "The Midlands—The Industrial heartland of America. Perhaps of all the regions of the United States, here can be found the greatest variety of railroading—heavy traffic trunk lines, fast freight bridge routes, tonnage arteries from mine to dock. And there are the shortlines." Rivals Chicago and St. Louis served as America's two premier rail hubs, and Iowa and Ohio had the highest line densities. Immediately prior to World War I, a local railroad official bragged that the Hawkeye State had a depot and agent located no farther than thirteen miles from any point within its borders. Surprising? Perhaps not. While Iowa has an unquestionable claim to the title of the most midwestern of states, it would be the Buckeye State that claimed more miles of railroad per square mile than any other midwestern state.

Multiple factors produced an imposing rail network. There was a rapidly increasing population that spiked after the Civil War. Federal censuses revealed that in 1860 the eight states had a combined population of 8,956,732, and by 1920 that figure had soared to 29,670,744. A favorable topography contributed to railroad expansion. Unlike mountainous, arid, or swampy regions, the geography of the Midwest offered fewer obstacles to railroad building; major river crossings posed the greatest challenges. The foremost example was the pricey Eads Bridge, which spanned the Mississippi River between East St. Louis, Illinois, and St. Louis and was completed in 1874; this bridge represents one of the foremost engineering and construction triumphs of the nineteenth century. This region, moreover, expanded its commercial agriculture; created extensive manufacturing, wholesaling, and retailing enterprises; and established varied mining and lumbering operations. These developments, together with population growth, resulted in booming freight, passenger, express, and mail traffic.

When it came to the electric interurban railway phenomenon, which burst upon the American scene near the close of the nineteenth century but collapsed during the post–World War I era, the Midwest became its epicenter in terms of mileage and number of companies. At the height of the Interurban Era in 1916, Ohio and Indiana led the nation with a combined total of approximately five thousand route miles, thereby operating nearly a third of all intercity "juice" lines. These two states were home to more than eighty carriers. The industry faltered before extensive corporate consolidations occurred and various urban freight beltways and other improvements could be constructed.

Although the Midwest did not have the country's first steam railroad prototypes—Maryland, South Carolina, and New York earned that honor—the iron horse appeared early on in what evolved rapidly into the more-than-century-long Railway Age. The midwestern region, however, can lay claim to the first electric interurban, one that sprouted forth in central Ohio. Whether steam or electric, this region enthusiastically embraced wheels-on-rails transportation.

Before the dominance of motorized vehicles—automobiles, buses, and trucks—and an expanding network of all-weather roads, steam railroads bound the Midwest to national and international markets. Even though railroad enterprises struggled initially, they expanded dramatically after the 1850s. Whether shippers or travelers, the burgeoning population benefited from reduced costs, increased speeds, and improved efficiencies. In time, though, complaints erupted about freight and passenger rates and service. Significantly, the first major response nationally to what citizens referred to as acts of "corporate arrogance" took place in the four Upper Mississippi River valley states of Illinois, Iowa,

Minnesota, and Wisconsin—the Granger movement of the 1870s. These same political units, led by Wisconsin and Iowa, participated in the progressive movement, a monumental housecleaning crusade that covered most of the country between the late 1890s and World War I. For carriers this meant local, state, and most of all federal regulation. These statutes and their implementation led to a long-lasting "enterprise denied" for the railroad industry.

By the 1930s the glory years for railroads in the Midwest had diminished. Excessive controls by the Interstate Commerce Commission (ICC) and modal competition from automobiles, barges, buses, pipelines, and trucks took their toll. The Great Depression likewise hurt carriers; company after company slipped into receivership. Yet when America entered World War II, railroads between 1941 and 1945 experienced their finest hour. Country depots and urban stations throughout the region were crowded with troops and civilians, and all trackage, whether mainlines or branches, experienced heavy volumes of traffic. The war resulted in most company bankruptcies ending and profits generated being paid out in dividends, earmarked for improvements, and stashed away as rainy-day funds.

Following the war midwestern carriers enjoyed an Indian summer, and optimism reigned. Betterments included widespread and cost-saving dieselization of motive power, upgraded streamliners, and new and remodeled stations. Summer turned into fall, winter, and then spring. By the 1950s every railroad, irrespective of location, encountered greater road competition, highlighted by state-sponsored turnpikes and thousands of miles of divided highways made possible by the Interstate Highway Act of 1956. Increased commercial airline operations, aided by the introduction of jet airliners in the late 1950s, captured a rapidly growing share of the long-distance passenger business. Outmoded labor agreements and harsh regulation hardly contributed to healthy balance sheets. Mergers, which began in earnest in the 1960s, helped financially, as did the creation of the National Railroad Passenger Corporation (Amtrak), launched in 1971, relieving nearly all of the remaining passenger-carrying roads of this money-losing burden. It would be the Staggers Act of 1980 that became the game changer for freight roads. This renaissance measure allowed substantial freedom in rate-making by reducing the power of the ICC. Railroads in the region and elsewhere would look much different in the twenty-first century—slimmed down in network size and exhibiting progressive policies. By now the Midwest had the services of the remaining Class I roads and an abundance of recently launched shortline and regional carriers.

This study rests on more than fifty years of reading, researching, and writing about railroads in the Midwest. The endnotes attest to my extensive work on both steam and electric carriers in these eight states. I believe that a regional approach to railroad history makes sense. In the mid-1970s, American geographer Donald Meinig made this astute assertion: "The regional concept has been too readily dismissed as a crude tool, whereas it is really a basic tool that has been used crudely." In 2022, historian Jon Lauck in his *The Good Country: A History of the American Midwest, 1800–1900* lamented that "the American Midwest [is] the most historically neglected region in the United States." He and other academics anticipate that the *Middle West Review,* launched in 2014, will enhance a better understanding of this "lost region."

This examination of midwestern railroads is not intended to be encyclopedic; it is impossible to be all-inclusive. In this case Indiana University Press has imposed a maximum limit of one hundred thousand words. Also, the approximately fifty illustrations cannot do justice to the visual complexities of midwestern railroading, but they offer varied glimpses into the past. More importantly, readers should keep in mind that this is an amazing region, contributing to multiple innovations and improvements and serving a constantly changing service territory. If one is to understand American railroad history, it is essential to consider what occurred in the Midwest. Hopefully, this study provides a good sense of the region's complicated and at times pathbreaking railroad heritage.

ACKNOWLEDGMENTS

ACKNOWLEDGMENTS ARE ALWAYS APPROPRIATE. DIFFERING from most of my previous books, I have with this study fewer institutions and individuals to thank. I remain indebted to the Information Sharing Office (formerly the Inter-library Loan Department) of the Robert Muldrow Cooper Library at Clemson University. Staff members worked diligently to locate multiple books and articles, including several that were difficult to obtain. The Center for Railroad Photography and Art in Madison, Wisconsin, especially Scott Lothes and Erin Rose, assisted with illustrations, as did Art Peterson, who manages the Krambles-Peterson Archive. These individuals also need to be recognized: Nick Fry, Ron Goldfeder, Tom Hoback, Don Hofsommer, Kevin Keefe, Ray Lichty, John Rebensdorf, Pete Rickershauser, Ed Robinson, Jim Rueber, Dan Sabin, Carlos Schwantes, and Ben Sill. Since 2006 I have been the beneficiary of the Kathryn and Calhoun Lemon Professor of History. This financial support has made my research and related expenses less of a financial burden.

H. Roger Grant
Clemson University
Clemson, South Carolina

RAILROADS IN THE MIDWEST

ONE

CREATION

1835–1860

SETTINGS

As the eighteenth century closed, the American West—especially the area located between the Great Lakes on the north, the Ohio River on the south, and the Mississippi River on the west—emerged in the minds of countless citizens as a land of milk and honey, the proverbial promised land. Following the Revolutionary War, thousands of Euro-American settlers discovered that its eastern sections offered much: fertile soil, abundant timber, a moderate and reasonably predictable climate, and ample rainfall. These features together with relatively cheap land, including blocks that were free to veterans of the Revolution, drew agriculturalists to the trans-Appalachian West. This led to the rapid development of the Northwest Territory, created by the federal Ordinance of 1787. This new political division further increased its attractiveness after victorious wars against indigenous tribes between 1790 and 1795 and continuing government efforts at their removal.

As the nineteenth century evolved, the Northwest Territory (Old Northwest became its popular name) grew as a favored destination for settlement. A large influx of settlers from the original states, the British Isles, and northern Europe took up residence, especially after the War of 1812. Most of all the populations of Ohio and Indiana soared, increasing in the former from 231,000 in 1810 to 581,000 a decade later and in the latter from 25,000 to 147,000 during this period. The country's head count likewise surged, nearly doubling in twenty years from 7.2 million in 1810 to 12.8 million by 1830. And that pace generally continued.[1]

How could these pioneers reach the Old Northwest and cope with the tyranny of distance? Although there existed primitive roadways into the sprawling region in what became the states of Ohio (1803), Indiana (1816), Illinois (1818), Michigan (1837), and Wisconsin (1848), waterways usually provided easier access. For decades, the Ohio River served as the great avenue to the West. The Great Lakes also enabled access. Initially, Lake Erie was the most widely used. Yet these principal water routes took settlers largely around the borders of the Old Northwest, although both the river and the lakes retained their status as arteries of commerce long beyond the frontier period. Some settlers attempted to navigate the primitive roads with their horses, carts, and wagons. Not to be missed in the process of migration was walking, or what contemporaries called "ankle wagons." Just as Indians walked great distances, intrepid frontiersmen and settlers later did so as well.[2]

Residents of Ohio, Indiana, and Illinois realized that roads and natural waterways required augmentation. Each had limitations. Roadways frequently become impassable during wet periods, mainly following the spring snowmelt and accompanying rains. No wonder this seasonal exaggeration: "Roads were as deep as they were wide." There was also this concise observation made about Indiana's roads in the 1830s: "They are intolerable in summer and impassable in winter." Most of these early roadways were narrow, being glorified animal or Indian trails or hastily fashioned by the US Army during Indian conflicts and the War of 1812. The military needed to serve its widely scattered frontier forts. At times virtually every road was difficult or nearly impossible to negotiate, except perhaps by horseback. If they were passable, speeds were painfully slow and travels uncomfortable. Even a team of oxen could encounter mobility limitations. A mid-nineteenth-century settler remarked caustically about his midwestern trips, "The springless lumber wagon with a board for a seat was great for indigestion." When it came to public roadways, the federally financed National Road, "the Grand Portage of America," emerged as the leading land route to the West and also the avenue to herd livestock, mostly cattle and hogs, to eastern markets. Although first proposed in 1808 by US secretary of the treasury Albert Gallatin, the

National Road emerged slowly. At last this more than six hundred miles of largely improved roadway began in Maryland in 1811, reached the Ohio River in 1817, entered Columbus, Ohio, in 1833 and Indianapolis, Indiana, somewhat later, and headed westward toward St. Louis, Missouri, with an Illinois branch from Vandalia to Alton. Only limited construction of the "Pike" occurred beyond Terre Haute, Indiana, extending into the vicinity of Vandalia, the initial Prairie State capital. The principal explanations were that congressional funding ended in 1838, and much of the area's settlement in Illinois and Indiana had already taken place before the road's arrival. The "completed" western portions of the National Road remained studded with tree stumps and chuckholes.[3]

Interior rivers, the myriad of tributaries of the vast Mississippi-Ohio drainage system, generally had less value as transportation arteries. The ones in Ohio lacked depth and were relatively short. This explains why the state during the late 1830s and early 1840s financed improvements to much of the 111-mile Muskingum River to allow sustained steamboat usage. In Indiana the major exception was the Wabash River below Lafayette. Illinois had the serviceable Illinois River to its rapids near La Salle. Steamboats could travel the 210 miles from its mouth to Peru, and at high water they could go an additional eighteen miles. Michigan and Wisconsin mostly came up lacking. The Kalamazoo River in western Michigan provided modest access from Lake Michigan into the interior. The Wisconsin River, which flowed into the Mississippi, offered better transportation opportunities, as did the Fox River, a stream that emptied into Lake Michigan. Shifting sandbars caused navigation challenges on both streams, but swirling rapids and shallow portions further hindered travel on the Fox. When settlements began in the trans-Mississippi West, Minnesota benefited from the Upper Mississippi and Minnesota Rivers, while Iowa found the Des Moines and Iowa Rivers of some value. The former had a series of rapids near its mouth on the Mississippi near Keokuk, and some steam navigation occurred as far inland as Des Moines but rarely farther northwestward to Fort Dodge. There were steamboats plying portions of the Iowa River. Missouri boasted the lengthy Missouri River. The "Big Muddy" had drawbacks, ranging from snags and sawyers to its habit of annually changing course. All rivers hindered transport due to high and low water levels and extensive freezing and ice flows during the winter and early spring. "Rivers are ungovernable Things," as Benjamin Franklin astutely observed.[4]

The Great Lakes offered less dramatic changes. This massive water complex, which stretched approximately 1,500 miles from east to west and was the largest continuous fresh water body in the world, remained generally stable with its water depths. Yet there was this notable choke point: when water levels were low on the Lake St. Clair Flats, traffic between Lake Huron and Lake Erie was slowed or interrupted. Resembling most rivers, these lakes frequently froze over or largely so during the winter months. When open waters returned, vessels were susceptible to violent storms, not uncommonly sinking them and causing injuries and drownings. The value of these waterways increased, however. Improvements to deepwater transport came with the completion of the Welland Canal between Lake Ontario and Lake Erie in 1829 (rebuilt in 1848) and the St. Mary's Falls Ship Canal or Sault Canal, opened in 1855, which connected the lower lakes with Lake Superior. Before midcentury and later as well, the federal government financed lighthouse construction and harbor betterments. But this lament about the Great Lakes remained: midwestern rivers, with few exceptions, flowed away from the lakes and not toward them.[5]

CANALS

How could transportation be upgraded? While the network of roads gradually improved, and the Great Lakes were made safer but never tamed, artificial waterways—canals—offered attractive possibilities. For the growing population in the Old Northwest, they seemed to be the solution to long-distance transportation problems. Significantly, canals afforded a better alternative to turnpikes, which had been popular in the more densely settled East. Constructing "ditches" to enhance the value of river and lake travel did not represent a new technology. The concept dated back to ancient Egypt and the Grand Canal (Jing-Hang Canal) in premodern China. It was the Erie Canal, which linked the Hudson River with Lake Erie, that served as the harbinger of a canal craze. This 363-mile state-sponsored "artificial river," begun in 1818 and completed in 1825, inspired other states of the Old Northwest to follow suit. The principal reason was that the Erie Canal worked well for both freight and passenger traffic and developed quickly into a money machine for the State of New York. It was the canal that made America, reflected one commentator.

In the Old Northwest, Ohio led the way in canal construction with more than eight hundred miles. The Ohio & Erie Canal (or simply the Ohio Canal) became the state's premier interior waterway. Construction of this 308-mile publicly financed project, which started in 1825, continued until its grand opening in 1832. As its name implied, the canal connected West Portsmouth on the Ohio River with Cleveland, the busiest port on Lake Erie, and served Chillicothe, Circleville, Newark, Zanesville, Massillon, and Akron. The canal also forged a convenient water route between the Atlantic Seaboard and the Ohio River valley. No longer would people in its service territory be hindered by the limitations of navigable rivers. In time residents of the Buckeye State gained access to a second trans-state canal. This was the Miami & Erie Canal (Miami Canal), which opened in 1845. It tied Cincinnati with Dayton, Troy, Defiance, Junction (where Indiana's Wabash & Erie Canal would connect), and Toledo, creating a 274-mile waterway. Furthermore, Ohioans benefited from multiple "lateral" or "feeder" canals to its two principal arteries, including the Hocking Canal (Ohio Canal to Athens), the Walhonding Canal (Ohio Canal to Brinkhaven), the Sandy & Beaver Canal (Ohio Canal at Bolivar to the Ohio River), and the Pennsylvania & Ohio Canal (Ohio Canal at Akron to the Ohio River). There were also two short Ohio Canal feeders, one to Granville and a more important one to Columbus. Then there was the canalized Muskingum River from Dresden Junction on the Ohio Canal to Marietta. The Miami Canal had its feeders—namely, the Cincinnati & Whitewater Canal between Cincinnati and Lawrenceburg, Indiana, the Warren County Canal between Middleton and Lebanon, and the short Sidney or Port Jefferson Canal that linked Lockington with Port Jefferson via Sidney. The Board of Canal Commissioners sought to satisfy as many Ohioans as possible and thereby win sustained legislative support.[6]

Indiana lacked the mileage of Ohio canals, but the state boasted an impressive one. Its Wabash & Erie Canal (Wabash Canal), 460 miles long, was the longest canal in North America. The building process, which occurred from Ohio toward the Ohio River and, like most midwestern canals, was state financed, joined Toledo (via Junction, Ohio) with Fort Wayne, Lafayette, Terre Haute, and Evansville. Construction, begun in 1837, was slow; the Ohio River at Evansville was not reached until 1853. By the eve of the Civil War, however, the section below Terre Haute was virtually abandoned. The other important canal in the Hoosier State was the seventy-six-mile Whitewater Canal built between 1836 and 1846. It connected Lawrenceburg, located on the Ohio River, with Cambridge City, a town on the National Road, and a year later the Hagerstown Canal Company constructed a short extension northward to that community. Initially financed by the state and later by private investors, the Whitewater Canal struggled to survive, but like all ditches it had a favorable developmental impact on its service territory. This was especially true for the Wabash Canal. It was "the single most important development in the political and economic life of Indiana during the mid-nineteenth century," concluded canal historian Ralph Gray. The obvious exception was the Central Canal, designed to link Indianapolis with the Wabash Canal. Workers completed only nine miles, connecting the Capital City with Broad Ripple; it literally went from somewhere to nowhere in particular.[7]

Illinois showed less aggressiveness with its canal building. Still, canal fever infected area residents. For decades it was realized that there was a practical way to establish water passage between Lake Michigan and the Mississippi River. This artificial river could be dug across their watersheds, and only a glacial moraine stood as the principal obstacle between the Chicago and Illinois Rivers. The state's lone commercial project became the ninety-six-mile Illinois & Michigan Canal. Knowing the value of the Erie Canal, lawmakers in the mid-1820s created a Board of Canal Commissioners, and its members knew that an inland boat passage between New York and New Orleans could be forged. But construction did not begin until 1836. The route stretched between Chicago, a rapidly growing city on the Chicago River and Lake Michigan port, and La Salle, located near the mouth of the Little Vermillion River and the rapids of the Illinois River. Below that point this stream provided a navigable avenue to the Mississippi River north of St. Louis. Although delayed by the Panic of 1837, which triggered nearly a decade of hard times and a state financial crisis in 1843, freight and passenger boat traffic finally commenced in 1848.[8]

Michigan and Wisconsin were sparsely settled during the height of the canal-building era, but surveys and construction nevertheless occurred. In the Upper Peninsula of Michigan, the Sault Canal, which measured less than a mile long, had immediate strategic value. Internal improvement proponents in Wisconsin Territory expressed more interest in canals and plank roads (an ill-fated road improvement scheme) than in railroads, viewing them as connections to bodies of navigable water and not as cross-country arteries. Wisconsinites saw possibilities in an artificial waterway spanning the short portage between the Wisconsin and Fox Rivers. Construction began on this Fox River Canal in the late 1830s but was not completed until 1853 after the state took control from a financially strapped private company. Later it returned this betterment to private hands. Yet efforts to create a functioning waterway at this point were ultimately abandoned. Some work took place on the projected Milwaukee & Rock River Canal, but it never achieved any meaningful value.[9]

Canals offered attractions. There is no question that they improved personal travel and freight transportation, created or expanded communities, increased real-estate values, and helped break down local isolation and parochial prejudices. Although packets and freighters moved "slow and steady" (three to four miles per hour), they offered safety and smoothness and could operate around the clock. Canals corrected the natural geography, placing usable waterways where Mother Nature had failed to do so. Furthermore, canal freighters could haul significant quantities of grain, coal, and other bulk commodities, perhaps as much as fifty times more than a wagon. In certain places their waters could be tapped for hydraulic power to operate grist and flour mills and other manufacturing concerns. Canals, however, were hardly the cure-all for transportation challenges. They suffered from multiple shortcomings. They were limited by geographical features and expensive to construct, maintain, and repair (their components included locks, aqueducts, dams, culverts, weirs, and the rare tunnel). Water levels needed to be kept at a standard depth of four feet or more; disruptive leaks and breaks caused by rodents, freshets, and floods disrupted operations; and winter temperatures often froze over these ditches.

Some canals came to be viewed as nuisances or worse. One example involved a faltering canal in Ohio. In 1852 Lisbon area residents attended a public meeting to express their displeasure about their local waterway. Their report said in part, "The Sandy Creek & Beaver Canal and its Reservoirs greatly obstructed the intercourse and business of the community by obstructing roads, and by breaking or dividing our school districts, injuring farms it passes through by flooding, for which for no compensation can be obtained, said company being bankrupt, further it is a great expense to our country by causing the need to build bridges across the Canal which the company refuses to maintain." The Wabash & Erie Canal also encountered this problem: At times farmers, most of all, objected to the presence of feeder reservoirs, fearing outbreaks of deadly fevers. Vigilante groups, known as reservoir regulators, sought to drain these perceived threats to public health, and their actions caused considerable expense to the state. Various canals also had the misfortune of becoming obsolete even before they opened. Still, they played a powerful role in shaping the urban geography of the eastern Midwest.[10]

The shipping and traveling public understood that with existing transportation options there were serious limitations. The land and water transport routes were often annoyingly seasonal. Changes in precipitation and temperature affected them differently. Dry summers and cold winters benefited road travel but not river, lake, and canal transport.

THE IRON HORSE DEBUTS

From the late 1820s onward, the railroad in the United States evolved steadily and at breakneck speed. This revolutionary means for dependable, long-distance transportation, for both freight and passengers and largely unencumbered by physical barriers, did not spring from the creative minds of US citizens as did the light bulb, television set, and personal computer. Although Americans made enormous contributions in perfecting the railroad, the British during the early nineteenth century made pioneering technological breakthroughs. On September 27, 1825, the twenty-six-mile coal-carrying Stockton & Darlington Railway became recognized as the first public railroad to use a steam locomotive.[11] Under the supervision of George Stephenson and his son Robert, Locomotion No. 1 performed well on that historic day. In October 1829, their improved locomotive Rocket continued to demonstrate their mechanical brilliance when it excelled against several competitors at the famous Rainhill trials, which were conducted on the nearly completed Liverpool & Manchester Railway (L&MR). A year later the Stephensons achieved another triumph with their steam power on the L&MR, the thirty-six-mile freight and passenger carrier between Britain's major seaport and leading manufacturing center. It became the prototype of the modern railroad.[12]

In less than a generation, British residents could travel and send their goods at speeds much greater than they could with carts, canal boats, and stagecoaches. Horseback riding was likewise eclipsed. Steam-powered trains, running on wrought-iron rails, had the capability of reaching the amazing speeds of thirty-five miles per hour or more.

The exciting railroad innovations did not remain confined to Great Britain for long. "It was clear that the British had achieved great things in the way of technology," observes historian David Gwyn, "and of railways in particular. Engineers from France, Austria, Prussia, Bavaria, Russia and the United States were sent to find out more and to report back." Within a generation the friendly transfer of this technology to America that ensued revolutionized commerce and travel. The iron horse literally became the engine for economic development and improved lifestyles; canals came to be viewed as old fashioned. Americans needed this mechanical wonder for multiple reasons, including conquering and serving their vast land mass, which roads, rivers, lakes, and canals had failed to serve adequately. Individuals engaged in farming, manufacturing, and most business activities required (and demanded) dependable, all-weather transport. With water carriers (except for canals) there were constant dangers, explaining why insurance rates to cover the loss of goods were often pricey. Then there was the desire for material gain and an improved standard of living. Commercial agriculture, for example, was much more profitable than the subsistence and semisubsistence alternatives. With the latter farmers faced the choice of either largely home consumption or selling or bartering their crops, produce, and livestock locally. Based on his extensive travel in the United States, French visitor Alexis de Tocqueville made this point in his 1835 book, *Democracy in America*—namely, that railroads could satisfy the "restless temper" of its citizens. Several decades later an Iowa farmer said it well: "What a restless race is the American!" From the times of the earliest settlements, mobility became a hallmark of the American character. Increased movement helped reduce provincialism and strengthen the nation.[13]

The first practical railroads for freight and passenger commerce did not appear in the Old Northwest but rather in Maryland, South Carolina, and New York. The Baltimore & Ohio (B&O), South Carolina Canal & Railroad (SCC&R), and Mohawk & Hudson Company made their debuts in the latter part of the 1820s. Historian James Dilts has identified the B&O as "the nation's first railroad." (This trail-blazing company relied on horses, not steam, for its initial motive power.) Optimism reigned. In September 1829 the *Niles Weekly Register* observed, "Rail roads shall become (as they one day must become) as common as turnpikes in this country." It would be the SCC&R that embraced steam with its New York City–built Best Friend of Charleston. On Christmas Day 1830, this Charleston-based carrier operated the nation's first steam-powered passenger train over a short distance of track. It did not take long before its rails stretched the 136 miles from Charleston to the navigable Savannah River at Hamburg, South Carolina. At that time, the SCC&R claimed to be the longest railroad in the world under a single management. Then in New York State on August 9, 1831, the steam locomotive DeWitt Clinton puffed along with several cars over the seventeen-mile Mohawk & Hudson Railroad, establishing a convenient connection between Hudson River steamboats and freight and packet boats on the Erie Canal.[14]

In the same year as the historic Charleston trip, the first railroad in the Old Northwest received a corporate charter. On July 31, 1830, lawmakers in Michigan Territory, desperate to improve local travel and commerce and to entice settlers, awarded backers of the Pontiac & Detroit Railway authority to build a twenty-five-mile line between the two municipalities in its corporate name. A year later Michigan chartered another railroad, and Ohio and Indiana followed with their first railroads. These legal documents, designed to attract investors, granted considerable powers to private-sector enterprises. They received the right of eminent domain for their construction and tax incentives. Their stockholders also enjoyed limited liability. Not to be overlooked, lawmakers liked charters since they did not require the expenditure of public funds. The movement away from canals and the determination of how intercity rail transport would be financed had begun in the Old Northwest.[15]

Granting the legal rights to build a railroad never guaranteed that one would soon or would ever be built. There were literally thousands of "paper" railroads throughout what became the Railway Age of industry expansion, and hundreds or perhaps more were in the Midwest. In some cases much of this paper was worthless; eager backers, however, thought they were making wise investments. Michigan Territory did see its first chartered railroad take shape; it came later with the Detroit & Pontiac, the company name being reversed.

Michigan iron rails did not arrive until the latter 1830s. In April 1833 territorial lawmakers incorporated the Erie & Kalamazoo Rail Road (E&K)[16] to construct an approximately 180-mile line connecting near the mouth of the Maumee River on Lake Erie (present-day Toledo, Ohio, then called Port Lawrence) with the Kalamazoo River. The latter stream, which was practical for mostly small craft and log floats, was navigable for only approximately seventy-five miles inland from Lake Michigan. The intent of the E&K was common among railroads during this period: being feeders to waterways. "Nearly all the lines then in operation were local or isolated works," noted the federal census of 1860, "and neither in extent nor design had begun to be formed into [a] vast and connected system."[17]

Whether shortlines or somewhat longer, the belief emerged that railroads offered varied advantages. The appearance of the iron horse would mean safer transport, lower shipping and insurance costs, expanded trade territories, better military defense, improved mail service, and increased land values. For investors there existed the possibilities of advancing share prices and hopefully regular dividend income.

It would be wrong to assume that everyone wanted a railroad. This new transportation technology had its critics. Take what occurred at a board of education meeting held at Lancaster, Ohio, in 1838: "You are welcome to the use of the schoolhouse to debate all proper questions in, but such things as railroads are impossibilities and rank infidelity. There is no work of God about them." Continued the board's chair, "If God had designed that His intelligent creatures should travel at the frightful speed of 15 miles an hour by steam, He would clearly have foretold it through His holy prophets. It is the device of Satan to lead immortal souls down to hell." A strong and deeply felt statement, indeed.[18]

IMPOSSIBLE DREAMS?

Local or regional projects were not always in the minds of the initial core of railroad enthusiasts. At an amazingly early date, visionaries proposed exceptionally long-distance railroads. Likely the foremost pioneering advocate was William Redfield, who served as the first president of the American Association for the Advancement of Science. In 1829 he wrote a forty-eight-page pamphlet with a revision the following year. It featured a lengthy albeit descriptive title: *A Sketch of the Geographical Rout of the Great Railway by Which It Is Proposed to Connect the Canals and Navigable Waters of New-York, Pennsylvania, Ohio, Indiana, Illinois, Michigan, Missouri, and the Adjacent States and Territories.* Redfield focused on reaching the Mississippi River valley from the Eastern Seaboard, but he went so far in his 1830 tract as to suggest advancing an iron way to the Pacific Ocean.[19]

Only a year after the second edition of the Redfield pamphlet, another suggestion for a transcontinental railroad appeared. This time it was not in a similar format but rather in a newspaper editorial. Judge Samuel Dexter, a contributor to the *Western Emigrant* (published in Ann Arbor, MI), wrote in part, "It is in our power to build up an immense city at the mouth of the Oregon [Columbia River], to make it the depot for our East India trade and perhaps for that of Europe—in fact to unite New-York and the Oregon by a railway by which the traveler leaving the city of New-York shall, at the moderate rate of ten miles an hour, place himself in a port right on the shores of the Pacific." He made this puissant point: "It is one of those great projects which none but a great nation could effect—but peculiarly adapted to the enterprising character of the people of the United States."[20]

There was another proposal of note. It would begin not in New York or some other coastal city or state but on the western shores of Lake Michigan. This railroad would cross present-day Wisconsin to the Mississippi River opposite Dubuque, Iowa. In 1838 the dreamer was John Plumbe Jr. In 1831–1832 this young Welsh immigrant had assisted in surveying a rail route across the Alleghenies and believed that railroads should be expansive. Writing in a local newspaper in his adopted hometown of Dubuque in the Iowa District of Wisconsin Territory, he drew attention to his first scheme. It made an impression, enough so that George Wallace Jones, the congressional delegate who represented the territory, submitted a petition to the US House of Representatives "praying for the survey of a route for a railroad from the Mississippi River, at Du Buque, to Milwaukee, Wisconsin Territory." His colleagues' response was discouraging: "It produced a great laugh and hurrah in the house, members singing out to me that it would not be long before my constituents would ask Congress to build a railroad to the moon." No action, of course, followed. Yet this was hardly a wild dream; after all, Baltimore railroad proponents a decade earlier had proposed to link that city's harbor to the Ohio River valley, a distance of 380 miles. Plumbe also became a Pacific railroad enthusiast, suggesting a railroad from the Mississippi River to the Oregon Country. Years later Dubuquers recognized him for his "original" thinking. In 1847 a group of them passed this resolution: "Resolved, Unanimously, that this meeting regards John Plumbe, Esq. as the original projector of the great Oregon Railroad." Although this is historically incorrect, he was unmistakably an early proponent of a transcontinental rail artery.[21]

The honor of being the most tenacious advocate for a long-distance railroad goes to Asa Whitney, a merchant who had traveled widely overseas and earned the title "the Railroad Projector." In the mid-1840s, this New Yorker began his quest for a Pacific artery, proposing rails from Lake Michigan to the Oregon Country. Whitney considered such an undertaking to be technologically practical and a way to revolutionize world trade, especially for Americans to tap the riches of China and the Far East. He also saw it as the best way to unite the nation. Whitney did more than any of his contemporaries to seek a Pacific railroad, and he attracted considerable attention. After spending much of his personal wealth on behalf of this endeavor, his efforts (and enthusiasm) convinced an increasing number of Americans that such a scheme no longer represented lunatic thinking. Although the first transcontinental railroad, the Union Pacific–Central Pacific, would not bind the East and West until May 10, 1869, at Promontory, Utah Territory, Congress in the mid-1850s sponsored several railroad surveys throughout the trans-Mississippi West. Another positive step occurred in 1854 when the Washington and Mexico City governments signed the Gadsden Purchase agreement for the US to acquire nearly thirty thousand square miles in the future states of New Mexico and Arizona for a potential low-grade southern transcontinental route.[22]

A growing number of Old Northwest residents had read or heard about long-distance railroad proposals. At this time railroad advocates needed to consider lines that were realistic in length. No matter their mileage, this transportation alternative produced increasing excitement about future connectedness. "Many of the people [in the 1830s] had never even seen a railroad or locomotive and hence were greatly elated over the coming of this new thing into the community which gave promise of such great prosperity," commented one historical writer. Some midwesterners realized that railroads were a necessity if communities were to survive and prosper. By the mid-1840s Americans began to subscribe to the concept of "manifest destiny." John O'Sullivan in his expansionist organ, the *United States Magazine and Democratic Review*, declared that foreign governments were seeking to obstruct the annexation of Texas in order to prevent "the fulfilment of our manifest destiny to overspread the continent allotted by Providence for the free development of our yearly multiplying millions." Railroads would play a key role in achieving that noble objective.[23]

MICHIGAN

The first functioning railroad in the Old Northwest, the Erie & Kalamazoo, represents the general characteristics of railroads constructed during the first two decades of what became the Railway Age. This modest, privately financed road developed slowly. It took three years after receiving its charter in 1832 before construction began. And this work occurred on what would be its only completed section, the thirty-three miles between Port Lawrence (Toledo), Blissfield, Palmyra, and Adrian, Michigan; it finally opened on October 1, 1836. Initially the E&K operated entirely in Michigan Territory, but a boundary dispute with Ohio, resolved in 1837 as a condition of Michigan statehood, shrunk its southern border. The company thus operated twenty-one miles in the Wolverine State and a dozen miles in the Buckeye State.[24]

The building of the E&K shows that at this early date it was possible to construct a railroad even with an acute shortage of talent. "Men, and even civil engineers, who had practical training in railroad building, were scarce in any part of the country and particularly in the states west of the Allegheny Mountains where building was then hardly begun," observed a scholar a century later. "It was therefore difficult to secure men in the local community capable of performing the various kinds of work to be done." Still, American ingenuity made this railroad and other pioneer projects materialize.[25]

The significance of the E&K is more than being the first railroad to turn a wheel in what was once the Northwest Territory. Its construction and equipment represented the swiftly changing nature of American railroads. By the 1840s the E&K had lost its corporate identity, becoming an appendage of the Michigan Southern. This can be considered part of the initial wave of system building, a consolidation process that has been ongoing to the present day.[26]

The E&K began as a largely wooden railroad and replicated to a degree a previously established practice in Great Britain, the Germanies, and America. These first railroads, best described as tramways, were tiny. A score or more of them appeared from the 1800s to the 1820s, being widely scattered in the seaboard states and used frequently by contractors. There may have been at least two in the Old Northwest, one in Shelby County, Indiana, and another linking a coal mine in Illinois to the Mississippi River in the greater St. Louis area. The innovative Beacon Hill Railroad, opened in 1805 outside Boston and sometimes called "America's first railroad," represents this genre.[27]

How wooden was the E&K? The answer: very. Seeking to exploit local materials and to keep expenses to a minimum, laborers cut large quantities of white oak trees from the woodlands adjoining the line survey. The railroad's crossties, bridges, culverts, and rails were made from these harvests. Stone "sleepers" might have been selected as crossties, but management fortunately did not use them as they proved structurally unsound. In spring 1837 the E&K opted for a better way to run the road's short, slow-moving trains. (Speeds were less than ten miles per hour for passenger trains and half that for freight movements.) Strips of flat strap or "flat bar" wrought iron measuring about two and a half inches wide, half an inch thick, and fifteen to twenty feet long were fastened to these wooden rails or "stringers," which permitted heavier loads and faster speeds. About this time wealthier eastern roads began to use solid wrought-iron "U," "T," or the much rarer "V" or "Barlow" rails, since they provided greater reliability and longevity. But E&K management considered them too expensive. Tons of secondhand strap rail came on the market, most of which went to poorer western and southern roads. Those carriers that installed strap rails faced a constant safety threat, however. The running of even light and slow trains like those on the E&K created a rolling action that might cause the strap rail to curl and break apart. These detached "snake heads" could spear through a car floor and cause derailment or injury and perhaps death to those onboard. Wooden stringers could splinter and also derail a train. Rolling stock, too, was largely wooden, paralleling river, lake, and canal boats.[28]

As with tramways, the B&O, and some other contemporary railroads including the E&K, horses supplied the initial motive power. But steam soon appeared on the E&K. On July 4, 1837, the first locomotive, appropriately named the Adrian No. 1, with a 4-2-0 wheel arrangement,[29] arrived from the recently opened Baldwin Locomotive Works in Philadelphia.[30] It "evoked complete satisfaction." By the early 1840s, the company owned two Baldwin products, four four-wheeled passenger coaches, and twenty freight cars (sixteen roofed and four open), proving to be "completely sufficient for the traffic." The E&K resembled contemporary carriers in that its passenger business generated greater revenues than freight; the road was not constructed substantially enough to haul large amounts of the latter.[31]

Several years after the Adrian No. 1 pulled its inaugural train, Michiganders received a second functioning railroad. Although the first chartered Pontiac & Detroit Railroad flopped, a successor using the same route emerged. In 1834 the Detroit & Pontiac Railroad received a charter. Yet it struggled to connect with its designated terminals, reaching only Birmingham from Detroit by 1839. At last in 1843 this poorly engineered and lightly constructed road opened for through service.

While the Pontiac & Detroit sought to build to completion, Michigan accomplished considerable construction of other railroads by mid-century, notwithstanding its extensive land mass and relatively small (albeit growing) population. As elsewhere in the Old Northwest, railroads during the 1840s and 1850s were viewed as important by the vast majority of Michiganders, especially farmers, and they had to be built.

Shortly before the Panic of 1837 struck, states like Michigan, Ohio, and Indiana authorized massive programs of publicly financed railway construction. Why? Local capitalists lacked the ability to finance these projects; capital was scarce and competitive. Funds could most likely come from the state government through the sale of bonds in eastern and foreign markets. Michigan's internal improvements board would oversee this building. Its beginning step focused on surveys for three trans-state routes. The northern one was projected from St. Clair (Palmer) to Grand Haven, the central from Detroit to St. Joseph, and the southern from Monroe to New Buffalo. The latter two were the first to materialize. By 1846 the central project had trackage that stretched from Detroit to Kalamazoo, and the southern one extended only from Monroe to Adrian, where it connected with the E&K. Being publicly owned, both duplicated how Ohio, Indiana, and Illinois had funded their principal canals. Yet "state socialism" did not endure. Before their anticipated completion, they fell into private hands, spearheaded by Boston merchant John Murray Forbes, New York financier John Brooks, and Detroit lawyer James Joy. Unlike what happened later in Illinois with its state-owned Northern Cross Railroad, Michigan fared much better with its two liquidations. The Central was acquired for $2 million in state indebtedness and the Southern for $500,000, also with public debt. "Once the lines were sold, the state was glad to be out of the railroad business," concluded Michigan railroad historian Graydon Meints. "Each section insisted on a project for itself and demanded it be continued even after financial difficulties began to appear. If the state had been able to concentrate its efforts after 1841 on its most promising project, the Central line, it might have been able to avoid many of the difficulties and much of the embarrassment that ensued." The central trackage emerged as the Michigan Central Railroad, and the southern one became the Michigan Southern Railroad. Both built to their anticipated in-state destinations, and by the early 1850s each had managed to reach Chicago.[32]

As the Michigan Central and Michigan Southern evolved, they bolstered their passenger traffic by investing in Great Lakes boat transportation. In 1849 the Michigan Central began service between Detroit and Buffalo with its palace steamer *May Flower* and later expanded its fleet. Two years earlier the Michigan Southern had gone waterborne with a steamboat connection from Monroe to Buffalo. Later it made Toledo its principal connecting port. In the 1850s other midwestern roads took advantage of the Great Lakes for joint rail-boat service for both freight and passengers. However, the Panic of 1857, which struck the nation and was especially severe in the Midwest, badly disrupted business on the Great Lakes. Railroads withdrew from operations on Lake Erie as water traffic dropped dramatically. Furthermore, passengers who wished to reach Chicago and points beyond could now go by the faster and safer all-rail alternative.[33]

OHIO

The opening of the Erie & Kalamazoo Rail Road had little impact on Ohioans. By the time rails extended from Toledo into nearby Michigan, the Buckeye State had an array of internal improvements, sporting the National Road and several other improved roadways, navigation and harbor improvements on Lake Erie, canalization of much of the Muskingum River, and an expansive canal system. But the existing network lacked perfection. Residents likely understood that the iron horse must become an integral part of the state's transportation infrastructure. And soon it did beyond the E&K. Luckily for that small interstate carrier, it would share what became known as "Ohio Gauge" of 4 feet 10 inches rather than the more widely employed "English Gauge" of 4 feet 8½ inches.[34]

During the canal-building frenzy, some Ohioans realized that long-distance ditch digging could never create swift, dependable all-weather

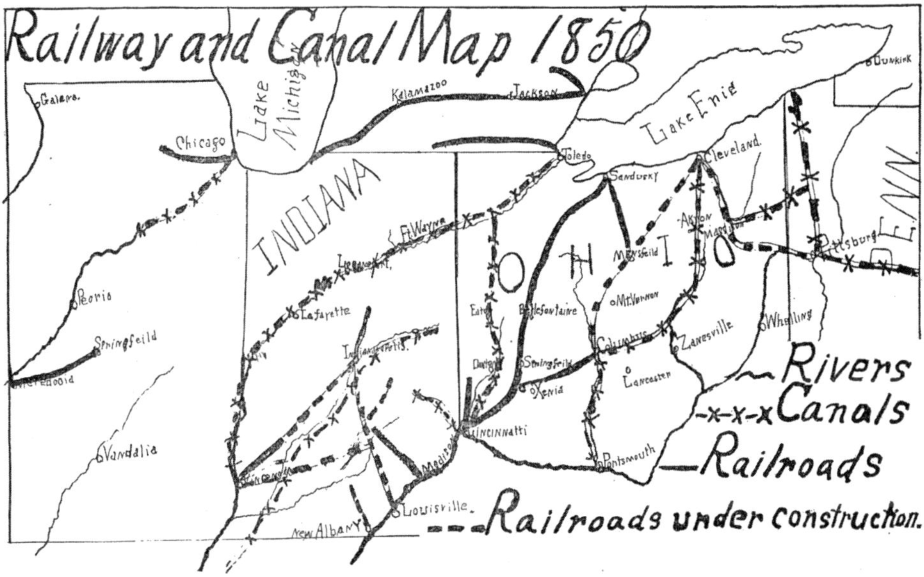

By 1850 railroad construction had diminished interest in canal building in Ohio, Indiana, and Illinois. Even though packet boats had largely disappeared by midcentury, the iron horse did not end canal usage. Take the Ohio & Erie Canal. Freight shipments, principally coal, remained active for decades to come. *(Author's collection)*

transport. The north-central region, largely counties and communities between Columbus and Sandusky, would be unable to achieve convenient access to canals. Public roads could be built and improved, but animal-powered travel would always be slow, and horses, mules, and oxen could not pull wagons with large load capacities. In 1826 Sandusky resident Eleutheros Cooke daringly suggested that the state finance a railroad between Lake Erie at Sandusky and the proposed Miami Canal at Dayton. Cooke understood that it was not the terrain that prevented canal construction as much as the lack of water to maintain adequate canal depths. There were no suitable places for feeder designed reservoirs.[35]

The earliest railroad maps of Ohio revealed extreme fragmentation. In 1840 only thirty-nine miles of spindly track were in operation. "The state is still too young and underpopulated," Franz Anton Ritter von Gerstner, an Austrian civil engineer who visited America's network of canals, railroads, and waterways between 1838 and 1840, opined several years later, "and it lacks sufficient capitalists able to assemble funds necessary for such projects. Still a few minor roads have already been completed and several larger ones begun." While rails did not immediately link Sandusky to the south or southwest, by the mid-1840s that hopeful connection between Lake Erie and the Ohio River took shape in pieces. Soon the Sandusky, Mansfield & Newark installed fifty-six miles between Sandusky and Mansfield. About that same time, the Mad River & Lake Erie laid down 102 miles of track from Sandusky to Bellefontaine, and in 1848 it completed another thirty-two miles from Bellefontaine to Springfield. Two years later the company pushed farther toward the southwest by spanning the twenty-four miles between Springfield and Dayton. There its rails met the Cincinnati, Hamilton & Dayton, which had recently completed a sixty-mile line from Cincinnati. At last a through railroad route had opened. Ohio lawmakers wisely never attempted to create railroads like they had done with most of their canals; the Michigan approach with taxpayer dollars would not be emulated. Yet during the formative years, the legislature authorized the state treasurer's office to loan its credit up to $200,000 for railroad projects and allowed some counties to subscribe certain amounts, ranging from $25,000 to $60,000, toward the capital stock of a company. The Springfield municipal government, for one, was permitted to subscribe $25,000.[36]

Paralleling other rail-building states and territories during the antebellum period, including those in the Midwest, legislatures entertained a rash of charter proposals. They usually authorized these requests. Lobbying by promoters might have been intense. Ohio may not have led the nation in granting these documents, but it surely ranked near the top. The public, of course, was anxious to obtain the iron horse; some organizers were operating in good faith, others solely for personal gain. Between 1830 and 1840, twenty-four companies were incorporated, in 1840 to 1850 twenty-three, and in 1850 to 1865 sixty-seven. Out of these 114 charters, only twenty-five roads were built either in part or in whole.[37]

Ohio was alone among the midwestern states in seriously attempting a dead-end construction scheme: a "railroad-on-stilts." This was a time when railroad builders debated the basic nature of the roadbed. The Ohio Railroad, chartered in 1836 and begun three years later, was designed to be built on a massive wooden superstructure, supported by heavy wood pilings. The idea was that it would reduce or eliminate grades, lessen the negative impact of heavy rains and floods, prevent frost heaves, and provide an easier way for snow removal. "Posts at least 10 inches in diameter are driven into the earth in 2 rows," observed a contemporary. "Those in each row are 5 feet apart, center to center, and the distance between the 2 rows is 7 feet 4 inches." The projected 177-mile route would largely hug the southern shore of Lake Erie from "a suitable point on the eastern border of the state" to the Maumee River. Trains, however, never operated over this platform or for that matter on terra firma. Before the company floundered (due in part to corrupt management), it had placed twenty-nine miles of this odd construction through the Black Swamp area between Fremont and the Maumee River. The Board of Public Works had loaned the company thousands of dollars and in 1844 sought to realize something from the state's investment. Its efforts were a colossal failure. "It was reported that this property had disappeared at the dissolution sale in 1842, and they were able to locate only one set of car wheels, one locomotive and one saw-mill."[38]

Railroad construction in the Buckeye State soon changed dramatically. Talk turned to the tangible. At midcentury route mileage soared to 792, and on the eve of the Civil War it reached an impressive 2,946 miles with more than thirty railroads. By 1867, when the state launched its railroad commission, there were thirty-five carriers, operating about 3,200 route miles. What is notable about how iron rails girdled Ohio is that they did not parallel the Ohio & Erie Canal corridor, the state's premier internal waterway. Instead they appeared largely on an east–west axis. Rails made it possible to connect directly with New York and Philadelphia and to link principal population centers conveniently with Chicago and St. Louis. Another result was that Cincinnati, "Queen City of the Ohio River," began to lose its preeminence in the state. "We need not tell our merchants that the trade which existed not many years ago between Cincinnati and Pittsburgh had been largely destroyed," lamented the *Cincinnati Gazette* in 1861, "and that the trade with the west from

Cincinnati in manufacturers of iron and glassware has been entirely diverted from us by competing [rail] routes." Added the newspaper, "Chicago supplies Pittsburgh with her manufacturers." The winners in Ohio would be Cleveland and Toledo, being situated on that strategic Chicago corridor. Still, river traffic continued, and Cincinnati also benefited indirectly from freight movements on the Ohio & Erie Canal between Cleveland, intermediate towns and cities, and West Portsmouth.[39]

INDIANA

Neighboring Indiana, which in 1836 had enacted its Mammoth Internal Improvement Act, focused on canals, but it also welcomed the iron horse. The Madison & Indianapolis Railroad (M&I) became its first railroad. In another example of contemporary building strategies, this pioneer pike tapped a busy waterway. It was designed to supplement rather than supersede river transportation. As the corporate name implied, the M&I sought to construct a northwesterly route from Madison, a blossoming community on the Ohio River, toward Indianapolis, the state's seat of government since 1826. (Madison was the nearest river community to the capital.) Financed heavily by a loan from a Madison capitalist, work began in 1837 from the Madison Hill, which overlooked the river. Spring witnessed the start of construction of this standard-gauge line, and by November laborers had completed the fifteen miles to Graham's Ford Bridge. A celebration ensued, becoming an oft-repeated event throughout the region. Unfortunately, the first steam locomotive, built by Baldwin, was lost at sea, but the Lexington & Ohio Railroad, which operated in Kentucky between Lexington and Frankfort, came to the rescue. It loaned the Elkhorn, and on November 29, 1838, this small steamer pulled the first passenger train in the Hoosier State. The impact of the Panic of 1837 delayed reaching Indianapolis, but in June 1839 the road entered Vernon, five miles distant. The initial track had strap rail, but the remaining mileage to Indianapolis would feature forty-five-pound T-rail. This iron was manufactured in Wales and transported via ship to connecting steamboats in New Orleans. Also in 1839 laborers completed a steam-powered inclined plane to reach the ridge top above

Madison from the river front. In an era of anemic-powered steam locomotives, this was the only feasible way for pioneer railroads to manage steep inclines. Indianapolis, eighty-six miles from Madison, waited until fall 1847 for M&I trains. Once again a lively celebration occurred. The inaugural train carried "an itinerant circus in addition to its hilarious excursionists."[40]

By the end of 1850, Indianapolis offered freight customers and passengers more than access to the Madison & Indianapolis. (In 1851 the entire railroad sported stronger sixty-pound wrought-iron T-rail.) The M&I through its auspices had three short feeders: the sixteen-mile Shelbyville Lateral from Edinburg to Shelbyville (1849), the twenty-mile Shelbyville & Rushville Railroad (1850), and the twenty-six-mile Knightstown & Shelbyville Railroad (1850). Indianapolis was emerging as a railroad hub. As in Michigan and Ohio, the iron horse would soon serve a wider population.[41]

The first boom in Indiana railroad construction occurred during the 1850s. The national economy showed strength, and London, Amsterdam, and other European investors exhibited an enhanced interest in American railroads. Furthermore, Indiana lawmakers achieved better control over their massive state debt. The peak of this optimism occurred in 1853, when at least twenty-five new railroads were discussed or launched. By 1855 there were 1,407 route miles in operation. The New Albany & Salem Railroad, reorganized on the eve of the Civil War as the Louisville, New Albany & Chicago, claimed the greatest length with 288 miles and connected the Ohio River with Lake Michigan via Bedford, Crawfordsville, and Lafayette. At last the dream of linking these two bodies of water had been achieved. It overshadowed by approximately 180 miles the second-largest road, the Evansville & Illinois (E&I), an Evansville to Terre Haute carrier. A more important railroad was arguably the Indianapolis & Bellefontaine (I&B) between Union, Ohio (later Union City), on the Ohio-Indiana state line and Indianapolis. This road gave the Hoosier State its first rail tie-in to major cities on the Eastern Seaboard. Initially, though, the I&B used Ohio Gauge; it was an Ohio company. Significantly, the E&I and I&B built on an east–west axis, and this directional orientation meant that by 1860 additional construction

The railroad map of the United States as of 1851 reveals how a web of interregional iron rails had expanded from the tidewater into the eastern part of the Midwest. *(Author's collection)*

allowed more Indiana locales to gain access to New York, Philadelphia, and Baltimore as well as Chicago and St. Louis.[42]

As the decade progressed, Indiana railroad mileage climbed to 2,163, ranking it third among the states of the Old Northwest but not far behind either Ohio or Illinois. A key component of the expanding networks was the Lake Erie, Wabash & St. Louis Railroad (LEW&StL). This Indiana firm won incorporation in 1852, and the following year its future Ohio partner, the Toledo & Illinois Railroad (T&I), received its charter. Backers of both projects grasped the "ideal" location of their intended route. "*Nature* has marked the Wabash Valley as the *best route* of a great commercial thoroughfare [by railroad] from the cities of Boston and New York to St. Louis." The anticipated plans involved the T&I building 74 miles largely through the Maumee River valley in Ohio and the LEW&StL constructing a 241-mile segment mostly along the Wabash River in Indiana. Between Toledo and Lafayette, this route would generally parallel the Wabash & Erie Canal.[43]

Construction of this future Toledo and St. Louis artery began rapidly. In early 1854 its backers bragged that their companies had completed their "maps, profiles, plans, drawings and specification of the Road, bridges, &c." They added that "rights of way, with inconsiderable exceptions, have been obtained along the whole route, and station and machine grounds have been secured at all the principal points, including most valuable grounds in Toledo."[44]

Typical of many railroad-building projects, both before and after, the LEW&StL and T&I relied heavily on local support. As early as June 1852, railroad boosters gathered for a "Rail Road Convention" in Logansport where they discussed matters of finance; their actions led units of local governments and individuals to invest liberally in the trans-Indiana line. It was common for a township or county to subscribe to company stock and perhaps to acquire its bonds. Property owners frequently made donations and concessions for rights-of-way and station facilities, all designed to guarantee that their community would have a railroad. Their logic became universal: "Rapid development of a new country is only possible through a system of railroads, affording speedy, regular, safe and economical transportation."[45]

The building of the LEW&StL went along rather smoothly. Topography posed limited problems, but an outbreak of "Asiatic cholera" in the summer of 1854 caused widespread illness and death to the workforce composed mostly of area residents and Irish laborers. The latter likely had previously been involved in ditch digging and possibly in railroad construction as well. The ninety-four-mile section between Toledo and Fort Wayne opened in August 1855, and by the end of January the following year, residents of Wabash, 136 miles from Toledo, heard the shrill whistle of the locomotive. On June 18, 1856, the first train steamed into

Lafayette, completing 203 miles of line. By August 1, crews had installed another thirty-nine miles of rail, forging a strategic connection at the Illinois border with that state's Great Western Railroad. "The whole work has been done in the most perfect and permanent manner," crowed the LEW&StL and T&I, "so as to make it in all respects a first class Road."[46]

Before the first work train reached the Great Western connection, the LEW&StL and T&I leadership decided to merge. This would become an early example of corporate consolidation in Ohio and Indiana. Realistically, it made no sense to remain separate entities. For all practical purposes, the T&I functioned as the eastern division, and the LEW&StL served as the western division. Investors of what emerged as the Toledo, Wabash & Western Rail Road (TW&W) prospered with this unification. The combined carrier generated a thriving and profitable freight and passenger business. Former canal towns became railroad towns as the road reached Fort Wayne, Peru, Logansport, and Lafayette. The TW&W sapped traffic from the dying canal, an occurrence that may have saddened some citizens. Stockholders, boosters, and most on-line residents surely had few if any tinges of nostalgia.[47]

Although the Toledo, Wabash & Western Railroad did not serve a rapidly growing Indianapolis, the capital city continued to attract rail lines, and more were anticipated. In what became a brilliant decision, Indianapolis and railroad executives decided in 1849 to create a General Passenger Depot or union depot. (There were seven stations either in operation or proposed.) This landmark facility opened in 1853 with multiple railroad owners. Historian Jeffrey Darbee concluded that this structure has a legitimate claim of being the nation's first union station. He admits that Columbus, Ohio, likewise might deserve that honor. Yet Columbus had only a single-carrier-owned depot and a lone tenant; in 1851 the Columbus & Xenia rented space to the Cleveland, Columbus & Cincinnati. Whatever is correct, the concept of one rather than multiple depots meant that passengers did not need to change stations, street traffic could become better organized, and hotels, eateries, and other support services could be clustered more conveniently. The completed Hoosier capital facility would be operated by the jointly owned Indianapolis Union Railway Company.[48]

TOLEDO AND WABASH RAIL WAY.

For the Government and Information of Employees only, and is not intended for the Information of the Public. The Company reserves the right to vary therefrom as circumstances may require.

No. 3. To take effect Sunday, March 20, 1859, at 12 o'clock, Noon.

TRAINS WILL RUN AS FOLLOWS

WESTWARD.						EASTWARD.		
No. 1. Mail Express.	**No. 2.** Express.	**No. 3.** Freight.	Distance between Stations	STATIONS.	Distance.	**No. 4.** Mail Express.	**No. 5.** Freight.	**No. 6.** Express.
Le. 1.00 A. M.	Le. 4.50 P. M.	Le. 9.00 P. M.		.... TOLEDO	9.243	Ar. 4.00 P. M.	Ar. 8.20 A. M.	Ar. 6.40 A. M.
" 1.25 "	" 5.10 "	" 10.00 "	9	. MAUMEE CITY .	8.234	" 3.35 "	" 7.30 "	" 6.20 "
" 1.50 "	" 5.27 "	" 11.00 "	8	. WHITEHOUSE .	9.226	" 3.10 "	" 6.55 "	" 6.00 "
" 2.15 "	" 5.45 "	" 12.00 A. M.	9	. WASHINGTON .	10.217	" 2.45 "	" 6.10 "	" 5.45 "
" 2.45 "	" 6.10 "	" 1.00 "	10	. . NAPOLEON . .	6.207	" 2.15 "	" **5.20**Pass"	" **5.20**Pas"
" 3.00 "	" 6.30 "	" 1.40 "	6	..... ADAMS	9.201	" 2.00 "	" 4.35 "	" 5.00 "
" **3.30M** "	" 7.00 "	" **2.50M** "	9	... DEFIANCE ...	10.192	" 1.30 "	Le. **3.30M**" Ar. **2.50M**"	" 4.30 "
" **4.00** M. P. "	" 7.30 "	" **4.00** Fd. M. "	10	... EMERALD ...	11.182	" 1.00 "	" 1.30 "	" **4.00M**"*
" 4.35 "	" 8.05 "	" 5.00 "	11	... ANTWERP. ..	8.171	" 12.30 "	" 12.10 A. M.	" 3.30 "
" 5.00 "	" 8.30 "	" 5.35 A. M.	8	.. STATE LINE ..	8.163	" 12.05 P. M.	" 11.20 "	" 3.05 "
" 5.30 "	" 9.00 "	" 6.20 "	8	. NEW HAVEN .	7.155	" 11.40 "	" 10.40 "	" 2.45 "
Ar. 5.50 " Le. 6.10 "	Ar. **9.20M** " Le. 9.35 "	Ar. 7.00 " Le. 7.15 "	6	FORT WAYNE	16.149	Le. 11.20 " Ar. 11.15 "	Le. 10.05 " Ar. **9.20M**"	Le. 2.20 A. M. Ar. 2.15 "
" 6.40 "	" 10.05 "	" 8.20 "	16	... ROANOKE ...	1.133	" 10.35 "	" 8.00 "	" 1.45 "
" 6.50 "	" 10.15 "	" 8.40 "	1	.... MAHON	7.132	" 10.30 "	" 7.35 "	" 1.40 "
" 7.10 "	" 10.35 "	" 9.15 "	7	. HUNTINGTON .	6.125	" 10.10 "	" 6.50 "	" 1.20 "
" 7.25 "	" 10.50 "	" **9.55M** "	6	.... ANTIOCH	7.119	" **9.55M** "	" 6.15 "	" 1.05 "
" 7.45 "	" 11.05 "	" 10.35 "	7	..... LAGRO	5.112	" 9.30 "	" 5.35 "	" 12.45 "
" 8.00 "	" 11.20 "	" 11.00 "	5	.... WABASH	14.107	" 9.15 "	" 5.00 "	" 12.30 A. M.
" **8.35M** "	" **11.50M** "	" 12.10 P. M.	14	...... PERU	8. 92	" **8.35M** "	" 3.35 "	" **11.50M**"
" 8.55 "	" 12.15 A. M.	" 12.55 "	8	NEW WAVERLY	8. 85	" 8.10 "	" 2.50 "	" 11.20 "
" 9.20 "	" 12.45 "	" **2.00M** "	8	. LOGANSPORT .	4. 77	" 7.45 "	" **2.00M**"	" 10.55 "
" 9.35 "	" 1.00 "	" 2.20 "	4	... CLYMERS ...	10. 73	" 7.30 "	" 1.35 "	" 10.40 "
" 9.55 "	" 1.25 "	" 3.05 "	10	.. ROCKFIELD ..	7. 63	" 7.05 "	" 12.55 "	" 10.10 "
" 10.15 "	" 1.45 "	" 3.40 "	7	.... DELPHI	8. 56	" 6.45 "	" 12.20 P. M.	" 9.45 "
" 10.35 "	" 2.10 "	" 4.20 "	8	.. BUCK CREEK ..	8. 48	" 6.20 "	" 11.40 "	" 9.20 "
Ar. 10.55 " Le. **11.00M** "	Ar. 2.35 " Le. 2.40 "	Ar. 5.00 " Le. 6.00 "	8	.. LAFAYETTE ..	7. 40	Le. 6.05 " Ar. 6.00 "	Le. **11.00M**" Ar. 10.00 "	Le. 8.55 " Ar. 8.50 "
" 11.20 "	" 3.00 "	" 6.30 "	7	... WEA, W, S. ...	2. 33	" 5.40 "	" 9.20 "	" 8.30 "
" 11.30 "	" 3.05 "	" 6.45 "	2	.. WEST POINT ..	5. 31	" 5.35 "	" 9.00 "	" 8.20 "
" 11.40 "	" 3.20 "	" 7.00 "	5	.. NEBRASKA ...	2. 26	" 5.20 "	" 8.40 "	" 8.05 "
" 11.50 "	" 3.25 "	" 7.15 "	2	INDEPENDENCE	5. 24	" 5.15 "	" 8.20 "	" 8.00 "
" 12.00 M.	" 3.40 "	" **7.45M** "	5	..... ATTICA	3. 19	" 5.00 "	" 8.05 "	" **7.45M**"
" 12.10 P. M.	" 3.50 "	" 8.00 "	3	WILLIAMSPORT	5. 16	" 4.52 "	" 7.50 "	" 7.35 "
" 12.25 "	" 4.05 "	" 8.30 "	5	WEST LEBANON	4. 11	" 4.37 "	" 7.25 "	" 7.20 "
" 12.40 "	" **4.25M** "	" 9.00 "	4	. MARSHFIELD .	7.	" **4.25M** "	" 7.00 "	" 7.05 "
Ar. 12.50 "	Ar. 4.45 "	Ar. 9.30 "	7	STATE LINE, ILL.		Le. 4.00 A. M.	Le. 6.30 A. M.	Le. 6.45 P. M.

* Meet Freight and Passenger.

SIGNALS.—One Puff of the Whistle signifies that the brakes must be tightened; Two Puffs, to be loosed; Three Puffs, to back up; and a continuous sound, approaching a station

HAND SIGNALS.—A Lamp swinging across the track, signifies stop. A lamp raised up and down, back up. A lamp swinging over the head "Go ahead."

All Engines, with or without trains, will come to a full stop at and before the crossing of the Ohio and Indiana, and Lafayette and Indianapolis Railroads and Draw-bridge at Attica.

The speed of Engines with, or without Trains, must not exceed 8 miles per hour within the city limits of Lafayette.

The time as shown by the clock in Superintendent's office at Toledo, wll be the Standard time. Conductors will compare their watches daily by this time.

Freight Trains will not be allowed to arrive at Stations more than 10 minutes ahead of Card time. Conductors and Engineers will be held equally responsible for the safety of their Trains.

General Superintendent's Office, ☞ N. B.—Observe Rules 1 and 20 on the other side.

The Toledo & Wabash Railway became one of the early long-distance routes in the Midwest, stretching between Toledo and the Indiana-Illinois state line. As was common on antebellum railroads, the volume of freight and passenger traffic was modest, as revealed in this 1859 employee's timetable. *(Author's collection)*

ILLINOIS

Illinois was slower than Michigan, Ohio, and Indiana to greet the iron horse. Residents depended heavily on watercraft plying the Ohio and Mississippi Rivers and the Great Lakes for their transport needs, and they found a large section of the Illinois River useful as well. Lesser streams proved problematic, especially for steam-powered vessels. The state's troublesome road situation resembled other parts of the Old Northwest, hindering personal travels and making cargo deliveries slow (if they happened at all) and expensive. "Bulky farm products could not pay high transportation charges and compete [for buyers] in eastern markets," explained historian John Krenkel. A rapidly growing population, of course, wished to shrink time and space as much as possible. During the early years of statehood, internal-improvement advocates proposed a canal to connect Lake Michigan with the navigable portion of the Illinois River. Throughout the region that would benefit from such a project, this idea gained support. In the 1830s most of all citizens of Chicago, a former military post and an incorporated town in 1833, saw that being a Lake Michigan port and being connected to the Illinois River could make their community a major metropolis. Prosperity would abound for its residents, whether they were land speculators, business owners, manufacturers, or professionals. Yet at the inception of the Illinois & Michigan Canal (I&M), the president of the Board of Canal Commissioners admitted (correctly) that a railroad would prove to be a better link between lake and river. His reasoning: "First, it would be cheaper to construct; second, it would be open to commerce all the year, whereas the water in the locks of a canal might often be frozen while the Illinois River and Lake Michigan were navigable; third, it would be a more rapid, and a better mode of transportation and travel than the canal." A young Abraham Lincoln agreed, saying during his first campaign for the state legislature in 1834, "No other improvement that reason will justify us in hoping for can equal in utility the railroad. It is a never failing source of communication, between places of business remotely situated from each other." Many thought the future president insane. The seed, though, had been sown, suggesting that canals might become rapidly outdated.[49]

On July 4, 1836, shortly before the Panic of 1837 ravaged the Midwest, dignitaries ceremonially turned the first shovels of earth for the Illinois & Michigan Canal. Nevertheless, the railroad alternative continued to be promoted. In the same year as canal excitement spread, the state legislature granted a charter to the Galena & Chicago Union Railroad (Galena). The corporate name revealed that backers considered Galena, the center of lead-mining activities in northwestern Illinois and southwestern Wisconsin, to be more important than Chicago. But hard times prevented the development of either a canal or a railroad. The sad state of the economy likewise stymied the first railroad charters that had been given a year before to the Chicago & Vincennes and the Jacksonville & Meredosia Railroads and the dozen or so additional projects when Galena backers received their legal go-ahead.[50]

The proposed Galena and other Illinois chartered railroads triggered great expectations along their projected routes. It was realized that local capital would be inadequate to turn dreams into reality. To satisfy the vast majority of residents statewide about the possibility of obtaining the iron horse, the General Assembly during its 1836–1837 winter session passed "an Act to establish and maintain a general system of Internal Improvements." A historian a century later wrote, "It was more than bold; it was foolhardy." This measure focused on railroad construction, amounting collectively to 1,342 miles. The price tag for this combined network of rail and waterway undertakings totaled $10.2 million, a staggering amount considering that the state counted only 400,000 mostly impecunious citizens. This improvement frenzy, of course, was not limited to Illinois.[51]

The projected rail routes crisscrossed the state. Four major and three branch lines were designated to be built on an east–west axis and a north–south one to extend from Galena to Cairo near the mouth of the Ohio River. Construction started on several of these proposed lines, but only the Northern Cross Railroad actually turned a wheel. It was expected to run from Quincy on the Mississippi River through Meredosia, Jacksonville, Springfield, Decatur, and Danville before reaching Indiana. Because of the deepening depression, it is remarkable that the Northern Cross evolved as much as it did. After it conducted surveys in the spring of 1837 and awarded construction contracts, the right-of-way began to take shape. By December 1838 workers had nearly completed the roadbed between Meredosia on the Illinois River and Jacksonville, and only eight miles of grading remained unfinished between Jacksonville and Springfield. Rails (wooden stringers with strap iron) followed, and by mid-1838 the track had reached Morgan City, a distance of twelve miles. At year's end these spindly rails entered Jacksonville. That November the locomotive Rogers, built by Rogers, Grosvenor & Ketchum of Newark, New Jersey, and allegedly the first iron horse in the Mississippi Valley, assisted with construction. What had become a twenty-four-mile railroad stalled at Jacksonville. Springfield, the new state capital, situated on the shallow and snag-infested Sangamon River, did not see the iron horse until February 1842.[52]

Largely a casualty of hard times, the Northern Cross rapidly deteriorated. The Rogers and two other locomotives either broke down or were too heavy for a worsening track structure, and horses and mules (called "hauling engines") became the motive power. Beginning in 1843 a series of leases followed, and no operator did much to improve the property. Finally, in 1847 Illinois sold the railroad, which included a short extension to Naples (like Meredosia, on the Illinois River), at a substantial financial loss. The state treasury received a mere $21,000, but that amount came in the form of state indebtedness rather than cash.

The Northern Cross nevertheless had a phoenixlike future. Private investors upgraded the dilapidated property as the Sangamon & Morgan Railroad and later as the Great Western. Under the latter corporate banner, track extended eastward between 1854 and 1856 from Springfield through Decatur and Danville to the Indiana border, where it connected with the Toledo, Wabash & Western. Ultimately the property became a part of the interregional Wabash Railroad.

The Illinois approach to becoming a participant in the budding Railway Age had been badly misguided. The internal improvements plan, as historian Simon Cordery explained, "was simply too ambitious for a young, undeveloped state, and it suffered from its political parentage. Everyone wanted 'their' line immediately, with the result that none were completed, and only a small fraction of one was built." And this apt observation: "Instead of building trial railroads, completing them, deriving experience from them and possibly obtaining revenue for further construction the legislature permitted sectional jealousy to dictate."[53]

With the exception of a generous and precedent-setting federal land grant to the Illinois Central (IC), private investments did much to expand railroad mileage. Domestic capital was gradually being accumulated for multiple projects, and this led to the rapid growth of Illinois. In 1847 it ranked an impressive eleventh in population among the states. In 1848, the same year as the publicly financed I&M Canal opened, the privately financed Galena made its modest debut from Chicago, operating over less than a dozen miles of secondhand strap rail. Although chartered a decade earlier, it sprang to life as the economy improved, and the Rockford Rail Road Convention of 1846 did much to energize this languishing project. What became a history-making railroad received able guidance from William Butler Ogden, the Lakefront City's first mayor, a leading citizen, and the company president. More building followed. The immediate focus was not on rails to Galena but on the forty-two miles to Elgin. Backers concluded that this section could immediately generate traffic. They took heart that construction would not be too difficult even though the terrain in the immediate Chicago area was often marshy. This was a sensible decision. In late October 1848, the ten-ton Pioneer, a Baldwin-built locomotive, first plied the Lilliputian line. Construction continued, although Elgin was not reached until January 1850. Business boomed. The firm's third annual report, issued in mid-1850, indicated that its four locomotives, sixty-seven freight cars, and eight passenger coaches could barely handle the volume of goods and people. Two years later a local Chicago newspaper claimed that the Galena had earned a 40 percent return on its investment capital. Although the company never reached Galena, it did arrive in Freeport, 121 miles from Chicago, and instead pushed westward toward the Mississippi River. In late 1855 its rails touched its eastern bank at Fulton. (Northwestern Illinois could be reached from Chicago via the IC in Freeport.) In 1864 the Galena became a core component of the recently organized Chicago & North Western Railway. By this time Chicago had established itself as the inevitable railroad center of the nation. Boosters crowed that their bustling city had grown into the "Rome of Railroads."[54]

The first steam locomotive to serve Chicago was the tiny 4-2-0 Pioneer owned by the fledgling Galena & Chicago Union Railroad. Remarkably, this historic engine escaped scrappers and achieved star status in 1948 and 1949 at the Chicago Railroad Fair. *(Author's collection)*

While Chicago got a major economic and psychological boost with its first railroad and claimed a population of 23,722 in 1850, the Illinois Central holds significance as one of the first major carriers in the Midwest. In 1850 Congress agreed that Illinois, Mississippi, and Alabama should receive 3,736,005 acres of public lands for a north–south railroad. The grant allotted to the IC would be Connecticut sized. Plans called for this iron way to run between La Salle, Illinois, on the I&M Canal, and Mobile, Alabama, on Mobile Bay. A year later the IC received a charter, allowing it to build the northern leg of this seemingly "wrong-way" transcontinental. Its tracks were expected to connect Dunleith on the east bank of the Mississippi River (near Galena) with Cairo, allowing

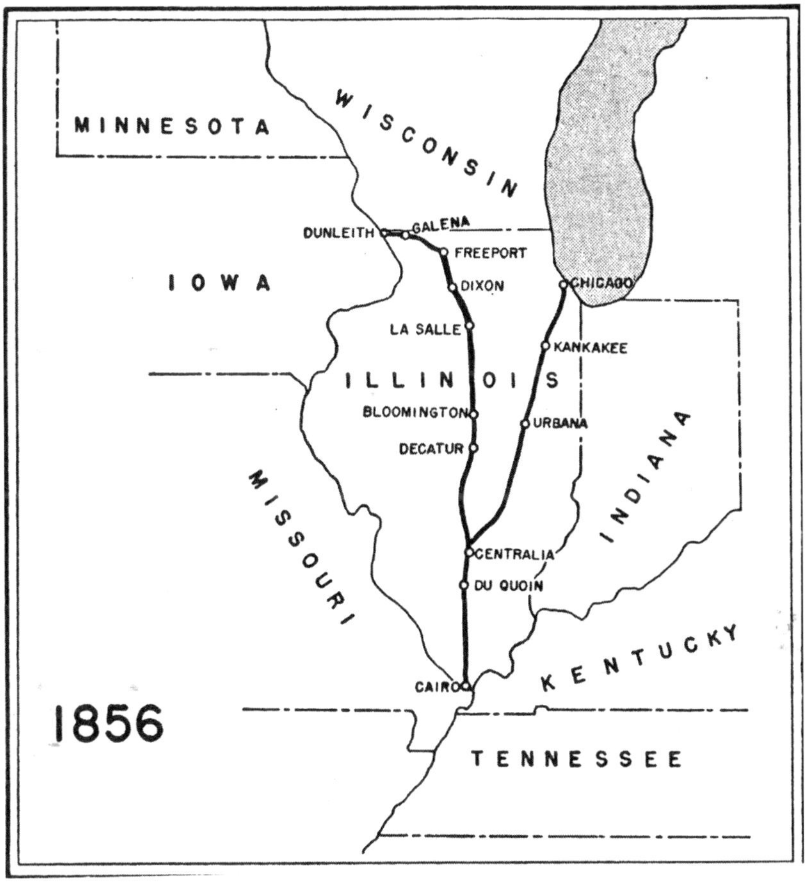

By the mid-1850s, the Illinois Central had emerged as the standout example of the progress made by railroad builders in the Midwest. By this time the company had installed a branch from Centralia to Chicago, the gestating hub of the nation's rapidly expanding interregional network of iron ways. The IC's 705 route miles made it the longest railroad in North America. *(Author's collection)*

direct access to the ice-free Mississippi to Memphis and New Orleans. If successful, this route could tap Upper Mississippi River traffic. The projection of midwestern railroads, however, developed on the east-to-west axis to reflect the direction of the moving frontier. The directors of the IC soon made a smart decision. Recognizing that Chicago was a promising and well-situated metropolis, they decided to build a "branch" from Centralia northeastward to this natural crossroads for transportation, a destination reached in 1854. It didn't take long for the branch to become a profitable part of the core stem. Two years later workers completed this 705-mile all-Illinois railroad, and it claimed to be the world's longest. Initially, the IC appeared to be more of a real-estate enterprise than a transportation company, busily selling more than 2.5 million acres of largely fertile prairie lands. Every farm and townsite sold meant increased freight and passenger traffic. Another positive for the IC was that its congressional land grant secured IC bonds, and investors (including Brits and Europeans) found these securities attractive.[55]

In the vanguard of the east-to-west rails in the Prairie State was the Chicago & Rock Island Railroad (C&RI). Chartered in 1847 as the Rock Island & La Salle Railroad (RI&LS), this projected eighty-two-mile line planned to connect the Illinois & Michigan Canal at La Salle with the Mississippi River at Rock Island. This undertaking received widespread support from interests in western Illinois and eastern Iowa. Resembling so many paper companies, the RI&LS sputtered; capital-raising efforts failed to permit construction. Why? The likely explanation is that only a modest population lived between La Salle and the Rock Island area. Moreover, Rock Island and cross-river Davenport really had not advanced much beyond the frontier stage. Major investors, who possessed a larger view of railroad construction, were required.

In early 1851 a new day dawned for the stillborn railroad. New Englanders Henry Farnam and Joseph Sheffield brought money, vision, and personal integrity to the project. Illinois lawmakers permitted the Rock Island & La Salle to become the Chicago & Rock Island. A not-so-surprising stipulation came with the new company's charter. The C&RI must pay the canal trustees when the railroad operated in direct competition for all freight transported by rail at the same rates the waterway charged. "The legislature was not about to damage the heavy investment of public funds in the waterway (which totaled about $6.5 million)," observed a latter-day historian. "Yet the lawmakers were not unreasonable. The C&RI would not have to pay on shipments of livestock; fees were due only when the canal was open; freight shipments were exempt from tolls if they came from or were destined for points twenty miles beyond

La Salle; tolls would stop when the canal indebtedness had been retired, and taxes on railroad property could be deducted from all tolls paid."[56]

The C&RI charter contained a loophole, and soon the competitive restrictions became moot. Since the line would parallel the I&M, canal trustees needed to grant a right-of-way strip through its lands. "If the trustees refused to comply before the first Monday in June (1851) after passage of the act," noted a scholar of the formative years of the Rock Island, "the railroad company could build without any restrictions in relation to tolls." Bad advice about their legal obligations resulted in I&M officials not acting by the set deadline: "The canal's refusal to grant a right of way annulled the toll provisions of the act, and the railroad company was thus relieved of conditions which might have strangled it in its infancy."[57]

The Chicago & Rock Island gained the distinction of being one of the best public-spirited undertakings during the formative years of railroad building in the Old Northwest. The firm of Sheffield, Farnam & Company signed a remarkable contract with the directors of the C&RI. The partnership offered to acquire the right-of-way for this trans-Illinois line, conduct the grading, install bridges and track, and provide rolling stock, depots, and other facilities. For their work they agreed to accept 7 percent first mortgage bonds in the amount of $2 million, cash at the rate of $25,000 per month up to $500,000, and certificates that bore 10 percent interest payable in railroad stock when the road was finished. The firm could operate completed sections and receive all earnings until it transferred the finished project to the directors.[58]

The Sheffield and Farnam firm faithfully fulfilled its contractual obligations. On Washington's birthday in 1854, the C&RI became the first Lake Michigan to Mississippi River line. There was rejoicing in Illinois and neighboring Iowa. A lavish steamboat trip for dignitaries between Rock Island and St. Paul, Minnesota, closed the celebration. *Hunt's Merchants' Magazine* summed up the new road this way: "One could scarcely believe that a railroad, 181 miles long, could be built, and well built, too, in the short space of one year ten months and twelve days."[59]

The Sheffield organization did not stop at Rock Island. It gained lasting fame for being involved in constructing the first bridge to span the Mississippi River, linking end-of-track with Davenport. Its satellite

Railroad Bridge Company began work in 1853, and after more than two years and eight months the first C&RI trains steamed over to the Iowa side. But on May 6, 1856, disaster struck. The steamboat *Effie Afton* hit the bridge next to the open draw, and flames erupted. The boat was incinerated and the wingspan badly damaged, knocking the complex out of service. Rivermen rejoiced about the railroad's misfortune. Although repairs allowed trains to resume their movements in early September, a landmark legal dispute followed, pitting the steamboat's owner against the bridge company. In the case of *Hurd et al. v. the Railroad Bridge Company,* Abraham Lincoln performed masterfully for the defense, eventually leading Jacob Hurd, backed by St. Louis steamboat interests, to fail in his lawsuit. During this time the Sheffield and Farnam partnership became involved with the Mississippi & Missouri Railroad, which was destined to reach the Missouri River at Council Bluffs, Iowa, and was a core component of what became the Chicago, Rock Island & Pacific Railroad (Rock Island).[60]

In the 1850s several Chicago-based railroads also pushed toward the Mississippi River. Another pioneer was the Aurora Branch Railroad, born in 1849 and the nucleus of the future Chicago, Burlington & Quincy Railroad (Burlington). Unlike the Chicago & Rock Island, which under a single banner constructed a trans-Illinois iron way, the Burlington would consist of several predecessors before it achieved a unified route. The physical building of the Aurora railroad (strap rails initially) began at Turner Junction (later West Chicago) on the Galena and extended six miles south to Batavia. It next added the seven miles to Aurora, a small industrial and trade town located on a popular stagecoach route thirty-eight miles southwest of Chicago. On October 21, 1850, passenger service commenced over this little pike to Chicago. It was not until October 1853 that the company, renamed the Chicago & Aurora Railroad and later the Burlington, installed fifty-eight miles of track westward from Aurora to Mendota, where it interchanged with the Illinois Central. (A direct Burlington connection to Chicago would not be achieved until 1864.)[61]

In the burst of 2,679 miles of railroad construction in Illinois during the 1850s, the gestating Burlington absorbed three independent companies. Each possessed its own corporate charter and built modest mileage.

The Central Military Tract Railroad completed eighty miles of line between Mendota and Galesburg in 1854; the Peoria & Oquawka Railroad ninety-three miles between Galesburg and the Mississippi River opposite Burlington, Iowa, and between Galesburg and Peoria, the former segment in 1855 and the latter two years later; and the Northern Cross Railroad one hundred miles between Galesburg and Quincy. The Burlington took control of the Central Military Tract in 1856, the Peoria & Oquawka in 1864, and the Northern Cross in 1865. System building had begun in the Prairie State.[62]

Another successful Lake Michigan to Mississippi River project slowly evolved during the 1850s. It would not be speedy like the Chicago & Rock Island but rather shared the characteristics of the Burlington. This carrier was initially the Alton & Sangamon, chartered in 1847 and reorganized on several occasions, becoming the Chicago & Mississippi in 1852, Chicago, Alton & St. Louis (CA&StL) in 1855, and Chicago & Alton (C&A) in 1861. Notably this railroad built in a reverse fashion across Illinois. It started from the Mississippi River town of Alton and pushed northeastward to Springfield, Bloomington, and finally Joliet in 1854, creating a 220-mile route. A year later the Joliet & Chicago Railroad provided entry into the Lakeside City, and this property was leased in perpetuity. The CA&StL also served St. Louis, not by rail but by its own Mississippi River steamboats for the twenty-mile downstream trip. It was not until 1865 that the C&A rails reached East St. Louis (née Illinoistown).[63]

Another railroad to enter East St. Louis was the Ohio & Mississippi Railroad (O&M). This Cincinnati-based carrier was financed heavily by British investors. One significant aspect about the O&M was that it was built to "Erie Gauge" of six feet between its iron rails. It was also long, being 340 miles between its two terminals. With its rail connection in Ohio, the distance when it opened in 1857 made for a 900-mile route between the Atlantic Ocean and the Mississippi River. As with other railroads seeking to reach St. Louis, the O&M used the services of the Wiggins Ferry Company, but winter ice and dangerous ice flows could disrupt operations for weeks, even months. The break in gauges, however, meant that O&M rolling stock remained on the east bank.

Gauge standardization came in 1871, and the opening of the Eads Bridge three years later allowed for the free flow of commerce to St. Louis and the West.[64]

WISCONSIN

While the percentage increase in railroad mileage during the 1850s in Illinois reached an impressive 2,413 percent based on its 111 miles at midcentury, Wisconsin claimed a much higher figure, a 4,425 percent growth. Its mileage in 1850, however, stood at a trifling twenty miles. A decade later it had climbed to 905 miles, placing it ahead of Michigan of the five Old Northwest states. Yet the gap between these two was only 126 miles.[65]

Even though Wisconsinites had access to two remarkable bodies of water, the Great Lakes and the Mississippi River, there were few internal streams that could offer reliable transport. Internal transportation options were poor at best, the prime exception being the scattered military roads. "Oh, for a good road across the territory!" opined the editor of the *Grant County Herald* in 1843. "For want of it, the western part of Wisconsin Territory is actually going into decay!" His thoughts reflected those of other contemporary midwesterners. No wonder railroad fever developed.[66]

During the formative years of the Railway Age, the core strategy of Badger State railroad building centered logically on linking Lake Michigan with the Mississippi River. The primary route would serve the thriving southwestern lead-mining district. Early on, proponents of this artery contended overoptimistically that lead transport alone would justify its cost and would yield enormous savings for lead transportation charges to eastern markets as well as foreign ones via New Orleans. Time would also be saved. As happened elsewhere in the region, there were canal and plank road proposals, but interest in the iron horse alternative intensified during the middle and late 1840s. By the time of statehood in 1848, territorial lawmakers had chartered nine railroads, but none of them became more than paper entities. "The panic of 1837 and the six-year depression that followed it were partly to blame," explained a student of early Wisconsin railroads. "But even after the depression lifted in 1842, there had been too few people, too little capital, and too little product in the territory to make building or operating a railroad a profitable venture."[67]

What would be the best way to finance railroad construction? It had become widely recognized that state sponsorship of internal projects had been the wrong course of action for Michigan, Indiana, and Illinois taxpayers. Bonding by counties, townships, and municipalities was a possibility, but would eastern and foreign investors acquire these financial instruments? The popular thinking among railroad proponents was that would be unlikely. Stock sales possibly could yield the necessary funds. When it came to the Milwaukee & Waukesha Rail Road (M&W), Wisconsin's first functioning railroad, chartered in 1847, public and private stock subscriptions proved inadequate to ensure construction of this twenty-mile westward-bound road. What emerged was a creative means of locally based financing. This self-help endeavor became the farm-mortgage plan.

How did this scheme work? August Derleth, a prolific fiction writer and anthologist turned historian with his centennial history of the Milwaukee Road, explained this concept that helped finance the M&W and its soon-to-be successor, the cross-state Milwaukee & Mississippi Railroad (M&M):

> Farmers along the right of way were invited to purchase stock, and lacking money with which to pay for it, they could give personal notes secured by mortgages on their farms, payable in 10 years, and bearing 8 per cent interest. The railroad stock was to pay a 10 per cent dividend, and the company planned to subtract interest due on mortgages from accruing dividends, permitting the 2 per cent difference in stock dividends to accumulate on the books until the time when the notes were paid. The plan called for sale of the mortgages as collateral security for its bonds, and it appealed to the settler, who felt that his stock would be worth far more than the price he had paid by the time his note came due, when he could either sell his railroad securities and cancel his mortgage, or keep the stock as an investment.[68]

At first the farm-mortgaging plan failed to yield construction money. That problem was resolved when the City of Milwaukee agreed to accept these mortgages in exchange for its municipal bonds. Eastern bankers accepted these instruments for cash, guaranteeing funding for the startup carrier. (This scheme resembled modern "conduit" financing for funding large-scale projects through the issuance of municipal bonds.) By the time the Panic of 1857 disrupted the financial world, the M&M and several other Wisconsin railroads had embraced this fundraising method. It generated approximately $5 million collectively and about $900,000 for the M&M. As for the M&M, its backers' dream of a trans-Wisconsin iron way succeeded. In 1850 its predecessor company, the M&W, began to take shape. Not surprisingly, a festive celebration took place on November 20, 1850, when the company's directors, journalists, and prominent citizens of Milwaukee enjoyed a ride over the first five miles of this line. "No state in the union, and no country in the world, has ever heard the snorting of a locomotive at so early a period of its settlement," were the excited words of a participant. "No wonder the editors have thrown up their caps and made a joyful noise." Rails reached Waukesha (twenty miles from Milwaukee) in early 1851, Madison in 1854, and Prairie du Chien near the confluence of the Wisconsin and Mississippi Rivers, 225 miles west of Milwaukee, in 1857.[69]

Although the farm-mortgage plan led to important railroad achievements, it did not become the financial windfall that participating farmers anticipated. Those who engaged in this mortgage-for-railroad scheme faced a good chance that they would encounter financial problems once depression haunted the state. When Wisconsin railroads entered bankruptcy, their stock became worthless or nearly so, and farm foreclosures followed. Antirailroad feelings also erupted.[70]

The Milwaukee & Mississippi did not become the sole trans-Wisconsin railroad opened during the 1850s. The second long-distance carrier, La Crosse & Milwaukee Railroad (LC&M), chartered in 1852, built to the north of the M&M. Between 1855 and 1858, it installed two hundred miles of track from lake to river. The LC&M benefited from farm-mortgage funding and from a state land grant. The latter, though, led to a monumental scandal. Byron Kilbourn, who previously had been involved with the M&M and served as president of the LC&M, had committed bribery in obtaining that real-estate gift. He delivered $631,000 in company bonds to lawmakers and public officials in Madison, including $335,000 to fifty-nine assemblymen and $50,000 to the governor himself. Kilbourn avoided jail and remained a powerful political force in his hometown of Milwaukee.[71]

Not to be missed was the Racine & Mississippi Rail Road. The culmination of two earlier unbuilt projects in southern Wisconsin and northern Illinois, this 104-mile carrier emerged between 1855 and 1859 from Racine, a lake port south of Milwaukee, to Freeport, Illinois, and a connection over the Galena to Chicago. It would not be long before the major Wisconsin railroads, which appeared during the 1850s, came under the control of the Milwaukee & St. Paul, launched in 1863 and the nucleus of the future Chicago, Milwaukee & St. Paul.[72]

MISSOURI, IOWA, AND MINNESOTA

As settlers flocked to lands west of the Mississippi River in the vast Louisiana Purchase domain, interest in railroads took hold. Even though Missouri had entered the Union in 1821, Iowa in 1846, and Minnesota in 1858, river transport dominated. Roads, resembling those in the Old Northwest, were miserable, although there were a few improved ones (mostly constructed by the US Army), and a limited mileage (concentrated in southeastern Iowa) that were planked. As for the latter, backers preferred railroads: "While we regard our plank roads as emphatically the farmer's highway to market and prosperity, yet we ardently look for the time when the Mississippi shall be connected with the Missouri by railway."[73]

In the late 1840s and 1850s, Missouri slowly began to embrace the iron horse. While residents, most of all St. Louisans, were wedded to water commerce, taking advantage of Mississippi and Missouri Rivers and their principal tributaries, the feeling grew that railroads enhanced wealth and reduced the burdens of distance. In 1850 a railroad advocate worried about this dependence on natural waterways and their impact on St. Louis. "The age in which we live forbids that Iowa and Minnesota should continue to send their mineral and agricultural products to St. Louis, for no other reason than that the Mississippi runs southward!" Missouri lawmakers concurred. Their response: the state prior to the Panic of 1857 authorized the "loaning of state bonds" that totaled nearly $25 million to multiple startup carriers. Missouri enjoyed good credit, and its obligations generally sold at par. To protect taxpayers the state took a first lien on all railroad recipients. Missouri still became saddled with huge debt, and by 1860 it ranked fourth among the states in terms of railroad-created encumbrances. It took another fifty years before the state retired these obligations. Lawmakers surely smiled, however, when they realized that they did not need to undertake canal- and state-owned railroads as had Michigan, Indiana, and Illinois, states that racked up even greater public indebtedness.[74]

Unlike other midwestern states, Missouri encountered an investment-raising problem when it came to attracting eastern money. The explanation was that it was the only one that had legalized slavery, resulting from provisions in the Compromise of 1820 that allowed it to enter the Union the following year. Wealthy Yankees frequently objected to the existence of the peculiar institution after the passage of the Kansas-Nebraska Act in 1854 and the Dred Scott decision by the US Supreme Court three years later. If they wished to invest in midwestern rail projects, they had opportunities elsewhere. "Especially during the second half of the 1850s, the flow of investment capital into Missouri from New England, New York, and Pennsylvania dwindled and nearly dried up," according to historians Peter Hansen, Don Hofsommer, and Carlos Schwantes, "dropping from providing 68 percent of the investment capital reaching Missouri in the late 1840s to 17 percent by the late 1850s, while dollars directed to Illinois greatly increased."[75]

Prior to the Civil War, three major railroads appeared in Missouri: the Hannibal & St. Joseph (H&StJ), the Pacific Railroad of Missouri (Pacific), and the North Missouri. The first to receive a charter was the H&StJ. In 1847 the state granted its backers, "solid men" who included John Murray Forbes of Boston and James Joy of Detroit, the right to build between the two river towns in its corporate name. The project also provided a potential link at Quincy, Illinois, via a Mississippi ferry, with the newly organized Burlington, a company controlled by these same shrewd investors. (The Father of Waters would not be bridged until 1868.) Early on the H&StJ was conceived as a possible link in a transcontinental railroad. Westward construction began at Hannibal in 1851, and by late 1858 its standard-gauge rails had reached the mid-Missouri town of Brookfield, one hundred miles from milepost 0. Unusual for construction in the antebellum Midwest, work also commenced at the opposite end, moving eastward. This became possible because materials could be transported by Missouri River steamboats to St. Joseph, the state's second-largest city. The building was noteworthy as well. The contractor made early use of steam shovels and excavators, helping mitigate a labor shortage. On February 13, 1859, the final spike was driven at a remote site between Chillicothe and Cream Ridge, forging a 204-mile trans-state artery and easy access to Weston (née West Town), a jumping-off place for wagon trains on the Santa Fe, Oregon, and California Trails. While private capital did much to finance this trans-Missouri road, Congress made a substantial contribution. In mid-1852 it granted the company a hard-won land grant, ultimately totaling 611,323 acres of mostly productive agricultural real estate. There were strings attached. The H&StJ was required to carry the US mails "at such price as Congress may by law direct" and to transport US government troops and property at no charge. As for the former, the H&StJ on April 3, 1860, dispatched a special train that arrived in St. Joseph with letters for the inaugural run of the Pony Express, a lauded public service that the completion of the transcontinental telegraph soon made obsolete.[76]

The other two antebellum railroads began in St. Louis, the quintessential and dominant American river city. For decades its citizens believed that communities grew and prospered along great waterways, but that attitude was about to change. Among an increasing number of St. Louis interests, railroads, not steamboats, were deemed to be the transport of the future. In 1849 the Pacific Railroad of Missouri received its charter to build westward through the "City of Jefferson" and terminate at the Kansas border "with the view that the same may be continued hereafter to the Pacific Ocean." It became the first railroad in the nation to use "Pacific" in its corporate name. On July 4, 1851 (the most patriotic date on the nation's calendar), festive ground-breaking ceremonies took place in downtown St. Louis, a commercial center of 77,860 residents. Yet more than a year passed before the first locomotive, the twenty-two-ton Pacific, a 4-4-0 product of Taunton Locomotive Works, reached St. Louis. On December 9, 1852, this diminutive steamer made its maiden run over the five miles of broad-gauge iron rails (5 feet 6 inches) between downtown St. Louis and Cheltenham, a village renowned as the state's first (but short-lived) secular utopia, Icaria, led by French communitarian Etienne Cabet. St. Louis boosters, being no different from other forward-looking midwesterners, dreamed of a Pacific railroad, a feeling that intensified with the acquisition of Oregon in 1846, the Mexican Cession of 1848, and California statehood in 1850. After 1849 came the national mania of the California Gold Rush.[77]

The Pacific Railroad crept westward. There were continuing frustrations, notwithstanding that the company had won a federal land grant of approximately 125,000 acres in 1852 and received state financial assistance. The topography, for one thing, presented challenges. Building through hilly terrain and bridging numerous streams and rivers took time and money. Only twenty miles west of St. Louis, the workers needed to bore a tunnel to maintain an acceptable ruling grade. Outbreaks of deadly cholera also caused delays. To worsen matters, public confidence was badly shaken by one of the great railroad disasters of the nineteenth century. In fact, it was the deadliest railroad bridge disaster to date. On November 1, 1855, the 760-foot temporary wooden-truss structure over the Gasconade River gave way as the locomotive Missouri pulled an excursion train that carried well-wishers to celebrate the completion of the line to Jefferson City. Only the last car of this thirteen-car consist remained on the rails. Forty-three individuals perished (earlier the accident report claimed thirty-one fatalities), including the chief construction engineer, a prominent merchant, and several state legislators. By the early months of the Civil War, rails had extended to Sedalia, 189 miles west of St. Louis yet still miles from Kansas.[78]

The Pacific Railroad launched another line of later significance. Known as the Southwest Branch (the future St. Louis & San Francisco Railroad), it completed nineteen miles of broad-gauge track in 1858 between Franklin (later Pacific) near the St. Louis County line and St. Clair. More followed. Twenty-four miles opened the following year, and by the eve of the Civil War rails had reached Rolla on the edge of the Ozarks, creating a seventy-seven-mile extension.[79]

The North Missouri Railroad became the third major Show-Me State railroad before the Civil War. Just as the Pacific Railroad encountered problems with the terrain, this St. Louis–based company faced a more serious and expensive obstacle: spanning the wide and treacherous Missouri River. It was chartered in 1851, but construction failed to start for another three years. Workers and materials finally appeared

By the 1850s the most popular type of steam locomotive had become the American Standard 4-4-0. The Minnesota, the early workhorse on the broad-gauge North Missouri Railroad, allegedly pulled the initial train from St. Louis to St. Charles. This piece of motive power, built in 1852 by Swinburne, Smith & Company of Patterson, New Jersey, served this emerging road well. *(Author's collection)*

along the St. Louis area survey. In August 1855, after nearly thirteen months of sporadic building, the fledgling road opened nineteen miles of broad-gauge line between center-city St. Louis and a ferry landing on the Missouri River opposite St. Charles, the former state capital. This iron road connection pleased St. Charles residents, realizing that they were twenty-one miles nearer to St. Louis than by the circuitous and potentially dangerous Missouri-Mississippi water route and much closer in terms of travel time.[80]

Supporters of the North Missouri, who resembled those of the Pacific Railroad, were forward-looking St. Louisans and ambitious with their railroad plans. They expected (hoped) to reach Iowa and penetrate farther northward, perhaps reaching Minnesota. Their core strategy was to protect and enhance St. Louis trade, being most concerned about the growing economic influence of Chicago due to its expanding network of iron rails. "The early completion of the North Missouri road is indispensably necessary," editorialized the *St. Louis Pilot*. "It is true that the early completion of this road is vital to the interests of St. Louis, as it will secure to her a trade which is now in danger of being lost."[81]

The North Missouri struggled financially. Unlike either the H&StJ or the Pacific Railroad, the company failed to receive a federal land grant, due principally to inept lobbying in Washington. Still, it got both private and public support. As with other contemporary railroad projects, the North Missouri cobbled together funds from county and municipal stock and bond sales and individual investors.[82]

Throughout its formative years, North Missouri boosters expressed optimism about how their railroad would develop the region north and west of St. Louis. "The North Missouri road [will run] near midway between the Mississippi and Missouri rivers, one of which is closed by ice from one to three months of the year, the other closed by ice and low water for five or six months of the year and of dangerous navigation the other six months," opined a supporter. "We say the North Missouri Road must take nearly all the business of the country lying between these rivers." The North Missouri also expected to establish a thriving interchange with the H&StJ at Macon City (later Macon), diverting freight and passenger traffic to and from the northwestern part of the state to St. Louis and beyond. Said its president, "There is no reason to doubt that this Road when finished to the crossing of the Hannibal & St. Joseph Road will prove one of the best paying Roads in the West."[83]

Tracklaying proved sluggish. At last in 1857 rails reached Warrenton, fifty-eight miles from St. Louis, and a year later Allen, near the future townsite and railroad hub of Moberly. In early 1859 Macon City welcomed its first North Missouri train, creating a connection with H&StJ and 172 miles from St. Louis. (Much of the anticipated traffic from this interchange flowed to Chicago and not to St. Louis.) The growing impact of the depression and the Civil War delayed further expansion; Macon City remained the northern terminus until 1868.[84]

By 1860 the North Missouri hardly ranked as a model railroad. "It was not yet in a fully completed condition, being deficient in depot buildings, water stations and many other things," wrote an observer. The explanation involved money. Although construction costs had not been excessive, the national depression, which began in September 1857, led to declining revenues, resulting in a funding drought. Moreover, individuals who had subscribed to earlier stock were either unable or slow to make their installment payments. And its nonstandard gauge obviously did not help. Finally, it reduced the track width in 1867. "Now the North Missouri conforms to the gauge of all the roads in Iowa and Illinois, and the Hannibal & St. Joseph road," reported the *American Railroad Journal*. "The work of changing the gauge, the distance being 170 miles, was accomplished in three days."[85]

Still another antebellum railroad of importance appeared in Missouri, the St. Louis & Iron Mountain (StL&IM). Its backers sought to serve the iron-mining district of southeast Missouri. This industry had to cope with difficult and expensive transportation problems, and the iron horse became its salvation. In 1856 workers laid twelve miles of rails south of St. Louis, extended a year later another thirty-four miles, and in 1858 reached Pilot Knob, producing an eighty-six-mile mainline and also a short branch to Mineral Point.[86]

By the time the Civil War erupted, Missouri also claimed about twenty miles of the Cairo & Fulton Railroad (C&F). Its supporters entertained visions of building from the Missouri side of the Mississippi River (close to Cairo, Illinois) to Fulton, Arkansas, near Indian Territory. This project potentially could become a link in a transcontinental railroad that would use the low-level route made possible by the Gadsden Purchase. Happily for this gestating undertaking, it had secured nearly two million acres of public lands. Although Chicago, Cincinnati, and Louisville interests hoped that the C&F would prevent St. Louis from penetrating the Southwest, this did not happen. In 1867 St. Louis investors took control of the St. Louis & Iron Mountain and the C&F, and these roads became the St. Louis, Iron Mountain & Southern Railroad (Iron Mountain). By 1873 the road operated between St. Louis and Little Rock, and soon it reached the Texas border. As historians Hansen, Hofsommer, and Schwantes concluded, "By connecting with Texas railroads at Texarkana, the Iron Mountain opened to Saint Louis a vast new trade territory of seemingly limitless possibilities."[87]

Although Missouri ultimately became laced with railroads, trunk roads, their branches, and shortlines, they faced a disadvantage that was largely missing in rival Illinois. Chicago benefited; St. Louis did not. Extending rails outward from St. Louis, builders encountered "pot and kettle" country and, for the St. Louis & Iron Mountain, the Ozark foothills. There was no expansive Illinois-like "Grand Prairie" with its vast open areas of tall grasses. Spanning streams, most of all the mighty Missouri River, increased costs and created its own engineering challenges.

Iowans were not immune to railroad fever before 1860. Although the North Missouri failed to reach the Hawkeye State prior to the outbreak of Civil War, the first railroad charter dated back a decade with the organization of the Davenport & Iowa City Railroad. Enthusiasm for this fifty-five-mile project produced solely a paper reality. Yet within a few years, its supporters flocked to the Mississippi & Missouri Railroad, affiliated with the Chicago & Rock Island and after 1866 part of the Rock Island. For one thing, they and others realized that their state lay in the path of the most direct route between a burgeoning Chicago and the Pacific Ocean. They wanted the iron horse and connections to the Lakeside City and points east.[88]

Backers of the Mississippi & Missouri won the honor of being the first to break ground for an Iowa railroad. The place was Davenport, the year 1853. The company board of directors sought to extend rails in three directions: one west to Iowa City (the state capital until 1857) and onward through Fort Des Moines (now Des Moines) and toward the general vicinity of Council Bluffs, another into southern Iowa and perhaps deep into the Southwest, and a third northwestward, aiming toward Minnesota Territory through Cedar Rapids. Resembling so many contemporary projects, progress was painfully slow. Not until mid-1855 did workers start to lay rail, and soon afterward the first locomotive arrived, the Antoine Le Claire, a 4-4-0 from the Rogers Locomotive and Machine Works. By year's end sixty-eight miles had been installed between Davenport and Iowa City and on the Southwestern Extension to Muscatine, another Mississippi River town. Before the economic impact of the Panic of 1857 took hold, the latter line was lengthened thirty-eight miles southwestward to the county-seat town of Washington, and there it stalled until after the Civil War. Construction was also suspended at Marengo, forty miles west of Iowa City. Nothing appeared on the hoped-for line to Cedar Rapids and points toward Minnesota. Nevertheless,

Mississippi & Missouri trackage had considerable value, being linked to Chicago by the only bridge to span the Mississippi River, and its service area was reasonably well populated. Iowa had also received a generous land grant from the federal government in 1856, and the Mississippi & Missouri got a sizable share of this largess, amounting to more than 480,000 mostly fertile acres.[89]

The antebellum years saw other railroad construction in the Hawkeye State. It was not that impressive, however. The Keokuk & St. Paul Railroad, designed to build along the west bank of the Mississippi River, never achieved much of its intended goal. Still, between 1857 and 1859 the company completed the short distance between Keokuk and Fort Madison. During this period the Des Moines Valley Railroad, which paralleled the east bank of the Des Moines River, likewise pushed out from Keokuk. And it achieved greater mileage, although by 1861 it terminated at Eddyville, a river-crossing community, ninety-two miles from its starting point.[90]

Notwithstanding the advantages that the Mississippi & Missouri had with its early start and its bridge over the Mississippi River, two other companies penetrated farther into the Iowa interior. One was the Burlington & Missouri River Railroad (B&MR), tied to the Burlington and its Boston investors. Although incorporated in 1852, the B&MR did not see a locomotive in Burlington, a bustling Mississippi River town, until four years later. Aided by land-grant acres and eastern money, tracks arrived in Ottumwa on the Des Moines River in 1859, a distance of seventy-five miles. There its railhead remained until after the Civil War. Fortunately, the company served a rapidly developing area and profitably hauled grain and livestock outbound and lumber and merchandise inbound.[91]

The second Iowa road that evolved during the antebellum years was the Chicago, Iowa & Nebraska Railroad (CI&N), financed principally by eastern interests. Construction started soon after its official organization in 1856. Tracklaying commenced at Clinton on the opposite bank of the Mississippi River from Fulton, Illinois, western terminus of the Galena. Similar to what took place in much of the Midwest, the Panic of 1857 delayed advancement, but in mid-1859 the CI&N completed the eighty-two miles to Cedar Rapids. Resembling the B&MR, its service area was relatively populated, and traffic grew steadily. The CI&N, however, never extended beyond Cedar Rapids; its backers and local interests decided to launch another company, the Cedar Rapids & Missouri River Rail Road (CR&MR), designed to build toward the Missouri River. (The CI&N had initially considered aiming toward Minnesota.) The CR&MR endeavor also benefited from a substantial land grant, one originally intended to assist the failed but partially graded Iowa Central Air Line. Although the outbreak of war caused shortages of labor and materials, the road marched slowly westward and by 1865 had reached Boone, 121 miles from Cedar Rapids. Two years earlier, the Galena had leased both the CI&N and the CR&MR.[92]

Less impressive than either the Burlington & Missouri River or the Chicago, Iowa & Nebraska-Cedar Rapids & Missouri River Railroads was the Dubuque & Pacific Railroad. It, too, dated from the mid-1850s and by 1859 connected Dubuque on the Mississippi with Independence. Two years later its rails extended to Cedar Falls, making for a ninety-nine-mile pike. At that time the company flew the more realistic corporate banner of the Dubuque & Sioux City Rail Road.[93]

While railroad construction in the Hawkeye State included south-to-north lines, the thrust developed east-to-west, a direction that would dominate. Iowans by 1860 could not boast about the state's railroad mileage as they could a generation or two later. Iowa had 655 miles, yet far more than what California of the trans-Mississippi states had that year. The Golden State had a meager twenty-three miles. In the Midwest only Michigan had less mileage than Iowa with 437 miles. Nevertheless, the opening of the Hawkeye State's modest railroad mileage helped spark heavy in-migration, especially from the East and sections of the Old Northwest; the population swelled from 192,214 in 1850 to 674,913 a decade later.[94]

On the eve of the Civil War, Minnesota remained a railroad desert. In 1858 the closest rail head to St. Paul, the state capital and headwaters of Mississippi River steamboat traffic, was La Crosse, Wisconsin. Minnesotans realized that they required more than river transport on the Mississippi, Minnesota, and Red River of the North to obtain long-term prosperity. There was a need to replace the heavy, all-wooden Red River two-wheeled carts pulled often by oxen that lumbered along a

The William Crooks, a classic 4-4-0 locomotive, ushered in the Railway Age in Minnesota on June 28, 1862. In 1908 the refurbished William Crooks finds James J. Hill, builder of the Great Northern Railway, standing on the steps of the tender. This historic locomotive eventually became the property of the Minnesota Historical Society and was later loaned to the Lake Superior Railroad Museum in Duluth. *(Author's collection)*

primitive roadway between St. Paul and Pembina, near the international border. Although railroads promised a solution to most transportation shortcomings, they were expensive to construct. In 1857, a year prior to statehood, territorial lawmakers granted incorporation to the Minnesota & Pacific Railroad (M&P), an undertaking that came with high expectations. Its promoters, being not that different from their contemporaries elsewhere, had ambitions beyond reason—in this case, extending a line from the Wisconsin border to the Pacific Ocean. Soon the M&P embraced more achievable goals. It intended to install track from St. Croix on the eastern territorial boundary to Breckenridge on the border with Dakota Territory with a branch from St. Anthony (later part of an expanded Minneapolis) to St. Vincent near the mouth of the Pembina River. Why this configuration? In 1857 Congress had passed a land-grant measure for the territory, and St. Paul politicians agreed to its provisions.

The federal government made it clear how its largess must be awarded, designating various paths for the iron horse across the vast wilderness. The concept was to follow established land routes.[95]

The deepening depression (which raged from 1857 to 1862), the Sioux Uprising in 1862, and the need for investment capital stymied actual railroad service. The M&P in 1858, however, succeeded in finishing about sixty miles of grading and bridging north of St. Paul to Clear Lake. The M&P morphed by the early 1860s into the St. Paul & Pacific, and that company succeeded in installing a line between St. Paul and St. Anthony. On June 28, 1862, the William Crooks, a classic 4-4-0 steam locomotive, pulled the first train in the North Star State, a harbinger of better transportation to come. As the 1860s closed, the state claimed 766 route miles. Within several decades a surge in population together with thriving business, farming, and mining activities made Minnesota a banner railroad state.[96]

WORKING ON THE RAILROAD

The coming of the iron horse meant that these emerging railroads needed to hire suitable workers. Midwestern carriers were no different from earlier upstarts in the East. For operating personnel they required locomotive engineers, sometimes referred to as engine runners. Ideally these individuals possessed a mechanical bent, were reasonably strong physically, and had good character, meaning that they were nondrinkers. These men may have been involved in blacksmithing and foundry work or familiar with agricultural equipment. Conductors, who were officially in charge of the train, might previously have been employed as stagecoach drivers or canal or steamboat captains on the Great Lakes, coastal waters, or inland rivers. This meant that they had experience supervising employees, managing passengers, and overseeing freight shipments and US mail. Firemen and brakemen might have had backgrounds similar to those of engineers and conductors and probably expected to be elevated to those positions. The frontline workers, who more than any others were in the public eye, were the station agents. These men (women were rare until the advent of telegraphy) needed to be literate and to have basic mathematical abilities. Ideally they possessed people skills and could handle less-than-carload-lot freight shipments and station equipment. Such individuals might have worked in hotels or taverns where they had been in charge of a stagecoach stop, or maybe they hailed from a local commercial business.[97]

Throughout America, young men often wished to leave an agricultural life, and the Midwest was no exception. The daily and yearly cycles of farming were monotonous; railroading represented a more exciting career. This occupation might generate greater income, and there was the possibility of advancements. Not to be overlooked, the steam locomotive represented an exciting technology; it oozed modernity.

What about compensation? The engineers usually received the highest pay, followed by conductors, agents, firemen, and brakemen. Salaries might be modest, even for the man at the throttle. It was not unusual for employees to augment their railroad income, and they might do so while working at their assigned jobs. Trainmen, baggagemen, and US postal workers were known to buy produce in villages and towns along the line and sell it profitably in the larger communities. In the 1850s an Indiana editor had this to say about the practice: "We understand that the mail agents on the New Albany and Salem Railroad are largely engaged in the produce business." He added lightheartedly, "We think that the Postmaster General ought to provide them with an extra car to make room for the mails that are now crowded out by the heavy shipment of eggs, butter, etc."[98]

TRAINS AND TRAVEL

In the antebellum period, denizens of the Midwest saw a remarkable change in the physical railroad. After all, this can best be described as the "Demonstration Period." An individual in 1860 had only to examine the track. Although there were places where strap rail could still be found, rolled, all-metal wrought-iron rails had come into common usage. By the 1850s midwestern states started to outlaw dangerous strap rail; Michigan did so in its general railroad law of 1855. A year later a Hoosier State carrier told its shareholders that workers had replaced the last six miles of strap rail with iron T-rail, noting that "it will relieve us from the bad name of having to run over it, which has had a very unfortunate influence upon our passenger business." These all-metal rails were usually spiked to hardwood ties and were placed on a graded earthen right-of-way and not installed on wooden platforms or stilts. Gauges, though, reflected diversity rather than uniformity. What had become the standard gauge of 4 feet 8½ inches between the rails dominated, and it was the only width found in Iowa, Michigan, and Wisconsin. Illinois, too, had mostly standard gauge. Missouri initially sported the broader 5-foot-6-inch width. Ohio and Indiana had the greatest mixture: standard, 4 feet 10 inches, 5 feet 4 inches, and 6-foot gauges. This hodgepodge mostly remained until the Civil War era, the exception being the short-lived narrow-gauge (3 feet and 3 feet 6 inches) phenomenon of the 1870s that continued into the following decade.[99]

Motive power and rolling stock captured the greatest attention. By the time of the Civil War, the basic appearance of steam locomotives had evolved into what they would look like for decades to come. They featured a closed cab, steam and sand domes, a bell, a whistle, an oil-burning headlight, and perhaps a cowcatcher and spark arrester. There were an array of new devices, including engine brakes, equalizing levers, and springs. While the 4-4-0 wheel arrangement dominated, locomotives had greater weight and produced more steam pressure. In 1845 the typical locomotive weighed thirteen tons and maintained eighty pounds of steam pressure, but fifteen years later the former had increased to twenty-five tons and the latter to 110 pounds of pressure. Even though wood usually filled the tender, coal was being adopted. In 1860 the Illinois Central studied the performance of fuel consumption on its freight and passenger locomotives and learned that wood burners cost the company 13.4 cents a mile to operate, but coal-fired burners cost it only 6.2 cents a mile. The days of wood fuel for railroads in the Midwest were numbered, although the changeover was gradual. The Michigan Central, for example, burned 100,835 cords of wood and 59,450 tons of coal in 1872. These iron horses were often colorful, being painted in bright colors and occasionally adorned with elaborate brass or bronze ornamentation. The Antoine Le Claire, the first locomotive in Iowa, featured two bronze statues of its corpulent namesake, the owner of the popular Le Claire House in Davenport.[100]

Passenger cars on midwestern railroads improved noticeably during the antebellum period. The earliest ones offered little in the way of amenities. "The seat ran along each side, like those of the omnibus, and the coaches equally destitute of any and every other appliance for the comfort or conveyance of the traveler, other than to sit down and 'hand-on'—if he could," observed a rider on the Northern Cross Rail Road. "A sudden lurch of the coach would often slide a sitter half the length of the coach and land him, or her, with gruesome bump in the middle of the floor." Novelist Charles Dickens made an extended tour in the United States and Canada in 1842, which included a cold-weather train trip between the Ohio towns of Tiffin and Sandusky. He commented in a not-so-flattering fashion on the overall quality of its rolling stock: "The cars are like shabby omnibuses, but larger: holding thirty, forty, fifty people. The seats, instead of stretching end to end, are placed crosswise. In the centre of the carriage, there is usually a stove. It is insufferable close, and you see the hot air fluttering between yourself and any other object you may happen to look at, like the ghost of smoke." By 1860 coaches might provide reclining seats and were most likely found only on prosperous roads. This equipment made overnight traveling somewhat less wearing before sleeping cars became available. Car heating also improved. Stoves became nearly universal (perhaps two per car), and coal replaced wood. Ventilation, too, became better with roof intake units. About 1860 came the introduction of the clerestory roof, characterized by a row of small windows directly under the roof that provided greater air circulation. The clerestory design also improved natural lighting. At night lard oil or compressed coal gas lamps superseded candles for illumination. Lard oil fixtures had their drawbacks. These were suspended in the center of the car and, owing to the motion of the train, were continually smoking. Passengers surely enjoyed access to water tanks (they usually drank from an attached common cup), and toilets were available, being simply a wooden box with a circular hole cut in the top for the seat. Even the color decor might be striking, with pale tones of blue, grey, red, and yellow. Since dining cars were absent, there were trackside eating houses, but the time to partake of food and drink was usually limited to fifteen to thirty minutes. Travelers frequently brought their own food, or they purchased these items from a young entrepreneurial news butcher who also sold a variety of oddments. Although passenger coaches remained largely wooden, their capacity increased, ranging up to sixty-five or more occupants. Ride quality improved noticeably as track structures became stronger, car suspension was enhanced, and additional sets of wheel trucks were installed. In the late 1850s, the Illinois Central, for one, constructed in its shops a twelve-wheel car that made for a more pleasurable trip.[101]

Passengers (and freight patrons) began to experience the convenience of company-owned and designed depots. When railroads first appeared, they often relied on existing establishments, especially hotels and taverns, to shelter travelers, sell tickets, and conduct other business. Franz Anton Ritter von Gerstner, the visiting European railroad expert, noted in 1843 that Ohio's Monroeville & Sandusky City Railroad "has not constructed any *buildings* on the line. The warehouse [for freight] in Monroeville, which is served by several spurs, was built by private individuals." By 1860 it became more common to have a railroad-constructed depot (or a converted dwelling or business structure) even in small communities. There would be dedicated space for waiting, freight and baggage storage, and an agent's office.[102]

With improving equipment and creature comforts, travel by rail became faster and at least tolerable if not exhilarating. Americans craved speed, and railroads outdid competing forms of transportation, whether stagecoaches or steamboats. A rail journey from St. Louis to Boston in the late 1850s took about forty-eight hours rather than an additional day or longer. Shorter trips also made better time than alternative modes, including the fastest stagecoaches.

As with all travelers on public conveyances, there were complaints. By 1860 they involved late trains, dirty cars, surly and rude crew members, and annoying and noisy passengers, ranging from intoxicated, smelly, or excessively talkative seatmates to screaming babies and misbehaving children. As with alternative forms of transportation, there was always the worry about contagious diseases, especially cholera, smallpox, or the grippe, spread by fellow passengers. The absence or inconvenience of acceptable food and drink options was a popular lament. Patrons might fuss about some depots being located far from the town center. Most of these travel concerns remained for generations. In some ways a love-hate relationship developed in the public mind about railroad travel, an attitude that knew no geographical bounds. Always, too, the fear persisted of the possibility of a serious derailment, head-on collision, or bridge failure.[103] But to assume that all railroad trips had their annoyances would be incorrect. As early as 1850, a traveler from Sandusky to Cincinnati enjoyed his experiences. The *Cleveland Herald* noted that he commented favorably on "the excellent management of the road (Mad River & Lake Erie), the competency and carefulness of the engineers, the attention and politeness of the conductors, the freedom from rowdyism and the excellent language of subordinates and the frequent distribution of cold water through the train." A majority of folks agreed that rail travel had become a magic carpet. "The future is a grand and glorious gift just waiting to be opened by the railroad," remarked an Ohioan on the eve of the Civil War.[104]

During the antebellum years, more midwesterners gained access to an expanding network of iron rails. In 1850 Iowa, Missouri, and Minnesota lacked railroads, and Wisconsin had but twenty miles; the other four states continued to claim only modest trackage. Ohio led with 575 miles, followed by Michigan with 380 miles, Indiana with 228 miles, and Illinois with 110 miles. A decade later the railroad picture had changed dramatically. Illinois ranked first with 2,867 miles, and Ohio was next with 2,299 miles. These states were followed by Indiana with 2,125 miles, Wisconsin with 922 miles, Missouri with 817 miles, Michigan with 770 miles, and Iowa with 679 miles. The Midwest and the rest of the nation were drawing closer together. Few residents would question that the iron horse had already redefined spatial relationships. Greater expansion in mileage had just begun.[105]

TWO

DEVELOPMENT

1860–1890

EXPANSION

Shortly before Citadel cadets fired on federal forces at Fort Sumter in the harbor at Charleston, South Carolina, on April 12, 1861, triggering a four-year American bloodbath, more than thirty thousand route miles of railroad operated nationwide. A substantial portion of this mileage served the Midwest. During the 1850s this region installed nearly ten thousand miles, significantly more than in either the Northeast or the South. At this time Chicago, whose population had ballooned from a scrubby frontier town of 4,470 in 1840 to 109,000, soon became the "New York of the West," eclipsing its rival St. Louis. Although the Lakeside City claimed eleven railroads, its citizens hungered for more. "Railroads are the magic carpets that bind the Republic," opined a local merchant: "They are the only mode of travel between most points. They give life to those they serve." What made these iron arteries, which radiated in and out of Chicago, so consequential was that they had established the city as the place where East meets West. With growing sectional tensions, this relationship meant that the Midwest had become closer aligned economically, socially, and culturally with New England and the Middle Atlantic states and, unlike St. Louis, less so with the South.[1]

Chicago's penetration reached most points on the compass. Affiliates of the New York Central (NYC) and Pennsylvania (PRR) provided connections with the Eastern Seaboard. To the south the Illinois Central (IC) connected at Cairo with "perpetual navigation" river traffic on the lower Mississippi. Shortly before the Civil War erupted, the Mobile & Ohio Railroad completed its 472-mile line northward from Mobile, Alabama, to Columbus, Kentucky, where a short link was made with the IC via transfer steamboats. To the west, the Galena & Chicago Union reached interior Iowa, as had the Mississippi & Missouri and the Burlington & Missouri River Railroads. To the north trackage extended into Wisconsin. The Milwaukee-based Milwaukee & St. Paul Railroad offered important interchanges with that state's expanding rail network.[2]

The outbreak of the Civil War soon ended the impact of the depression spawned by the Panic of 1857, which had severely affected the Midwest, yet the war years saw only modest line construction. Railroad iron was pricey, if obtainable, and labor was scarce and expensive. The trackage already built, however, helped enable a Union victory by April 1865. This came about, in part, due to the closure of the lower Mississippi and the Port of New Orleans during the early months of the conflict, thus diverting river traffic to the rails. There existed multiple routes from the East to Chicago and connections to the Mississippi and Ohio Rivers. These links allowed massive movements of federal troops and their military and support supplies. The most spectacular example of the tie-in of the Midwest to the Union cause came in September 1863 when the Eleventh and Twelfth Corps of the Army of the Potomac traveled by special trains across the Appalachians to Indianapolis and south to the Ohio River. By transporting these twenty thousand troops quickly, they saved the bottled-up federal forces in Chattanooga. Several Ohio and Indiana carriers made this possible: Central Ohio, Columbus & Xenia, Little Miami, Indiana Central, and Jeffersonville Railroads. Ten years earlier it would have been impossible for these two corps to have reached East Tennessee in time for this pivotal victory. Midwestern railroads met the needs of not only the military but also civilian passengers and freight customers. At times, though, they were nearly overwhelmed by the volume of wartime traffic.[3]

Once peace returned, major railroad construction resumed. National route mileage soared to 52,922 in 1870, reached 92,147 in 1880, and the following year for the first time exceeded 100,000 miles. It soon exploded, reaching 193,346 in 1890. The Midwest became an integral part of this rapidly spreading network of iron (and soon steel) rails. The eight states saw these dramatic mileage gains: Michigan, 1,638 in 1870 and 7,243 in 1890; Ohio, 3,538 in 1870 and 7,912 in 1890; Indiana, 3,177 in 1870 and 5,971 in 1890; Illinois, 4,823 in 1870 and 10,214 in 1890; Wisconsin, 1,525 in 1870 and 5,584 in 1890; Missouri, 2,000 in 1870 and 6,004 in 1890; Iowa, 2,683 in 1870 and 8,366 in 1890; and Minnesota, 1,092 in 1870 and 5,466 in 1890. When plotted on a national map, the middle point of railroad mileage reveals how the Midwest emerged as the center of land transportation. In 1860 it stood sixty miles south of Mansfield, Ohio; twenty years later it had moved thirty miles northwest of Logansport, Indiana; and by 1890 it was ninety miles northwest of Chicago. The Lakeside City itself mushroomed, especially during the Gilded Age. Its population grew from 503,185 in 1880 to 1,099,850 a decade later, an increase of slightly more than 118 percent. Mark Twain wrote of Chicago, "She is always a novelty; for she is never the Chicago you saw when you passed through the last time."[4]

Because of politics and geography, the first transcontinental route sliced through the trans-Chicago West region. Since the 1850s lawmakers had shown interest in forging a coast-to-coast rail route, but sectional disputes prevented anything of consequence from happening. To protect slavery, southerners agitated for a transcontinental line that stretched westward to California from New Orleans, Memphis, or possibly St. Louis. Northerners wanted to build west from Chicago, roughly along what became the Overland Route of the Chicago & North Western (North Western), Union Pacific, and Central Pacific Railroads. Americans generally assumed that there would be only a single transcontinental, due largely to high costs and construction challenges. Even this was impossible because congressional lawmakers from the North and South could not compromise on a projected route. This issue would not be resolved until the outbreak of the Civil War when southerners departed Washington, DC, for Montgomery, Alabama, the newly established capital of the Confederacy. The first Pacific Railroad Act, signed by President Abraham Lincoln on July 1, 1862, advanced this initial transcontinental railroad. The designated starting point was Council Bluffs, Iowa, located on the east bank of the Missouri River opposite Omaha, Nebraska Territory.[5]

Extending west from the Mississippi River to meet the gestating Union Pacific became the goal of three railroads. Fortunately for Iowans their state lay directly in the federally mandated path, contributing ultimately to its ranking as a top mileage state. A subsidiary of the North Western won the race to be the first Chicago road to reach what became milepost 0 for the Union Pacific, doing so under the banner of the Cedar Rapids & Missouri Railroad. This historic date was January 22, 1867. The Chicago, Rock Island & Pacific (Rock Island) entered Council Bluffs in May 1869, and the Burlington & Missouri River, controlled by the Chicago, Burlington & Quincy (Burlington), completed its trans-Iowa artery in January 1870. The Burlington, however, had earlier established its presence in Council Bluffs when its affiliate St. Joseph & Council Bluffs Railroad arrived in 1867. Later, in 1879 the Wabash-controlled Omaha & St. Louis Railroad entered the city from its parent company's trans-Missouri route at Brunswick. In the early 1880s, the Chicago, Milwaukee & St. Paul (Milwaukee Road) completed its Chicago to Council Bluffs line. These arteries collectively made Council Bluffs an important node on the national railroad map, and its population rose accordingly.[6]

Extensive system building occurred throughout the Midwest during the postwar decades. In fact, the 1880s became the golden age of railroad expansion. This came about through construction, merger, and lease and ranged from the monumental to the less impressive. "I have long been of the opinion that sooner or later the railroads of the country would group themselves into systems," reflected Charles Elliott Perkins, vice president and general manager of the Burlington, "and that each system would be self-sustaining—or cease to exist & be absorbed by those systems near at hand & strong enough to live alone." *Railway Age* concurred. Opined this national trade journal, "It is not to be denied that the public is far more efficiently and cheaply served by the consolidation of numerous disconnected often poverty-stricken roads into grand systems under superior management and provided with the most perfect equipment." Some of America's greatest and most powerful companies emerged or expanded. Several representative giants stand out. These include the NYC and the PRR east of Chicago and the North Western and Rock Island to its west.[7]

The NYC itself began as a collection of small railroads in New York State, but Cornelius Vanderbilt, its visionary leader, sought more mileage by embracing consolidation, through either merger or lease. His New York Central & Hudson River Railroad, launched in 1869, invested heavily in carriers that served Michigan, Ohio, Indiana, and Illinois. The Vanderbilt firm took control of the Lake Shore & Michigan Southern, Michigan Central, and the Cleveland, Cincinnati, Chicago & St. Louis Railway (known as the Big Four). The latter emerged in 1889 by uniting the Cincinnati, Indianapolis, St. Louis & Chicago and the Cleveland, Columbus, Cincinnati & Indianapolis Railroads.[8]

Resembling the Vanderbilt system, the PRR, chartered in 1846, bought or leased various railroad properties, including Pennsylvania's state-owned Main Line of Public Works in 1857. What became its route between Pittsburgh and Chicago operated for decades under the banner of the Pittsburgh, Fort Wayne & Chicago Railroad (PFtW&C). This company consisted of several independent roads, having been created in 1856 from the Ohio & Pennsylvania, Ohio & Indiana, and Fort Wayne & Chicago Railroads. A similar corporate-type history involved the Pittsburgh, Cincinnati & St. Louis Railroad (PC&StL), popularly known as the Panhandle. Included in this PRR-controlled property were several carriers that linked Pittsburgh, Columbus, and Cincinnati, specifically the Pittsburgh & Steubenville, Steubenville & Indiana, Central Ohio, Columbus & Xenia, and Little Miami Railroads. Also part of this complex were the Terre Haute & Indianapolis and the St. Louis, Vandalia & Terre Haute Railroads. In 1890 a corporate consolidation resulted in the PC&StL and several smaller properties becoming the Pittsburgh, Cincinnati, Chicago & St. Louis Railroad (Vandalia). The PRR also made possible the completion of the moribund Grand Rapids & Indiana Railroad ("Good Fishing Line"), forging a route between Fort Wayne and Mackinaw City, Michigan. This satellite firm for years operated largely as an independent railroad. To manage a growing and substantial rail network west of Pittsburgh and Erie, Pennsylvania, management launched

While having a less extensive midwestern network than either the New York Central or Pennsylvania, the Baltimore & Ohio by the 1870s had forged a through line between Baltimore and Chicago, a distance of 839 miles. In Chicago Junction, Ohio (Willard after 1917), the Chicago line diverged westward, and the Sandusky, Ohio, line extended northward to that Lake Erie port community. This ca. 1878 image shows the Chicago trackage on the left and the Sandusky trackage on the right. The large building houses the depot and division offices. *(Author's collection)*

an operating firm, the Pennsylvania Company, in 1869, and until 1920 the PRR had its lines east of Pittsburgh and its lines west of Pittsburgh and Erie. Lines west consisted of two units: the Northwest System, which contained the traffic-heavy PFtW&C, and the Southwest System, which had the Panhandle and Vandalia as its core. That structure, which created two largely independent halves, worked well. The equipment west of Pittsburgh was marked "Pennsylvania Lines" rather than "Pennsylvania Railroad."[9]

Consolidations were not always applauded by midwesterners. Indiana can be considered representative. As the NYC and the PRR became the dominant carriers in the Hoosier State, the *Indianapolis Journal* likely grasped the pulse of public sentiment. In early 1873 it editorialized, "The transportation of our people is at the mercy of men who never see us, who know nothing of us, and care nothing for us."[10]

Paralleling the evolution of the NYC and PRR, the North Western claimed a complicated corporate genealogy. It made its debut in 1859 as the Chicago & North Western Railway, emerging from the bankruptcy of the Chicago, St. Paul & Fond du Lac. This company operated in both Illinois and Wisconsin. Soon the North Western added more trackage in the Badger State, gaining access to Green Bay and subsequently extending into the copper-mining country of the Upper Peninsula of Michigan. Arguably of greater importance was the consolidation with Galena & Chicago Union Rail Road in 1864 and two years later the leasing of the Chicago & Milwaukee Railroad that opened in 1855 between these two cities. During the 1870s and 1880s, subsidiary firms constructed lines, often branches, in Iowa, Minnesota, and Dakota Territory. In the mid-1880s the North Western took control of the Fremont, Elkhorn & Missouri Valley, a property serving northern Nebraska and the Black Hills. As the last decade of the century began, it acquired the Milwaukee, Lake Shore & Western, a road that provided a connection between Milwaukee and Superior, Wisconsin, a busy port on Lake Superior.[11]

The North Western had a special relationship with the Chicago, St. Paul, Minneapolis & Omaha Railway, known as the Omaha. This sprawling property, which by the early twentieth century consisted of approximately 1,700 miles, served Wisconsin, Minnesota, Iowa, Nebraska, and South Dakota. As expected, the Omaha had predecessors, principally the St. Paul & Sioux City and the West Wisconsin Railroads. The North Western made the Omaha part of the North Western System in 1882, yet it remained a semi-independent property until the 1950s.[12]

The Rock Island lacked any special distinction with its system building. The core Chicago & Rock Island (C&RI), which in 1854 linked Chicago with the Mississippi River, became closely tied with the Mississippi & Missouri Railroad as the latter pushed toward Council Bluffs. Already the C&RI had leased the Peoria & Bureau Valley Railway, a valuable feeder that provided access to Peoria and the Illinois River. In 1865 and 1866, a complicated corporate arrangement between the Illinois and Iowa firms led to a unification, creating the Chicago, Rock Island & Pacific Railroad Company.[13]

The spurt in Rock Island expansion came after the national economy rebounded from the Panic of 1873. There was the leasing of the 162-mile Keokuk & Des Moines, a step that made sections of Iowa Rock Island country. New construction carried the company into other parts of the Hawkeye State and Missouri. Its footprint in the Midwest also increased in the late 1870s when it took a major financial position in what became the more-than-thousand-mile Burlington, Cedar Rapids & Northern, a firm that it absorbed in 1902. Under the generalship of Ransom Cable, the Rock Island became heavily involved in the trans-Missouri West. Its Chicago, Kansas & Nebraska put on a building blitz in Kansas during 1887 and 1888. Affiliated companies also gave the Cable road a presence in Colorado, Oklahoma Territory, and Texas. The road became truly "the Great Rock Island Route" and continued to grow freight and passenger traffic radiating in and out of Chicago. Observers thought the company becoming a bona fide "& Pacific" seemed a realistic possibility.[14]

Less famous railroads consolidated existing properties and built new lines. Take the Chicago, St. Paul & Kansas City Railroad (CStP&KC), a company that in 1892 became the Chicago Great Western Railway. Founder Alpheus Beede Stickney (usually referred to by his initials) and his business associates used the dormant charter of the Minnesota & Northwestern Railroad (M&NW) to build not northwesterly from the Twin Cities but in a southerly direction. In 1884 it opened a 110-mile line between St. Paul and Mona, Iowa, abutting the Minnesota border. This trackage forged a connection with an Illinois Central property that allowed entry into the Chicago gateway. Interestingly, railroad gossip speculated that the M&NW would likely be gobbled up by the IC. "The Illinois Central is now a large system, and well backed financially, and, with other large systems, must in time have its own line to the Northwest and become a direct competitor for the wheat and milling traffic," observed the *St. Paul Globe*. "By securing this road [M&NW] it would have a splendid line, a thing it has been wanting for some time past."[15]

The Stickney property had no plans to sell; it would not be taken over by the Illinois Central, Rock Island, or any other trunk road. Access on its own rails into Chicago became the immediate objective. This evolved by the M&NW absorbing Dubuque & Northwestern and connecting that Mississippi River city with M&NW rails. Next under the banner of the Minnesota & Northwestern Railroad Company of Illinois, Stickney's road at last reached its goal. In early 1888 through service commenced between St. Paul and Chicago.[16]

A. B. Stickney sought more expansion. In a corporate revamping, the CStP&KC emerged in 1885. It would take charge of the strategic Wisconsin, Iowa & Nebraska Railroad, which was known as the Diagonal and in the mid-1880s built from Waterloo to Des Moines, and connect it to the Stickney mainline at Oelwein, Iowa. These roads combined legally, and by 1891 additional construction and trackage rights arrangements provided the CStP&KC an avenue via Leavenworth, Kansas, into the Kansas City, Missouri, gateway. By this time the nearly nine-hundred-mile carrier had also added modest feeders. Its system building, albeit less than spectacular, had become part of the story of midwestern railroad growth. Not to be overlooked (or discounted) were the large number of railroads, often Chicago-based, that had the prefix "Chicago & . . ." in their corporate names, attesting again to the importance of this dynamic midwestern metropolis.[17]

Perhaps the most sensational railroad construction project in the Midwest during the postwar era of expansion, which involved Chicago and Cleveland, was the New York, Chicago & St. Louis Railroad, the famed Nickel Plate Road (NKP). In 1882 a group of investors, the "Seney Syndicate," led by New York City banker George Seney, opened a rail line between Buffalo and Chicago. This 521-mile steel roadway, which had been rapidly surveyed and constructed, was designed to become a formidable competitor to the Lake Shore & Michigan Southern (LS&MS), a Vanderbilt moneymaker. Unlike what contemporaries believed (and others later reported), this was not planned as a "hold up" road–a scheme to sell it to another road. Rather, its owners expected to have "glittering prospects" with their new property. When in operation, this well-engineered and well-built property, which boasted of being nineteen miles shorter than the LS&MS and sporting a spectacular steel span over the Cuyahoga River and the adjoining "Flats" in Cleveland, alarmed Vanderbilt management. Although W. H. Vanderbilt publicly belittled the NKP, he privately coveted the road. In October 1882, however, the owners sold the NKP to the Vanderbilt interests at a handsome profit.

The reason involved more than direct competition for freight and passenger traffic—it was the fear of a disastrous rate war that no pooling agreement would likely prevent.[18]

Often neglected in this Golden Age of line expansion were the industrial and terminal railroads. The Terminal Railroad Association of St. Louis (TRRA) earned the honor of being the foremost example in the Midwest and the nation. Launched in 1889, it came to monopolize all terminal and switching operations in St. Louis, including control of the strategic Eads Bridge, opened between St. Louis and East St. Louis in 1874. The principal architect of the TRRA was Jay Gould, who at this time controlled the Missouri Pacific and Wabash Railroads. He forced an agreement among six roads (three terminating in East St. Louis and three terminating in St. Louis) for a coordinated and efficient means of handling freight and passenger movements on both sides of the Mississippi River.[19]

Throughout the development decades, an important aspect of railroad expansion and betterments throughout the Midwest involved the transition from strap to wrought-iron to steel rails. As the 1860s began, a few smaller railroads continued to use strap rail, but they rapidly abandoned this inferior track choice. It had been cheap at first but quickly became an operational and maintenance nightmare. Iron became the replacement, although there were differences in quality. The Illinois Central, for one, opted for the best grade, and that meant either English- or Welsh-made wrought-iron rails. Then came steel in the 1860s and 1870s, and it was less likely to fail and could safely support more powerful locomotives, larger freight cars with their heavier loads, and faster passenger train speeds. It was not in Pittsburgh or some eastern city but in Chicago where the first American Bessemer rails were rolled, occurring in 1865. Yet the domestic market for some time saw steel imported from Britain, France, and Prussia (Germany after 1871). During the early domestic production of this metal, Illinois led the nation in the number of steel mills, having two such works in Chicago and one in Joliet. Much of this rail weighed fifty-six pounds to the yard, which long served as an industry standard. The NYC, however, adopted eighty-pound steel rail in 1884, and more carriers followed.[20]

TRAVELS

During the post–Civil War decades, dubbed the "Gilded Age" by novelists Mark Twain and Charles Dudley Warner, travelers experienced a steadily improving railroad network. If they boarded a train or changed trains in a great midwestern metropolis, they might be awed, perhaps confused by the hustle and bustle of the terminal station. The busiest places passengers encountered in the Midwest were Chicago and St. Louis. The former city lacked a union terminal, having multiple facilities, ranging from Dearborn to the North Western passenger stations. If travelers needed to move from one of these places to another, they could access a free transfer service by showing their interline ticket to the omnibus driver. The Parmalee Transfer Company, launched in 1853, transported them and their baggage conveniently and reliably. This monopoly operation made station interchanges somewhat seamless. The Parmalee firm also picked up passengers at downtown hotels, offices, and residences. St. Louis had a union depot for most carriers, although not initially. In 1875 this much-desired structure opened, yet from the start it was too small for the volume of business. Its inadequacies led the TRRA to seek a functional union station that consolidated all intercity passenger traffic under a single roof. In 1894 the magnificent Romanesque-style St. Louis Union Station held its grand opening. Patrons raved about the wide and attractive concourse with its retail shops and services, its one-hundred-room Terminal Hotel with its spacious and elegant dining room, and the massive steel train shed, described as the largest in the world. The station became an instant city landmark.[21]

Midwestern residents who did not live in or near large cities experienced depots that lacked complexities, being usually small and single-story. These were the ubiquitous "country" stations. By the post–Civil War years, all but the poorest companies wanted buildings designed for their needs rather than repurposed houses, hotels, or other existing structures. Throughout the region railroad patrons became intimately familiar with the combination depot: waiting room, central office, and freight and baggage room. In the late 1880s, the Ohio Commissioner of Railroads and Telegraphs reported that his state had "2,199 depots–seven stone, 85 brick, and the remainder wood." Those railroads that served larger towns were more likely to erect brick structures, and they became a replacement type in growing communities. New depots by the 1870s showed more exterior ornamentation then they had earlier, and that trend continued for some time. In rural areas, where there was a critical housing shortage for agents and their families, companies might erect two-story depots with "cozy" upstairs apartments. They were most commonly found in the Upper Peninsula of Michigan, in northern Wisconsin, throughout Minnesota, and in the Ozarks of Missouri.[22]

Of all the bourgeoning cities of the Midwest, railroads in Chicago developed the most extensive commuter service. No one questioned that it was the epicenter of such operations. The city's remarkable population surge continued: 298,963 in 1870 and 1,698,575 by the end of the century. Commuter traffic was reflected in how the Illinois Central increased this business. It climbed from roughly 200,000 passengers in 1870 to approximately 1,500,000 a decade later and reached 4 million in 1890. By the 1880s rail lines fanned out in fifteen directions, creating a pattern that resembled the spokes of a giant wheel. Communities like Winnetka, Des Plaines, Elmhurst, Downers Grove, Lockport, Flossmoor, Crete, Hammond, and East Chicago either emerged or grew rapidly. Suburban commuter runs extended outward for thirty to forty miles. It was not uncommon for specially designed depots and station space to appear, having in mind the flow of inbound and outbound commuters. Trains often stopped at every station, but some called at only the busiest places. One innovation stands out, and it took place on the IC. It introduced locomotives known as "double enders." They could run equally well forward or backward. Rapid acceleration from stops also became possible. Irrespective of motive power, these Chicago commuter roads appeared dedicated to offering reliable service. A descriptive publication titled *Chicago and Its Suburbs* praised the North Western for providing excellent commuter trains that were "adopted to the wants of city workers."[23]

The developing Railway Age had passenger trains that varied in quality and services provided. As branch or feeder trackage increased, these movements likely consisted of older rolling stock. Happily, most of the wholly obsolete cars by the Gilded Age had been retired. Maintenance of equipment assigned to these lines or used for mainline locals might also be modest. On branches, especially, a wooden day coach or

This broadside issued in 1877 by the Detroit & Milwaukee Railroad, successor to the Detroit & Pontiac Railroad (and a year later becoming the Detroit, Grand Haven & Milwaukee Railroad and later part of the Grand Trunk Western Railroad), immodestly boasted that this road was the "Cheap, Pleasant & Expeditious Route." *(Author's collection)*

two or maybe a combination car (baggage, mail, express, and passenger) were attached to a string of freight cars. These slow-moving "mixed" consists, which handled "hogs and humans," provided basic transportation. Commuter trains, whether in Chicago, St. Louis, or other cities, might use older coaches, but they lacked "head-end" cars. Perhaps there was a news butcher on board, but newspapers, oddments, and the like were often available in the station or at a nearby newsstand.

It was on main routes that passengers encountered the latest equipment. Still, this remained the wooden-car era. All-metal passenger cars would not appear until the early twentieth century. After all, hardwoods were plentiful and relatively inexpensive, and this lumber could easily be shaped and crafted by master carpenters. And their interiors could be elegant, reflecting popular Victorian tastes.[24]

Riding in a coach could be a pleasant experience. The Chicago & Alton Railroad (Alton), which by the 1880s linked Chicago, St. Louis, and Kansas City ("Three Great Cities of the West"), proclaimed on the cover of its March 1889 public timetable that it offered "Ladies Palace Day Cars and Palace Reclining Chair Cars FREE of Extra Charges." The Alton was not alone in providing comfortable equipment to patrons who traveled to and from midwestern destinations.[25]

What surely caught the eye of passengers was the advent of dining, sleeping, and parlor/observation cars. While riders continued to bring their own food on board, meals could be purchased on trains by the 1860s. This practice of eating and traveling was not novel; food had been part of the transportation experience for decades, occurring on canal packets, river and lake boats, and coastal steamers. Train travelers found it annoying (and time consuming) to stop along their journeys for meals, especially when they were eager to arrive at their destinations. Shortly after the Civil War, one of the earliest "hotel cars" came from the Aurora Shops of the Burlington. This piece of rolling stock could sleep thirty and feed up to forty patrons. In 1877 Florence Leslie, wife of the publisher of *Frank Leslie's Illustrated Newspaper,* traveled cross country in style. When she departed Chicago westbound on the North Western, she offered these thoughts about being aboard a Pullman hotel car: "We find everything closely resembling our late home, except that one end of the car is partitioned off and fitted up as a kitchen, storeroom,

CHICAGO ROCK ISLAND AND Pacific Railroad.

GREAT OVERLAND ROUTE

CHICAGO & OMAHA SHORT LINE.

THE

Best Equipped Road with the Smoothest Track

IN THE WEST.

MAGNIFICENT PALACE SLEEPING CARS

ON ALL THROUGH TRAINS.

GREAT OVERLAND MAIL

GOES OVER

ROCK ISLAND ROUTE.

A. M. SMITH, General Pass. Agent.

Form B 7.

A. KIMBALL. General Sup't.

CAMERON, AMBERG & CO., PRINTERS, CHICAGO.

Facing and above, In 1879 the Chicago, Rock Island & Pacific ballyhooed its Chicago to Omaha route, proclaiming that it was the "Best Equipped Road with the Smoothest Track in the West." This pocket timetable and system map also lauded its passenger comforts: "This Company Runs *The Only Line of Dining and Restaurant Cars* in the nation between Chicago and Omaha." Such self-promotion was typical and would continue throughout the Railway Age. *(Author's collection)*

scullery—reminding one, in their compactness and variety, of the little Parisian *cuisines,* where every inch of space is utilized, and where such a modicum of wood and charcoal produces such marvelous results." The main meal also pleased her: "At six the tables are laid for two each, with dainty linen, and the finest of glass and china, and we presently sit down to dinner. Our repast is Delmonican in its nature and style, consisting of soup, fish, *entries,* roast meat and vegetables, followed by the conventional dessert and the essential spoonful of black coffee."[26]

A better alternative came from business genius George Pullman. Although his Chicago-based company manufactured hotel cars, it introduced in 1868 the first dining car, named the Delmonico to honor the acclaimed New York restaurant. This car offered well-prepared and efficiently served meals in an attractive setting, complete with table linens, silverware, crystal glasses, and china dishes. Not until the 1880s did dining cars become standard parts of first-class passenger consists.[27]

George Pullman gained his greatest acclaim for his sleeping cars. Although he was not the inventor and had competitors, principally the

Mann Boudoir Car Company, Union Palace Car Company, and Wagner Palace Car Company, his name became synonymous with luxury rolling stock. By the end of the century, the Pullman Company (née Pullman Palace Car Company) monopolized the sleeping-car business. In 1865 Pullman's luxurious sleeper Car "A" or Pioneer became associated in public lore with President Abraham Lincoln's funeral train procession over the rails of the Alton between Chicago and Springfield, Illinois.[28] What is better known is his company town of Pullman, Illinois, founded in 1880 and located nine miles south of Chicago. It was designed to be a fully self-contained model community. Before long the Pullman population soared, totaling 10,680 residents in the 1890 federal census. Here the company manufactured and maintained its dining and sleeping cars and constructed even more freight cars. The sprawling site also operated its own industrial railroad. The place, however, became famous or infamous for a bitter labor strike in 1894 due to Pullman's unwillingness to reduce rents on housing and maintain wages during a catastrophic national depression. Workers, too, complained about the town being puritanical and undemocratic in its governance.[29]

A Pullman car offered patrons "perfection." In a detailed letter written in 1888 by Frank Blowers, a Chicago & Grand Trunk Railway office worker, to his sister in England, he describes this icon of Gilded Age travel. In this lengthy missive, which includes drawings of the car that he rode from Detroit to Chicago, Blowers writes, "The Car is well carpeted throughout. All windows are of plate glass and are double-fitted with roller blinds. The panels of glass over the windows and around the top of the car are beautifully cut frosted. I was very much struck with the quantity of fine carving, all of which is done by hand." Continued his commentary, "The water supply is carried beneath the car in a large tank and is forced to the various taps by compressed air. The hot water pipe passes through the furnace and the Ice water pipe through chambers filled with ice." Blowers explains how his sleeping berth was made up: "The seats are turned over. The lower portion of the backs taken out and laid across the seats and form the lower berth. Reaching up he [porter] turns a handle set into the top of the sloping panel above, which immediately falls outward on its hinges and is held in a horizontal position by chains which run over a wheel containing a spring. When the panel is closed up, the spring recoils and winds up the slack chain on the wheels. This process forms a top to the lower berth and the bed of the upper berth. The mattresses, quilts, pillows, etc., which are stowed away in the upper berth are then put in their places." He closes this portion as follows: "Wooden panels are slid along the backs of the seats and locked into position completely closing the sides. Clean sheets and pillow cases are put on. The front is closed by thick tapestry curtains hung by leather covered hooks to the curtain rods along the top of the car and there you are."[30]

Passenger equipment luxuriousness did not stop. In the same year as Blowers's trip to Chicago, Horace Porter in an article published in *Scribner's Magazine* realized that improvements should be expected. "While it would seem that the luxuries of railway travel in America have reached a maximum, and the changes a minimum, yet in this progressive age it is very probable that in the not far distant future we shall witness improvements over the present methods which will astonish us as much as the present methods surprise us when we compare them with those of the past."[31]

During these development decades, midwesterners witnessed changes in freight rolling stock. Not only did cars get bigger, albeit usually of wooden construction, but there were new types to observe. One kind stands out: the tank car. Following the success of Colonel Edwin Drake's oil well near the northeastern Pennsylvania town of Titusville in 1859, a boom ensued. Initially, workers at the wellhead placed the crude petroleum in wooden barrels and loaded them in boxcars and gondolas for upstart refineries. Then in 1865 the first wooden vat-type tank car appeared. Some shipments likely went to Cleveland, where the Excelsior Refinery Company had recently opened. Soon these vat cars disappeared, being replaced by the horizontal iron tank car that became the basic style. By 1870 that original Cleveland refinery became part of the Standard Oil Company, led by John D. Rockefeller and Henry Flagler. These men and their associates stabilized this chaotic industry by combining refineries and centralizing management. Their innovative "trust," which came to dominate oil refining, made its debut in 1879. By the 1880s the ever more powerful Standard Oil operated the Union Tank Line as a subsidiary, and it emerged as the largest tank car operator in America.

Ohio, too, continued to be a leading petroleum state. It had more than the sprawling refineries in the Cleveland Flats. In the 1880s oil was being produced and refined in the Lima-Findlay area of western Ohio. And to help serve it, various tank car manufacturers, including the Lima Car Works, supplied the transportation needs to this burgeoning industry. By now tank cars had become a common part of freight train consists.[32]

More exciting than any parade of tank cars were coal-burning locomotives, ones that had become more powerful and featured additional sets of wheels. These improvements allowed them to handle mainline "Limiteds" with their heavyweight diners and sleeping cars at greater speeds, ranging from forty to fifty or more miles per hour. In 1881 the Pennsylvania introduced the New York–Chicago Limited, and its initial westbound run took twenty-six hours, thirty-six minutes to make this 908-mile trip. The fastest previously scheduled trip had taken seven hours longer. Trains, including this PRR named train, could accomplish this feat due in part to more miles of mainline having heavier steel rail. Other technological advances ensured less dangerous operations—for example, sturdy Janney couplers, which by the 1880s had become the standard automatic coupling devices that replaced link and pins; Westinghouse air brakes; and vestibule-styled cars.[33]

No matter whether passengers made their trips in coach or Pullman, they might experience a "time problem" prior to the early 1880s. In the days of dominant travel by stagecoach, canal packet, and steamboat, travelers adjusted comfortably to "God's time" or sun time (based on its passage across the local meridian) and set their timepieces accordingly or perhaps only their internal body clock. With the advent of longer railroad journeys, each railroad selected its own setting, using the solar time of its headquarters city or principal terminal. This resulted in a crazy-quilt pattern of times. A major union station served by multiple carriers required more than a single clock. There would be Cleveland, Chicago, St. Louis, or some other city-based solar time. When it was twelve noon in Chicago, it was 12:07 in Indianapolis, 12:13 in Cincinnati, and 12:24 in Cleveland but still morning to the west—11:27 in Council Bluffs, 11:41 in St. Paul, 11:48 in Dubuque, and 11:50 in St. Louis. Such differences frequently confused passengers. "The traveler's watch was to him but a delusion," commented one disgusted traveler, "clocks at stations staring

F. C. N.-G. RAILWAY CO.

TIME TABLE NO. 2.

TO TAKE EFFECT TUESDAY, SEPT. 7th, 1880.

GOING SOUTH.			*GOING NORTH.*	
No. 3.	No. 1.	Stations.	No. 2.	No. 4.
	a. m. lv.		*p.m. ar.*	
	7:50	CUBA.	7:30	
	8:45	LEWISTOWN.	6:45	
	9:20	WATERFORD.	6:15	
	9:45	WEST HAVANA.	6:00	
	a. m. ar.		*p. m. lv.*	

Trains will run daily except Sundays.

Section men will see that no ties, cord wood, or other material, are piled within five feet of the rail. Engineers will sound the whistle for all public crossings at least 300 yards from the crossing.

Great care must be taken to avoid killing stock. Trains will come to a full stop, if necessary. Engineers will be held accountable for carelessness in killing live stock.

SIGNALS.

1. The whistle blown once means, apply the brakes; twice, let go the brakes; three times, back up; four whistles shall be the signal for switch, or for calling in flag man.

2. A stationary red flag upon the side of the track signifies that the track is out of order and must be run over slowly. If placed between the rails, it signifies that the track is impassible and that trains must come to a full stop.

3. A lantern swung across the track is the signal to stop. A lantern raised and lowered is to go ahead. A lantern swung in the circle is the signal for backing.

CAUTION.

Carefulness is earnestly enjoined. Always take the safe side in case of the least uncertainty.

Chicago time will be taken as standard time.

S. H. MALLORY,
Ch'f Eng'r and Gen'l Man.

When the gestating Fulton County Narrow Gauge Railway, located in western Illinois, issued its second operating timetable (effective in September 1880), the company made certain that its employees knew that "Chicago time will be taken as standard time." This was not unexpected. It was not "God's time" that locals used before the creation of standard time zones on November 18, 1883. *(Author's collection)* each other in the face defiant of harmony either with one another or with surrounding local time and all wildly at variance with the traveler's watch, baffled all intelligent interpretation."[34]

It would be the railroad industry and not the federal government that created standard time zones. The General Time Convention, spearheaded by William Frederick Allen, who was associated with the *Official Guide of the Railways and Steam Navigation Lines*, solved this challenging conundrum. The big day occurred on Sunday, November 18, 1883, becoming the day of two noons. Approximately six hundred railroads abandoned the fifty-three arbitrary times and adopted Greenwich-indexed meridians that defined the times in each of four zones: Eastern, Central, Mountain, and Pacific.[35] These demarcations generally ran along the 75th, 90th, 105th, and 120th meridians. Changes occurred, however. Ohio, for example, initially used Eastern time but later entered the Central time zone. Washington lawmakers finally legitimized these railroad-created zones with the Standard Time Act of 1918.[36]

Not only were uniform time zones created in the 1880s; this became a decade of standardization. By the early 1880s, gauges were fully established at four feet eight and a half inches; earlier gauge size had been a matter of corporate preference. As of 1870 an indication of still gauge variations in the Midwest includes these examples: Atlantic & Great Western, six feet; North Missouri, five feet six inches; Portsmouth Branch (Portsmouth, Columbus & Michigan), five feet four inches; Central Ohio, four feet ten inches; Sandusky, Mansfield & Newark, four feet nine and a half inches; and Lake Erie & Louisville, four feet nine and a quarter inches.[37]

While standardization reigned, there was one short-lived but memorable exception. A narrow-gauge craze erupted in the Midwest, which led to hundreds of miles of line being constructed to three feet or three and a half feet wide during the immediate post–Civil War years. Promoters believed mistakenly that a reduced gauge would be less expensive to build and operate. They also understood that communities wanted a first or a second railroad. Residents, whether living in towns or on farms, knew that public roads were wretched, and the horse and the railroad were the mainstays of travel. Moreover, these narrow-gauge enthusiasts were often rank amateurs. The prime advocate behind the Toledo, Delphos

& Indiana Railroad was Joseph Hunt, a Delphos, Ohio, druggist best known as the maker of Slippery Elm, a health tonic. The spark plug for the sixty-one-mile Fulton County Narrow Gauge Railroad (FCNG) was William Davidson, editor of the *Lewiston Democrat*. He sought to end the isolation of his hometown, Lewistown, Illinois, and to make it the county seat. This narrow-gauge pike took shape between 1879 and 1882 and ultimately connected West Havana with Galesburg, Illinois. In 1906 the Burlington leased the property and completed the process of standardization that began a year earlier, but the FCNG had lost almost $850,000 during its independent years. Davidson and his backers, though, surely took pleasure when Lewiston became the seat of Fulton County. Notwithstanding the slowness of the FCNG to change its gauge, most slim-width mileage in the Midwest by 1890 had become standardized. The 146-mile St. Louis & Cairo Railroad (originally the Cairo & St. Louis) is representative. By 1875 this three-foot-wide road linked the river town of Cairo with East St. Louis. After a decade the C&StL, principally a coal carrier, became the leased property of the Mobile & Ohio (M&O). In 1885 the five-foot-gauge M&O converted to standard dimensions, and within a year it widened the former C&StL, allowing access to or through the St. Louis gateway via the Eads or Merchants Bridge and creating a seamless interchange with connecting carriers.[38]

The push for standardization included freight cars. Railroads and manufacturers, including those in Chicago, Detroit, and St. Louis, agreed to standardize their components and dimensions. As with track widths, this meant that freight rolling stock could be interchanged throughout the Midwest and nationally and also operate in Canada and Mexico.

GRANGERS

By the 1870s railroad patrons nationally began to express their unhappiness with the industry. Yet there had been earlier public criticisms. A common concern involved line locations. Residents of established communities nearly always wanted the iron horse and fussed when that did not occur as rapidly as they expected or perhaps not at all. Additional complaints existed, and they were largely service related. For example, would passenger trains operate on Sundays? Some wanted them; others objected because of their Sabbatarian beliefs. In time these localized irritations became overshadowed by the "railroad problem," particularly rate discriminations and related business practices. The Midwest emerged as the epicenter for this discontent, centering in the four states of the Upper Mississippi River valley: Wisconsin, Illinois, Iowa, and Minnesota.[39]

The initial regulation of railroads, whether in the Midwest or elsewhere, had been largely confined to their charters. Although several eastern states prior to the Civil War had launched railroad commissions, they possessed limited legal authority and could not control rates, even if they were egregious, or respond to customer charges of discrimination. Simply put, they functioned largely as advisory agencies. That soon changed. New regulatory bodies emerged with enhanced powers.

Why did residents of the Midwest turn from being primarily railroad boosters to becoming advocates of regulatory controls? The explanation: a perfect storm struck. Following the Civil War, most farmers had become heavily dependent on railroad transportation for marketing their crops, livestock, and dairy products and for receiving their necessities, ranging from lumber to machinery. In the late 1860s, agricultural prices fell, especially for grains, and rising postwar inflation plagued the region. Debt levels increased for farmers and other residents as their buying powers decreased. Next came the Panic of 1873, which badly disrupted the entire national economy.

Complaints varied, but they focused on trunk line monopolies. Shippers, largely farmers, did not understand why certain rates were excessive (especially relative to commodity prices) and discriminatory. In some cases farmers decided to burn their corn as fuel rather than to ship it to market. An often-cited example of what were considered to be unreasonable rates came from Galva, Illinois, where the Burlington enjoyed being the sole carrier. A carload of grain sent from this community to Chicago, approximately one hundred miles away, cost more than to ship it from Chicago to New York City, a distance roughly seven times greater. This situation reflected classic long- and short-haul discrimination. Also troubling was the practice of railroads generally charging lower rates for large shippers, including manufacturers and wholesale firms, and those who lived in certain places (Chicago, for example). Others in Galva and elsewhere also wondered why it cost four or five cents for passengers to travel a mile rather than two or three cents. The road's unequal treatment of consumers and localities sparked this reform crusade. "The uprising of the people of the Western States was not against the aggregated amount of the rates being collected by the railways, but against the discrimination they were practicing in collecting their revenues," remarked A. B. Stickney, a frequent industry critic. "This fact should be thoroughly mastered by every mind which desires to comprehend the meaning of the so-called Granger legislation."[40]

Farmers together with a coalition of merchants and commercial interests, impacted by high rates and rate discriminations, did not accept the justifications made by railroad officials who often hailed from far beyond the borders of the Midwest, hinting of an underlying colonial complex. The trunk lines argued that free competition and the laws of supply and demand offered the only effective form of regulation. Some consumers believed that these sentiments allowed carriers to charge what the market would bear, being capitalism at its worst. The public likely ignored the fact that railroads, particularly those who had been actively engaged in line expansions and acquisitions, faced high fixed costs and growing competition from an expanding regional rail network. Midwestern carriers agreed that switching and terminal expenses were the same for short as for long hauls, and hence they preferred long-haul traffic at lower rates per mile than those for short distances. Not to be overlooked, the industry was perpetually capital and labor intensive and forced to deal with business and traffic cycles.[41]

Hope for aggrieved consumers came from the newly organized National Grange of the Patrons of Husbandry, better known as the Grange. Launched in 1867 by US Department of Agriculture clerk Oliver Hudson Kelley, an idealistic and indefatigable worker, this first American agricultural advocacy group initially sought to reduce rural isolation through social activities and to improve agrarian life through scientific agriculture. Some local units backed the formation of mutual fire-insurance companies and other cooperative businesses. Soon this mushrooming farm-centered organization, which became widely prevalent in the Midwest, sought to deal with transportation inequities. Farmers discovered in these newly formed Grange lodges a congenial vehicle to air their complaints and saw the potential for change through the political process. "[The organization] is a power which no party can afford to ignore," remarked one Granger. In 1874 it reached its peak strength with nearly eight hundred thousand members nationally.[42]

In the early and mid-1870s, the clearly defined issues of railroad misbehavior overshadowed everything in the legislatures of these four Granger states. "Because of the highly competitive nature of commerce in the upper Mississippi Valley," concluded historian George Miller, "rate abuses affected that area more acutely than any other." The popular rhetoric can be found in an 1873 book published in Chicago by Edward Winslow Martin (pseudonym of James Dabney McCabe), who cried out, "The railroads have debauched and demoralized our courts and legislatures . . . have robbed the nation of an empire of domain . . . will cover the whole land with ruin and suffering." The belief grew that railroads must be servants of the people and not their masters.

Take what occurred in Illinois. Its revised state constitution, ratified in 1870, gave the legislature authority to regulate railroads and elevators. The following year lawmakers, working through the region's dominant Republican Party, created a board of railroad and warehouse commissioners, fixed maximum passenger rates, and established freight rates based on distance. Two years later this body expanded its "Granger Codes," allowing the commission to prepare a schedule of reasonable maximum freight rates.[43]

The Granger legislation that took place in neighboring Wisconsin became the bugbear for that state's railroads. Its Potter Railroad Act, which became effective in May 1874, formed a three-member board of railroad commissioners. What infuriated Badger State carriers, especially the Milwaukee Road and North Western, was that the measure arranged freight and passenger traffic into classifications and established maximum rates for items within each category. Generally, it ended the practice of carriers setting a higher rate per ton mile and passenger mile for shorter hauls. This law established the precedent of inflexibility in rates, and it accepted the mistaken assumption that "reasonable" charges must be based solely on distance. Charles Frances Adams Jr., architect of railroad legislation in Massachusetts, called the statute the "most ignorant, arbitrary, and wholly unjustifiable law to be found in the history of railroad legislation." He continued with these comments about this reform crusade: "If ever a problem called for wise legislation, founded upon careful and patient study, this one certainly did. The Granger legislatures, however, went like so many bulls at red rags." When a state district court upheld the Potter Act in July, its backers rejoiced, but railroads and company supporters fumed. Reports circulated that carriers responded by using decrepit rolling stock and providing erratic service. There were "Potter cars" and "Potter time." The Milwaukee Road went so far as to announce that it would no longer build additional mileage in the state.[44]

When Wisconsin regulated its railroads, Iowa did so as well. Cyrus Clay Carpenter, its popular Republican governor, spearheaded this legislation, saying, "In my judgment the time has arrived when a limit to freight charges on our Iowa railroads should be fixed by law." Carpenter's words rang true with the state's nearly forty thousand members of the Patrons of Husbandry. Yet the final law lacked their full backing, failing to create a board of railroad commissioners as these agrarians had wanted. It did impose a maximum rate or "cast-iron tariff" on freight charges. This especially pleased eastern Iowa merchants who had campaigned vigorously for the lowest possible freight charges.[45]

Interestingly, Hawkeye State Grangers did not direct their anger toward the North Western. Its short-haul charges were next to the lowest in the state, and its long-haul rates to Chicago were the cheapest. Moreover, consumer sentiments were that the railroad provided dependable service and kept its lines in good condition. The Burlington, most of all, did not escape their wrath.[46]

What took place in Minnesota duplicated for the most part the regulatory happenings in Illinois, Wisconsin, and Iowa. In fact, its network of state Granges, which began in St. Paul with the North Star Grange Lodge in 1868, was likely influenced by ongoing Grange agitation in Illinois and Wisconsin. Public criticisms of railroads, which emanated from farmers and merchants, became acute between 1871 and 1874. The impact of the Panic of 1873 made financial conditions much worse for farmers and those who depended on the agricultural economy. This involved "mortgage foreclosures, bank failures, and a steep price decline," noted historian Martin Ridge. "The greatest blow to the farmers was the downward march of wheat prices from more than one dollar a bushel to eighty cents by September 18 [1873]." Grangers complained about oppressive freight rates and discriminatory practices. They did not appreciate, for one thing, the cozy anticompetitive relationship between the St. Paul & Pacific Railroad, core of the future Great Northern Railway, and William Davidson for grain-elevator services in the Twin Cities. In 1871 lawmakers required railroads to classify freight, and rates were set for both freight shipments and passenger travel. They also established the office of state railroad commissioner, granting him the authority to subpoena both individuals and records and making it a felony to refuse such requests. The following year other measures became law, including amended rate legislation and the requirement that companies install and maintain rights-of-way fencing and cattle guards. A bona fide railroad and warehouse commission likewise emerged. In 1874 the legislature directed it to create "reasonable maximum rates" for all carriers operating in the state. Minnesota railroads were not pleased, and they continued to employ their legal resources to negate most of these regulatory controls.[47]

The Granger movement led to setbacks together with lasting victories for its backers. Between 1875 and 1878, weaker regulatory measures replaced harsher statutes. The most restrictive ones became only unpleasant memories for the affected companies. In 1876 Wisconsin lawmakers repealed the Potter Act. It returned policymaking duties to the state's railroads, including the all-important matter of rate-making. Iowa followed with a friendlier railroad rate measure. Legislators felt industry pressures and realized that there had been mistakes in their lawmaking, as the laws were poorly drafted and inflexible.

The impact of the Granger regulatory movement established the principle of active public supervision of quasi-public companies, and it found advocates in other states as well as in the US Congress. Much to the grief of the railroad industry, judicial challenges to the concept of state regulation received a stunning defeat in 1877. It came on March 1 when the US Supreme Court in the landmark case of *Munn v. Illinois* ruled in favor of the defendant. In this test case, Chicago grain elevator owner Ira Munn argued for exemption from an Illinois law that fixed the rates his firm charged. The plaintiff claimed that he was engaged in interstate commerce and that these controlled rates deprived him of legitimate profits without due process of law. Chief Justice Morrison Remick Waite, an Ohioan, wrote for the majority. He based his ruling on Anglo-Saxon law, laying down the maxim that the owner of any property "clothed with a public interest must submit to be controlled by the public for the common good." Waite noted that it had long been customary, both in Britain and America, to fix by law maximum rates of charges for ferry operators, hackmen, innkeepers, and others. In his opinion he also argued that "for the protection against abuses by legislatures the people must resort to the polls, and not to the courts." This decision affected more than terminal elevators; it affirmed the constitutionality of the Granger codes until another Supreme Court ruling a decade later altered their impact.[48]

What was the Granger regulatory legacy? There existed a growing feeling nationally that the *Munn v. Illinois* decision was flawed. Consumers, particularly those associated with merchant-dominated organizations, objected to the practice of some railroads recouping revenues lost on regulated local business by raising unregulated through rates. Clearly the post-Granger reform era revealed that the rate-making process had become complex and contradictory. By the early 1880s, a range of individuals and groups concluded that only the federal government could deal effectively with the "railroad problem." Observed historian Russel Nye, "Grangerism was the earliest form of Midwestern progressivism."[49]

In 1886 the opportunity for resolving the rate-making dilemma came before the US Supreme Court in the case of *Wabash, St. Louis and Pacific Railway Company v. State of Illinois*. The receivers of the company appealed a decision by Illinois regulators that involved a Gilman, Illinois, shipper. The Wabash asked that Bailey & Swannell pay sixty-five dollars (or twenty-five cents per hundred pounds) to transport a carload of grain from Gilman to New York. On the same day, the road charged Elder & McKinney of Peoria thirty-nine dollars (or fifteen cents per hundred pounds) for a similar load to the same destination. This loaded boxcar traveled eighty-six miles farther than the one from Gilman. "The freight being of the same class in both instance, and carried over the same road, except as to the difference in distance, it is obvious that a discrimination again Bailey & Swannell was made in the charges against them," argued Illinois officials.[50]

Observers realized that at first glance a discriminatory act had occurred. In its defense, the Wabash pointed out that the Peoria customer used its services more often, and the actual cost was switching at the point of origin. The court, however, was unmoved by these arguments. In the view of the justices, the key issue involved interstate versus intrastate commerce. Illinois controlled the latter but not the former. Interstate movements must be regulated by Congress exclusively, and this was allowed by "that clause of the constitution which empowers it to regulate commerce among the states."[51]

Even before *Wabash* overturned the *Munn* decision, US senator Shelby Cullom of Illinois led an investigation into railroad practices, especially those that smacked of discrimination. The actions of the Supreme Court, the Cullom Report, and pressures from certain shippers and carriers led a reluctant Congress to pass an interstate commerce bill, which President Grover Cleveland signed on February 4, 1887. This historic measure created the Interstate Commerce Commission (ICC), which provided the regulatory arm to ensure that railroads would establish reasonable and just rates, refrain from using traffic pools, and file rate tariffs and annual reports with the ICC. The commission did not receive the right to establish maximum rates. In the ensuing decades, however, it grew into the premier independent agency in the federal government.[52]

Adding to the complexity of regional charges were the periodic outbreaks of rate wars. In 1870 three roads, Burlington, North Western, and Rock Island, formed the Iowa Pool to limit cutthroat competition and to stabilize rates between the Chicago and Omaha gateways. This "gentlemen's agreement," which was not legally binding, eventually fizzled, although in 1882 the Wabash joined the pool. It collapsed in 1884 because its participants became dissatisfied with the traffic arrangements, in part due to their expansion beyond the Missouri River, either realized or planned.[53]

One well-publicized rate eruption involved passenger fares. In 1880 the Wabash sought to gain market share in the busy Chicago and St. Louis corridor by reducing ticket prices. Its four competitors matched these cuts, including the Chicago & Alton, operator of the most popular trains between these two cities. "The Alton has succeeded in its object to destroy the [profit] of all through travel from St. Louis eastward," observed the *Railroad Gazette*. It took nearly two years before the rivals ended their pricing combat. In the interim ticket prices fell by 50 to 90 percent, to the delight of the traveling public. Some believed (or hoped) that cheap travel would become permanent.[54]

LABOR UNREST

During the Gilded Age, consumers in the Midwest were not the only ones who sparred with the railroad industry. Workers did so as well. The region gained recognition as a breeding ground for railroad brotherhoods. The Brotherhood of Locomotive Engineers (BLE), the first permanent union launched by railroad workers, began in Detroit in 1863. Engineers on the Michigan Central became angered by recent wage cuts and extended working hours, and so they banded together. In 1868 the first conductor's organization was launched in Amboy, Illinois, by a group of Illinois Central conductors, and soon another group was started in nearby Galesburg by Burlington conductors. Later that year their representatives gathered in the conveniently located junction town of Mendota to form the Conductor's Union. It was not designed to be merely an Illinois-based organization; it was created to organize fellow workers nationwide. In 1873 the Brotherhood of Conductors emerged, and six years later it rebranded itself as the Order of Railway Conductors (often called the "Big O"). Although the Brotherhood of Locomotive Firemen was launched in Port Jervis, New York, in 1873, Hoosier State native Eugene V. Debs, who later emerged as America's foremost railroad labor activist, served the union in the 1880s, including a stint as a fireman for the Terre Haute & Indianapolis Railroad and editor of *Locomotive Firemen's Magazine*. It took longer for railroad telegraphers to organize. In 1886 a meeting of telegraphers in Cedar Rapids, Iowa, was spearheaded by Ambros Thurston, publisher of the trade journal *Railroad Telegrapher* in neighboring Vinton, Iowa. This conclave led to the formation of the Order of Railway Telegraphers of North America. But it took years before this body emerged as more than a fraternal organization.[55]

The Wabash, St. Louis & Pacific owned this unusual 0-4-2 switch engine. The date and location of this photograph are unknown. Likely the time is in the 1880s, and it may have been taken in Fort Wayne, Indiana. The engineer, fireman, and brakeman take a break from their assignments to pose for their picture. *(Author's collection)*

Brotherhoods, whether launched by workers in the Midwest or elsewhere, might best be labeled "conservative." Their emphasis was on "Benevolence, Sobriety and Industry." Members needed to practice hard work, self-reliance, honesty, and temperance. They sought to be professional and respectable, unquestionably highly regarded Victorian-era values. Strikes were usually not included in their playbook. These brotherhoods emerged largely as fraternal and mutual aid societies. In an era when such male-only organizations and lodges attracted tens of thousands of members, these incipient railroad unions sponsored various activities, ranging from ritualistic initiations to evening suppers and dances. And they assisted fellow members and their families. Some contemporaries referred to them as "coffin clubs." Why? They offered disability and burial insurance. These became critical benefits since members relied totally or nearly so on the wage system, and no effective public or private safety nets existed to care for their wives and dependents. The cost of this much-wanted and needed security was manageable. A member might make monthly payments of a dollar or less.[56]

Yet strikes erupted and affected railroads throughout the Midwest. The first significant worker action took place in July 1877. This struggle, often referred to as the "Great Strike of 1877," burst forth between labor and management, and though bitter, it was short-lived. The unrest was a direct result of the prolonged depression triggered by the Panic of 1873. With the national economy still in the doldrums, multiple companies, including the Baltimore & Ohio (B&O), PRR, and Union Pacific, slashed wages and cut jobs. There were other matters of contention. The B&O lengthened freight trains without increasing crew sizes in order to reduce labor costs. Violence exploded. The PRR encountered the worst outbursts when strikers and their supporters in Pittsburgh destroyed railroad and urban property valued in excess of five million dollars. Troubles spread quickly to the Midwest, including Chicago, East St. Louis, and St. Paul. In July freight and passenger operations either stopped or became limited; in fact, the strike halted nearly all freight traffic in the Midwest. Widespread damage to railroad facilities likewise occurred, and a Burlington switchman in Chicago was killed. The arrival of federal troops restored peace, and normal freight and passenger train operations resumed. Fortunately for railroad operatives, the economy picked up, and in the 1880s, except for a brief mid-decade recession, overall worker pay and working conditions generally improved.[57]

Better times did not guarantee labor-management harmony. Strikes flared up in 1885 and again the following year. This unrest centered on the so called Gould Roads, a network of midwestern and southwestern carriers headed by Jay Gould, the "Money Monarch" or for some the "most hated man in America." Much of this labor conflict erupted in Moberly, Missouri, on the then-bankrupt Wabash, St. Louis & Pacific Railway (Wabash) and in Marshall, Texas, on the Texas & Pacific Railroad (T&P). The reason for worker discontent: slashed wages.[58]

The "Southwest Strikes" involved disgruntled shopmen through their local units of an expanding Knights of Labor. Differing from the newly launched American Federation of Labor, which focused on "bread and butter" issues, the Knights failed to fully accept the wage system and dabbled with cooperative businesses, including coal mines and cigar factories. Shop workers, long unhappy about their inadequate wages, responded negatively to a 10 percent wage reduction announced in February 1885. A walkout occurred, but soon relative peace returned. When the Wabash started to lay off shopmen who belonged to the Knights, tempers flared, and in August another work stoppage erupted. Their actions stunned both Terence Powderly, who headed the Knights, and Gould himself. Neither wanted a strike. Powderly agonized about what it might do to his fragile organization, and he had reason to worry. Gould backed down on the wage cuts, and order was restored. At this point the Knights experienced a brief meteoric growth in membership. But when a wildcat walkout took place the following year on the T&P, Gould and his managers were prepared. Replacement workers were quickly employed. Public opinion, moreover, turned against the Knights. When some strikers vandalized Wabash equipment and property in Moberly, the local newspaper editorialized, "Moberly has had enough." The train brotherhoods expressed little or no support for the job actions of 1885 and 1886 and seemed content to take a neutral stance in disputes with the Gould properties.[59]

Two years of relative labor tranquility in the Midwest ended abruptly in 1888. A nasty strike on the Burlington, led by engineers who received support from firemen and switchmen, surprised the railway world. There had been growing unhappiness among engineers, the potentates of railroad workers; their actions were unexpected considering that they belonged to the ultraconservative BLE. Burlington engineers focused their complaints on the unwillingness of management to set uniform mileage pay. A trip of one hundred miles in both freight and passenger service, they believed, should constitute a day's work. If more miles were run, pay should be on a pro rata basis. Also, if fewer than one hundred miles were covered in ten hours, overtime pay should be granted. Another issue involved what constituted a first-class engineer (one who received extra compensation) and a related matter of job protection for these senior enginemen. There was also general disgust that the Burlington paid their engine crews less than other Granger trunk roads, including the North Western and Rock Island. In 1886 the Burlington granted the BLE union recognition but failed to accommodate it on matters of mileage pay and classifications. Relations deteriorated the following year when a new general manager showed no sympathy toward the brotherhood's concerns.[60]

A strike loomed. On February 27, 1888, engineers, joined by a number of firemen, "hit the bricks." "All trains in transit were delivered to the nearest terminal, regardless of the hour," noted BLE historian Richard Cook, "and 2,000 locomotive engineers and firemen stepped out of their cabs. This had not been done, however, until the men had exhausted every possible recourse in order to avoid striking." The Burlington responded by hiring strikebreakers. These engineers did not hail from the Midwest; most came from the Philadelphia-based Reading Railroad. Soon service returned to near-normal conditions, although for a time engineers on the Wabash and Santa Fe refused to handle Burlington rolling stock. Then conditions for management and the traveling and shipping public worsened. A complicated series of events followed, including court injunctions, switchmen joining the work stoppage, and violence. Strikers attacked scabs and company-hired Pinkertons, and disabled locomotives. That summer protestors dynamited several trains. Finally, the switchmen called off the strike, but for the other participants it lingered officially until January 4, 1889. The engineers failed to achieve their demands, and many left the employ of the Burlington. Senior management did make a positive response to this labor unrest. Later in 1889 it launched what was called the Relief Department, designed to pay accident, sickness, and death benefits to those who joined voluntarily.[61] Participants had modest monthly payroll deductions. This gesture, designed to improve worker morale, apparently succeeded.[62]

RAILROAD TOWNS

A railroad strike could devastate a community, especially where the company was the largest or sole employer. Creston, Iowa, location of a Burlington division point, a running-repair facility, and the "largest engine house in the West" (a dubious booster claim), served the east–west Chicago to Denver mainline and north and south branches. Founded shortly after the Civil War by railroad interests, Creston grew rapidly and captured the Union County seat from nearby Afton; it registered a population of 4,081 in the 1880 federal census. If a resident did not work for the Burlington, he probably lived next door to someone or had a close neighbor who did. Creston lacked another carrier; much to the disappointment of community interests, it was a single-railroad town. Unlike the three other Burlington division points in the state, Creston, most of all, felt the sting of the 1888–1889 walkout by locomotive engineers. It took this railroad community years to recover from this event. Local merchants, who were adversely affected, had extended credit to strikers and their families. They frequently found collecting on these accounts difficult if not impossible. A prominent butcher, for one, who faced hundreds of dollars of uncollected debt, decided to leave Creston and seek his fortune in another Iowa locale, where he ultimately prospered.[63]

There were other Crestons. Scores of towns, large and small, depended heavily on a railroad payroll. They might be division points and the location of shops, repair facilities, and marshaling yards. Examples include Ann Arbor (Michigan), Bradford (Ohio), Fond du Lac (Wisconsin), Galesburg (Illinois), Brookfield (Missouri), Perry (Iowa), Peru (Indiana), and South St. Paul (Minnesota). Remarked a resident of Oelwein, Iowa, hub for Chicago Great Western operations, “Railroaders here spend, but those farmers who come to town watch their pennies.” This statement rang true for generations.[64]

The presence of a working-class railroad-employed population could easily be detected by an outsider. In some ways these communities resembled older river and canal towns. Railroad-spawned businesses appeared close to the depot and adjoining facilities; they usually included a hotel, boarding house, saloon, and restaurant (“beanery”). Such places could be abundant. The drinking and sleeping establishments were often singled out by the “church-going crowd” as public nuisances and threats to “village virtues.” A railroader-oriented hotel might offer attractive room rates, clean and bug-free bedding, and access to bathing and meals, but “women of the night” might be found plying their ancient trade. Pool and card sharks could also be present. There always seemed to be “ne’er-do-wells and hooligans” in the railroad corridor, vagrants in particular. Sedalia, Missouri, a community dominated by the Missouri–Kansas–Texas and Missouri Pacific Railroads, was one such place. In 1877 the *St. Louis Post-Dispatch* described Sadalia as “the Sodom and Gomorrah of the Nineteenth Century." That charge contained an element of truth: multiple brothels flourished. It was here that Scott Joplin, the Ragtime King, played piano. At the end of the century, when his famous "Maple Leaf Rag" was published, it honored Sedalia's Maple Leaf Club, a "leading house of disrepute."[65]

Railroad management sought to cure the ills of the most troubling aspects of workers' time spent along the railroad corridor. This involved more than the enforcement of "Rule G," which banned the use of intoxicants. During the Gilded Age, some companies opened reading and entertainment rooms in crew-change points, thereby providing an alternative to saloons and thus hopefully controlling alcohol consumption. Sober crews meant safer railroads. An imaginative overall solution involved the spread of facilities operated by the Railroad Division of the Young Men's Christian Association, known as the "Railroad Y." The movement began in Cleveland in the fall of 1872 when several rooms in the Lake Shore & Michigan Southern station were set aside for railroaders, largely designed to be a substitute for the saloon, hotel, and boardinghouse. Supporters believed that if the off-work surroundings could be altered in a positive fashion, it could substantially change workers' behavior and make their jobs more pleasurable. This might be considered a version of Reform Social Darwinism—"change the environment and you change the person." Railroad Ys provided convenient, clean, inexpensive sleeping rooms and economical dining to members, who paid modest annual dues.[66] These facilities brought an alternative to bug-infested beds and unsavory food. Railroad Ys also allowed these railroaders opportunities to spend their leisure time constructively, having access to card rooms (gambling was forbidden), libraries, and other public areas. If a member were found with a prostitute, he would be barred permanently from the Ys. Not every worker responded positively to the presence of these specialized railroader-oriented facilities with their strict rules, but most did. A positive testimonial came from a brakeman who in the early twentieth century worked for the Wabash and was based in Decatur, Illinois: "I carried a membership card, which cost me five dollars a year, and this card entitled me to the many privileges given to members, such as free baths, and reduction on room rent, meals, and many other things." He added, "There was a bowling alley, and pool room down in the basement, and lounging rooms on the first floor where the boys could play games, such as cards, checkers, and dominoes, and there was nearly always some boomer around there that could play the piano that sit in one of the rooms, and there was also a wonderful library of good books." Railroaders might not have been anxious to attend regular nondenominational religious services, especially if they practiced a liturgical faith or had none at all. Reflecting cultural norms, the Railroad Y movement created several "Colored Branches," including ones in Chicago and other large cities.[67]

It is understandable that Railroad Ys most often appeared in division points and near major railroad terminals. St. Louis is an example. Once the city had its Union Station, a magnificent monument to the Railway Age designed by Theodore C. Link, an impressive four-story brick Railroad Y (also the work of Link) was built immediately west of the train shed. Its location provided a short walk for member railroaders to obtain a room or meal or wait in its library or other public spaces.[68]

Some towns in the Midwest, although fewer than those that claimed a Railroad Y, had railroad-sponsored hospitals. As the industry evolved, major carriers wrestled with how best to meet the medical needs of their employees and how to treat injuries arising from train accidents. A leader in the railroad medical field was the Wabash, which operated its highly successful (and popular) Wabash Employees Hospital Association. Before its creation in 1884, the company and its predecessors relied on local physicians to treat workers and passengers who suffered injuries, paying them on a case-by-case basis. In the late 1870s, the railroad began offering retainers to a select group of reputable on-line physicians and surgeons who could attend to its medical needs. This change lessened the possibilities of medical mistakes and of physicians bilking the company. It also meant better quality control in an era of medical quackery.[69]

By the post–Civil War years, trunk carriers throughout the Midwest commonly had or would start some form of regularized medical system. The number of accidents increased as lines expanded, freight and passenger traffic burgeoned, and train speeds rose. Most officials believed that providing medical assistance was humane, reduced lawsuits, and

One of the iconic urban stations in the Midwest and the nation was in St. Louis, being that magnificent creation by architect Theodore Link. Not long after it opened in 1894, a local photographer captured this sprawling structure. *(Emil Boehl photograph, St. Louis Mercantile Library at UMSL)*

engendered goodwill among employees and the public. With the exception of trespassers, who were likely vagrants, the Wabash provided medical attention for all accident victims.[70]

Even before establishing its hospital department, the Wabash had gained national attention in railroad and medical circles for having launched the first systemwide professional association of railway surgeons. In late 1881 and early 1882, Dr. J. T. Woods, "a good organizer and an inventive genius in the preparation of appliances for the relief of the injured," led this movement. A former Union Army brigade surgeon from Toledo who had recently been named chief surgeon of the railroad, Dr. Woods called together other Wabash-retained surgeons. At an 1882 meeting in Decatur, Illinois, division point and location of the largest system shops, he told associates that "prior to any organization, if such step be deemed best, I desire to call your attention to the fact, as a formal meeting of railroad surgeons, this is the first that has ever occurred. Whatever the result, we, so far as I know, in the matter are pioneers." Dr. Woods and twenty-two fellow doctors formed what they called the Wabash Surgical Association. Later that year the Surgical Society of PRR affiliate Pittsburgh, Fort Wayne & Chicago (PFtW&C) was also created. Within a decade or so, surgeons on the B&O, Erie, and other roads emulated the Wabash and PFtW&C. In 1888 an umbrella organization, the National Association of Railway Surgeons, assembled in Chicago, and this new body expanded rapidly. This event meshed well with the ongoing national crusade for professional organizations. Historian Robert Wiebe contends in *The Search for Order, 1877–1920* that the new middle class of the post–Civil War decades sought to bring about a modern, orderly society through bureaucratic means.[71]

While the Wabash led the way with a professional association of surgeons, it followed other railroads by establishing a network of hospitals. In 1869 the Central Pacific Railroad blazed the way, opening a temporary hospital in Sacramento, California. A year later it constructed a permanent facility. In 1882 Dr. Woods urged the Wabash to establish its own hospitals. Although management endorsed his proposal, some workers objected: "The leaders were especially against [company hospitals], wouldn't have it in any way. While they didn't suggest anything to take its place, they wouldn't have any blankety-blank hospital or any doctor for that matter." (A few, in fact, embraced the rapidly growing Christian Science faith.) Resistance among employees soon crumbled, likely because of several well-received hospitals opened on other Gould roads, especially the well-equipped Missouri Pacific hospital in St. Louis.[72]

The Wabash opted for what is best described as a mutual benefit association, which additional railroads, including the B&O and PRR, also found attractive. A number of nonrailroad businesses, ranging from farm machinery to stove manufacturers, also embraced this approach. Although the Wabash underwrote the hospital buildings and some related expenses, employees paid much of the costs for their medical care. Those who joined this voluntary program were assessed a modest monthly fee, based on income, with a track laborer contributing less than half of what a locomotive engineer paid.[73]

With a modest bureaucracy in place, the Wabash rapidly implemented its medical program. The company purchased four large houses that could be converted into hospitals. These remodeled structures soon opened in Danville, Illinois; Kansas City, Missouri; Peru, Indiana; and Springfield, Illinois. In what might appear to be an unusual arrangement, the Wabash engaged several Roman Catholic nursing orders to help staff its hospitals. The nuns received a small monthly stipend, along with room and board. Somewhat after the Wabash opened its Kansas City hospital, it sold it to Frisco affiliate Kansas City, Fort Scott & Gulf. The Wabash did not abandon the state, however. Rather, it relocated to Moberly, an important shop town and division point. On donated land, the railroad invested $40,000 for the construction and furnishings of a state-of-the-art facility. It also replaced the original hospital in Peru with what an industry trade publication called "one of the completest and best equipped railway hospital buildings in the country." Communities with Wabash medical facilities were pleased with what the railroad had accomplished.[74]

One midwestern town claimed something highly unusual. The place was West Lafayette, Indiana, home of Purdue University, the state's public land-grant school. The facility was an instructional building that was designed to test steam locomotives. The initial laboratory, conceived in 1891 and opened three years later, claimed the distinction of being the world's first permanent installation for such research. Under the direction of W. F. M. Goss, professor of experimental engineering, students working in a wing of the recently constructed engineering building studied Schenectady No. 1, an American standard locomotive that the university had acquired from the Schenectady Locomotive Works. Why a testing laboratory? With advances in engineering and technology, it became possible to check steam locomotives for fuel and water consumption and mechanical and thermal efficiency. The data collected was used to develop more power at less cost. Although early on a fire severely damaged the Purdue facility, repairs were made, and the testing continued until the late 1930s. Other collegiate locomotive testing facilities appeared in the Midwest, including ones at Iowa State College of Agriculture and Mechanic Arts (today's Iowa State University) in Ames and the University of Illinois in Champaign.[75]

ADDITIONAL HAPPENINGS

As the Gilded Age waned, midwesterners likely paid attention to the opening of several transcontinental systems. These rail lines would not be under a single corporate banner from coast to coast, yet they connected the Chicago and St. Louis gateways with the Pacific Coast. By the 1880s the Union Pacific–Central Pacific (Southern Pacific after 1885) lost its claim as the sole transcontinental carrier. The Southern Pacific also forged a link. The company took advantage of breaks in the mountains made possible by the Gadsden Purchase and pushed eastward from Los Angeles, via Yuma, Arizona Territory, to El Paso, Texas. In 1881 Southern Pacific rails met the Santa Fe at Deming, New Mexico Territory, to form a second transcontinental route and a connection to Kansas City and other midwestern rail centers. Six years later the Santa Fe succeeded in opening its own line to California. The expanding company also established better connections to the East. In 1888 it constructed a direct line from Kansas City to Chicago.

The Northern Pacific experienced a more daunting challenge in creating its route to the Pacific. In 1864 President Abraham Lincoln signed legislation for a northern transcontinental. To offset construction expenses, this measure included the largest federal land grant in history, amounting to nearly sixty million acres. The projected path was from Lake Superior at Duluth, Minnesota, to the Pacific Northwest. Even with ample agricultural and forest lands to sell, financial difficulties haunted the project. By 1873 the mainline had been extended only to Bismarck, Dakota Territory. A combination of aggressive management and additional capital, both domestic and foreign, allowed the Northern Pacific to reach Portland, Oregon, and soon Tacoma, Washington Territory. In the summer of 1883, this transcontinental at last opened for through service. To honor this momentous occasion, financier and company president Henry Villard staged an extravagant and costly celebration. Special trains transported hundreds of guests to and from Gold Creek, Montana Territory (near present-day Helena), for the golden-spike ceremony. To add to the splendor of this day, speeches and other happenings were relayed to the nation by telegraph from this remote site.[76]

By 1890 midwesterners could ship or travel with northern, central, and southern options to the West Coast. More transcontinental mileage was in the immediate offing: the Great Northern Railway under the direction of James J. Hill entered Seattle from the Twin Cities in 1893.[77]

As in all parts of America, travel mishaps occurred. Some passengers worried about accidents, and they had realistic concerns. Although railroads in the Midwest and the nation saw safety improvements during the post–Civil War period, including better signaling, double tracking, knuckle couplers, air brakes, and other operating and equipment betterments, tragic accidents still occurred. On December 29, 1876, the westbound Pacific Express, a Lake Shore & Michigan Southern passenger train bound for Chicago, broke through a faulty Howe truss bridge over the Ashtabula River near Ashtabula, Ohio. At least eighty people died as a result of the fall and subsequent burning of the train. More than a decade later, on August 10, 1887, another bridge collapse shocked the nation. This catastrophe, which occurred three miles east of Chatsworth, Illinois, involved a Toledo, Peoria & Western excursion train with two locomotives and fifteen cars headed from Peoria for Niagara Falls, New York. A portion of the consist derailed due to a burning wooden culvert, the result of an earlier area grass fire. Nine cars promptly "piled up as high as telegraph poles." The number of dead ranged from 81 to 85 and those injured from 169 to 372. Whatever the actual number of killed and injured, this was a human disaster of considerable magnitude.[78]

Train robberies caused widespread excitement throughout the Midwest. Although they were far less frequent and dangerous than wrecks, they grabbed newspaper headlines and resulted in well-publicized law-enforcement responses. Thanks to pulp fiction, motion pictures triggered by the 1903 *Great Train Robbery* classic, radio, and television, the public likely associates these events with the Wild West where the Dalton Gang, the Hole-in-the-Wall Gang, and other train robbers became famous. Yet the Midwest also experienced these criminal acts; in fact, it claimed the earliest ones. Likely the first passenger train heist took place in May 1865 near North Bend, Ohio, west of Cincinnati, on the Ohio & Mississippi Railroad. After derailing the locomotive, tender, and baggage-express car, one group of gang members entered the express-baggage car and

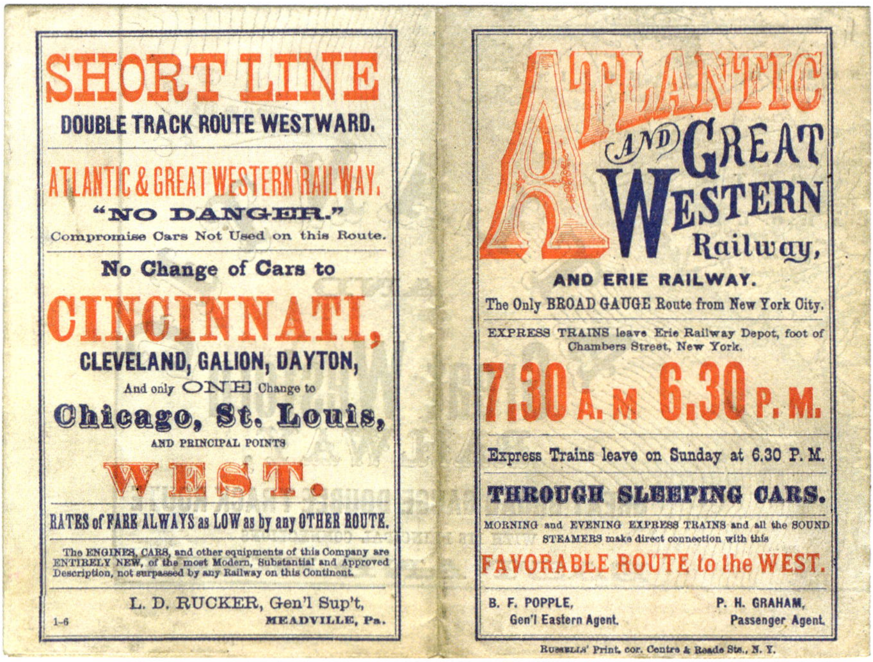

SHORT LINE

DOUBLE TRACK ROUTE WESTWARD.

ATLANTIC & GREAT WESTERN RAILWAY.

"NO DANGER."

Compromise Cars Not Used on this Route.

No Change of Cars to

CINCINNATI,

CLEVELAND, GALION, DAYTON,

And only ONE Change to

Chicago, St. Louis,

AND PRINCIPAL POINTS

WEST.

RATES of FARE ALWAYS as LOW as by any OTHER ROUTE.

The ENGINES, CARS, and other equipments of this Company are ENTIRELY NEW, of the most Modern, Substantial and Approved Description, not surpassed by any Railway on this Continent.

L. D. RUCKER, Gen'l Sup't,
MEADVILLE, Pa.

1-6

ATLANTIC AND GREAT WESTERN Railway,

AND ERIE RAILWAY.

The Only BROAD GAUGE Route from New York City.

EXPRESS TRAINS leave Erie Railway Depot, foot of Chambers Street, New York.

7.30 A. M 6.30 P. M.

Express Trains leave on Sunday at 6.30 P. M.

THROUGH SLEEPING CARS.

MORNING and EVENING EXPRESS TRAINS and all the SOUND STEAMERS make direct connection with this

FAVORABLE ROUTE to the WEST.

B. F. POPPLE, Gen'l Eastern Agent.
P. H. GRAHAM, Passenger Agent.

RUSSELLS' Print. cor. Centre & Reade Sts., N. Y.

WABASH LINE

THE U.S. MAIL ROUTE.

THE FAST LINE!

THROUGH

Ohio, Indiana and Illinois

TO

SOUTH'N IOWA, MISSOURI, KANSAS, ARKANSAS, NEBRASKA, COLORADO, TEXAS, &c.

PASSENGERS WESTWARD BOUND

are specially directed to the Official Time Table within, showing the arrivals of our trains at Principal Western Points, which will be found to be considerably in advance of those of other Lines.

For safety and comfort, combined with all the modern improvements, this Line cannot be excelled, every train being equipped with MILLER'S SAFETY PLATFORMS, and WESTINGHOUSE'S NEW AND IMPROVED AUTOMATIC BRAKE, pronounced the only absolutely safe Brake under all possible circumstances, and attached to Express Trains are PULLMAN PALACE SLEEPING CARS and new Palace Day Coaches (no extra charge for seats in the latter), which run through to the Mississippi and Missouri Rivers without change—advantages afforded by no other Line.

The Trains of this Line now run direct to Peoria.

Through Tickets via the "Wabash Line"

Are on sale at all the Principal Ticket Offices of connecting Roads and at the Company's terminal points and principal Stations. For further information apply personally or by letter to either of the following named Agents:

I. F. WILEY, Eastern Passenger Agent, ...263 Broadway, NEW YORK.
S. FARNSWORTH, Eastern Passenger Agent,....................WORCESTER, Mass.
J. P. POWARS, Traveling Agent,..................................TOLEDO, Ohio.

Or to W. L. MALCOLM,
General Passenger & Ticket Agent, TOLEDO, Ohio.

June 18, 1876.

SPECIAL INFORMATION! TO RETURNING CENTENNIAL PASSENGERS VIA

WABASH LINE

FAST U. S. MAIL ROUTE to

FT. WAYNE, LOGANSPORT,
WABASH, LAFAYETTE,
PERU, DANVILLE,
TOLONO, DECATUR,
BLOOMINGTON, SPRINGFIELD,
PEORIA, JACKSONVILLE,

ST. LOUIS,

Quincy, Hannibal, Keokuk,

AND PRINCIPAL POINTS IN

Illinois, Missouri, Kansas, Colorado, Arkansas, Texas and Nebraska.

Location of Depots and Ticket Offices in Philadelphia

OF ROADS RUNNING IN CONNECTION WITH WABASH LINE.

RAILROAD.	TICKET OFFICES.	DEPOTS.
Pennsylvania	838 Chestnut Street. 1348 Chestnut Street. 116 Market Street. Exhibition Grounds.	Thirty-second and Market. Exhibition Grounds. Kensington. Market Street Ferry.
Philadelphia & Reading	838 Chestnut Street. 624 Chestnut Street. 732 Chestnut Street. 317 Arch Street. Exhibition Grounds. Ninth and Green Sts.	Thirteenth and Callowhill. Exhibition Grounds. Ninth and Green Street.
New York & Philad'lp'a New Line, North Pennsylvania, Lehigh Valley Route,	434 Chestnut Street. 732 Chestnut Street. Exhibition Grounds.	Berks and America Sts. Exhibition Grounds.
Philadelphia, Wilmingt'n & Balti'e Baltimore & Ohio Route,	700 Chestnut Street. 838 Chestnut Street. Exhibition Grounds.	Broad and Washingt'n Av. Exhibition Grounds.

For information as to the Time of Arrival and Departure of Trains, see Daily Papers, Travelers' Official Guide, or inquire at Railroad Ticket Offices.

This is the Only Route running PULLMAN SLEEPING CARS through from

CLEVELAND TO ST. JOSEPH AND ATCHISON,

And DAY CARS from

TOLEDO to KANSAS CITY Without Change!

R. ANDREWS, Gen'l Sup't, Toledo, O.
J. F. WILEY, East'n Pass. Ag't, 263 Broadway, N. Y.
W. L. MALCOLM, Gen'l Pass. Ag't, Toledo, O.

Facing, Railroads sought to reassure travelers that their equipment was modern, safe, and comfortable. In 1867 a public timetable of the broad-gauge Atlantic & Great Western Railway crowed that it was the smart way to travel over portions of the eastern Midwest—"NO DANGER." An 1876 Wabash, Toledo & Western Railway public timetable did much the same with these words: "Every train being equipped with MILLER'S SAFETY PLATFORMS, and WESTINGHOUSE'S NEW AND IMPROVED AUTOMATIC BRAKE." *(Author's collection)*

blew open the Adams Express Company safe, and another "relieved passengers of their watches and money." The perpetrators escaped across the Ohio River to Kentucky and were never caught. The following year the Reno brothers, who have been incorrectly credited with committing the first post–Civil War train robbery, operated in the same region, but they were eventually brought to justice. Their good luck ended dramatically when a group of vigilantes caught them and strung them up.[79]

The bandits who gained the greatest national, even international, attention (and lasting fame) were members of the James Gang. These outlaws had had good training with banditry, having been part of the pro-Confederate William Quantrill guerrilla band in Missouri. On the evening of July 21, 1873, the gang held up a Rock Island passenger train near Adair, Iowa, about eighty miles east of Council Bluffs. Jesse and Frank James and their accomplices believed that eastbound train No. 2 carried a large shipment of gold bullion destined for New York and worth an estimated $75,000. In the process of this holdup, the gang wrecked the locomotive, killing the engineer, but there was no huge quantity of gold; Wells Fargo & Company had shipped it on an earlier train. These desperadoes did not leave empty handed. They found about $2,000 in gold in the express car and took as much as $6,000 in cash, jewelry, and watches from the frightened passengers. In what was called the "Blue Cut Robbery," which took place in September 1881, the James Gang held up a Chicago & Alton passenger train near Kansas City. After members stopped the locomotive and took command of the engine crew and the express messenger, they robbed the express safe and passengers. The final take was less remunerative than their Adair heist.[80]

As the 1880s ended, railroad leaders must have felt confident about the overall nature of their industry in the Midwest (and elsewhere, too).

Since the Civil War, there had been a host of improved and replacement technologies for railroad operations. Take what Thomas Edison, the "Wizard of Menlo Park," did for communications. He perfected the quadruplex telegraph for sending two messages simultaneously in each direction over a single wire, increasing capacity and reducing the need to install and maintain additional wires. This increased efficiencies for dispatchers, depot agents, and tower operators. Similarly, Alexander Graham Bell's invention of the telephone, which he patented in 1876, led several railroads in the 1880s to use this novel device to regulate train movements, although none were large carriers. Yet the telephone held enormous promise for future use.[81]

The actual railroad itself experienced a sea change of betterments. Steel rails rapidly replaced iron ones, locomotives became more powerful, and sleeping and dining cars had evolved as standard equipment on the better long-distance passenger trains. These improvements hardly exhausted the list of how railroads had advanced since 1860.

Railroad personnel had reason to feel comfortable about their future. Not only had there been important advances in communications and improvements to the physical railroad, but they did not perceive threats from other forms of land and water competition. The iron horse held dominance. The automobile had yet to become a plaything of the rich, let alone the principal means of transportation for the average citizen. No one had thought of a motorized truck; this was the age of the horse and mule for local haulage. And nearly all public roads remained primitive, making most road travels tiring and exasperating ordeals. At this time the electric interurban hardly appeared as a potential challenger. Still, there were signs that it might do so. In 1889 the seven-mile Newark & Granville Street Railway, in reality a rural trolley, opened between the two central Ohio towns of its corporate name. As the twentieth century emerged, this pioneer "juice" road gained the distinction of being the first electric line to become part of a general network of highly competitive interurbans for short- and medium-distance passenger traffic and for less-than-carload-lot freight, express, and US mail. Their appearance usually did not sit well with their steam road neighbors. After all, the decades-old railroad land monopoly had a potential challenger.[82]

THREE

MATURITY

1890–1930

HARD TIMES

The 1890s did not start off auspiciously for the nation's midsection and its railroads. As the previous decade closed, farmers on the Great Plains and in western sections of the Midwest began to experience several years of crop-damaging droughts. The adage "When there's no rain on the plains, there's no grain in the trains" often rang true. The price for wheat, oats, and other grains had plummeted since 1880 to distressing levels, often failing to cover the cost of production. Those midwestern agrarians who focused on corn-hog and dairy production fared better than grain-dependent growers. Fortunately, the overall level of farm debt throughout much of the Midwest was lower than that in the trans-Missouri West.

It was early May 1893 when most Americans began to suffer financially, including the wealthiest families. A devastating panic struck Wall Street. When shares of the National Cordage Company, the recently formed hemp trust, plummeted from 140 to 70, it helped trigger a five-year depression. No security seemed immune. Confidence and credit vanished; the economy sank in irretrievable collapse. Business after business failed, including a sizable portion of the railroad industry. By 1895 more than 150 railroads, representing approximately 40,000 route miles, were under court protection. During the boom years of the 1880s, companies had underwritten their construction projects, acquisition activities, and betterments through high-interest bonds. After the onset of the national depression, rapidly shrinking freight and passenger revenues made scheduled payments on these fixed-debt obligations difficult, if not impossible. The sprawling Atchison, Topeka & Santa Fe (Santa Fe), which a few years earlier had extended its mainline from Kansas City to Chicago, fell into the hands of receivers. Other victims that served the Midwest included the Baltimore & Ohio (B&O), Erie, and Northern Pacific Railroads. Even if companies remained solvent, their leaders (and investors) worried about their short- and long-range futures.[1]

During this time of national distress, midwesterners continued their dependence on railroads. Unlike earlier in the century, there was no agitation for a replacement mode of transport. Railroads reigned, bankrupt or not, and they needed to reach every town, village, and hamlet, become faster and safer, and operate in the public interest. This sentiment would largely hold true until the World War I era, when internal combustion vehicles grew in popularity for individual travel and short-haul freight movements, and all-weather road mileage increased.

What gained the public's attention during the catastrophic depression of the 1890s were not reports of "horseless carriages" but rather the Pullman strike of 1894, a direct result of hard times. This bitter dispute jarred Chicago, the Midwest, and the nation. It emerged as one of the most acrimonious strikes in American history, comparable to the railroad worker unrest of 1877 and the shopmen's strike of 1922.

The background of what occurred in Pullman, Illinois, early on could not have been predicted. George Mortimer Pullman, a smart, resourceful, and self-confident Chicago entrepreneur who possessed a liberal Universalist Church heritage, believed that his perfection of the sleeping car would become his greatest personal and financial triumph. This led him to launch the Pullman Palace Car Company in 1867. Although facing stiff competition in the sleeping-car business, he succeeded in placing his cars on several midwestern roads and soon prospered. Pullman provided patrons with a quality product and benefited from railroads never having been particularly pleased with their own sleeping-car operations. A decade later he had some six hundred cars in revenue service throughout much of the country and employed approximately two thousand workers. As the national economy sprang back to life following the Panic of 1873, Pullman opened a massive car plant fourteen miles south of

Chicago in what became the place he named after himself and his company. This "sleeping car king" orchestrated more than the construction of an industrial complex; he built a "model town" of all-brick structures with employee housing, stores, a hotel, and other support facilities. The surrounding grounds offered a parklike atmosphere in a largely rural setting and featured the artificial Lake Vista. Because Pullman was an ardent prohibitionist and defender of "village virtues," there were no saloons, brothels, gambling dens, or other "temptations." The community delighted Pullman and impressed visitors, becoming a popular tourist attraction. And it gained international notoriety. Workers, however, came to view the place with less enthusiasm. The feeling developed that life there was puritanical and undemocratic. When economist Richard Ely visited Pullman in the mid-1880s, he observed, "It is not the American ideal. It is benevolent, well-wishing feudalism." Still, employment until the Panic of 1893 was usually steady, and payrolls were met.[2]

It did not take long into the depression for George Pullman to respond; after all, his operations, which included freight car construction, had slowed significantly, and revenues had diminished. He laid off workers, and those who remained had their wages cut. The pay reductions were hardly insignificant, amounting to about a third. Yet housing rents and prices at the company stores remained at predepression levels. Also troubling was that Pullman and his associates did not take a corresponding reduction in their salaries. The stubborn and irascible Pullman, who had no tolerance for organized labor, refused to participate in collective bargaining. He preferred to discuss matters of wages, rents, and store prices on an individual basis. Moreover, he "had no conception of the true state of affairs in his shops, nor the injustices being heaped upon his employees." The response? On May 11, 1894, the suffering workers, who numbered about four thousand, decided to strike. The final straw was the dismissal of three operatives, likely because of their activities on a workers' grievance committee.[3]

Outside support rapidly developed for Pullman strikers. The recently launched American Railway Union (ARU), designed to be a potent industrial labor organization and led by the homespun and charismatic activist Eugene V. Debs (former editor of the *Fireman's Magazine*), soon joined the Pullman labor unrest. Already the ARU basked in its initial successes, most notably a recent albeit brief walkout in April 1894 against James J. Hill's Great Northern Railway. A union spokesman claimed that this work stoppage had achieved most of its demands, including restoring a pay cut made to maintenance-of-way workers. Despite the unfriendliness expressed by the more conservative operating brotherhoods, ARU membership soared, reaching about 150,000 railroaders. The union also gained considerable public support.[4]

What became the role of the ARU in the walkout by Pullman workers? The Debs union declared his sympathy toward the strikers. They were eligible to join the ARU because the Pullman Company operated an industrial railroad from its manufacturing and maintenance facilities to connections with area trunk roads. On June 26, 1894, the ARU took action by launching a sympathetic boycott of all trains that had Pullman cars in their consists. Debs instructed strikers to avoid any criminal acts and to move the US mails, lest the federal government intervene.

The boycott led to violent acts by ARU members and supporters. Widespread damage and destruction of property occurred, mostly concentrated in the Chicago area. This involved the torching of rolling stock, the derailing of locomotives, and the wrecking of the Diamond Special, a Chicago–St. Louis passenger train operated by the Illinois Central (IC). Although all trunk roads in Chicago suffered, the Pennsylvania (PRR) and IC sustained the greatest financial losses. The final cost of the strike for the IC alone exceeded $700,000. This "Debs Rebellion" also resulted in the Pullman Company losing property and business and experiencing extra operating expenses.[5]

The ARU was the ultimate loser. The Pullman strike destroyed this infant industrial labor organization. The powerful twenty-four-member General Managers' Association of Chicago (GMA), which included representation of all carriers with terminals in the city, agreed that the union must be crushed, and it responded accordingly. By mid-July the GMA succeeded in ending the work stoppage. It did so through the recruitment of strikebreakers, deputized US marshals, state militia, and federal troops, and court injunctions. It was a short but painful experience for the ARU. The boycott, though, never officially ended but merely dissolved. ARU officials, including Debs, served time in jail for defying a federal injunction. (Debs emerged as a hero to many in the laboring class and later became a perennial candidate for the US presidency on the Socialist Party ticket). Although a majority of strikers would be rehired by their respective companies, some faced blacklisting. This forced them to find work on friendly carriers or perhaps to change their names and identify themselves under a new "flag" or alias. This was often workable before passage of the Railroad Retirement Act of 1937 and other federal and state measures. Some former ARU members left railroading permanently. A lasting legacy of the Pullman strike is that it served as the impetus for establishing Labor Day as a national holiday.[6]

During the frenzied 1890s, the nation had one of its most important and emotional presidential elections. Voters had a choice in 1896 between Republican William McKinley, former governor of Ohio and then member of Congress, and William Jennings Bryan, former congressman from Nebraska and the Democratic and People's Party nominee. McKinley advocated the gold standard and protective tariffs, and Bryan sought "free silver" and free trade. Each approach would theoretically be a pathway to permanent national prosperity.

The campaign activities of these two standard-bearers were dramatically different, yet midwestern railroads played important roles for both men. Because of Mrs. McKinley's fragile health and on the advice of his campaign manager, Mark Hanna, William McKinley remained at home in Canton, Ohio. From the front porch of their unpretentious house, McKinley conducted his campaign. The people came to him. These delegations, which ranged from members of the Grand Army of the Republic to the Women's Christian Temperance Union, arrived by tightly coordinated schedules worked out by the McKinley staff and the railroads, largely the PRR, whose Pittsburgh-to-Chicago mainline served Canton. The PRR operated cut-rate excursion trains from throughout the Midwest. From the station visitors either walked the several blocks or took carriages to McKinley's front yard, perhaps joined by a brass band. Thus, without leaving his doorstep, McKinley met thousands of well-wishers.

William Jennings Bryan and his handlers realized that the nominee faced an uphill battle for the presidency. The Midwest needed their close attention; the region had emerged as the principal political battleground. Soon after Bryan's nomination at the Democratic convention in Chicago on July 11, 1896, the Bryan party began its extensive whistle-stop tours.

The four major ones, which involved an astonishing 18,009 miles by rail and multiple roads, consumed more than three months. At first "the silver orator of the Platte" rode observation cars that belonged to the individual roads, but toward the end of his campaign the Democratic National Committee leased a private car with that essential rear observation platform, the Idler ("a most inappropriate name, it seemed to me," quipped Bryan), and happily he "was robbed of the inconvenience which necessarily attends a frequent change of cars."[7]

The election outcome? Even with his exhausting campaign by rail, Bryan lost to McKinley, who collected 271 electoral votes to his 176. Yet in the Midwest Bryan generally ran ahead of other Democratic candidates. The election of 1896 was important for more than culminating in a McKinley victory. It was what political scientists call a "realigning" or "critical" election, meaning after 1896 Republicans became the dominant national party, remaining so until the Democratic landslide of 1932. But the use of a whistle-stop campaign endured. President Harry S Truman's barnstorming rail tour through the Midwest in 1948 became second only to Bryan's.[8]

EXPANSION

With the crushing national depression, rail line construction dropped dramatically throughout the country, including the Midwest. As the economy started a sustained comeback on the eve of the Spanish-American War, prospects looked much brighter for greater expansion. New route miles or "first main tracks" rose nationally from 2,109 in 1897 to 3,265 in 1898 and reached 4,569 the following year. In 1900 the American rail network reached 218,101 miles. Building progressed. The year 1906 proved to be especially active. More miles of railroad were constructed that year across the United States than during any year since the construction boom of the late 1880s That trend continued until 1916, when national mileage peaked at 254,037 miles. Yet the previous year saw fewer miles of lines built than in any year since 1864. Then the decline began. Multiple factors came into play, including the impact of World War I on domestic and international money markets, federalization under the US Railroad Administration, and the increased presence of automobiles, barges, pipelines, and trucks. Starting in 1917 railroads abandoned more miles of line than they installed. The railroad monopoly had ended, and a new era of modal competition had dawned.[9]

What did railroads in the Midwest build during the final years of line construction? Unlike what occurred in the trans-Missouri West, where several carriers installed considerable mileage (highlighted by the 1,375-mile Pacific Coast Extension from South Dakota to Puget Sound, built by the Chicago, Milwaukee & St. Paul [Milwaukee Road]), the eight-state region experienced less spectacular additions. Two examples illustrate the scope of the new rail lines. In 1911 the Minneapolis, St. Paul & Sault Ste. Marie Railroad (Soo Line) opened a seventy-three-mile link between Boylston, south of Superior, Wisconsin, and Frederick, Wisconsin, forging the shortest route between the Twin Cities and the Twin Ports of Duluth and Superior on Lake Superior. It allowed the Soo Line to compete effectively with the Great Northern, Northern Pacific, and Chicago & North Western (North Western) affiliate Chicago, St. Paul & Minneapolis & Omaha (Omaha Road) between these two points. A much smaller albeit strategic construction involved the PRR. In its final expansion in the Midwest, the company at last served Detroit. Access to one of America's greatest industrial centers—including the sprawling two-thousand-acre Dearborn, Michigan, River Rouge complex of the Ford Motor Company, which took shape after 1917—was achieved by gaining trackage rights north of Toledo into the Wayne County region from Pere Marquette, Ann Arbor, and Wabash. The PRR, however, needed to construct a portion of its desired route. It did so in 1922 by installing twenty miles between Carleton, Michigan, and the Ford complex under the banner of the Pennsylvania-Detroit Railroad Company.[10]

By the 1920s Henry Ford's River Rouge facilities in greater Detroit claimed the largest private or industrial railroad in the Midwest and the nation. This famed automobile maker believed that vertical integrated production was essential for his firm's prosperity and dominance. For transportation, the company owned a fleet of Great Lakes freighters and the 454-mile Detroit, Toledo & Ironton Railroad (DT&I), the former providing access to iron ore mines in the arrowhead county of Minnesota and the Upper Peninsula of Michigan and the latter to the bituminous coal fields of southern and southeastern Ohio. At "the Rouge"

Ford's railroad by the late 1920s operated approximately one hundred miles of track and owned a fleet of steam locomotives and rolling stock, including specialized cars that served its three blast furnaces. Fanatical about cleanliness, Ford made certain that his motive power was kept in tip-top condition, including having their external components nickel plated. "The purpose of the nickel plating was to create an environment of cleanliness and to detect rough usage, plus it enhanced locomotive appearance," explained railroad writer David Guay. This industrial road also operated some of the earliest electric box-cab locomotives, acquiring them from General Electric between 1928 and 1930, attesting to the progressive outlook of Ford. Yet this automotive magnate received more renown for having the seventeen miles of the DT&I between the River Rouge complex and Flat Rock Yard electrified with a novel Westinghouse 22,000-volt, 25 AC power system.[11]

This general period stands out for the rebuilding or expanding of hundreds of miles of existing lines. Railroads, whether in the Midwest or elsewhere, are never completely finished. Such improvements are usually intensive rather than extensive, but there are exceptions. These include cutoffs, designed to shorten mileage and reduce troublesome grades and extensive curvatures. Between 1925 and 1928, the IC constructed a remarkable one between Edgewood, Illinois (fifteen miles south of Effingham, IL), and Fulton, Kentucky. This 169-mile length of trackage, known as the Edgewood Cutoff, had several objectives: to increase capacity and reduce distance on the company's main north–south line, to obtain a second crossing of the Ohio River (complementing its bridge at Cairo, IL), and to reduce the number of public grade crossings on this freight route. When completed, the line claimed a low-level route though the eastern foothills of the Ozarks, made possible by three tunnels of 800, 2,600, and 6,985 feet and sixty-three miles of largely tangent track south of Edgewood.[12]

Often as part of such improvements, companies increased their capacities where traffic was particularly dense, installing double or even triple tracks along stretches of their principal arteries. E. H. Harriman, whose railroad empire included the Chicago & Alton and Union Pacific Railroads, went so far to dream of universal double-tracking along all trunk routes. Bridges, too, were strengthened or replaced. As a case in point, the Chicago, Burlington & Quincy (Burlington) in 1909 embarked on the double-tracking and straightening of its more-than-two-hundred-mile water-level line between Savanna, Illinois, and St. Paul, Minnesota. Although the company completed a substantial portion by 1915, the entire project was not finished until 1929. Owing to such costly upgrades, one could say that the Burlington and other midwestern railroads were built twice, once in the nineteenth century and again in the twentieth century.[13]

Newly launched independent shortline railroads throughout the Midwest contributed to the mileage increases. These building endeavors help explain why regional expansion between 1900 and 1920 climbed from 64,010 to 71,633 miles. This mileage growth would have been greater had there not been an explosion in electric interurban trackage. By World War I, there existed regionally a somewhat disconnected grid of 8,081 miles of these frequently competing passenger, less-than-carload-lot (LCL), express, and US-mail-carrying traction operations. Some electric lines also handled carload freight interchangeable with steam roads. The Illinois Traction Company and the Cedar Rapids & Iowa City Railway represent these "electric steam railroads." Some steam shortlines converted to electric power. The Cincinnati, Georgetown & Portsmouth Railroad is an example. Built in 1886 as a forty-one-mile narrow-gauge steam road between Cincinnati and Georgetown, in 1902 this now-standard-gauge road came under wire.[14]

It was more than mileage that made the interurban era in the Midwest noteworthy. Major investments took place in manufacturing and support enterprises. A leading example involved car builders. These included American Car Company in St. Louis; American Car & Foundry Company in Jeffersonville, Indiana; Barney & Smith Car Company in Dayton, Ohio; Cincinnati Car Company in Cincinnati; Danville Car Company in Danville, Illinois; Jewett Car Company in Newark, Ohio; G. C. Kuhlman Car Company in Cleveland; McGuire-Cummings Manufacturing Company in Chicago and Paris, Illinois; Niles Car & Manufacturing Company in Niles, Ohio; and St. Louis Car Company in St. Louis.[15]

Every midwestern state had multiple "twilight era" steam shortlines. Most were modest. Take a cluster that appeared between 1907 and 1913 in western Iowa. Three of the four railroads that opened—Creston, Winterset & Des Moines; Iowa & Omaha Short Line; and Iowa & Southwestern—averaged seventeen miles long. The longest, Atlantic Northern & Southern Railroad (AN&S), installed fifty-four miles of track. These little roads were designed principally to serve inland communities, to meet the needs of local farmers (movement of grain and livestock to market), and in two cases to offer improved rail service to towns dominated by a single carrier. As with many late-date shortlines, these railroads failed early. All had become junk by 1920 except seventeen miles of the AN&S, reconstituted as the Atlantic Northern Railroad. It remained in operation until the mid-1930s.[16]

The Midwest claimed some much longer twilight shortlines. Two stand out: the 169-mile Akron, Canton & Youngstown (AC&Y) and the 120-mile Detroit, Bay City & Western (DBC&W) Railroads. The former was in some ways an oddball road. It began officially in 1907 with this construction plan: Magadore, Ohio, several miles east of Akron, to Youngstown, Ohio, a distance of fifty miles, and south from Magadore to Canton, Ohio, twenty miles. The AC&Y, however, never built to either Youngstown or Canton. Initially it was largely an industrial road, which linked the nineteen miles between Magadore (an interchange point with the Wheeling & Lake Erie Railway) and Copley Junction (an interchange with Northern Ohio Railroad). The AC&Y served a rapidly growing Akron, a city that had emerged as a center for the manufacturing of tires and related rubber products. Before long, the AC&Y became firmly associated with its largest customer, being known as the "Road to Goodyear." On March 1, 1920, the AC&Y took control of the 152-mile Northern Ohio Railroad, a property built in the 1890s by the Pittsburg, Akron & Western that later had been leased by the Lake Erie & Western Railway, a New York Central (NYC) affiliate. This allowed the Akron-based railroad to establish a seamless connection between Goodyear and Detroit automakers (principally the Ford Motor Company) by interchanging with the DT&I at Columbus Grove, Ohio.[17] The AC&Y thrived as an industrial, agricultural, rock, and bridge-line carrier. In the process it became a part owner of the forty-mile Akron & Barberton Belt Railroad, opened in 1902 by the "Match King," Ohio Columbus

Major interurban companies in the Midwest commonly maintained private cars for their officials and important guests. The pride of the Northern Ohio Traction & Light Company was the Josephine. This photograph, taken about 1910, shows the car in front of the Akron carbarn. The three-member crew, including an African American porter, awaits orders to take this luxury car out on the road, perhaps to Cleveland, Canton, or some other destination along its extensive Ohio network. *(Author's collection)*

Barber, founder of the Diamond Match Company. Much later, in 1964, the Norfolk & Western (N&W) leased the AC&Y, which in 1944 had officially taken ownership of the Northern Ohio. Later the N&W absorbed the Akron road, and in 1990 it was sold to the Wheeling & Lake Erie, a startup regional carrier. It was during this time that the western portion of the AC&Y between the Ohio towns of Carey and Delphos was retired.[18]

It might appear that Michigan, most of all its Lower Peninsula, was adequately served by railroads. As of 1900 the Wolverine State sported a 7,946-mile web of rails. The southern part of the Lower Peninsula also had a network of well-built interurbans, including giants Detroit United Railway and Michigan United Railway. At its peak the state claimed nearly a thousand miles of electric lines.[19]

As in other midwestern states during the early twentieth century, promoters continued to believe that more miles were needed, and ones that could be profitably operated. This explains why the four Handy brothers of Bay City, headed by Thomas Handy, sparked the formation of the Detroit, Bay City & Western Railroad. Although their hometown seemingly had adequate steam and interurban service, they saw the potential of extending rails eastward into the "Thumb Country," the state's geographical mitten and the self-proclaimed "Garden Spot of Michigan." The Handys likewise saw a vibrant Detroit south of Port Huron as a desirable destination. If the Motor City could be reached, more businesses could be served and interline traffic increased. The brothers had the resources and the entrepreneurial talents to accomplish their ambitions. By 1907 the Handys had prospered in their wooden box manufacturing and coal mining enterprises, and they had taken a flier with the woebegone one-hundred-mile Pontiac, Oxford & Northern Railroad (Polly Ann), selling it in 1909 to the Grand Trunk Railway of Canada for a handsome profit. Two years before the Polly Ann sale, the Handys had launched the DBC&W.[20]

The Handy Route failed to materialize overnight. Construction pushed slowly eastward from Bay City, taking nearly a decade before rails reached Port Huron, a distance of 102 miles. As the road opened in segments, it generated decent revenues, coming largely from coal, sugar beets, and general merchandise. Shortly before federalization in 1917, the Handys organized the nineteen-mile Port Huron & Detroit Railroad (PH&D). The following year its rails reached Marine City, but they never entered Detroit.[21]

Unlike the AC&Y, the Handy properties ultimately failed to prosper. A combination of the unexpected death of the two brothers (one by suicide), a deepening agricultural depression that began after World War I, and rapidly increasing automobile and truck usage aided by better roads forced a receivership in 1922. Initially, there was hope that a successful reorganization could take place, but that failed to happen. The original

DBC&W would be abandoned except for what became the forty-eight-mile Detroit, Cairo & Sandusky Railway. Designed principally as a sugar beet hauler, the road held on until 1953, although it retired portions of its line, operating at the end only the thirty-one miles between Cairo and Sandusky.[22]

While the Detroit, Cairo & Sandusky revealed that there was life to a portion of the Handy properties, the PH&D proved more enduring. It thrived as an industrial switching operation. Ultimately this upgraded shortline, which the Duffy family had owned since 1922, fell into the hands of the Chesapeake & Ohio Railroad and subsequently became part of the Chessie System and then today's CSX Transportation Company. Much of the trackage continues to serve customers.[23]

The trajectory of what the Handy brothers created became the opposite of the AC&Y experience. The former went from large shortline to industrial switching; the latter developed from an industrial-designed property to a major shortline. Although each road eventually had its mileage reduced through abandonment, neither can be considered a failure.

CONSOLIDATIONS

While the decades that brought maturity for railroads in the Midwest involved line construction of varying types, there were important consolidations, and they occurred in different ways. To streamline their corporate structures, controlled properties were regularly fused into the parent. The Burlington is one example. Between 1899 and 1901, this Chicago-based carrier absorbed a host of entities. Some affiliates were being operated directly by the Burlington, but others operated separately. While these arrangements generally functioned adequately, a bewildering complex of corporations needed to be restructured. As company historian Richard Overton explained, "From the financial and corporate standpoint, the existence of countless independent companies required a mountain of paper work and made calculation exactly how the entire Burlington system was doing as a whole extremely difficult." At last the Burlington owned and operated nearly all of its lines. Only a few of its smaller stock-controlled roads and its modest narrow-gauge mileage in Colorado functioned separately, and in time these too disappeared into the Burlington.[24]

When it came to corporate restructuring, the greatest impact on midwestern carriers prior to the "merger madness" of the 1960s and the megamergers of the late twentieth century took place in the 1920s with the work of the two Van Sweringen brothers. Who were the "Vans"? These prim, reserved, and inseparable bachelors, Oris Paxton (O. P.) Van Sweringen (1879–1936) and Mantis James (M. J.) Van Sweringen (1881–1935), grew up in a poor, religiously strict Ohio family. Early on O. P. dominated his younger brother, referring to him as a "clerk." (A less harsh description would be O. P. the "thinker" and M. J. the "doer.") Their father, a Union Army veteran who had been seriously wounded, could not engage in hard manual labor and therefore resorted to an array of low-paying odd jobs. At one time the family became homeless, but through the kindness of a Wooster, Ohio, businessman they lived for a short period in his summer house. More relocations followed. Eventually the family settled on the east side of Cleveland, but life continued to be a struggle. This family of six children suffered further when their mother died from consumption at age forty-one. As Clevelanders, O. P. and M. J. attended public schools, but their formal education ended with the eighth grade. Yet they were avid readers and determined workers. After a series of jobs, the Vans decided on careers as Cleveland-area real-estate promoters, and they did so with impressive results. The brothers gained local prominence and wealth as developers of the exclusive and innovative Shaker Heights Village, becoming an Ohio Horatio Alger success story par excellence.[25]

The Vans achieved national fame not for their real-estate endeavors but for amassing a railroad empire. In the process of completing their Shaker Heights residential and commercial developments, they sought to build a seven-mile rapid-transit line to link their planned community with Public Square, Cleveland's downtown business and commercial hub. To construct their electric railway, they needed access to the right-of-way of the New York, Chicago & St. Louis Railroad (Nickel Plate) that the NYC owned. This route was the only practical avenue between these endpoints. In 1916 the brothers got an offer that they couldn't refuse. The two principal reasons: federal officials threatened to take the NYC to court for violating the recently enacted Clayton Antitrust Act, and the brothers enjoyed a friendship with NYC president and former Clevelander Alfred Smith. He not only made it possible for the Vans to gain their desired right-of-way but also asked them to acquire the Nickel Plate. They agreed. The Vans borrowed heavily and launched a highly leveraged holding company, Nickel Plate Securities Corporation, to provide the legal vehicle for the takeover. This 523-mile railroad became the first component of the brothers' future rail domain. Thanks to Smith, investment bankers J. P. Morgan & Company, who also served the NYC, became their financial agent. Smith also arranged for them to hire John Bernet, a capable NYC executive, to take charge. Historian Richard Saunders speculated that the Vans were merely stalking horses for Smith and the NYC, and perhaps for a time they were.[26]

The Nickel Plate, which became steadily upgraded and effectively managed by Bernet and his leadership team, burgeoned into a profitable operation by focusing on fast-freight service between Chicago and Buffalo. The Vans quickly developed an appetite for more acquisitions; the railroad "bug" had infected them. With Interstate Commerce Commission (ICC) approval in 1923, they merged the Nickel Plate with two adjoining carriers, the Toledo, St. Louis & Western (Clover Leaf Route) and the smaller and less robust Lake Erie & Western (LE&W). This created a 1,700-mile system in what became the only important *formalized* railroad merger of the 1920s. With the Nickel Plate purchase, the brothers had learned the ins and outs of how to utilize a leveraged holding company and would use their newly found skills again and again.[27]

Soon the Vans expanded beyond the Nickel Plate, Clover Leaf Route, and LE&W. Working quickly and quietly, they made astounding acquisitions; they were the "invisible giants," in the assessment of biographer Herbert Harwood Jr.[28] The brothers purchased from railroad magnate Henry Huntington and his associates the 2,100-mile Chesapeake & Ohio Railway (C&O), a heavy coal hauler that connected Columbus and Cincinnati with tidewater Virginia. Included in this transaction was the C&O-controlled Hocking Valley Railway, a 350-mile carrier with a Toledo-to-Gallipolis, Ohio, stem with branches extending into the southeastern Ohio coalfields. Next the brothers took a major position in the 2,250-mile Pere Marquette, a mostly Michigan carrier with a prime Chicago connection, and they bought heavily into the 2,453-mile Erie Railroad, which served New York, Buffalo, Akron, Cleveland, and Chicago. By the mid-1920s the brothers reigned over more than 9,000 miles of rail line and seriously challenged competitors B&O, NYC, and PRR for interregional freight and passenger traffic.[29]

The timing for the Vans to acquire control of multiple railroads came at an opportune moment. The 1920s was a decade of business consolidations. Not since the turn of the twentieth century had political, economic, and social factors created an environment so conducive to architects of vast corporate enterprises. In the case of railroads, Congress had passed the Transportation Act of 1920, known also as the Esch-Cummings Act. A key provision instructed the ICC to prepare a unification plan that fashioned a limited number of competitive companies of roughly equal financial strength. After two failed attempts to generate an acceptable one and the coming of the Great Depression, these efforts were abandoned. Still, congressional intent favored massive, albeit federally supervised, system building.[30]

The financial transactions of the Vans became progressively more complex as they assembled their sprawling empire. They grasped the current economic and political forces and managed their railroads through holding companies rather than with formal mergers. In 1924 the brothers dissolved the Nickel Plate Securities Corporation, its original purpose having been served. Next they transferred its assets to other "paper" firms to facilitate their expansion objectives. The Vans embraced this holding-company strategy for multiple reasons. This business arrangement gave them control in a leveraged fashion, yet they could attract investors through financial inducements. The brothers held the majority of the voting common stock, while others owned nonvoting preferred shares with attractive fixed dividends. They also could assemble railroads without ICC interference. Not to be overlooked was the fact that if they structured a rail system through holding companies, they might later present a formal merger application to the ICC as a fait accompli. Their approach to consolidations revealed true brilliance.[31]

The Vans continued to refine their railroad empire. In early 1925 they concluded that it was an auspicious time to consolidate their affiliated properties. To achieve this objective, they needed ICC approval. The brothers asked the commission to allow them to merge the C&O, Erie, Nickel Plate, and Pere Marquette into a supersystem. A year later the ICC rejected their request. Even though the Vans' proposal appeared to be in the public interest, financial considerations, most of all complaints from C&O minority stockholders, derailed their efforts. These investors maintained that their equity in a strong road would be diluted by weaker carriers, particularly the Erie. Notwithstanding this adverse decision, the Vans kept on planning how to strengthen their holdings.[32]

The brothers still wanted a railroad merger. Undaunted by the earlier ICC decision, they returned to that body in 1928 and asked authority to unite the C&O with the Erie and Pere Marquette. A modest victory followed. Fifteen months later the commission authorized only a C&O–Pere Marquette union. Concern about the financial health of the Erie again precluded a complete consolidation. Frustrated, but always seeking to advance and protect their empire, the Vans in January 1929 created a master holding company, the Alleghany Corporation. The firm immediately absorbed all railroad assets and provided the brothers with personal control. Capital came from bonds, notes, and nonvoting stocks. Unfortunately, the Wall Street crash of October 1929 began to shatter their empire. By 1931 the deepening depression meant serious financial troubles, causing large-scale personal losses for the Vans. After their deaths in the mid-1930s, a slimmed-down Alleghany Corporation resulted. But on the eve of disaster, the brothers made a major (and lasting) contribution to Cleveland, completing on Public Square the Midland Building for railroad and other offices and the landmark Terminal Tower skyscraper, featuring shops, hotel, and a magnificent passenger station.[33]

REGULATION AND FEDERAL CONTROL

By the time that the ICC disappointed the Van Sweringens, federal regulation of the industry had already become all-powerful. In 1887 Washington had passed the Act to Regulate Commerce (better known as the Interstate Commerce Act), but for passenger and freight users this landmark legislation, which created the ICC, had only a modest positive consumer impact. Although railroad officials frequently fretted about federal interference, they soon realized that the law was weak. In 1892 Richard Olney, a Boston corporation lawyer who would shortly become US attorney general in the Grover Cleveland administration, told Burlington president Charles Perkins not to press for repeal of the statute and not to worry: "My impression would be that, looking at the matter from the railroad point of view exclusively, [repeal] would not be likely to succeed; if it did not succeed, and were made on the ground of the inefficiency and uselessness of the Commission, the result would very probably be giving it the power it now lacks." He continued, "The Commission, as its functions have now been limited by the Courts, is, or can be made, of great use to the railroads. It satisfies the popular clamor for a government supervision of railroads, at the same time that that supervision is almost entirely nominal." Olney added, "Further, the older such a Commission gets to be, the more inclined it will be found to take the business and the railroad view of things. It thus becomes a sort of barrier between the railroad corporations and the people and a sort of protection against hasty and crude legislation hostile to railroad interests." While correct about the impact of the then-current legislation and the nature of a regulatory commission, Olney did not foresee the forthcoming progressive movement.[34]

By World War I, the ICC had become significantly strengthened. Although the Granger movement of the 1870s suggested an attitudinal change in the popular view of the industry, historian Michael Kammen observed that during the formative years of the twentieth century "the railroad shifted from being a symbol of dramatic and unimagined progress to representing abusive and regressive economic power." Business historian Albro Martin agreed, arguing that public anger (and misunderstandings), concentrated heavily in the Midwest, resulted in this widespread antirailroad sentiment. He argued that the ICC, empowered greatly by two key laws, brought about what he called "enterprise denied" for the industry. This legislation damaged both railroads and ultimately the public. Companies faced the reduced ability to raise capital in a period when they faced costly modernization needs; after all, this was the "Age of Reconstruction." By 1915 a staggering one-sixth of all railroad mileage was under court protection.[35]

The two principal pieces of federal legislation haunted railroad officials and also bankers and others in the financial world. The first came in 1906 when Representative William Hepburn, a progressive Iowa Republican and chair of the House Commerce Committee, spearheaded passage of a rate-control bill. President Theodore Roosevelt enthusiastically signed the measure. The Hepburn Act empowered the ICC to set freight rates based on complaints from shippers, putting teeth into the Interstate Commerce Act and upending conservative court decisions about the role of this regulatory agency. There were additional provisions, including granting the ICC power to control divisions of rates and charges made for switching services. It also required standardized recordkeeping and reporting.[36]

The second statute was the Mann-Elkins Act. Sponsored by Representative James Mann, a progressive Republican from Illinois, and Senator Stephen Elkins, a Republican industrialist from West Virginia, it sailed through Congress in 1910. President William Howard Taft, who backed this legislation from its inception, readily signed the bill. The ICC emerged even stronger. This measure gave it the power to suspend proposed rate increases for a stated period while it considered their legality, and it placed the burden of justifying rate hikes directly on the carriers.[37]

Other pieces of federal legislation, inspired by reformers—Republicans, Democrats, or Progressive Party members after 1912—added to the concern of industry officials and their investors. These ranged from the Hours of Service Act, or the "sixteen-hour law," passed in 1907 to the Valuation Act of 1913, designed to determine the actual value of a railroad's real property. "It will be a sorry day for the Republic," remarked Frederick Delano, president of the Wabash Railroad soon after the latter measure became law, "when regulation is carried to such an extreme."[38]

President Delano and other railroad executives were hardly thrilled with still another "intrusive" federal measure. In 1916 the railroad brotherhoods, flexing their growing powers, announced their intention to win an eight-hour day. If the industry rejected their demand, they threatened to launch a national strike. They set Labor Day 1916 as the potential (and symbolic) date for their job action. President Woodrow Wilson did not want a paralyzing strike in the midst of his bid for reelection; he faced a tight race with his Republican challenger, Charles Evans Hughes. Wilson asked Congress to deal with this potential labor crisis; lawmakers quickly responded with the necessary legislation. The Adamson Act, which bore the name of the Georgia progressive Democrat William C. Adamson (who chaired the House Interstate Commerce Commission), established the eight-hour day for operating-craft employees and telegraphers. The measure averted a disastrous worker shutdown of an industry already struggling to manage increased traffic created by the Great War in Europe and a vibrant national economy. Carriers experienced escalating labor costs; annual wages soared from an average of $567 in 1900 to $880 in 1916, and they continued to rise.[39]

An unhappy industry responded to the Adamson Act. Railroad officials did more than fret; they tested the legality of the law in the courts. Their efforts turned to dross. In March 1917 the Supreme Court upheld the statute by a single vote.[40]

Due to the combination of the Hepburn, Mann-Elkins, and Adamson Acts and other Progressive Era measures, railroads, whether operating in the Midwest or elsewhere, found themselves in a serious economic bind. Historian Maury Klein correctly described the situation: "The [federal] government had taken over both sides of the ledger, income and expenses, and the mechanisms for regulating one were in no way coordinated with those for adjusting the other." Yes, enterprise denied.[41] Then there were the restrictive legislative actions taken by midwestern states. "Full-crew" laws long impacted the bottom lines of regional carriers. By the time of World War I, most of the eight states had them on their statute books. Designed to protect public safety broadly defined, these Progressive Era reforms were largely the same. A representative example was the one passed by the Indiana legislature in 1913, a body dominated by reform-minded men, being a coalition of consumer-sensitive Democrats and Republicans. It required five crewmen on all freight trains that handled less than fifty cars. Additional crewmen were mandated for longer trains. Legislators did not ignore crew sizes on passenger trains. They also required five employees and included this provision: "Said brakemen or flagmen shall not be required to perform duties of baggage masters, express messenger or porter."[42]

In late 1917 a shocking event came for all carriers—federalization of much of the railroad network. Since the 1850s private ownership in the Midwest had been fully established; only Michigan and Illinois had been directly engaged in the railroad business. Now the US Railroad Administration (USRA) assumed operations of all trunk steam roads and many of the lesser ones, including terminal companies, together with selected interurbans. This controlled trackage was operated as a single system, headed by the director general of railroads, and supported by three regional directors. Midwestern rails were either in the Eastern Region (east of Chicago and the Mississippi and north of the Ohio and Potomac Rivers) or the Western Region (west of Chicago and the Mississippi River).[43]

Why federalization? The short answer was the inability of the nation's railroads to respond adequately to wartime traffic both before and after April 6, 1917, when the United States declared war on the Central Powers (Germany, Austria-Hungary, Bulgaria, and the Ottoman Empire). These nations had been battling the Allies (Great Britain, France, and Russia) since August 1914 and Italy since 1915. Months before America's formal entry, a severe freight-car shortage had developed. As of November 1, 1916, a shortfall of tens of thousands of freight cars plagued railroads and their customers. There was also need for more motive power and other equipment, including baggage and express cars. Wartime traffic generated by the Allies had spiked, and chaos reigned in Atlantic and Gulf terminals. Loaded freight cars clogged sidings at port side while shippers pleaded for empties. Part of this congestion stemmed from deadly German submarine attacks on merchant maritime vessels, causing shipping companies to become reluctant to leave the major US ports.[44]

The railroad industry responded to the growing traffic snarls as best it could. The Railroads' War Board, a voluntary organization of company executives launched six days after the declaration of war, sought to create a normal traffic flow but failed. Old rivalries, jealousies, and suspicions thwarted their good intentions. The movement of goods between Chicago and New York, for example, was hampered by the lack of cooperation between the B&O, Erie, NYC, and PRR. Each carrier sought to maximize its business at the expense of its rivals. These roads admitted that some arteries were usually overtaxed. They were not wrong. Railroads in 1917 carried the greatest volume of freight and passenger traffic in their history.[45]

The Wilson administration had no choice but to take unprecedented action. At noon on December 28, 1917, essential carriers came under the authority of the USRA—January 1, 1918, for accounting purposes. Although it was one of the most powerful federal agencies ever established, this was not nationalization. Under the terms of the Railroad Control Act of March 1918, Washington promised annual compensation to the federalized roads on the basis of net operating income for the three years preceding June 30, 1917. There was also the assurance that the government would provide adequate maintenance.[46]

Federalization generally accomplished the core goals of the Wilson administration. It did much to coordinate service, reducing traffic on the most congested routes and increasing it on those that operated below capacity. The USRA likewise worked to bring about standardization in maintenance and equipment. As for the latter, it created five standard freight-car designs that led to the building of approximately one hundred thousand units and a dozen standard designs that produced more than five thousand steam locomotives, including the most popular type for both freight and passenger power, the Mikado or "Mike" with its 2-8-2 wheel arrangement. Although much of the new equipment went to hard-pressed eastern-based carriers, Chicago-based ones were also recipients, ranging from the Great Western to the Chicago, Indianapolis & Louisville (known as the Monon). In fact the USRA designs formed the basis for a majority of locomotives built during the remaining years of the steam era. Furthermore, there were sizeable wage increases for workers during federal operations, a direct response to labor shortages and wartime inflation, while initially there were only modest freight-rate hikes. Common laborers, including coach cleaners, engine wipers, and freight handlers, might be individuals of color, Hispanics, women, and teenage boys, but their postwar employment usually ended. The USRA also made the eight-hour day standard throughout much of the industry.[47]

No operation, whether sponsored by federal authorities or private interests, happens without flaws. Overlooking the positives, especially the unsnarling of wartime traffic and the quest for standardized power and rolling stock, railroad executives complained that after twenty-six months of government control, Washington had failed to maintain their roads in the same or better shape than they were at the time of federalization. Erie officials rightly grumbled that their property was returned in a "battered condition." (They did not mention that their personnel repeatedly stole track materials, mostly rails, switches, and ties that the USRA had supplied to neighboring railroads. The Erie was not alone in committing thievery.) And of similar significance, the USRA for more than a year refused to push for freight-rate and passenger-fare hikes. All railroads, irrespective of location, saw their monthly deficits grow. After March 1, 1920, the date the USRA relinquished control, companies commonly had to battle with the government over the issue of fair compensation. Financial adjustments occurred, but for many the process took years.[48]

There were additional concerns about the impact of federal control, historic traffic patterns were disrupted, and the general goodwill of some carriers was damaged. During the immediate postwar years, business solicitation became a prime activity. This seemed especially true for the PRR, the "Standard Railroad of the World." The USRA furthermore made mistakes. Take locomotive allocations. In 1917 the Rock Island purchased thirty new locomotives and took delivery the following May. Then the government allocated to the railroad twenty road and ten switching locomotives that came with a $1.4 million price tag. Management protested; this power was not needed to handle existing freight and passenger movements. "At the date our objections were filed 23 Rock Island locomotives, including 15 of the 30 that had just been purchased, were being used on foreign lines," explained Board Chairman Charles Hayden, "so we felt that it was not fair to the Rock Island to buy new power for it when the power it already had was not being used on its own road." He added, "At this time there are approximately 90 idle locomotives on the system, so this protest is even more meritorious now than when it was first made."[49]

Midwestern railroad leaders had concerns other than those that involved their USRA experiences; they worried about the rising power of railroad labor. Within the ranks of the brotherhoods and backed by socialists and other advanced progressives, including Republican senator

Robert M. La Follette Sr. of Wisconsin, and also winning support from farmers and miners, demands grew for government ownership. This replicated the People's Party 1892 Omaha Platform plank that sought to end private railroad ownership. In the immediate postwar period, the Plumb Plan League (named for Glenn Plumb, legal counsel for the major brotherhoods) called for nationalization. In early 1918 this proposal, which won backing from the Big Four operating brotherhoods, shopmen, and other nonoperating crafts, demanded a publicly owned rail network to be overseen by an operating corporation that represented equally the federal government, railroad labor, and railroad officials. The buyout of private railroad owners would be financed through the sale of government bonds with half of the operational profits earmarked to pay interest and to retire the debt and the other half going to railroad employees.[50]

Even though the Plumb Plan League fizzled, it garnered considerable attention. Railroad executives and investors objected strenuously. The proposal, however, was doomed by strong antilabor sentiment that dominated Congress. Still, federal lawmakers and President Wilson sought additional railroad legislation. The future of the industry would instead be impacted by the Transportation Act of 1920, a measure that contained a requirement for industry consolidation. Another provision included creation of the Railroad Labor Board, which received jurisdiction over labor disputes involving wages, working conditions, and other grievances. The Transportation Act also required the ICC to establish rates that would guarantee a "fair rate of return" on total railroad investments. Originally the amount was set at 5.5 percent, with the requirement that one-half of any income in excess of 6 percent would be subject to recovery by the federal government. Yet for the industry, the 1920s saw the annual net railway operating income yield an average rate of return of only 4.5 percent; the best year for Class 1 carriers was 1926, when it reached 5.35 percent. Only three other years during this time, 1925, 1928, and 1929, saw the amount exceed 5.0 percent. The following decade this return would fall dramatically short of what had occurred during the Roaring '20s.[51]

During the 1920s midwestern railroad executives began to fret about increasing modal competition from automobiles and trucks and to a lesser degree from intercity buses. Local passenger traffic dropped, and it could be striking. Midwesterners bought both new and used cars in increasing numbers. One Michigander said about the Ford Model T, "It's the modern mobile utopia." The North Western is illustrative of this change. Since the company had historically been a "heavy passenger line," management watched traffic trends closely. Although its long-distance patronage generally increased during the decade, short-haul ridership decreased dramatically. In 1917 the total was 16,702,885, but six years later it had plummeted to 8,133,518, reflecting soaring automobile usage. Companies, though, seemed less worried about declines in their LCL business. It might be only marginally profitable, but truckers were claiming a greater share of these shipments. Railroaders might express a naive view about their rubber-tired competition. An NYC official who worked for the Toledo & Ohio Central in the 1920s remembered, "I heard railroad men belittling the automobile and truck menace by pointing to the interurban lines, which were on the way out, as an indication of what would probably happen to the automobile age."[52]

MOTIVE POWER

In the 1920s the modern steam locomotives made their debut. Their birthplace was the western Ohio city of Lima and the company the Lima Locomotive Works, the nation's third-largest producer of motive power. Already steamers had become bigger and more powerful. In 1910 the dominant Baldwin Locomotive Company had built for the Great Western ten monster Mallet-compound locomotives with their 2-6-6-2 wheel arraignment. They featured two sets of drivers under a single boiler that used steam twice. These behemoths appeared several years after the Great Northern became the first carrier to employ articulated Mallets on a large scale. But the Great Western disposed of its fleet of 2-6-6-2s within a few years. Although good pullers, they were exceedingly slow, prone to derailing, hard on track and bridge structures, and expensive to maintain.[53]

The philosophy of Lima designers, led by William Woodard (known as the "Wizard of Steam"), was to create a powerful yet fast freight and passenger locomotive. Unlike poky Mallets the Ohio firm concluded that with adequate boiler capacity and ample firebox size, it would be possible to provide sustained horsepower production and to operate at competitive speeds. Their iron steeds would also have multiple Lima innovations, including improved superheaters and trailing-truck booster engines to assist in starting trains. This Lima prototype became the Mikado 2-8-2. In 1922 this first new-breed engine joined the fleet of the Michigan Central Railroad, an NYC subsidiary, and it gave stellar over-the-road service. Soon seventy-five of these new-breed locomotives joined the parent's properties.[54]

Lima designers did not stop with this upgraded 2-8-2; there would be the bigger and better 2-8-4, becoming a bona fide Super Power locomotive. Initially called the A-1 when introduced in January 1925, this husky product became known as a Berkshire, honoring its performance in the Berkshire Hills on the Boston & Albany Railroad, an NYC subsidiary and initial customer. "The year 1925 marked the beginning of a new era in railroading, the steam locomotive came of age," concluded Super Power expert Richard Cook. "The antiquated short train handled by light motive power, or the drag freight moving at snail's pace was soon to be a thing of the past."[55]

During an exhaustive testing period, the A-1 appeared on various midwestern railroads, running over sections of the IC, Milwaukee Road, and Missouri Pacific. "When the first A-1 first came [to the IC], it was used primarily in test runs between Centralia and Cairo through the southern Illinois hills, commonly referred to as the Illinois Ozarks," recalled a locomotive engineer who had firsthand operating experience with this Lima product. "The grades on the line approximate three-quarters of a per cent, and the curves in this hilly area range from three to five degrees. Frequently one can find four or five such curves within the distance of a single mile. The use of the Limas in the Illinois Ozarks eliminated the pusher or helper locomotives and crews needed to assist tonnage trains up those hills." He added, "The 2-8-4's were a powerful locomotive and they were fast, too."[56]

The experimental phase of the A-1 impressed the Van Sweringen brothers. They sought the best locomotives for their railroad empire and quickly embraced Super Power. It did not take long before these 2-8-4 Berkshires from both Lima and the American Locomotive Company (Alco) in Schenectady, New York, appeared on the C&O (where

The evolution of steam locomotives from the 1840s to the 1930s is revealed in this view of Chicago & North Western motive power. On the left is the company's pride and joy, the "H-Class" 4-8-4, which it claimed to be the largest dual-service locomotive in the world, being capable of hauling 150 loaded freight cars at a speed of fifty miles an hour. This locomotive type appeared soon after the Lima Locomotive Works introduced its "Lima Super Power" in the mid-1920s. *(Author's collection)*

they were called Kanawhas), Erie, Nickel Plate, and Pere Marquette. Nickel Plate authority John Rehor offered this assessment of that road's Berkshires: "There are those who assert that the Nickel Plate Berkshire was the most successful steam locomotive ever built for freight service, and their argument is hard to resist. Certainly, no locomotive was more perfectly designed for the job it had to do." The Pere Marquette reached a similar conclusion. Its initial order of fifteen Berkshires worked well in "highballing" freight trains between Chicago and Detroit. "Today fast freight schedules must parallel those of fast passenger trains," opined management. "The performance of these first fifteen Class N [Berkshire] locomotives has been so successful that twelve more were ordered in 1941 and an additional twelve in 1944, making a total of thirty-nine that are now being used in this same service."[57]

Additional experiments with steam power continued almost until the era ended. The PRR's 6-4-4-4 duplex-drive passenger locomotives stand out. Two of these powerful, technically advanced, and streamlined T-1 class speedsters were introduced in 1942, and fifty more were built by the company between 1945 and 1946. The company assigned them to the Broadway Limited and other trains between Harrisburg (the west end of its electrified lines) and Chicago. Unfortunately, they failed to prove their worth. Operating and maintenance issues were the culprits; diesels became the better alternative.[58]

During the first three decades of the twentieth century, inventors sought to create a cheaper, less labor-intensive, and superior form of propulsion. The general focus involved internal rather than external combustion. Attention centered on building single-unit, self-propelled railcars, ones designed to accommodate passengers, mail, and express. They might also be able to pull a passenger coach or two. These all-in-one vehicles would be less expensive to run, being operated by fewer crew members, and they would be cleaner (no soot or cinders) and as comfortable as traditional passenger equipment. The objective was to have a practical alternative to standard steam trains for lightly trafficked appendages and perhaps for local service on main and secondary lines.

The process to construct successful railcars led to dead ends, and initially they involved steam propulsion. The Kobusch-Wagenhals Steam Car, an oil-fueled steam contraption, was one of these failed ventures. The prototype unit, built in 1906 by the St. Louis Car Company, went to the Missouri Pacific. Two additional cars operated on the St. Joseph & Grand Island and Crystal City & Uvalde Railroads, but their time in revenue service was limited. Throughout their operational life these Kobusch-Wagenhals cars were haunted by slow acceleration and required a vertical boiler that limited steaming capacity. A contemporary railcar was the Ganz Steam Motor Car, a product of the Ganz Works of Budapest, Hungary. The Rock Island tried one on its Indianola, Iowa, branch, but it proved unsuccessful. Another albeit somewhat larger steam car came from the Baldwin Locomotive Works. It sold one to the Cincinnati,

Hamilton & Dayton Railroad, where it was assigned to its fourteen-mile Hamilton to Middleton, Ohio, branch. But after several months it was withdrawn from service for similar reasons. And there were these problems: Passengers complained of rough-riding cars that reeked of coal smoke. Other builders tried steam vehicles; collectively, about one hundred cars were built or remained in service until World War I.

Another albeit unsuccessful alternative to steam self-propelled passenger cars involved the Edison-Beach Storage Battery Car. The basic concept of this early twentieth-century experimental vehicle was also to slash operating costs and to offer passengers a clean, comfortable environment. In this case, the storage battery car was designed to eliminate the need for the overhead wire network used by streetcars and interurbans. While there had been earlier efforts to build such a car, a breakthrough of sorts came in 1909 with the launching of the Thomas Edison–controlled Railway Storage Battery Car Company. The expectation was that an advanced power source—namely, a nickel-iron alkaline storage battery—would be revolutionary. The company made this advertising pitch: "If you are operating steam equipment on branch line or local service and desire to increase the earnings—look to Beach cars." Although several major railroads tested the Edison car, only the Long Island Railroad, a largely commuter road, acquired two. Beginning in April 1911, it assigned them to suburban service on its two-mile Bushwick appendage. There were a few additional purchases but none by midwestern roads. Battery life, weight, and related mechanical problems doomed this Edison firm.[59]

The early focus on experimental self-propelled railcars was understandable. Power designers, manufacturers, and officials were mostly "steam men" who thought in terms of external-combustion engines. The new century began to see individuals who, like contemporary automotive pioneers, believed in gasoline-engine propulsion. One of the first reports of a gasoline-powered rail motor car dates from 1903. This piece of rolling stock operated over the eleven-mile Tabor & Northern Railway between the Iowa towns of Tabor and Malvern. The *Street Railway Journal* described this "gasoline railway car" as being similar to the "auto coaches which are such familiar sights in Chicago streets." As for the all-important power source, "Its two-cylinder engine produced 25 horsepower and had a top speed of twenty miles per hour. The cost of the gasoline was calculated to be one cent to the mile."[60]

Although the fate of the Tabor & Northern's tiny gasoline motor car is not recorded, the development and impact of the McKeen Motor Car is well known. Its creation and production centered on the work of William R. McKeen Jr., an Indiana native, son of Terre Haute & Indianapolis Railroad president William Riley McKeen, and trained at Rose Polytechnic Institute in Terre Haute. As superintendent of motive power and machinery for the Union Pacific Railroad (UP) in Omaha, he won the encouragement of President E. H. Harriman to experiment with a new type of railcar. The foremost attraction was to reduce operational costs on lightly patronized branch lines. Potential savings included fuel and the maintenance expenses of steam locomotives. There would also be fewer crew members. These cars would feature a gasoline engine, a chain-drive transmission, and a radical body type.[61]

What did William McKeen create? In 1905 a prototype of his famous knife-nosed, rounded-tail, and all-metal vehicle appeared. The idea for this early attempt at streamlining was that it would reduce wind resistance and result in better fuel consumption. No one denied that McKeen's airflow concept was revolutionary and that he introduced the internal combustion engine to regular, practical railroad service. These technological advances resulted in McKeen cars being capable of achieving sustained speeds of forty or more miles per hour. Improved versions emerged from the UP's Omaha shops (originally 100 horsepower but later upgraded to 200 horsepower), and from the start they were eye-catching. These futuristic McKeen cars, famous for their "warlike-looking submarine design" and highlighted by a rich maroon enamel-painted body and jet-black trucks, featured a drop-center door opened by a foot treadle (reducing the need for a trainman to operate the door), air-tight "dust-proof" porthole windows, and a ventilating system that screened and changed the air. Their roomy passenger section provided comfortable seats, good lighting, and an electric heating system. As they evolved, they could pull a trailer when operated on a line with modest grades, increasing their capacity for mail and express. Later ones could

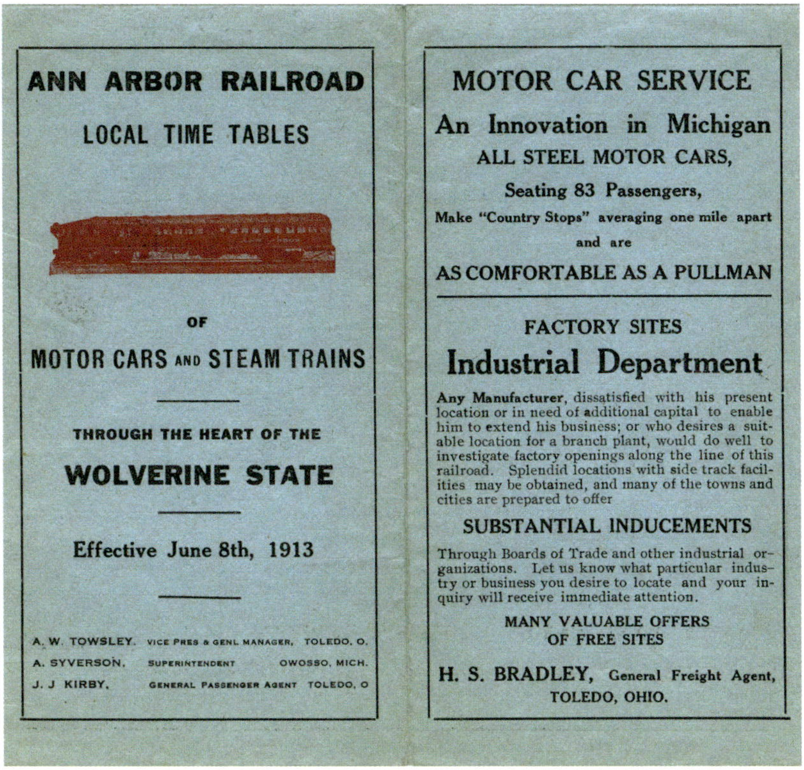
ANN ARBOR RAILROAD

LOCAL TIME TABLES

OF

MOTOR CARS AND STEAM TRAINS

THROUGH THE HEART OF THE

WOLVERINE STATE

Effective June 8th, 1913

A. W. TOWSLEY. VICE PRES & GENL MANAGER, TOLEDO, O.
A. SYVERSON. SUPERINTENDENT OWOSSO, MICH.
J. J KIRBY. GENERAL PASSENGER AGENT TOLEDO, O

MOTOR CAR SERVICE

An Innovation in Michigan

ALL STEEL MOTOR CARS,

Seating 83 Passengers,

Make "Country Stops" averaging one mile apart

and are

AS COMFORTABLE AS A PULLMAN

FACTORY SITES

Industrial Department

Any Manufacturer, dissatisfied with his present location or in need of additional capital to enable him to extend his business; or who desires a suitable location for a branch plant, would do well to investigate factory openings along the line of this railroad. Splendid locations with side track facilities may be obtained, and many of the towns and cities are prepared to offer

SUBSTANTIAL INDUCEMENTS

Through Boards of Trade and other industrial organizations. Let us know what particular industry or business you desire to locate and your inquiry will receive immediate attention.

MANY VALUABLE OFFERS
OF FREE SITES

H. S. BRADLEY, General Freight Agent,
TOLEDO, OHIO.

The cover of the June 8, 1913, Ann Arbor Railroad public timetable includes an image of one of its McKeen Motor Cars. The reverse side contains this promotional message: "Motor Car Service. An Innovation in Michigan ALL STEEL MOTOR CARS, Seating 83 Passengers, Makes 'Country Stops' averaging one mile apart and are AS COMFORTABLE AS A PULLMAN." *(Author's collection)*

haul several loaded freight cars. Refined models expanded passenger space, accommodating seventy-eight riders.[62]

Backed by the robust Union Pacific, McKeen cars after 1908 became the product of the McKeen Car Company. From manufacturing space in a former UP car shop in Omaha, the firm built 152 cars until production largely ended in 1917. (The company shut down in 1920.) McKeen cars appeared on multiple Class I midwestern carriers: Ann Arbor, Erie, Great Western, Hocking Valley, IC, North Western, Rock Island, and

In 1937 a Chicago Great Western gas-electric motor train is being "worked" at the Austin, Minnesota, station. No. 1009 has an attached McKeen trailer. *(Author's collection)*

Soo Line.[63] Several shortlines also acquired the McKeen product: Butler County Railroad (MO), Charles City Western Railway (IA), Electric Short Line Railway (MN), Hocking & Sandy Creek Traction Company (OH), Toledo, Port Clinton & Lakeside Railway (OH), and Woodstock & Sycamore Traction Company (IL). The majority, though, operated on the UP and its affiliated roads.[64]

McKeen cars were hardly perfect. They were known for their mechanical shortcomings, often breaking down inconveniently away from a station. The cars were also noisy, particularly when tackling a stiff grade. "These defects did not encourage sales," opined John White Jr. in his encyclopedic *The Railroad Passenger Car.* "Except for the closely associated Union Pacific, few repeat orders were placed. Most lines bought one or two cars as an experiment." Still, a few McKeen cars (although often heavily modified) operated for decades, but they had replacement power plants, perhaps a heavy-duty Winton engine, and other mechanical upgrades. Their bodies also might be altered noticeably. In the late 1920s, the Oelwein, Iowa, shops of the Great Western fashioned three seventy-foot McKeen units into a "De Luxe Motor Train." These cars received a 300-horsepower Electro-Motive Corporation gasoline engine and an electric transmission to traction motors rather than its original mechanical drive. Known as the Blue Bird, it operated for several years between the Twin Cities, Red Wing, and Rochester, Minnesota, catering to patients of the Mayo Clinic. Its two trailing cars featured buffet, lounge, and sleeping sections.[65]

About the time that the first McKeen car appeared, the General Electric Company (GE) entered the self-propelled railcar market. It and McKeen dominated the first generation of motor cars. With the experience of GE with electric motors and appliances, company engineers correctly concluded that the biggest weakness in the McKeens was their mechanical transmissions; GE opted instead for electrical ones. After several years of trials with demonstrator models, GE cars became popular with both trunk and shortline roads. An exemplary user was the never-electrified Minneapolis, St. Paul, Rochester & Dubuque Electric Traction Company. Commonly known as the Dan Patch Line for a famous racehorse owned by its promoter Marion Savage, it was reorganized in 1918 as the Minneapolis, Northfield & Southern Railway. By 1910 this "wireless interurban" consisted of a forty-two-mile line between Minneapolis and Northfield, Minnesota. Four years later it briefly assumed operations of the Great Western's Northfield-Mankato branch (and for decades trackage rights remained). GE gas-electric passenger cars and freight motor No. 100, acquired in 1913 and the first of its kind ever built, successfully operated over this 107-mile route. The use of cheap naphtha fuel reduced operating costs, making it far less expensive then steam power.[66]

During this burst of rail motorcar activities, additional firms entered what became a crowded field. These included the J. G. Brill and St. Louis Car Companies and the smaller Hall-Scott, Kuhlman, and Strang Gas Electric Car firms. A few poor albeit creative shortlines fabricated their own cars. The Atlantic Northern Railroad in Iowa, for one, placed a wooden boxlike contraption on a Model T frame. Some shortlines replaced the tires on Model Ts, Overlands, or other automobiles with

In 1927 the Northern Ohio Power & Light Company distributed a small brochure describing its newly acquired "Deluxe Electric Line Chair Car." The cover of this publication features this G. C. Kuhlman Car Company product. This Buckeye State interurban hoped that it could survive automobile competition by providing the best modern equipment. *(Author's collection)*

flanged wheels and operated them to transport passengers, mail, and express. On trunk roads repurposed automobiles usually served as track inspection vehicles. The seventy-mile St. Joseph Valley Railway, for example, which linked Elkhart, Indiana, with Columbia, Ohio, with the nine miles between Elkhart and Bristol under wire, owned both Brill and Hall-Scott motor cars. The short-lived company also possessed an automobile equipped with flanged wheels for varied purposes.[67]

While a McKeen car and other gas electrics might be seen pulling one or more freight cars or conducting switching chores, forward-thinking inventors, designers, and manufacturers came to believe that the diesel engine would be a superior source of propulsion. Invented in 1892 by Rudolf Diesel, the engine as perfected offered power, compactness, durability, and economy, being ideally suited for heavy freight movements. Passenger units could also benefit.

A pioneer in what became the diesel revolution was the Electro-Motive Engineering Company, founded in Cleveland in 1922. (A year

The Erie Railroad emerged as a pioneer in the use of internal-combustion locomotives like its No. 20. In 1926 this sixty-ton diesel-electric switch engine was built jointly by the America Locomotive Company, General Electric, and Ingersoll-Rand. *(Author's collection)*

later it dropped "Engineering" from its corporate name and added "Corporation.") EMC and partner Winton Engine Company, also based in Cleveland, manufactured the gas-electric engines (or prime movers) and the electric transmissions that powered the multiple railcars produced mostly by the St. Louis Car Company. Their initial gas-electric car went to the Great Western in 1924 and the second to the Northern Pacific. By the late 1920s, EMC-Winton dominated the railcar market, yet it continued to have private contractors construct these units. In 1930 General Motors acquired EMC and Winton to form the Electro-Motive Division of General Motors (EMD). Management turned its energies to the development of diesel-electric locomotives. General Motors, moreover, knew how to market a product, and within five years the first practical freight road diesel, the EMD FT, appeared.[68]

Although EMD became the dominant manufacturer of diesel-electric freight and passenger power, the world's first commercial diesel locomotive resulted from a joint venture between GE, Ingersoll-Rand,

and Alco. This historic piece of rolling stock was the sixty-ton box-cab switcher, No. 1000, owned by the Central Railroad of New Jersey, known simply as the Jersey Central. The No. 1000 featured a six-cylinder inline 10×12 Ingersoll-Rand diesel engine and a GE transmission, and an Alco body housed these two principal components. On October 22, 1925, No. 1000 went to work in the New York City area, and for more than thirty years it remained in active service on the Jersey Central. It would not be a one-of-a-kind switcher. A year later the North Western acquired two of these cab units for use in the Chicago Loop because of a smoke abatement ordinance. In 1928 the Erie had a similar diesel at work switching the Firestone Tire & Rubber Company plant near downtown Akron to avoid the fire hazard of a coal-fired steamer. By the early 1930s, more than thirty of these workhorses, which could operate continuously, used cheap fuel oil, and were environmentally friendly, were found in scattered places throughout the region.[69]

MORE TECHNICAL ADVANCES

Freight shipments developed into the bread-and-butter revenue makers for railroads in the Midwest and elsewhere. The leading commodities carried during the late nineteenth century and into the twentieth century included coal, grain, livestock, lumber, merchandise, and manufactured products. As might be expected, steady improvements occurred in the efficiency and reliability of the rolling stock needed to handle these rapidly increasing cargoes. No one, though, ever considered freight cars to be romantic or attractive; they were everyday workhorses.

The age of maturity witnessed the transition from largely wooden cars to those made wholly or mostly of steel. This changeover could have occurred earlier; small metal-type cars could be found on British rails by the close of the eighteenth century. Several factors explain why the wood-car era lasted so long. For one thing, the nation had ample supplies of hard woods, including white oak and yellow pine. Furthermore, car builders, whether private firms or railroads themselves, could hire workers who possessed woodworking skills and who generally took pride in what they were able to accomplish. When efforts accelerated to switch to metal, conservative car builders and their employees resisted change. They wanted small, wooden freight cars. Also, their unit costs were reasonable, especially important for carriers with limited resources. The Panic of 1873 likewise retarded the metal car revolution. During these years a number of midwestern roads fell into the hands of court-appointed receivers. Investment dollars needed to be spent carefully.

Although the rise of metal freight car builders was not limited to the Midwest, the region became a leader in constructing these more durable, larger, and pricier pieces of rolling stock. An early replacement advocate was ironically lumber baron T. W. Harvey, who sought to create an industrial town similar to Pullman, Illinois; his townsite was located three miles to the south. Not only was it to be a manufacturing center; Harvey and his son, resembling George Pullman, wanted to ensure Protestant Christian values among its residents, including temperance. Before Harvey, Illinois, appeared, the Harveys had several experimental cars built in the Aurora, Illinois, shops of the Burlington. The first one was a gondola, and it appeared in 1890. When the Harvey car shop started production, it planned to make more than gondolas. Box, refrigerator, stock, and tank cars were on the construction agenda. Although a small number of steel cars were built and sold, the Panic of 1893 and the ensuing depression ended the Harvey operation. The initial buyer had been the Milwaukee Road, acquiring twenty-five stock cars. Several other midwestern-based railroads purchased a variety of these metal cars. Total production amounted to about one hundred units.[70]

Other midwestern steel car manufactures achieved greater success than the Harveys. Take the Michigan-Peninsular Car Company. Based in Detroit, this firm by the late 1890s had become the city's largest manufacturer prior to the rise of the automobile industry. Soon the Michigan-Peninsular Company became an important producer of all-metal rolling stock, selling a large number of steel boxcars to the Erie in 1897. The Haskel & Barker Car Company, long located in Michigan City, Indiana, also stands out. Not only was it a large producer of freight cars and cabooses; it was also innovative. Following a major fire in 1913, the firm abandoned the building of freight cars in stalls, which made production slow and inefficient, and instead set up the first straight-line production track for assembling its all-metal products.[71]

By the early twentieth century, the revolution in freight-car construction had at last occurred. In 1908 the PRR had 8,700 steel and steel-framed freight cars in its constantly modernizing equipment roster, and a growing number were owned by other railroads that served the region. Discarded wood cars, ones that were not dismantled or burned, might end up on farmsteads or in other locations such as chicken coops, toolsheds, or miscellaneous storage structures.[72]

All rolling stock required more than basic bodies. During this time two critical components evolved: knuckle couplers and air brakes. Initially, the most common way to connect cars was to fasten a chain to a pin on the end of each car. These chain couplings made starts and stops so jerky that pioneer trainmen often put chunks of wood between the cars to hold them apart and to keep these chains taut. As cars became heavier, the link-and-pin coupler came into general prominence. This device consisted of a slotted wrought-iron drawbar fastened to the end of the car. A long oval-shaped link was then inserted by the brakeman and held in place by an iron pin dropped into a hole in the drawbar after the coupling had occurred. This attachment method proved dangerous for brakemen and switchmen, causing serious and sometimes fatal injuries. The most common accidents involved the loss of fingers and thumbs and related hand impairments.[73]

A better method came with the knuckle or Janney coupler. This dramatic breakthrough came after the Civil War when Eli Janney, a mechanically gifted former Confederate Army officer, fashioned a coupler that resembled the knuckles of the human hand and was known formally as the "Vertical Plan Janney-Style Coupler." After successful testing by a subsidiary of the PRR, the Janney Car-Coupling Company sold its product widely by the 1880s, becoming the standard automatic coupling device. The knuckle coupler, which competitors modified for patent purposes, worked well. One feature was that it permitted the mating of cars even when track levels were different. This replacement device also resulted in fewer injuries and deaths of trainmen and sped up the assembling and disassembling of trains.[74]

Hand-in-hand with the perfection of modern car coupling came a dramatically better breaking system. Before the Civil War, the railroads in the Midwest and elsewhere generally used what was called the "double-acting" brake system. The first involved a linkage mechanism that allowed the engineer to reverse the locomotive while operating at speed. The second allowed the brakeman to set the brakes on all wheels of a car with a single brake wheel. This improved method of controlling a train produced glaring shortcomings. Reversing the locomotive created enormous wear on the linking and driving wheels. It also damaged rails, particularly at station stops. Since brakemen needed to scamper along swaying freight cars to set or release brakes, the job was difficult and dangerous, especially during inclement weather.[75]

In the post–Civil War era, the modern train brake appeared. Although George Westinghouse did not "invent" a continuous train-braking system, he did much to perfect and market it. In the 1870s Westinghouse devised a method whereby air pressure was used to keep the brakes *off* rather than to activate them. A triple valve made this possible. The valve was appropriately named; it carried out three distinct functions: "[It was] a pressure-sensitive valve that could admit air from the train line into the reserve tank, readmit air from the same tank to the brake cylinder, and exhaust the air to release the brake." To make the Westinghouse system work, each car needed such a valve as well as its own air tank. "It was a remarkable chunk of cast iron no larger than a grapefruit," noted historian John H. White Jr., "and so amazing to mechanics of its day that some of them half expected it to speak."[76]

The earliest triple-valve air brakes worked well for passenger cars, but they were not always effective on long, fast freight trains running downgrade. Consequently, during the summers of 1886 and 1887, the Master Car Builders Association conducted exhaustive test runs on the "Burlington Hill," located immediately west of Burlington, Iowa, on the Chicago–Denver mainline of the Burlington. The results led to Westinghouse and his associates developing a faster, heavy-duty triple valve that met all the necessary requirements. The key was the addition of vent pipes on each car that increased the speed of the system sixfold. This meant that brakes on each car activated almost simultaneously. There were other "Westinghouses." Frederick Eames is remembered for developing the vacuum brake, but it failed to gain the same popularity, being used mostly outside North America.[77]

Even though major technological breakthroughs had occurred with couplers and air brakes, the American railroads were slow to adopt these devices, especially the air brake. Cost considerations are largely the explanation. Although the price tag for refitting passenger cars with couplers and air brakes was reasonable due to the relatively small numbers involved, the freight car situation was strikingly different. A major company did not complain much about spending roughly $100 each for installing air brakes on a few hundred passenger cars, but doing so for thousands of freight cars was another matter. The expenses would have been lower had Westinghouse not held a patent monopoly. Moreover, this replacement technology was not really labor saving; brakemen continued to face a multitude of tasks.[78]

The catalyst for adopting these two technical advancements arguably came from an unexpected source: the crusading efforts of Lorenzo Coffin, Civil War chaplain, politician, and social reformer. As an appointed member of the Iowa Board of Railroad Commissioners, this public-spirited official, who frequently rode on freight and passenger trains, learned about railroad workers who had lost fingers, hands, and even their lives attempting to make couplings with links and pins. Coffin also became aware of the danger when brakemen attempted to slow or stop trains with hand brakes. He demanded that railroads operating in the Hawkeye State immediately adopt knuckle couplers and air brakes. Asked Coffin rhetorically, "Why not have self-couplers that will couple automatically when the cars are pushed together and not require the men to go between the cars; and why not have air-brakes on freight as well as on passenger cars under the control [of] the engineer as on the passenger trains?" He drafted the first railroad safety law, and in 1890 lawmakers passed the Iowa Safety Appliance Act.[79]

Coffin did not stop in his quest for railroad worker safety. He focused on Congress and the White House. Coffin won. On March 2, 1893, President Benjamin Harrison signed the Safety Appliance Act. This statute gave railroads five years to equip all of their rolling stock with couplers that would automatically lock upon impact and to install air brakes. Because of the nation's economic collapse after the 1893 Wall Street panic, railroad revenues plummeted, and compliance faltered. The industry won an extension; August 1, 1900, became the reset deadline.

Railroad management came to realize that accidents were reduced and wear and tear on equipment were less. The Safety Appliance Act turned out to be a classic win-win for companies and their employees. During the year following President Harrison's approval of the measure, at least 2,837 railroad men were killed on the job and another 20,000–30,000 injured. Coffin observed: "Four years later there were 1,693 killed, making a saving of 1,044 lives, and there were about 5,000 fewer men injured by accidents." Still, for a few more years some midwestern roads failed to achieve this mandated goal.[80]

One technological advance that contributed to railroad safety involved enhanced communications. Even though the telegraph had been used in dispatching and train-control work since shortly before the Civil War and remained a backbone of how train movements were controlled, the telephone made its presence felt by the time of World War I. In the late 1890s, several railroads that served the Midwest, notably the Santa Fe, had found the telephone to be a promising communication device, especially for issuing and delivering train orders. This comment, made in 1904, suggested that telephone usage would become more common: "The telephone has not, as yet become an important factor in the operation of trains. This has been probably because the telegraph is a tried and proved servant, doing work economically and well." The prophecy (and the correct one): "The telephone will probably appear as a rival of the telegraph in this field. When this time comes, it will be natural that the telephone should be employed in the movement of trains."[81]

Technological improvements came rapidly. One involved a telephone selector device, allowing the dispatcher to select any station and to connect with it without signaling other stations as with the telegraph. It also became apparent that the telephone was faster for sending and receiving messages. This permitted an increasing volume of traffic to be handled, thereby reducing the number of on-duty dispatchers. In 1909 a signal engineer for the Burlington commented, "The introduction of the telephone for block purposes has made it possible for railroads to use a different and more permanent class of men for this work, which is bound to result in more efficient service in the future." Using a telephone eliminated the need to master Morse code. By the 1920s the telephone had come of age. In 1925, the Telephone and Telegraph Section of the American Railroad Association reported that Class I railroads had 132,850 miles of telephone lines used for the transmission of train orders along 249,398 miles of trackage. This was an increase of more than 13,000 miles since 1920. The appearance of the telephone would not soon eliminate the telegraph. Dots and dashes would be sent and received by dispatchers, agents, and tower personnel until the post–World War II decades.[82]

During the maturity era, there were two important events in the frequently changing world of midwestern railroading. These involved related innovations that ultimately altered the way that a substantial volume of the nation's freight shipments would be handled: "containerization" and trailers-on-flatcars (TOFC) or "piggybacks."

Railroads in the Midwest can claim to be the incubator of what became known as "magic boxes." During World War I and soon thereafter, several electric and steam roads almost simultaneously adopted containers for LCL freight. This form of transport modernization appeared to have appealing advantages. It permitted interurbans to compete more effectively with motor trucks for handling small shipments and steam roads to reduce terminal congestion that dispatched ferry or "trap cars" for pickups and deliveries. Generally, a customer would load some type of container onto a truck at a factory or warehouse and have that vehicle bring it to an awaiting flatcar. Then it would be lifted onto a flatcar, travel to its destination by rail, and finally be trucked to the consignee. In 1921 the financially struggling Cincinnati, Lawrenceburg & Aurora Electric Street Railway (CL&A), which had fallen into receivership in 1913, became an early transporter of containers (actually demountable truck bodies) that were placed by an electric hoist onto an extensively remodeled box motor car. This allowed containers to move in a seamless fashion between freight terminals in downtown Cincinnati and southeastern Indiana destinations. Why this creative act? CL&A's management "used its whits," desperately attempting to remain in business. Furthermore, the interurban faced a gauge problem. Resembling nearly all electric roads, the CL&A was constructed to standard width, but its rolling stock could not run over the broad-gauge (five feet two and a half inch) streetcar tracks of Cincinnati. The CL&A was modestly successful with its container service before the company collapsed in 1931. Other Midwest "juice" roads provided container services, including the Cincinnati & Lake Erie Railroad (C&LE), Detroit United Railway, and Rockford & Interurban Railway.[83]

The C&LE container experience revealed sophistication. Its entry into this business began in 1929. It was not a lone venture but a cooperative arrangement between Cargo Transport, Inc., which consisted of a group of Ohio trucking companies; Motor Terminal Companies of New York, which supplied the leased containers; and C&LE, which provided the flatcars, support facilities, and employees. The interurban operated overnight service between its end terminals in Cincinnati and Toledo as well as ones in Dayton, Lima, and Springfield. At these facilities truckers transported containers to customers in Kentucky, Michigan, and Ohio. This highway and rail operation would then be reversed. This bona fide intermodal operation provided point-to-point delivery. Apparently the C&LE had made a wise decision in entering the container business. The company faltered, though, as did most midwestern interurbans that lacked a healthy freight-car business with connecting steam railroads. As hard times accelerated in the early 1930s, the C&LE weakened, entering receivership in 1932, and by the end of the decade it was gone.[84]

Because of their size and importance, steam roads gained greater attention with this creative way of transporting LCL shipments. The Cleveland, Cincinnati, Chicago & St. Louis Railway (Big Four) led the way. In May 1917 this NYC subsidiary was the first to use metal boxes, being a customer of the Cincinnati Motor Terminals Company. The individual who sparked this creative and economical way to manage LCL was Benjamin Franklin Fitch, a salesman for the White Motor Company, a Cleveland firm that had expanded from sewing machine manufacturing to making automobiles and trucks. By 1919 all of the Cincinnati's railroads provided this LCL service. They benefited by reducing or ending their use of time-consuming and expensive trap-car operations. The Columbia Terminals Company offered a similar service in St. Louis. This became a popular way for shippers to send their goods, being much faster than the traditional trap cars that traveled through a warehouse district picking up and delivering LCL shipments. Furthermore, railroads could free up boxcars and crews that previously had been assigned to these operations. In 1921 the NYC started to employ containers in coordinated

In this undated photograph taken at an undisclosed location, Lake Shore Electric Railway motor No. 43 is "on the point" of a two-car train that includes one of its innovative Bonner Railwagons. *(Krambles-Peterson Archive)*

rail-truck intermodal service. The company introduced a specially constructed flatcar capable of carrying nine metal boxes. A crane transferred them on and off awaiting trucks. Later in the 1920s, the PRR launched its Keystone Container service, using equipment similar to what the NYC had introduced. This container episode, however, soon turned to dross, being a victim in the 1930s of regulatory restraints and most of all increased truck competition. Trucking firms slashed their rates and pushed their drivers to the limit to furnish fast door-to-door service. Not until after World War II did containerization return, and this time it would not be designed for only LCL freight.[85]

The first steam road, Great Western, embraced TOFC in the mid-1930s. This innovative freight-transport concept, however, would take two decades or more to become widespread in the Midwest and the nation. Two Chicago-based interurbans led the way. In 1926 the Chicago, North Shore & Milwaukee (North Shore Line), a Samuel Insull utility property, introduced its "Truck Ferry Service," and a year later another Insull-controlled interurban, the Chicago, South Shore & South Bend (South Shore Line), followed suit. In fact, the North Shore Line TOFC service served as the model for steam railroads for transporting truck trailers on flatcars. This large and well-constructed electric road could not bring freight cars into downtown Chicago, mainly because of the curvature on the city L system, handicapping its LCL business that dated from World War I. In 1932 the North Shore Line's creative venture into freight hauling saw a major improvement; it expanded its offering to include trailers or entire trucks owned by common-carrier motor carriers or shippers. And for more than a decade, this TOFC service prospered.[86]

Another type of coordinated interurban-highway offering involved the introduction of the Bonner Railwagon on the Cleveland-based Lake Shore Electric Railway (LSE). Service began in September 1930 and operated in conjunction with the Electric Freight Railway Company. This ingenious concept had been conceived by Toledo banker, politician, and entrepreneur Colonel Joseph Bonner in the late 1890s. In 1919 *Popular Science Monthly* lauded Bonner's creativity, explaining that "freight of less than a carload may be moved direct from the point of origin to the destination warehouse or wholesaler without rehandling!" LSE acquired six ten-ton, eighteen-foot truck trailers that could be transported on specially designed fifty-five-foot flatcars and also operate on roads, providing shippers door-to-door service. An eye-catching feature of the Bonner system was that the truck wheels rested below the flatcar's frame, giving the equipment a low profile that differed radically from the appearance of TOFC equipment on the North Shore and South Shore interurbans. "Railwagons are virtually side tracks on wheels," crowed the LSE. Although this revolutionary way to move freight between Cleveland and Toledo proved successful, it was short-lived. By 1932 a perfect storm killed the Bonner Railwagon: regulatory problems, unregulated "gipsy" truck competition, and the deepening national depression.[87]

TRAIN TRAVEL

The years between the end of World War I and the onslaught of the Great Depression can be considered a golden age for railroad passenger service. If their pocketbooks allowed, overland travelers selected trains that were the epitome of luxury and speed. Unlike the past decades, railroad executives realized that automobiles and intercity buses, which operated on a better network of public roads, cut deeply into short-haul passenger revenues. Yet long-distance rail travel offered hope for increasing passenger revenues. This meant a focus on named trains in the Midwest and nationally. When these standard heavyweight trains were either introduced or upgraded, they became emblems of modern travel comfort.[88]

Trunk roads, whether large or small, sought to make their flagship passenger trains the finest possible. Management felt that they could generate strong operating income with these top-notch trains, but they also allegedly provided a "marquee" value. This involved the belief that potential freight customers who enjoyed riding on such premier trains would direct their shipments to the same railroad. In a January 1926 advertisement in the *Saturday Evening Post*, the PRR pitched its flagship Broadway Limited between New York City and Chicago and ballyhooed "its great fleet of famous passenger trains." It also promoted its freight trains: "Less dramatic—but equally dependable—is the day-and-night movement of freight, 365 days a year, over the far-flung lines of the Pennsylvania System."[89]

While most travelers who rode crack passenger trains had no carload or LCL freight to send or to receive, they had options between popular destinations. Take journeys between Chicago and St. Louis. Three roads, Chicago & Alton, IC, and Wabash, were the major contenders on this speedway known as the "Rainbow Run."[90] Starting in 1925 Wabash management spent heavily to upgrade equipment on this competitive route. A year later the company distributed complimentary ink blotters that contained short promotional copy for its two premier trains that served this corridor. One proclaimed the "New All-Steel Banner Limited." The text read, "This is the day train to St. Louis, the Southwest and Mexico that seasoned travelers prefer. Observation and parlor car, diner service and other details contributing to travel comfort are unexcelled." The other described the "New All-Steel Midnight Limited to St. Louis." It was declared to be equally outstanding: "Men who use the WABASH speak enthusiastically of the feeling of fitness with which they arrive at their destinations. The courteous, unruffled service, the club car accommodations and the luxury of a good night's sleep while rolling over the rock-ballasted roadbed and all-steel trains have made WABASH synonymous with comfort, among men who travel."[91]

Although lightweight "streamliners" would not make their debut until the mid-1930s, several midwestern railroads sought another way to capture public attention and patronage. The approach was coordinated

What is likely a local train on the double-track mainline of the Chicago, Burlington & Quincy Railroad is rapidly approaching the station at Somonauk, Illinois, twenty-two miles west of Aurora. In this 1905 photograph, the agent appears to be rushing to load several express or LCL items. *(Author's collection)*

air-rail service, and it usually involved modest complexities. By the later part of the 1920s, each mode of transportation had qualities that made this a potentially attractive travel option. Since Americans loved speed and modernity, coordination met that desire. Passage of the Contract Air Mail Act (Kelly Act) in 1925, the sensational trans-Atlantic solo flight of Charles Lindbergh in his *Spirit of St. Louis* two years later, and dramatic advances in aviation technologies allowed a novel way to make long-distance journeys. Yet the newest aircraft could accommodate only a handful of passengers and could not fly above storms, cruising normally at altitudes between one thousand and four thousand feet, and usually avoided nighttime flights.

The foremost service that grabbed headlines and had a strong midwestern connection came in 1928 with the launching of TAT, officially Transcontinental Air Transport, Inc. Operations began between New York City and Los Angeles a year later. TAT proclaimed that its Ford

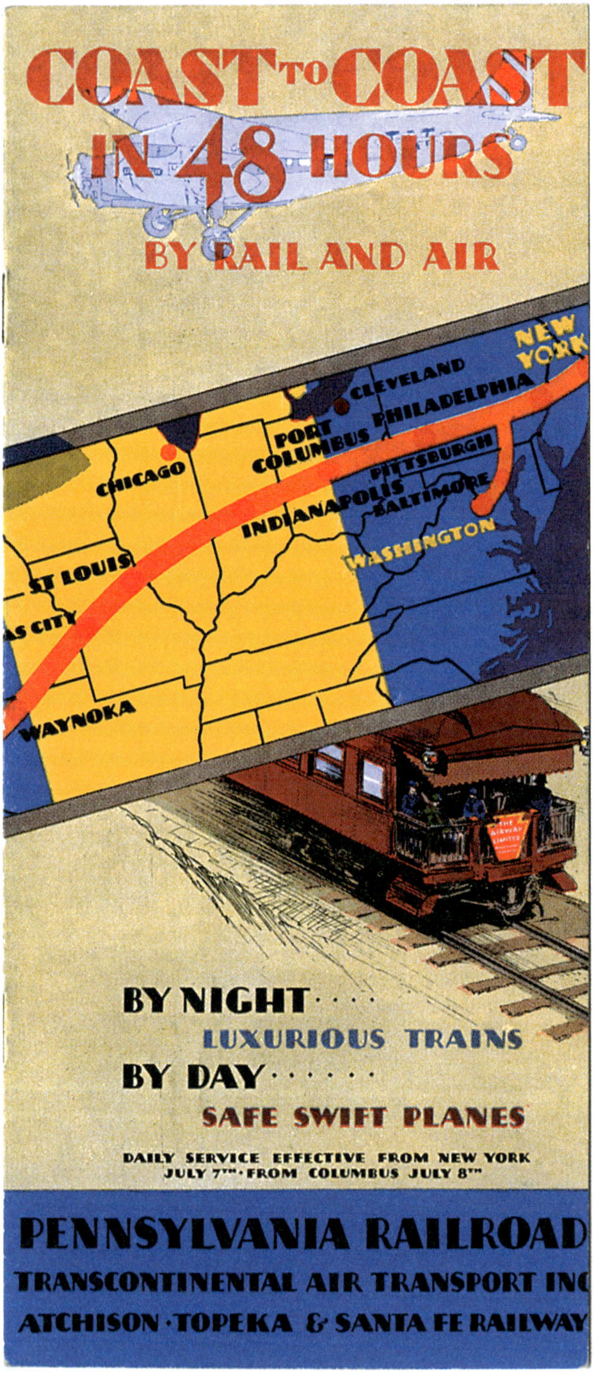
COAST TO COAST
IN 48 HOURS
BY RAIL AND AIR
NEW YORK
CLEVELAND
PHILADELPHIA
PORT COLUMBUS
PITTSBURGH
CHICAGO
INDIANAPOLIS
BALTIMORE
WASHINGTON
ST LOUIS
AS CITY
WAYNOKA
BY NIGHT.... LUXURIOUS TRAINS
BY DAY...... SAFE SWIFT PLANES
DAILY SERVICE EFFECTIVE FROM NEW YORK JULY 7TH · FROM COLUMBUS JULY 8TH
PENNSYLVANIA RAILROAD
TRANSCONTINENTAL AIR TRANSPORT INC
ATCHISON · TOPEKA & SANTA FE RAILWAY

Facing, The Pennsylvania Railroad distributed a lavish brochure-timetable to promote the Airway Limited and Transcontinental Air Transport rail-air coordination. This initial folder shows service that began from New York City on July 7, 1929, and from Port Columbus, Ohio, the following day. *(Author's collection)*

trimotored, all-metal, high-wing monoplanes offered a travel alternative "for those whose time is too important to waste." Gushed the *Highway Magazine* in early 1929, "It is Modern Transportation's answer to the demands for faster travel without sacrifice of safety or comfort." But TAT could not claim to be a standalone enterprise. Nighttime flying remained problematic, particularly over mountainous terrain, especially the expansive Appalachian chain. This coast-to-coast operator required ground support, and it came from the PRR. That railroad did not disappoint. The result was a westbound deluxe named train, the Airway Limited. This all-Pullman consist offered an array of amenities: "Barber, bath, valet, ladies' maid, train secretary, writing desk, stock quotations, magazines, newspapers, baseball and football scores (in season)." Was the PRR sprouting wings? Yes. It had invested in TAT with dedicated trains and in other ways.[92]

The joint TAT-PRR arrangement meant that the first leg of the cross-country trip involved a rail experience: "The night by train—The day by plane." In the inaugural trip, the Airway Limited departed Pennsylvania Station in New York at 6:05 p.m. on July 7, 1929, and sped overnight to Columbus, Ohio. The train with airplane-bound passengers stopped not at Columbus Union Station but instead at the newly established Port Columbus station, adjacent to the capital city's airfield seven miles to the east. Upon the scheduled arrival at 7:55 a.m., connecting passengers, who numbered ten or less and had already had breakfast in the diner, walked under a canopy to an awaiting Ford "Tin Goose." Soon they were airborne to Indianapolis, St. Louis, Kansas City, and points southwest. After landing that evening near Waynoka, Oklahoma, they boarded a set-out Pullman on which the Santa Fe's Missionary would take them to Clovis, New Mexico. On the second day, TAT delivered these passengers to an airfield in Glendale, California, for a chauffeured ride to downtown Los Angeles. What happened to the Airway Limited?

After Port Columbus it continued to Columbus and Indianapolis. The eastbound trip involved a similar itinerary, with the plane leaving Los Angeles at 8:45 a.m. and arriving the following day at Port Columbus at 7:15 p.m. The connecting overnight train to New York was the American from Indianapolis. After dinner and breakfast in the diner, it steamed into Pennsylvania Station at 9:50 a.m. the next morning, where it also made connections with PRR service to Philadelphia, Baltimore, and Washington, DC. Both coast-to-coast trips were advertised to take only forty-eight hours rather than the seventy-five or longer by the fastest trains. While this was theoretically much faster than land transportation, weather and mechanical problems might badly disrupt the published schedule. At times this mandated additional travel by rail. Said one wag, "TAT stands for 'Take-A-Train.'" Another called TAT "Take a Train Airline." TAT never mentioned the high level of cabin noise, frequent or near-constant airsickness felt by passengers, or the possibility of brief unconsciousness caused by low levels of oxygen in body tissues (hypoxia) as the plane flew over the San Gabriel Mountains into the Los Angeles Basin.[93]

The end of TAT operations came with the advent of the Great Depression. The company, which merged with Western Air Express in 1930 and soon rebranded as Transcontinental & Western Air (TWA), failed to become profitable. It lost heavily on this coast-to-coast service, even though a one-way trip was pricy, costing roughly $350 or about sixteen cents per mile. When it shut down eighteen months after its start, the operation was $2.7 million in the red. The absence of a federal mail contract did not help. By the early 1930s, the US Department of Commerce had constructed enough rotating beacon navigation lights to negate the need for nighttime travel by rail. Moreover, a TAT plane in fall 1929 crashed during a thunderstorm at Mount Taylor, New Mexico, killing all eight persons on board, an event that likewise had an adverse effect. As for the PRR, it liquidated its stock holdings in TWA in 1936.[94]

While the mighty PRR entered the coordinated air-rail service, the Great Western, a much smaller and financially weaker carrier, did so as well. The company crowed, "Leading as Usual." As might be expected, this was a wholly midwestern service. Starting on February 25, 1929, this train-plane arrangement allowed passengers from Minnesota,

The repeatedly innovative Chicago Great Western Railroad publicized its joint rail and airplane service with Universal Air Lines in the May–June–July 1929 issue of its company magazine. *(Author's collection)*

Iowa, and Illinois to take the Legionnaire or Chicago Special for the Windy City and an airplane rendezvous. A chartered car transported them from Grand Central Station to the Municipal Airport. The next leg involved boarding a Universal Air Lines ten-passenger trimotor for either St. Louis or Cleveland. The early morning arrival of these two trains permitted an easy connection with the 9:45 a.m. flight to St. Louis, which landed at 1:00 p.m. The Cleveland plane did not take off until 4:00 p.m. for its four-hour-and-forty-five-minute trip. Still, the Great Western viewed this in a positive light: "A time saving schedule providing for a business day in Chicago, dinner in Cleveland, with plenty of time to make connections with faster trains for New York and other seaboard cities." As with TAT service, the Great Depression ended coordinated operations between the Great Western and Universal Air.[95]

While joint air-rail service almost exclusively involved steam roads, at least two midwestern interurbans provided a similar service. Beginning on May 5, 1928, the Cleveland, Southwestern Railway & Light Company (Southwestern), which operated between Cleveland and Bucyrus, Ohio, offered riders at select stations the convenience of purchasing tickets for two connecting flights on Stout Airlines, an air carrier launched in November 1927 that linked Cleveland with Detroit (Ford Airport in Dearborn) and soon Chicago. This relationship lasted only briefly; apparently few travelers opted for a joint interurban-air journey.[96] The North Shore Line had a longer one. Shortly after the Southwestern established its relationship with Stout, this Insull interurban introduced joint air-interurban service with airlines serving Chicago Municipal Airport (later Midway Airport). Notwithstanding what imaginative steam and electric railroads did to boost their own revenues and aid cooperating air carriers, the domestic airline industry as of 1930 claimed less than 1 percent of intercity passenger miles.[97]

MAIL AND EXPRESS

The association of the US Post Office with railroads dates back to the dawn of the industry. An American train first carried letters in 1832, and six years later Congress designated all railroads as "post roads." Letters traveled as "pouched" mail, placed in brass-locked canvas bags. A major upgrade came during the 1860s. It was largely a result of the unprecedented volume of mail generated by the Civil War and the ongoing demand by government officials and the public for more rapid movement of the mails. (This desire likewise helped increase passenger train speeds.)

The warmup for what became the "first permanent, complete, and official Railway Mail Service" took place on the Hannibal & St. Joseph Railroad (H&StJ). At the suggestion of William Davis, assistant postmaster at St. Joseph, this trans-Missouri carrier employed the first dedicated mail car. Pulled by the locomotive Missouri, a 4-4-0 American, in a single-car train, it carried oilskin-wrapped envelopes to St. Joseph over the course of four hours for the Pony Express, which on April 3, 1860, had started mounted runs westward. The H&StJ provided this 206-mile service from Quincy, Illinois, and eastern connections until the completion of a telegraph line to California that supplanted the Pony Express on October 26, 1861.[98]

Several years later the North Western used a mail car more effectively. The spark plug behind the introduction of what became known as railway post offices or RPOs was George Armstrong, an assistant postmaster in Chicago. Wishing to speed up mail deliveries during a time of growing war-related volume, he conceived of a "post office on wheels." Argued Armstrong, "It is well known to the public that passengers, traveling over railroad routes, generally reach a given point in advance of letters; when to that given point letters must pass, under the present system, through a distributing office, as is largely the case now, the tardiness of a letter's progress toward its place of destination is proportionally increased. But a general system of railway distribution obviates this difficulty." Armstrong continued, "The work being done while the cars are in action, and transfers of mail made from route to route, and for local deliveries on the way as they are reached, letters gain the celerity in transit as persons making direct connections." After presenting his case to Postmaster General Montgomery Blair in mid-1864, Armstrong received authority to test his idea. On August 28, 1864, the country's first railway post office, placed in a repurposed baggage car and furnished with letter and newspaper cases, rolled between Chicago and Clinton, Iowa, a distance of 140 miles. While the experimental run was not without problems, postal authorities, railroaders, and others realized that a sea change in how to handle mail had been effectively demonstrated. Between 1865 and 1867, company-built mail cars began daily operations between Chicago and Green Bay, Wisconsin, and Chicago and Omaha.

Although not an interior view of an early Railway Post Office car, this photograph, taken by the Burlington Railroad in 1948, reveals the basic layout of how clerks processed the mail. This is the Silver Post mail car initially assigned to Twin City Zephyr service to and from Chicago. *(Don Hofsommer collection)*

Other railroads acquired this specialized equipment, and soon railroads serving Chicago, including the Burlington, Erie, and Rock Island, placed RPO cars in their passenger train consists. Rather than handling locked sacks of mail, postal workers opened them, "worked" their contents, and repouched the mail for on-line destinations and for connections. The Post Office Department rewarded Armstrong with appointment as head of the Railway Mail Service, which began in 1869. It did not take long before the Armstrong innovation became the backbone of the regional and national intercity postal distribution system. Postal officials bragged that RPOs could achieve delivery times of twelve to twenty-four hours.[99]

Following the establishment of the RPO cars, more advancements in mail delivery took place in the Midwest. In 1875 an expedited, twenty-four-hour solid mail train had been established between New York and Chicago over the Vanderbilt Lines (New York Central and Lake Shore & Michigan Southern), but this service ended after ten months. Officials concluded that "the mail didn't begin to compensate for the high costs of speed." The Post Office Department sought another and hopefully permanent Fast Mail. It would travel from Chicago to Council Bluffs for West Coast connections. Several carriers rejected an exclusive offer to provide a roughly sixteen-hour transit time for such a train running over this approximately five-hundred-mile route six times weekly. One railroad executive remarked, "The mails can be massed east of Chicago, but they cannot be west. At Chicago they scatter out like the fingers on the hand." After considerable deliberations, the Burlington agreed. This service began on March 11, 1884. As railroad writer and editor David P. Morgan noted, "From the time the railroad secured the mail contract in 1884 until 1897, for example, the schedule was reduced upon ten different occasions, even while the load was rising from a couple of cars to six containing 150 tons of mail. The Burlington took pride in its achievements and went so far to sponsor a piece of sheet music 'The Fast Mail' and a booklet 'How the "Greyhounds" of the Burlington Beat the Rising Moon.'"[100]

Passenger trains, deluxe, local, or mixed, handled vast amounts of express shipments. As the population grew, more items needed to be transported by rail. Among the leading users of this service were two Chicago-based mail-order houses, Montgomery Ward (established in

1872) and Sears, Roebuck & Company (launched in 1887). The latter firm offered a bewildering array of items, ranging from hairbrushes to windmills. By the early twentieth century, its catalog, "the silent salesman," could be found in households throughout the Midwest and elsewhere.

During the maturity years, the long-established railroad express business underwent major changes—not so much in the mechanics of transporting packages in an express car, a section of a baggage or mail car, or a solid train, but in the structure of the business itself. At the turn of the twentieth century, four investor-owned companies dominated: Adams Express, American Express, Southern Express, and Wells Fargo. In 1913 a marked transformation occurred. William Howard Taft, in one of his last duties as president, signed the Parcel Post Act. Previously, the Post Office did not accept packages, although the new measure initially limited them to eleven pounds and width plus height of only seventy-two inches. More federal intervention followed. During World War I, the United States Railroad Administration took over the express companies to bolster the war delivery efforts. William Gibbs McAdoo, who headed this emergency agency, believed that if the four major express companies and the three minor ones were federalized, they could be merged into one efficient megafirm. On June 30, 1918, the American Railway Express Company made its debut. After the war Congress passed the Transportation Act of 1920, as with railroads and electric interurbans private investors regained control. In time the railroads decided that it would be in their interests to own the express operations. In December 1928 this led to the chartering of the Railway Express Agency. Then on March 1, 1929, the eighty-six Class I railroads chose not to renew their contracts with the American Railway Express; the Railway Express Agency (REA) took over the majority of the nation's express operations. The Southern Railway refused to be a party to this arrangement and organized its own express firm, Southeastern Express. REA was dominated by railroads that served the Midwest, being led by the Baltimore & Ohio, Burlington, IC, Milwaukee Road, NYC, North Western, PRR, and Santa Fe. They and other carriers hardly found the express business to be a moneymaker. At best those railroads that owned shares in the REA covered their operating costs.[101]

EDUCATION AND SAFETY

Education usually is not directly associated with the Railway Age. Yet railroads in the Midwest made important contributions to at least one large segment of the population: rural residents. Beginning in 1904 the Burlington, working in conjunction with Iowa State Agricultural College, operated specially outfitted passenger coaches for exhibiting the latest agricultural research and holding lectures. Success ensued. Within seven years this extension outreach reached an estimated 939,000 individuals who had boarded sixty-two "agricultural colleges on wheels" and heard more than seven hundred lectures.[102]

The Burlington was not alone. Other midwestern carriers became involved in rural education. One was the Wabash. In 1911 this railroad teamed up with the University of Missouri College of Agriculture and the Missouri State Board of Agriculture to send a "special lecture train" on a three-day, twenty-one-station whirlwind tour. Consisting of several baggage and passenger cars and staffed by university and state personnel, this train stopped at stations, often in county-seat communities, where onboard specialists informed farmers and townspeople who were involved with agribusiness activities about such topics as "corn improvement," "feeding the dairy cow," and the "College of Agriculture."[103]

To dispatch trains, whether freight, passenger, express, specials, or work extras, controlling their movements safely and efficiently became paramount. The industry historically had been plagued by deaths and injuries. National data in the late nineteenth century confirms that risks for American railroaders were significantly higher than for their counterparts in Great Britain. There were no immediate signs that domestic workplace safety was about to improve.[104]

Changes did occur. It would be the North Western that claimed to have originated the "Safety First" slogan and campaign.[105] About 1910 Ralph Richards, longtime general claim agent, started what he called the "safety-first" educational program. His actions were timely. That year railroads nationally killed a shocking 3,383 workers, although only 608 died in derailments or collisions. Backed by management (liability laws made accident claims no longer relatively inexpensive) and officially launched on January 1, 1911, Richards's efforts helped focus widespread attention on industry safety. He soon became known as the "father of the railroad safety movement," with his recognition due in part to his talent as a proselytizer.[106]

How did Richards seek to improve railroad safety? Safety committees were at the core of his plan, and they focused on "little accidents." These coordinated and localized units appeared on every operating division and in all roundhouses, shops, and terminal yards. Consisting of division officers, three of whom were permanent members, and one or more workers from "every class of labor employed in the shop, or from every class of labor employed in the roundhouse and in the yards," these committees met monthly to discuss "any defective condition or practice that is likely to cause an accident or that is likely to prevent accidents or likely to increase efficiency of our organization." Explained Richards, "These men are paid by the company for the time they serve on these committees, the same as if they were working, and they are paid their expenses for attending these meetings." Employees cooperated and proudly wore a "neat button" with the safety-first slogan.[107]

The safety work on the North Western produced positive results. In January 1914 Ralph Richards told a group of assembled workers that "there have been during the past three years 265 fewer deaths and 8,461 less injuries." That trend continued. His efforts paid dividends for the company and ultimately for other carriers, midwestern or not. In 1912 the American Railway Association, the industry trade group, endorsed the Richards plan, as did the USRA during World War I. Erie Railroad superintendent Robert Woodruff reflected in 1925, "If the avoidable accidents can be greatly reduced, railroad work will be no more hazardous than any other occupations, and that should be the aim of each supervising officer and foreman."[108]

Although lawmakers did not mandate the Richards approach, one federal law contributed to making railroads safer. In 1907 President Theodore Roosevelt signed the Hours of Service Act (HOSA). This measure, promoted by Senator Robert La Follette Sr., a progressive activist, prohibited carriers from requiring their employees to remain on duty for more than sixteen consecutive hours. After that time, the statute required that workers be given ten consecutive hours off duty.

It specifically restricted telegraphers and dispatchers to nine hours of work during a twenty-four-hour period in continuously operated stations or no longer than thirteen hours in daytime-only stations. There was this exception: these two groups could work four additional hours in case of an emergency. Railroads began to comply, and a US Supreme Court ruling in 1911 (*Baltimore & Ohio Railroad Company v. Interstate Commerce Commission*) upheld the legality of the HOSA and led to full compliance.[109]

Midwestern railroads made significant betterments to their physical plants, especially once the economy rebounded following the aftermath of the Panic of 1893. The early years of the twentieth century marked the high point of the second building of the industry. This involved a host of betterments ranging from double-tracking principal lines to replacement of depots and union stations.

One focus became safer bridges. All too often midwestern railroads had built quickly and by the cheapest means. Ohio and Illinois had some disastrous bridge failures—namely, at Ashtabula, Ohio (1876), the worst in the nineteenth century, and Chatsworth, Illinois (1887). Early on they commonly erected timber trestles and bridges. Wood was cheap, accessible, and easy to use for construction but prone to decay and fire. The next phase of building for durable structures involved using wrought or cast iron, necessitated by increased locomotive weights and operating speeds. A fundamental change took place with Eads Bridge, which connected East St. Louis across the Mississippi River with St. Louis. Opened in 1874, this steel arch structure emerged as an engineering triumph, being the nation's first major steel bridge. Steel became the metal of choice on the heaviest trafficked lines for large spans and for selective smaller ones as well. Wood continued to be employed, largely for crossing smaller streams on branches and shortlines, but new methods for preserving wooden components were also developed.[110]

During the first part of the twentieth century, midwestern cities became involved in extensive grade-separation projects. As urban vehicular volume increased, especially with automobile usage after 1910, local politicians and company officials agreed that track overpasses were required for public safety and traffic efficiency. Some cities, including Chicago, Cleveland, Detroit, Indianapolis, and Milwaukee, at various

In the mid-1920s the American Railway Association, the industry trade group, distributed thousands of safety posters throughout the Midwest. Agents placed them in their depot waiting rooms and other public areas to warn the public of the dangers associated with railroad crossings. More automobiles were on the roads during the Roaring '20s. In 1924 the number registered nationally stood at 15,460,649, a figure that continued to increase. *(Author's collection)*

times enacted compulsory grade-separation ordinances. These betterment projects were not cheap. The preponderance of railroads (trunk, belt, and terminal) that served Chicago, for example, spent heavily on these improvements, mostly between 1882 and 1930, although the majority took place between 1893 and 1925. Most Chicago-area carriers dispatched scores of trains, including frequent commuter runs that carried large volumes of riders daily. These grade separations reduced fatal and nonfatal accidents and allowed for faster train speeds.[111]

Whether trains operated in suburban service or on main or secondary lines, they required the best possible track signaling. Early on train movements had been relatively light and generally slow, but as traffic increased after the Civil War the industry sought to enhance safety by improving train control. This involved the manual block system, sometimes called the telegraph block system. In 1903 about thirty thousand miles of track featured these controls. The concept lacked complexity: it allowed only a single train to occupy a defined section of track at one time. In 1910, this section was less than five miles. But how was this accomplished? When a train entered the block, the station agent-operator set a signal to indicate that the track was occupied. When the train left the block, the operator telegraphed his counterpart at the entry point to display a clear signal, permitting the next train to enter the blocked section.[112]

Manual block signaling gave way to dramatic advancements. The next betterment involved automatic block signals (ABS). With this technology, signals were operated by electricity and actuated by all trains. As they moved, signals moved. In 1903, the Rock Island, for example, installed an ABS system on fifteen miles of mainline track west of Chicago, using three-position, upper-quadrant semaphores. Such upgrades became popular albeit expensive. In 1920, there were nearly forty thousand miles of line nationally controlled by ABS, and a decade later coverage soared to slightly more than sixty thousand miles. By this time every trunk road in the Midwest had this modern way to manage train movements on its principal lines. In the late 1920s, railroads began to install centralized traffic control (CTC). The first important installation took place in 1927 on the NYC at Fostoria, Ohio, and covered the forty miles between Berwick and Stanley, Ohio. CTC allowed dispatchers to control signals and switches. They could set meeting points, run faster trains around slower ones, and increase train volume. Contemporaries contended that this technology provided failsafe operations, yet engine crews had to observe the signals. Other carriers followed the NYC's lead. The Great Depression, however, limited expansion of CTC-protected lines because of the high costs involved (about $10,000 per mile). When prosperity returned, CTC became common on busy lines. Coinciding with these electronic improvements was the introduction of automatic train control. In 1914 the Chicago & Eastern Illinois claimed the first major use of these cab safety devices when it placed 107 miles of its mainline under this projection between Chicago and Danville, Illinois. This primitive automatic warning equipment used a magnetic device on the locomotive that a wayside indicator triggered if the engineer did not respond to a restrictive block signal indication.[113]

STATIONS

Roughly coinciding with advances in signaling came the upgrading or building of replacement "country" depots and urban stations. During these maturity decades, railroads in the Midwest assigned their bridge and building personnel to undertake remodeling or replacement of multiple smaller and usually single-agent structures. These often were the ubiquitous wooden combination depots, those that housed a waiting room, center office, and freight house. In busier places, especially county seats, brick structures (perhaps including a separate women's waiting area or maybe a lunch counter) frequently replaced wooden ones. Since depots were community gateways, local boosters and citizens appreciated these improvements.

There appeared large and not-so-large monuments to railroad travel—namely, urban stations that served more than a single carrier. In the eight midwestern states, various ones emerged between 1890 and 1930. Representative of this genre are the Michigan Central Station in Detroit (1913), Union Terminal in Cleveland (1930), Gary Union Station in Gary, Indiana (1910), Union Station in Chicago (1924), Milwaukee Road Station in Madison, Wisconsin (1903), Union Depot in St. Paul (1920), Union Depot in Des Moines, Iowa (1904), and Union Station in Kansas City (1914). The latter one became the capstone in its highly acclaimed City Beautiful movement. They were the pride of residents and pleased patrons. Few though were built during the following decades. Only Cincinnati Union Terminal, which opened in 1933, stands out. The Great Depression, World War II, and changing personal travel preferences explain the paucity of new union stations. At last the "Golden Age of Railroading" was coming to a close.[114]

FOUR

MODERN ERA

1930–PRESENT

TROUBLE ON THE TRACKS

Paralleling the era of maturity of railroads in the Midwest, the modern era began in a similar fashion. Another deep and long-lasting depression ravaged the country. When the stock market crashed on Black Tuesday, October 29, 1929, the Great Depression was in the offing. By mid-1931 a catastrophic economic downswing had swept the nation, continuing in varying degrees of severity until the outbreak of World War II. Why this calamity? These hard times resulted largely from Wall Street stock and real-estate speculation, best exemplified by the collapse in 1926 of the postwar Great Florida Land Boom. The Great Depression rivaled the Panic of 1893, which had sparked five years of widespread economic suffering and labor and political unrest. Unlike the pre-1893 period, average stock prices on the eve of the massive sell-off had more than doubled since the mid-1920s. Railroad shareholders generally benefited from substantial upticks in the value of their holdings. In one bizarre happening, unsophisticated albeit get-rich-quick investors in 1926 and 1927 acquired Seaboard Air Line Railroad stock, mistaking it for an aviation company. ("Air Line" means a direct rail route or "as the crow flies" and not an airline.) The explanation for this excitement was passage of the Kelly Air Mail Act in 1925, which allowed commercial airplanes to carry US mail and to become potentially profitable. Such companies for speculators became Wall Street darlings.[1]

The Great Depression became just that for American railroads, regardless of their service territory. The coming of hard times led to severe contraction in bread-and-butter freight traffic, reducing gross revenues by nearly half. In 1930 weekly freight car loadings ranged from about 800,000 to 1,000,000, yet two years later these numbers stood at nearly 550,000. The passenger business hardly fared better. In 1926 railroads carried 874 million riders; in 1932 it had dropped to about half that volume. Also in that year approximately three-quarters of the national railroad mileage failed to earn enough to cover interest charges or other fixed obligations. Bankruptcies followed. By the close of the 1930s, approximately fifty railroads had failed, including a substantial number of Class I carriers that served the Midwest. These included the Ann Arbor, Chicago & North Western (North Western); Chicago Great Western (Great Western); Chicago, Milwaukee, St. Paul & Pacific (Milwaukee Road); Chicago, Rock Island & Pacific (Rock Island); Erie; Missouri Pacific; St. Louis–San Francisco (Frisco); and Wabash, St. Louis & Pacific Railway (Wabash). Those roads that remained court-free saw their equity values dip sharply or nearly collapse as the economy worsened. In 1929 the Illinois Central (IC), for example, had its common shares trade as high as $153.50, but in 1932 they had plummeted to a low of $4.75. Giants New York Central (NYC) and Pennsylvania (PRR) barely managed to stay afloat during the Depression onslaught.[2]

Not to be overlooked was increased modal competition during the 1920s that seemed unceasing during the Great Depression. More automobiles, buses, and trucks traveled the nation's system of expanding all-weather roadways. Federal, state, and local lawmakers had poured millions of tax dollars into the road improvements. Washington had financed about 13,000 miles of roads by 1921, but by 1940 this total had soared to slightly more than 235,000 miles. In the 1930s Chicago remained the country's railroad mecca, but multiple US highways also served the city, including US 30, successor to the pioneer New York to San Francisco Lincoln Highway. Furthermore, the trucking industry until 1935 was unhampered by any meaningful regulatory controls. "Gipsy" drivers, often unemployed workers who acquired a secondhand truck, siphoned off some of the more lucrative shipments that previously went by rail. To worsen matters, pipelines captured a growing proportion of

Midwesterners endured the hardships of the Great Depression of the 1930s. Although the relief programs of Franklin Roosevelt and his fellow New Deal Democrats brought relief to countless Americans, hard times continued to near the end of the decade. When the "Roosevelt Revision" of 1937–1938 struck, it was the third worst economic downturn in the twentieth century. On June 30, 1938, a Chesapeake & Ohio passenger train from Cincinnati, powered by an Atlantic 4-4-2 locomotive, steams into the joint C&O-Erie station in Hammond, Indiana. Yet this scene reveals no sign of the economic malaise affecting the region. *(John F. Humeston photograph, author's collection)*

the petroleum business, and water carriers took a bigger bite out of the movement of low-value commodities like aggregates, coal, and grain. Commercial aviation gained a competitive position for long-distance travelers, especially once the Douglas DC-3 and the original Lockheed Electra entered airline fleets after the mid-1930s.[3]

Yet hope emerged for midwestern railroads. The federal government sought to alleviate their financial suffering, promising cash infusions. In early 1932 a reluctant President Herbert Hoover approved a congressional measure that created the Reconstruction Finance Corporation

(RFC), designed to make loans to insurance companies, railroads, and other major businesses in need of liquidity. For troubled carriers, the RFC, with its pool of several billion dollars, emerged as the banker of last resort. When Franklin Roosevelt and the New Dealers took control of the federal government in March 1933, the RFC rapidly increased its assistance to the distressed business sector. The Roosevelt administration proclaimed that preservation of the railroads was vital to the public interest, not only for essential transportation but also for maintaining its vast labor force and bolstering the consumption of a multitude of products and services. The RFC became a godsend for scores of troubled carriers, yet its loans failed to prevent multiple midwestern bankruptcies.[4]

Lawmakers in Washington also concluded that traditional bankruptcy proceedings were inadequate to handle the growing railroad crisis. The response led to adding Section 77 to the Bankruptcy Act of 1898. This amendment streamlined such proceedings and gave the Interstate Commerce Commission (ICC) enhanced powers to protect investors and the public interest. In reality it hastened the overall reorganization process, being tailored to the needs of the transportation sector.[5]

STREAMLINERS

All was not gloom and doom for midwestern railroads. One bright spot that captured widespread attention was the introduction of diesel-powered streamlined passenger trains, fast, seemingly noiseless, and reeking of modernity. They collectively helped cheer up residents of the Midwest and the nation. In the early 1930s, the most sensational diesel-electric passenger train was about to be born. Ralph Budd, the talented and daring president of the Chicago, Burlington & Quincy Railroad (Burlington), realized that his road needed to respond to increased automobile usage. The motorcar industry in 1929 had produced a record 4.5 million vehicles, and hard times did not shut down production. Automobile registration that year had climbed to 23 million. People who couldn't afford a new automobile might acquire a used one, perhaps a vintage Ford Model T. Budd sensed, too, that the public had developed the attitude that railroads were "tired" and lacked a progressive outlook. He challenged that perception.

In 1933 the Burlington placed an order with the Edward G. Budd Manufacturing Company of Philadelphia (whose head was a distant relative of the Burlington executive) for a high-speed, streamlined, three-car articulated passenger train with an estimated $200,000 price tag. This first diesel-powered streamliner would be fabricated from lightweight stainless steel, using technologies developed for the automobile and aviation industries. By employing aluminum and steel alloys (and using stainless-steel shot-welding), a train could be lightened without reducing car strength. Breakthroughs in aerodynamics would also be utilized, resulting in a shovel-nosed or slope-nosed locomotive front. Wind-tunnel tests at the Massachusetts Institute of Technology with a Budd Company model revealed that its resistance to motion at ninety-five miles an hour would be less than half that of a train with a steam locomotive and heavyweight coaches at that same speed. This seventy-passenger, 196-foot streamliner would have three distinct units: "The first car will contain the motor, baggage and mail compartment; second car, baggage and express, with a buffet and smoking compartment in the rear to seat 19 passengers; third car will be entirely devoted to seating space with a capacity of 51, which includes 12 parlor chairs." A two-cycle, eight-cylinder, six-hundred-horsepower diesel engine recently developed by Electro-Motive Corporation (EMC) would provide the power. What would this futuristic train be called? Budd, who had received a solid liberal arts education while earning his civil engineering degree at Highland Park College in Des Moines, named this radically new train the Zephyr. He recalled lines from Geoffrey Chaucer's *The Canterbury Tales* in which Zephyrus, winged Greek God of the West Wind, represents renaissance. That was exactly what Budd expected of this streamliner for these times of national angst.[6]

The event that grabbed headlines and brought broadcasters to their microphones came on May 26, 1934. Although the Burlington had formally received the Zephyr from the Budd Company on April 18, 1934, and subsequently sent it on an extended national tour, stopping in thirty eastern cities and sixteen cities along the Burlington, the crowning event was a nonstop run from Denver to Chicago. But there was more. Confident of the Zephyr's performance capabilities, Budd arranged with officials of the Century of Progress Exposition in Chicago to have the train arrive as the grand climax of the staged transportation pageant "Wings of a Century."[7]

The dawn-to-dusk dash of the Zephyr was breathtaking. Although a brief electrical problem occurred early on that nearly stopped the train, it continued onward from Denver toward Chicago. (Rumor circulated that the train made a secret fuel stop.) The Zephyr met all expectations. It covered the 1,015.4-mile nonstop trip in thirteen hours and five minutes, about half the normal schedule of twenty-five hours. It reached a speed of 112.5 miles per hour at one point, averaged 77.61 miles per hour, and rolled onto the pageant stage on time, much to the delight of the audience and, of course, to EMC and railroad personnel, including Budd, who were on board. "The train has demonstrated by this performance its capacity to maintain for a long period a high average speed and higher speeds for shorter distances, as well as low cost of operation at high speeds," noted company historian Richard Overton. The special run was more than an enormously successful publicity stunt. On November 11, 1934, the Zephyr (renamed the Pioneer Zephyr but still retaining its official No. 9900), entered daily revenue service between Kansas City, St. Joseph, Council Bluffs, Omaha, and Lincoln, complementing two steam passenger trains in each direction. It remained active until 1960, ending its career on a daily run between Galesburg and Quincy, Illinois. Ultimately, the company donated this historic train to the Museum of Science and Industry in Chicago. The popularity and efficiency of its initial streamliner prompted the Burlington during the following six years to add eleven more Zephyrs, each one larger and more powerful. When the Texas Zephyr was introduced in 1940, it operated with a four-thousand-horsepower diesel engine.[8]

Another lightweight streamliner coincided with the appearance of the initial Zephyr. The Union Pacific (UP) joined this emerging technological revolution. "Tomorrow's Train Today," officially the M-10000, with its striking yellow and brown livery, differed in several ways from its Burlington counterpart. Builder Pullman would use aluminum, it would run on distillate, it would feature a Winton engine, and it would accommodate 116 passengers and crew. UP officials had in mind a fast, comfortable, and economical long-distance train. They hoped that it could significantly reduce the operating schedule between Chicago (via

The Burlington Railroad had invested well in its original Zephyr. This train set would not be retired until March 20, 1960, when it departed Galesburg, Illinois, for Quincy, Illinois, a distance of fifty-three miles. *(John Gruber photograph, © Center for Railroad Photography and Art)*

the North Western) and the Pacific Coast. On the maiden voyage in October 1934, which followed a twenty-two state, thirteen-thousand-mile tour, the M-10000 made the run from Los Angeles to Chicago in less than thirty-nine hours, clipping six hours off the fastest previous run between these two cities. UP historian Maury Klein made these comparison points about the M-10000 and the Zephyr: "For years confusion and disputes have raged over which of the two companies developed the first streamliner. The answer is in fact simple and indisputable. The Union Pacific's train went public in February, the Burlington's in April." Continued Klein, "However, the Burlington's Zephyr included the newly perfected diesel engine from the start; the Union Pacific originally used the Winton before switching to the diesel, enabling the Burlington to claim rightly that it developed the first diesel-powered streamliner." This articulated UP train had a spark-ignition distillate engine rather than a diesel one. On January 31, 1935, the M-10000 became the City of Salina and served the 197-mile route between Kansas City, Missouri; Topeka; and Salina, Kansas. Unlike the venerable Pioneer Zephyr, it ended up on an Omaha scrap pile in 1942. On June 6, 1935, its companion train, M-10001, the City of Portland, began racing along the 2,272 miles between its namesake city and Chicago, shaving eighteen hours from the fastest regularly scheduled time. It won the distinction of being the first streamliner to include Pullman sleepers. Soon afterward, the joint UP–North Western diesel-powered City of Denver and City of Los Angeles (with the Southern Pacific) entered regular service.[9]

As the 1930s progressed, other railroads in the Midwest and elsewhere began to offer travelers the speed and comfort of streamliners. Steam-powered trains, however, could still provide attractive features. Take what occurred in the competitive Chicago–Milwaukee corridor. After July 15, 1934, the Milwaukee Road and North Western both operated traditional steam-powered equipment on ninety-minute schedules over this eighty-five-mile route. North Western management concluded that it would do the same between Chicago and the Twin Cities. This bankrupt company realized that a Zephyr or M-10000 clone would be too expensive, and it would take time to acquire such equipment from Budd, Pullman, or another manufacturer. It therefore needed to make a silk purse out of a sow's ear. Nevertheless, a remarkable train appeared.

Using its available resources, employees laid new rail, improved curve elevations for high-speed running, and converted four eleven-year-old Pacific-type locomotives (4-6-2s) from coal to oil. This reduced engine changes and eliminated fuel and water stops at several intermediate points. Other workers renovated a group of coaches, diners, and parlor cars, all of which were updated with air-conditioning.[10]

In December 1934 North Western personnel must have taken comfort in knowing that their deluxe passenger train was about to take to the rails. With everything in readiness, press releases and paid publicity began to appear for the 400. "Again 'North Western' makes railroad history clipping hours from the previous fastest morning time between Chicago, Milwaukee and the Twin Cities," announced a promotional piece. "400 miles in 400 minutes. FASTEST TRAIN ON THE AMERICAN CONTINENT." The name suggested sophistication and wealth: "The Four Hundred" in high society were the creme de la creme. "Besides being both unusual and easy to remember," noted one commentator, "[the name] told the whole story. In a way, with the possible exception of the [NYC's] *20th Century Limited,* it is the most effective train name ever devised." Perhaps, but debatable.[11]

On January 2, 1935, the 400s made their inaugural runs between Chicago and the Twin Cities, the exact distance being 409 miles. Everything went well: radio stations provided live broadcasts, crowds gathered at trackside, and the trains ran on time. Onboard passengers were pleased: they were comfortable and took pleasure in speeds that normally exceeded eighty miles per hour. These "new aristocrats of the rails" put midwestern railroading on the map.[12]

The 400s served the travelers well, but they were hardly the ultimate form of intercity rail transportation. A state-of-the-art 400 would have greater marquee value and would permit the North Western to battle successfully with the Burlington and Milwaukee Road in this competitive Chicago–Twin Cities market.[13] In December 1938 the North Western asked the bankruptcy court for authority to purchase twenty streamlined cars and four diesel locomotives. The judge agreed, authorizing the $2.3 million expenditure. Pullman-Standard and EMC would produce trains that revealed "exceptional imagination, research, care and study by the carbuilder, railway, and locomotive manufacturer." On September

Now!
NOT ONE "400"-
BUT A Fleet
OF THEM
To Milwaukee
To Green Bay
To Upper Michigan
To St. Paul-Minneapolis
To Southern Minnesota
To Madison
CHICAGO AND NORTH WESTERN LINE

Facing, Even though the Chicago & North Western had been pleased with the steam-powered 400s between Chicago, Milwaukee, and the Twin Cities, it took similar pride with dieselization of its flagship trains. By 1942 the company had expanded its 400 service, operating streamliners to more destinations in Wisconsin, Michigan, and Minnesota. *(Author's collection)*

24, 1939, with much fanfare, these replacement 400s entered service. As with other modern industrial objects of the 1930s, the 400s featured flowing lines and graceful contours. The North Western expanded its 400 service by the early 1940s from Chicago to Green Bay; Ishpeming, Michigan; Madison; and southern Minnesota.[14]

The Burlington and Milwaukee Road became keen competitors for Chicago–Twin Cities passengers. Unlike the North Western and Milwaukee Road, the Burlington had escaped bankruptcy, allowing it to introduce its Twin Cities Zephyr on April 21, 1935. This train's comfort and speed, which averaged more than seventy-five miles per hour over this 431-mile route, ensured strong patronage as it battled two entrenched rivals. The following year the Burlington upgraded this service: "Superseding the spectacular three-car Zephyrs that established the first streamline train service between Chicago and the Twin Cities each of these new seven-car super-Zephyrs supplies commodious coach accommodations for 120 passengers, luxurious parlor and parlor-lounge cars, a delightful full-length diner, and a convivial cocktail lounge."[15]

The Milwaukee Road did not follow the Burlington's approach but rather the North Western's—first steam and then diesel power. The Milwaukee Road used its West Milwaukee, Wisconsin, shops to fabricate lightweight passenger coach, diner, and observation cars of an improved design, and it received from the American Locomotive Company (Alco) two streamlined (shrouded) Atlantic-type (4-4-2) locomotives featuring options that sustained high-speed operations. On May 29, 1935, the Milwaukee Road introduced its Hiawatha service (affectionately called the Hi's). Several years later the company upgraded the motive power, and shrouded Hudson-type locomotives (4-6-4s) replaced the Atlantics. On September 20, 1941, two Electro-Motive Division (EMD)[16] diesel units propelled the high-speed Hi's.[17]

No matter the power or the carrier selected, the traveling public benefited. "Whatever road one rides, competition has made the Chicago-Twin Cities trip one of the best train rides in the United States—and one of the best patronized," opined *Trains* editor A. C. Kalmach in late 1941. His observation rang true for years to come.[18]

As the age of modern streamliners progressed, other railroads, whether Chicago- or St. Louis–based or serving the Midwest, followed the lead of the Burlington and UP. The Rock Island, for one, began in 1937 to introduce its fleet of diesel-powered Rocket streamliners. On September 29, 1937, its Peoria Rocket entered service between Illinois's two largest cities, being hailed as "a bright and beautiful thing to behold." On the company's Chicago–Omaha–Denver passenger route, its Rocky Mountain Rocket, likewise viewed as a "dashing streamliner," made its inaugural trip on November 12, 1939. For the time being, the joint Rock Island–Southern Pacific Golden State Limited remained with steam.[19]

The two most renowned passenger trains that served Ohio, Indiana, and Chicago, the 20th Century Limited on the NYC and the Broadway Limited on the PRR, embraced the Milwaukee Road streamliner model. This meant lightweight cars replacing traditional heavyweight ones and diesels replacing steam in the 1940s. As with other contemporary streamliners, they featured air-conditioning and additional amenities, including outlets for electric razors. The 20th Century Limited, "the most famous passenger train in the United States," experienced a new day on June 15, 1938. "The First All-Room Train in America—No Open Berth Cars," proclaimed the company. This iconic streamliner operated between New York City and Chicago on a sixteen-hour schedule and was powered by streamlined Alco-built Hudsons. Their art deco and modernist features were the joint efforts of the railroad's equipment engineering department and Henry Dreyfuss, a New York industrial designer. EMD diesels did not replace steam until 1945. Also on June 15, 1938, rival PRR dispatched its Broadway Limited with new Pullman-Standard-built streamlined cars. Notable features were the first private-room showers and the introduction of roomettes. The steam power for its train sets were Pacifics, including one that was streamlined. The PRR, though, employed streamlined GG1 heavy-traction electric locomotives between New York City, Philadelphia, and Harrisburg, Pennsylvania.

These eye-catching "juice" units were built by General Electric and the PRR shops in Altoona, Pennsylvania, between 1934 and 1943. Duplicating the 20th Century Limited, the Broadway Limited advertised a sixteen-hour schedule. Raymond Loewy, another New York industrial designer, participated in creating the art deco look of these trains. Dieselization came after World War II.[20]

Another streamliner was the Land O' Corn, a two-car unit built by the American Car & Foundry Company for the Illinois Central. The St. Louis firm believed that this diminutive version of a streamliner or what it called a Motorailer would sell well. Few, though, were purchased. At a glance this high-tensile-steel streamliner resembled a bus on flanged wheels. Unlike other new-breed passenger trains, this one lacked baggage, express, or mail compartments, although it featured a buffet section with a coffee shop, a lunch counter, and dining tables "serving inexpensive but tasty meals." The Land O' Corn provided its passengers (125-seat capacity) with "comfortable coach seats, attractively decorated interiors and all-weather air conditioning." The train made its inaugural run between Chicago and Waterloo, Iowa, a distance of 275 miles, on October 26, 1941. Although capable of reaching speeds over eighty miles per hour, its average speed was considerably less, usually about fifty miles per hour. The IC advertised a convenient schedule for the round trip and offered low-cost fares. Fewer crew members were required on the Land O' Corn than on the other two passenger trains that served this route, the Hawkeye and the Iowan—namely, an engineer, a conductor, a flagman, and a waiter-porter. Employees assigned to the train jokingly or perhaps affectionately called it the Can of Corn. Unfortunately, this popular train experienced a tragic end. On February 18, 1942, it struck a truck at Plato Center, Illinois, forty-five miles west of Chicago, killing the engineer and injuring twenty-five passengers. The train was not repaired or replaced; instead, the ICC restored steam and a regular consist of cars to the Land O' Corn.[21]

A footnote to the streamliner phenomenon involved the Fairmont Railway Motors Company of Fairmont, Minnesota. Although this firm had established itself as the leading maker of motor cars ("speeders") used mostly by maintenance-of-way workers, it constructed at least one streamlined vehicle. At the request of the Washington, Idaho & Montana

Railway, which sought to make its passenger service less costly than with conventional steam-powered trains, it arranged with Fairmont to build a lightweight railcar for handling passengers, mail, and express between Palouse, Washington, and Bovill, Idaho. Named the Potlatcher, this mini-streamliner, which measured thirty-three feet, operated over this forty-eight-mile route from 1938 to 1955.[22]

FT LOCOMOTIVES

Much less clamorous than the flashy streamliners that plied midwestern rails were the first mass-produced freight diesels that appeared on the eve of World War II. Even though diesel-powered locomotives had been used since the late 1920s, they were deployed largely for switching and transfer chores and substituted for steam locomotives in smoke-conscious cities like Chicago and St. Louis. Other municipalities also enacted stringent city-smoke-abatement laws, and railroads needed to comply. A dramatic change took place as the 1930s closed. This involved what railroad writer Wallace Abbey has called "the diesel that did it": the FT, an EMD product. It didn't appear overnight, taking about ten years of research and development. (The F stands for Freight, and the T likely represents Thirteen, being 1,350 horsepower per unit.) Compared to contemporary diesels, the FT was a giant; it became frequently a 5,400-horsepower locomotive when consisting of four units. This La Grange, Illinois, manufactured marvel revolutionized freight motive power. Between 1939 and 1940, the company sent a three-unit prototype model, numbered 103, on a national tour. (In eleven months No. 103 traveled 83,764 miles on twenty Class I railroads in thirty-five states.) On November 25, 1939, its initial revenue freight service began on the Burlington between Chicago and Kansas City. Soon extensive testing took place on the Atchison, Topeka & Santa Fe (Santa Fe). As a result of its positive tryout on that road, it placed the first order for two production copies; they entered revenue service in 1941. Wartime limitations on railroad equipment mandated by the War Production Board meant that a limited number of FT-type units were manufactured. Still, some railroads that served the region (for example, the Erie), put them in operation during the conflict. The

In May 1960 Monon Railroad shop workers in Lafayette, Indiana, replace a Fairbanks-Morse prime mover with an EMD model. The result: a "hybrid" diesel locomotive. *(J. Parker Lamb photograph, © Center for Railroad Photography and Art)*

FT continued to be the only American-manufactured freight diesel until 1945.[23]

The introductory FT road units were hardly perfect machines. Yet testing quickly led to mechanical improvements that produced greater dependability. The overall performance of this new breed of freight power often left railroaders breathless. Although initial acquisition costs were considerably more than those of comparable steam locomotives, their economic advantages of excellent fuel efficiency, low maintenance, enhanced availability, and faster startup speeds with heavy consists offset purchase expenditures. For one thing, a diesel set used little water, and so ultimately hundreds of trackside water tanks could be removed and water-supply personnel reassigned. Nevertheless, there were freight-diesel holdouts, at least until after World War II. Midwestern carriers like Chesapeake & Ohio (C&O), Nickel Plate, IC, and PRR and allies Norfolk & Western and Wabash resisted FT-type power. One factor was that the C&O, IC, PRR, and their affiliated properties were important coal haulers; managements did not wish to alienate their large-volume shippers. These railroads, moreover, had made substantial investments in steam locomotives and infrastructure and were reluctant to junk their costly commitments to the iron horse. Some officials remained optimistic that modern reciprocating locomotives had a place on their railroads. Not to be ignored were deeply entrenched habits among officials and workers. One Akron, Canton & Youngstown (AC&Y) locomotive engineer fretted about being able to make the change from steam to diesel. Could he master this new technology and thereby hold his job?[24]

By the time the freight diesel arrived shortly after World War II, an intense competition had developed among manufactures. EMD lost its monopoly. The established steam-locomotive builders, Alco, Baldwin, and Lima, also had to compete not only with EMD but also with Fairbanks-Morse, a longtime diesel engine manufacturer, and the General Electric Company. Several small midwestern-based gasoline and diesel-electric makers also participated: Atlas Car & Manufacturing Company of Cleveland, Davenport Locomotive Works of Davenport, Iowa, Fate-Root-Heath Company (Plymouth Locomotive Works) of Plymouth, Ohio, and Whitcomb Locomotive Works of Rochelle, Illinois. Their locomotives were designed for industrial, switching, and shortline usage.[25]

TRUCKS AND BUSES

In the post–World War I decades, midwestern railroads began to consider augmenting their freight and passenger operations with their own trucks and buses. Both forms of surface transportation burgeoned during the 1920s, especially motor carriers. This mode of transport benefited from vehicle improvements, heavy-duty pneumatic tires, better roads, lack of federal regulation, and its adaptability and convenience. By 1925 there were 2.4 million trucks registered nationally; five years later the total reached nearly 3.5 million. Emerging trucking companies and independent operators frequently served as feeders for railroads, whether for agricultural, industrial, or other types of less-than-truckload shipments. The door-to-door convenience whether to factory or farm and frequent service made trucks attractive to shippers. Early on, railroads often did not particularly care, knowing that their less-than-carload lots (LCL) movements were labor intensive and generally a modest revenue source. They considered trucks as a complementary rather than a competitive form of transportation. Furthermore, the trucking industry lacked dominant companies, consisting of numerous small firms that often lacked financial stability. By the late 1920s and early 1930s, an estimated 150,000 independent truckers appeared on the nation's highways. These were often called "gypsies," "wildcatters," or "fly-by-night" operators. Officially the federal government labeled them as "itinerant peddlers."[26]

Then came the Great Depression. Trucking firms seemed impervious to the economic downswing. Why? Most had low operating costs, including labor, and shippers eagerly sought to reduce their transportation expenses. As trucks cut into boxcar traffic, concern grew as these upstart competitors gained market share. By the time of the early 1930s, tires, for example, from the four major manufacturers in Akron traveled more frequently to automakers in Detroit by truck rather than via the AC&Y, Detroit, Toledo & Ironton, Baltimore & Ohio (B&O), or PRR. Toward the end of the 1920s, the latter company, in fact, had begun investing in trucking companies, including acquiring in 1930 a one-third interest in the rapidly expanding Chicago-based Willett Company. The common response by midwestern carriers was only for the pickup and delivery of LCL shipments. Roads that started such services included the Burlington, IC, Michigan Central, North Western, and PRR. The Burlington went so far as to create a truck division as part of its satellite Burlington Transportation Company, which had already taken to the highways with buses. Noteworthy is the fear expressed by some railroad executives that if they entered the trucking business on a large scale, they could face unpleasant regulatory consequences.[27]

The most creative (and enduring) response to the rise of commercial motor carrier competition came with the introduction of modern truck trailer-on-flatcar (TOFC) or "piggyback" service. The concept was appealing, combining the flexibility and door-to-door pickup and delivery ability of motor carriers with the cost-effectiveness of rail-line hauls. TOFC was not "invented" in 1935 by piggyback pioneer Chicago Great Western. Since the 1870s railroads throughout America had operated special circus trains, and they carried on flatcars their ornate circus wagons, the archetypal symbols of this beloved form of traveling entertainment. In the 1920s the Chicago, North Shore & Milwaukee (North Shore Line) interurban blazed the way by starting to transport truck trailers, initially to bring carload freight close to downtown Chicago. This successful operation would be extended to accommodate shippers in Milwaukee, although the company rejected haulage of livestock and perishables.

The Great Western became the breakthrough steam road. The Great Depression had plunged it into bankruptcy, and this 1,500-mile road desperately needed to increase its revenue stream. Early in 1935 the Great Western's alert Chicago-based traffic department called management's attention to the piggyback concept, and it agreed to the experiment. Company official Samuel Golden used the circus-train model. He borrowed a truck trailer from the Chicago-Dubuque Motor Transportation Company and worked with employees at the Oelwein, Iowa, shops to place it on a standard forty-foot flatcar. It was then attached as securely as possible to the flatcar using a set of chock blocks and other fasteners. No problems developed when the Oelwein-to-Dubuque local handled the experimental car on several round trips.

The piggyback experiment ultimately produced commercial results. If the Great Western could provide suitable rates, several appropriately fitted cars, and the necessary loading ramps, the Chicago trucking firm would be interested in moving trailers on a regular basis between the Windy City and Dubuque. Management agreed. The railroad applied to the ICC for the necessary tariffs (a process made easier since the Motor Carrier Act of 1935, which allowed the commission to set joint rail-truck rates), and it ordered shop workers to equip ten flatcars for this service. The Oelwein shop force made tie-downs, and a Chicago specialty equipment manufacturer provided moveable jacks. Although the Chicago-Dubuque Motor Transportation Company decided not to use the rails, the Great Western pushed ahead with the concept. Success followed. In May 1936 it signed a two-year contract with the fourteen-member Illinois-Minnesota Motor Carriers' Conference and filed the necessary documents with the ICC. To meet its anticipated needs, the Great Western assigned additional flatcars and leased more from the Chicago & Eastern Illinois (C&EI), creating a fleet of about fifty cars. By summer 1936 the TOFC service had been fully established. In the first full month, the railroad handled 870 trailers that yielded a modest profit. Although the New York, New Haven & Hartford Railroad entered the piggyback business between Boston, Providence, and New York shortly after the Great Western, the industry showed little interest in this intermodal arrangement, not embracing it with gusto until the mid-1950s. In 1952 only four midwestern railroads of the six offered TOFC service nationally on either a limited or on a general basis: Burlington, C&EI, Great Western, and Santa Fe. Why so late? Ossification permeated corporate thinking, and there was an unwillingness to make the necessary financial commitments. But their reasoning was more complex. Companies did not want to take TOFC freight away from more profitable boxcars. They also considered this question: Was there a market? Perhaps carriers failed to recognize the changing competitive transportation landscape of the post–World War II years.[28]

In the 1920s and 1930s, multiple railroad executives in the Midwest saw the possibilities of financial rewards by taking to the highways, either launching their own bus networks or establishing partnerships with bus companies. Not all railroads that operated in the eight-state region did, but some major ones, including the Burlington, Great Northern (GN), Missouri Pacific, NYC, North Western, and PRR, invested in bus operations. Take GN. As early as 1921, President Ralph Budd believed that buses and trucks were "here to stay" and that his company should enter "in short-haul business [on roadways] as part of its transportation activities." He recognized the financial and service advantages that a bus could offer. "For the cost of one train in each direction, say morning and evening, a bus could be run every two hours in each direction from 8 a.m. to 4 p.m." In 1925 the Budd-led carrier decided to invest in the emerging bus industry. He believed that often money-losing passenger train operations, especially on branch lines, could be cut or reduced by replacing them with buses. GN acquired a 90 percent interest in the Minnesota-based Northland Transportation Company, which had its roots beginning in 1914 as a jitney operation between Hibbing and Virginia in the Mesabi Iron Range of Minnesota. Before long, the rapidly expanding company dominated bus service in the North Star State. Even though this bus operator prospered, GN in 1929 sold most of its stock to what became the Greyhound Corporation, a coast-to-coast operator and future industry leader. As a counterweight to Greyhound bus operators, Burlington, Missouri Pacific, and Santa Fe launched the Trailways Transportation System in the mid-1930s, creating an affiliated system (unlike Greyhound's centralized ownership) that competed on a regional and national basis with Greyhound. After World War II, though, midwestern railroads had exited from the bus business. The Burlington, for one, sold its Burlington Transportation Company to the upstart All American Bus Company, which sought to establish itself as a competitor to Greyhound.[29]

Resembling some contemporary midwestern interurbans, including the Fort Dodge, Des Moines & Southern Railroad and Union Traction Company of Indiana, a few smaller railroads launched bus subsidiaries. One was the sixty-five-mile Missouri Southern Railroad, an Ozark carrier that linked Leeper with Bunker. Beginning in the summer of 1929, its Missouri Southern Transportation Company provided connecting bus service between Salem and Van Buren, Salem and St. Louis, and Salem and Popular Bluff. Its equipment lacked both size and elegance, being two seven-passenger Buick automobiles. These vehicles also handled small express shipments.[30]

INTERURBANS

As commercial trucking and buses became ubiquitous after World War I, the electric interurban industry in the Midwest experienced a rapid decline and an early death. But it was the automobile that was the disruptive technology hastening the demise of most interurbans. The region once boasted of having one-third of all US electric intercity railway mileage. This heartland of electrics soon witnessed abandonment after abandonment with the weakest intercity companies shutting down during and after the war. The healthier ones frequently had to fight for their survival, often through innovative freight and passenger efforts. One example of this creative response came with freight shipments. In 1928 the Northern Ohio Traction & Light Company, Penn-Ohio Public Service Company, and Lake Shore Electric Railway launched the Electric Railways Freight Company to provide a coordinated freight operation. Their managements sought to compete with both steam roads and trucks. Take Akron-to-Detroit tire shipments and car assembly parts. These three interurbans, in conjunction with the electric Eastern Michigan–Toledo Railroad, were pleased with these moves. Two years earlier Penn-Ohio had opened a freight house in Youngstown, and a year later the Northern Ohio had completed a similar albeit larger facility in Akron. Speed and just-in-time delivery allowed these roads to attract shippers, who paid a premium price for this freight service.[31]

Another imaginative response to truck competition came from the Northern Ohio. It launched one of the first mechanically cooled refrigerator cars. "Reefers" had been used for decades on steam railroads and occasionally on interurbans that had the capability to interchange rolling stock, but they used block ice that required replenishing at regular intervals. In 1924 the Akron-based company introduced several freight cars equipped with insulated walls and electrical refrigeration units. The result pleased the Cleveland Provision Company, a wholesaler that distributed meat and dairy products throughout northeastern Ohio. A few years later, the North Shore Line provided similar cars to transport dairy products from Wisconsin to the Chicago market.[32]

The public might not have noticed freight movements, although if they appeared on city streets and disrupted traffic, residents may have been annoyed or complained to local politicians. It became common to have municipal ordinances that permitted freight movements only during nighttime hours. Surely residents recognized the appearance in the 1920s of lightweight and, for companies, more economical passenger cars, usually products of the Cleveland-based G. C. Kuhlman Car Company (controlled after 1904 by J. G. Brill Company), Cincinnati Car Company, American Car and Foundry of St. Charles, Missouri, or St. Louis Car Company. Then came even better equipment, notably that found on the Cincinnati & Lake Erie (C&LE) and Indiana Railroads.[33]

A state-of-the-art car from Cincinnati Car Company grabbed national attention in July 1930. The spark plug for what took place can be attributed to Dr. Thomas Conway Jr., industry consultant and former professor of finance at the Wharton School of Finance and Commerce at the University of Pennsylvania. He believed that a profitable passenger market existed for a modernized interurban that linked not-too-distant urban centers. In this case it would be between Toledo, Columbus, and Cincinnati. In 1929 Conway and his associates unified core components of the onetime Ohio Electric Railway, specifically a mainline between Toledo and Cincinnati and a connecting link from Springfield to Columbus, creating a more-than-250-mile electric network. Soon the C&LE had extensive physical upgrades, including line relocations, upgraded power, and attractive new passenger cars. This replacement rolling stock consisted of ten coaches and ten coach-observation cars, which were lightweight and high-speed. They became known as Red Devils because of their striking Tuscan red paint scheme and their ability to accelerate rapidly and maintain speeds of fifty or more miles per hour. The interiors of the coach-observation cars were elegant, featuring comfortable individual upholstered chairs, writing desks, and table lamps. Boasted the company, "A fleet of De Luxe trains—operating on convenient and dependable schedules—serve daily, the business districts of each of these cities—Cincinnati, Columbus, Dayton, Hamilton, Lima, Middletown, Springfield, Toledo." It added, "They offer to everyone, a service that provides the long sought essentials in travel, namely speed with safety, greater comfort, greater economy."[34]

A Pathe News Weekly production may have surprised movie audiences nationwide. They watched a remarkable film clip that showed a staged and extensively publicized race on July 7, 1930, between car No. 126, one of the "C. & L. E.'s Luxurious Flyers," and a rather slow biplane. This action occurred south of Dayton on a section of improved track that had enhanced overhead power. This Red Devil outdistanced its aerial competitor by a car length and reached a speed of ninety-seven miles per hour. In another stunt a Red Devil won a contest with a road racer by fifteen lengths. This publicity made the cars an immediate hit. "By August 1930 C&LE ticket sales were up by more than 40 percent over the June level, and at Cincinnati sales increased by an extraordinary

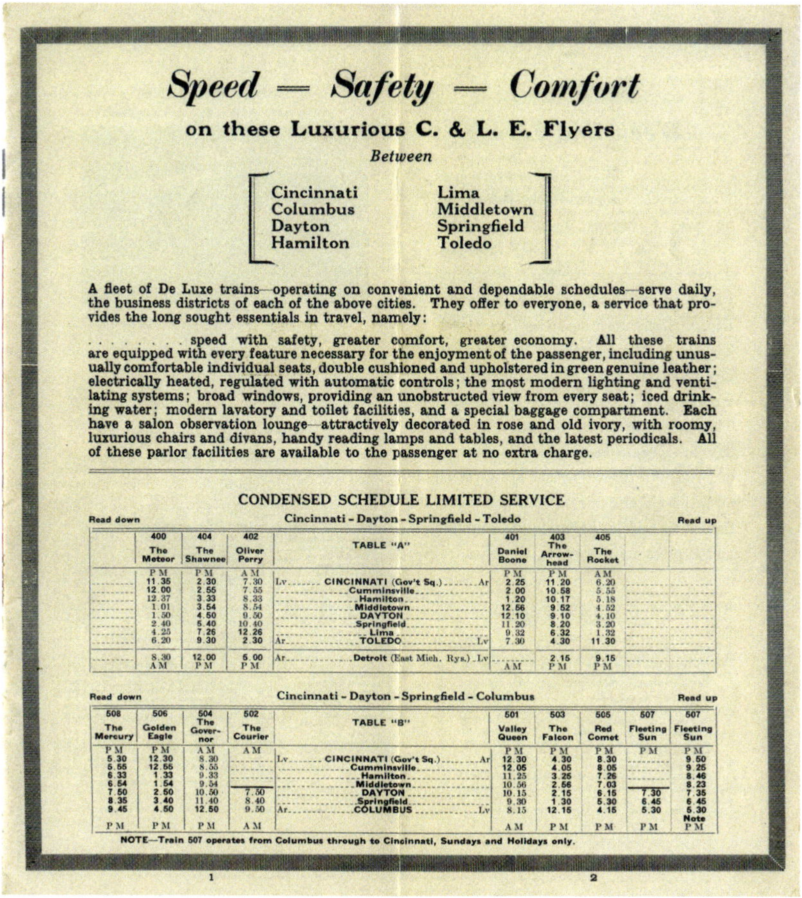

Speed — Safety — Comfort

on these Luxurious C. & L. E. Flyers

Between

Cincinnati	Lima
Columbus	Middletown
Dayton	Springfield
Hamilton	Toledo

A fleet of De Luxe trains—operating on convenient and dependable schedules—serve daily, the business districts of each of the above cities. They offer to everyone, a service that provides the long sought essentials in travel, namely:

. . . . speed with safety, greater comfort, greater economy. All these trains are equipped with every feature necessary for the enjoyment of the passenger, including unusually comfortable individual seats, double cushioned and upholstered in green genuine leather; electrically heated, regulated with automatic controls; the most modern lighting and ventilating systems; broad windows, providing an unobstructed view from every seat; iced drinking water; modern lavatory and toilet facilities, and a special baggage compartment. Each have a salon observation lounge—attractively decorated in rose and old ivory, with roomy, luxurious chairs and divans, handy reading lamps and tables, and the latest periodicals. All of these parlor facilities are available to the passenger at no extra charge.

CONDENSED SCHEDULE LIMITED SERVICE

Read down — Cincinnati - Dayton - Springfield - Toledo — Read up

	400 The Meteor	404 The Shawnee	402 Oliver Perry	TABLE "A"	401 Daniel Boone	403 The Arrow-head	405 The Rocket		
	P M	P M	A M		P M	P M	A M		
	11.35	2.30	7.30	Lv CINCINNATI (Gov't Sq.) Ar	2.25	11.20	6.20		
	12.00	2.55	7.55	Cumminsville	2.00	10.58	5.55		
	12.37	3.33	8.33	Hamilton	1.20	10.17	5.18		
	1.01	3.54	8.54	Middletown	12.56	9.52	4.52		
	1.50	4.50	9.50	DAYTON	12.10	9.10	4.10		
	2.40	5.40	10.40	Springfield	11.20	8.20	3.20		
	4.25	7.26	12.26	Lima	9.32	6.32	1.32		
	6.20	9.30	2.30	Ar TOLEDO Lv	7.30	4.30	11.30		
	8.30	12.00	5.00	Ar Detroit (East Mich. Rys.) Lv		2.15	9.15		
	A M	P M	P M		A M	P M	P M		

Read down — Cincinnati - Dayton - Springfield - Columbus — Read up

508 The Mercury	506 Golden Eagle	504 The Gover-nor	502 The Courier	TABLE "B"	501 Valley Queen	503 The Falcon	505 Red Comet	507 Fleeting Sun	507 Fleeting Sun
P M	P M	A M	A M		P M	P M	P M	P M	P M
5.30	12.30	8.30		Lv CINCINNATI (Gov't Sq.) Ar	12.30	4.30	8.30		9.50
5.55	12.55	8.55		Cumminsville	12.05	4.05	8.05		9.25
6.33	1.33	9.33		Hamilton	11.25	3.25	7.26		8.46
6.54	1.54	9.54		Middletown	10.56	2.56	7.03		8.23
7.50	2.50	10.50	7.50	DAYTON	10.15	2.15	6.15	7.30	7.35
8.35	3.40	11.40	8.40	Springfield	9.30	1.30	5.30	6.45	6.45
9.45	4.50	12.50	9.50	Ar COLUMBUS Lv	8.15	12.15	4.15	5.30	5.30 Note
P M	P M	P M	A M		A M	P M	P M	P M	P M

NOTE—Train 507 operates from Columbus through to Cincinnati, Sundays and Holidays only.

1 2

The recently launched Cincinnati & Lake Erie Railroad in its October 12, 1930, public timetable enthusiastically promoted its "Luxurious C. & L. E. Flyers," better known as "Red Devils." *(Author's collection)*

662 percent over those in June," noted interurban historian William Middleton. "Only three weeks after the new equipment entered service the Big Four Railroad threw in the sponge and discontinued its competing Cincinnati-Columbus *Senator*."[35]

The upgrades orchestrated by Dr. Conway failed to insure a financially healthy C&LE. The deepening national depression forced the C&LE into receivership in 1932, and competing automobile competition

The C&LE made the public aware of the victory that "Red Devil" No. 126 had achieved in its race with a biplane on July 7, 1930. This event was subsequently shown in a Pathe newsreel in movie houses from coast to coast. A few days after the staged race, Car No. 122 travels through downtown Dayton near the corner of Main and Third Streets publicizing that all week the State Theater would show this exciting contest. *(Krambles-Peterson Archive)*

led to its abandonment seven years later. The high-speed Red Devils, however, did not go to scrappers, some being sold to the Lehigh Valley Transit Company and others going to the Cedar Rapids & Iowa City Railway, known as the CRANDIC. On the latter road, they earned the nickname of Vomit Comets, likely coined by students at the University of Iowa due to these cars jarring passengers when speeding over rough sections of track.[36]

Although the C&LE died, two other midwestern interurbans, North Shore Line and Illinois Terminal (née Illinois Traction), later provided passengers with what can be described as bona fide streamliners. "In almost every aspect except their overall length [these cars] were essentially comparable to contemporary streamlined main line railroad

Six years after C&LE No. 126, "the World's Fastest Interurban," reached a speed of ninety-seven miles per hour in its winning race with a biplane, the somewhat battered car stops at Springboro Pike in Moraine City, Ohio, not far from where it had its memorable victory. In the background is a Frigidaire manufacturing plant. *(W. C. Janssen photograph, Krambles-Peterson Archive)*

equipment," opined William Middleton. In 1941 the North Shore Line introduced its two four-car articulated, air-conditioned Electroliners on its double tracked line between Chicago and Milwaukee. Eight years later the Illinois Terminal Railroad (IT) placed in service three blue and aluminum trains, two of which consisted of passenger-baggage combines, coaches, and parlor cars (the other lacked a parlor car). The St. Louis Car Company produced this twilight equipment; in fact, these interurban cars were the last ones built in America.[37]

The Electroliners were the more famous of the interurban streamliners. Colonel Albert Sprague, the North Shore Line's receiver, raised the nearly $300,000 for their purchase. Sprague wanted to modernize the bankrupt company's image and services and hopefully avoid

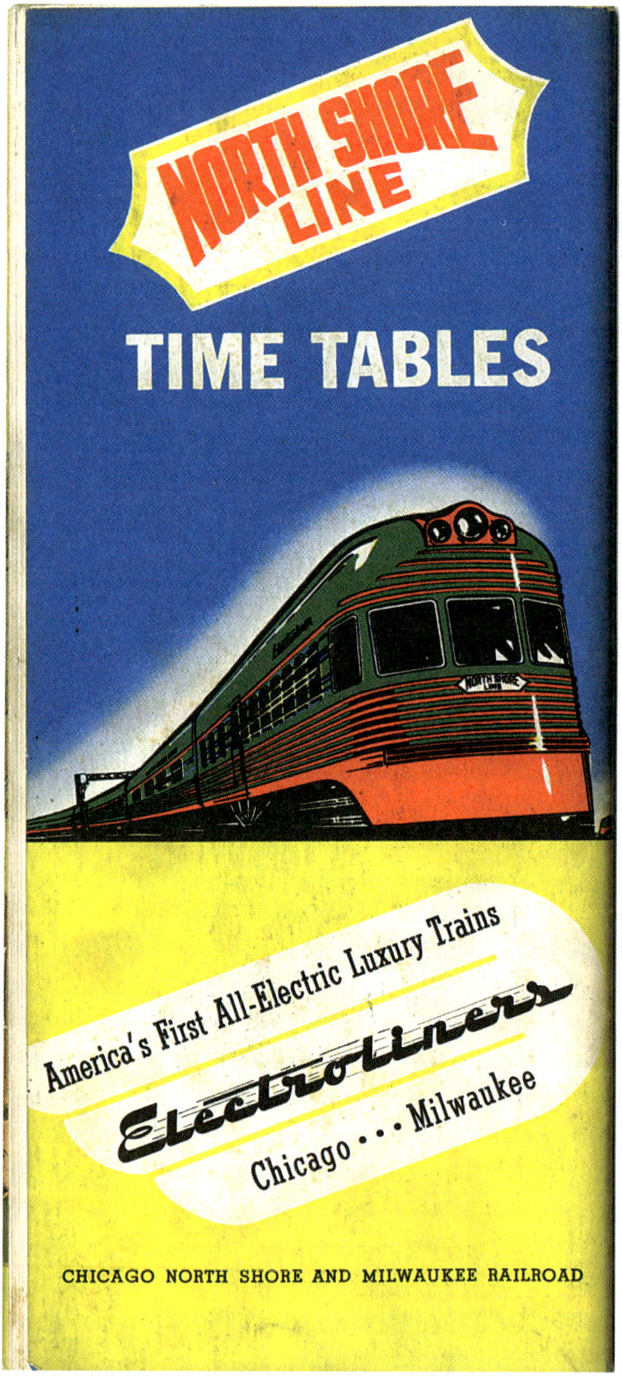
NORTH SHORE LINE
TIME TABLES
America's First All-Electric Luxury Trains
Electroliners
Chicago ... Milwaukee
CHICAGO NORTH SHORE AND MILWAUKEE RAILROAD

Facing, In its February 9, 1941, public timetable, the Chicago, North Shore & Milwaukee Railroad made certain that patrons knew that they could ride "America's First All-Electric Luxury Trains." And they did, especially during World War II. *(Author's collection)*

abandonment of this 114-mile road. The North Shore Line ballyhooed these state-of-the-art streamliners as "America's First All-Electric Luxury Trains." Promotional copy that appeared in its February 1941 public timetable said in part, "Thrill to an entirely new experience in smooth-flowing travel on swift, silent ELECTROLINERS—the North Shore Line's incomparable new 'trains of the future' in service today!" The hype continued: "Here are trains with ultra-modern appointments, luxurious equipment and club-like atmosphere unsurpassed in railroad service. Down to the last minute detail, every facility of the ELECTROLINERS is designed to give you *all-luxury* travel—at regular coach fares—on *all-electric* trains, electrically operated even to temperature control and electro-pneumatic brakes." Concluded the North Shore Line, "NEVER BEFORE TRAINS LIKE THESE! Deep-upholstered seats, separate smoking lounges, superbly equipped Tavern-Lounge Cars with softly cushioned settees and unique refreshment appointments. Here indeed is high-speed, all electric luxury travel, the first of its kind in America." Using the high-speed cutoff through the Skokie Valley west of the original Shore Line route, Electroliners were capable of traveling at eighty-five miles per hour for the eighty-seven miles between the Chicago Loop and downtown Milwaukee. These two train sets served the public and company well, remaining in service until the road's abandonment in January 1963.[38]

Unlike the North Shore Line streamliners, the ones acquired by the 466-mile IT proved to be a poor investment. It was an ill-advised million-dollar last-ditch attempt to remain competitive in the passenger business between numerous Prairie State destinations and St. Louis. Although in the late 1940s the IT had reduced or curtailed service on portions of its system, it introduced three air-conditioned streamliners, two with three cars (motor, trailer, and parlor) and one with two cars (motor and trailer), on November 7, 1948. The company had worked

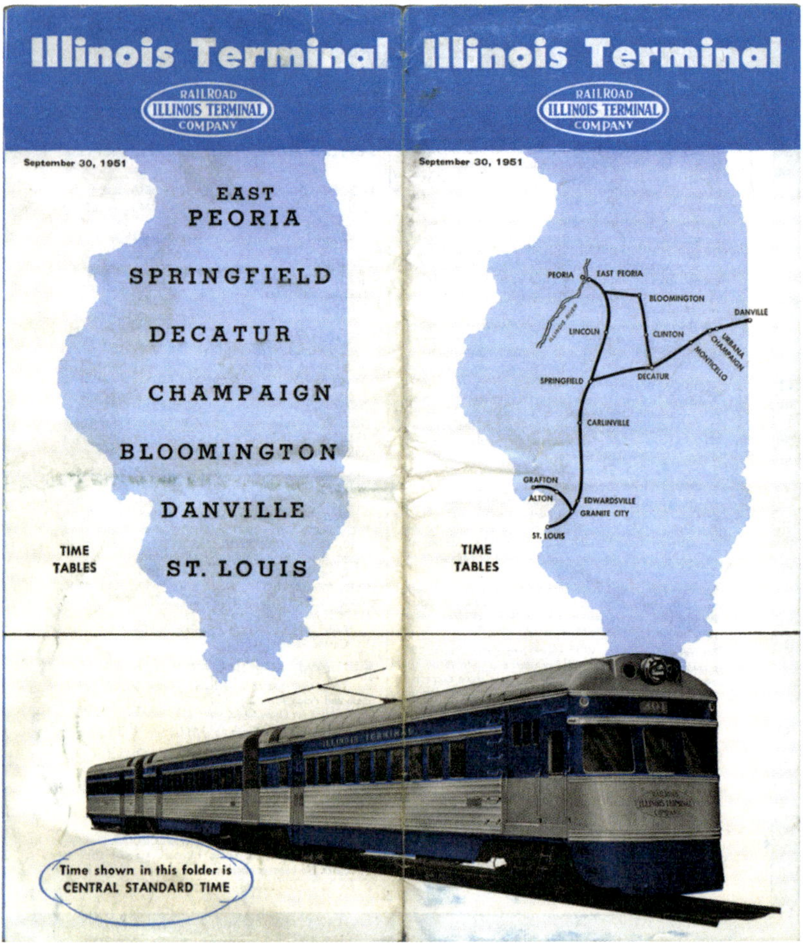

Resembling the North Shore Line, the Illinois Terminal Railroad incorporated an image of its streamlined interurban cars on the cover of its September 30, 1951, public timetable. But within several years, disappointing patronage led to the end of this service. *(Author's collection)*

carefully with the builder, but there was an initial flaw: its streamliners could not negotiate the tight curves into the downtown Peoria station, forcing passengers to use its new albeit less convenient depot in East Peoria. These nonarticulated train sets traveled less rapidly than did the Electroliners, needing to run over more city streets. Train No. 91, for example, left East Peoria at 9:00 a.m. and arrived in St. Louis at 1:45 p.m., a distance of 171 miles, making fifteen intermediate stops and additional ones when flagged. The IT also operated its third set between Decatur and St. Louis, leaving the East Peoria–St. Louis line at Springfield. Even though it bragged that "here is postwar luxury travel at its thrilling stream-lined finest," revenues could not long sustain operations. By the mid-1950s the company had won permission from the Illinois Commerce Commission to end virtually all of its passenger operations, including its streamliners, on March 3, 1956.[39]

Although interurban mileage in the Midwest had shrunk dramatically by 1940, passenger-carrying electric roads continued to serve the region. The epicenter of these activities was Chicago. Here the "Insull's interurbans," named for Midland Utilities Company magnate Samuel Insull, had since the mid-1920s provided frequent, dependable service in a multidirectional fashion from the Loop. In addition to the North Shore Line, the Insull empire included the Chicago, Aurora & Elgin (CA&E) and the Chicago, South Shore & South Bend (South Shore) Railroads. The CA&E continued to operate until the late 1950s, and the South Shore remains today with patrons being served by the Northern Indiana Commuter Transportation District. A private operator, Anacostia Rail Holdings Company, provides freight service as well. During World War II, this interurban network, especially the North Shore Line, experienced its greatest patronage.[40]

WORLD WAR II

Railroading in the Midwest in the first part of the 1940s hardly resembled what had taken place in the 1930s. "It has been either feast or famine," opined an Erie Railroad official in 1944. "We've experienced that long depression when traffic fell, workers were furloughed and our company went bankrupt, and now every resource is being taxed to the limit. We're being forced to hire high-school lads and pull men out of retirement." He added happily, "We're paying dividends on our company stock." This Cleveland-based railroad was extremely proud that it could declare a modest dividend in 1942, the first one in sixty-nine years. The press release, orchestrated by Robert Woodruff, its image-conscious president, said in part, "Wall Street tradition was shattered and Brokers were dazedly groping for reliable replacements for the immemorial dictums—When Erie Common pays a dividend, there'll be icicles in hell—and three things are certain—Death, Taxes, and no dividends for Erie Common."[41]

During the war years, railroads desperately sought workers. Enlistments and the draft had taken their toll. The public was hardly surprised to read newspaper advertisements like this one: "HIGH SCHOOL BOYS 16 OR OLDER RAILROADS NEED WORKERS. Back up America's fighting forces." The IC, for example, trained thousands of these youngsters who were ineligible for the draft. Women were not ignored, being hired for routine maintenance jobs, station and tower operators (using telephones rather than telegraph instruments), and other duties. They were the Rosie the Riveters of the rails. Midwestern carriers, especially Chicago-based ones, hired Mexican nationals for seasonal maintenance-of-way jobs. Retirees, particularly shop workers, were also asked to return "for the duration." The Wabash issued this general call for help: "Wanted—Males—Railroad carpenters, carpenter helpers, extra gang laborers, machinists, boilermakers, telegraph operators. Steady Work, good pay."[42]

Workers were not only in high demand to maintain railroad equipment and to operate trains; locomotive manufacturers in the Midwest also needed them during the ongoing war effort. EMD, Fairbanks-Morse, and Lima contributed to the cause by building locomotives for domestic and export use and supplying a range of armaments and marine propulsion products for the War Department. In a contemporary magazine advertisement, Fairbanks-Morse revealed how employees at its Beloit, Wisconsin, plant contributed: "Submarines and locomotives make similar demands on their engines. Both demand great power, compactness, heavy-duty construction, dependability, and easy, quick serviceability." Added the copy, "That's why it is significant to railroad men that the Navy uses more than two million horsepower of these [opposed-piston] Diesels."[43]

What about travelers? People who had forsaken trains for their automobiles or buses rediscovered that their communities had depots and likely passenger trains. They did so because gasoline, tires, and replacement auto parts were rationed. If one possessed an "A" ration gasoline coupon, how far could you travel on four gallons a week? The reverse side of the coupon contained this timely question: "Is this trip really necessary?" There was also a federally mandated thirty-five-mile-per-hour highway speed limit. A station agent in Iowa recalled that when individuals flocked to his depot during the war, a surprising number did not know how to interpret a public timetable or even to tell the difference between a.m. and p.m. There were those, too, who didn't fully comprehend that the Midwest was now on Central War Time (Daylight Savings Time). As inexperienced or first-time train patrons, they commonly asked questions. The range might (and probably did) annoy the ticket or station agent. "How do I know if the train is on time?" "Where do I find my seat on the train?" "Is there a diner?" "Does my train have toilets?" "Where do I put my 'grip' and will it be safe?"[44]

The war years of 1941 to 1945 proved to be the finest hour for American railroads. Carriers responded to the unprecedented demands caused by total mobilization that ultimately led to victory over fascist forces in Europe and Asia. "Without transportation we could not fight at all," contended Joseph Eastman, director of the Office of Defense Transportation, in 1943. No one in government, railroad circles, or elsewhere challenged his observation. Eastman's agency worked well, having a less cumbersome and far-reaching bureaucracy than the US Railroad Administration of the World War I era.[45]

The basic statistics of American rails during World War II were impressive. Between 1941 and 1944, railroads carried 83 percent of the increase of all traffic, and they handled 91 percent of all military freight and 98 percent of all military personnel. MAIN (Military Authorization Identification Number) extras crisscrossed the region. These trains moved frequently and transported tens of thousands of service men and women and their impedimenta. Freight traffic, measured in ton-miles, soared from 373 billion in 1940 to 737 billion in 1944. It took the industry until 1966—two decades of general prosperity and population growth—to surpass the latter figure. Passenger volume, expressed in revenue passenger-miles, skyrocketed from twenty-three billion in 1940 to ninety-five billion in 1944, a peak number never again attained. Unlike bus and trucking companies, railroads had surplus freight and passenger cars standing idle in yards and on sidings during the Great Depression, and with modest repairs they could press them into active service. There is no debate that during these forty-five months railroads helped win the war.[46]

The dramatic increase in freight and passenger traffic knew no geographical bounds, but the Midwest can arguably be considered the busiest region in the nation. There were steel mills in Cleveland, Gary, and Youngstown; tire plants in Akron, Detroit, and Findlay, Ohio; and automobile makers turned military hardware manufacturers in Detroit, Toledo, and South Bend. Extensive agricultural and agribusiness operations became widespread. Farmers frequently planted from fence line to fence line and labored in their fields throughout the planting, growing, and harvest seasons. Regional railroaders were also overworked. In October 1942 John Grover, a writer for the Associated Press who visited midwestern locations by traveling on a series of freight trains, described the situation: "Paperwork was multiplied as freight piles up and must be moved. The pressure on yard and roundhouse repair crews increases as equipment is speeded up and wears out. From the Big Guy worrying his brains out in the main office to the last gandy-dancer on the end of a pick on a branch line right of way, railroaders are working the hours it takes to move the freight that's got to move." Grover related a conversation he had overheard between two Erie employees in Marion, Ohio, the location of a major shops facility:

> "Yay, Smitty, how y' doing? Playing the horses lately?"
> "Playin' 'em, hell. I'm the horse. I've had only one day off since April."
> "Ya big sissy. What's a day off? I don't remember."

Continued Grover, "Everywhere among the nation's railroad men, the clock is the enemy. They're always fighting time. They hauled a crippled tank car out of the line at Marion, slapped a new set of wheels on it and had it ready to go along with us by the time our engine was serviced." He might have noted that established safety rules were often ignored during these hectic times.[47]

Tonnage moved. About the time that Grover rode freights, the positive impact of the FT diesel was graphically revealed. The B&O dispatched from Chicago a train with seventy-six loaded oil tankers for the 805-mile trip to Baltimore. It was a continuous run, except for crew changes and several refueling stops. A steam-powered movement would have taken considerably longer.[48]

Taking virtually any train through one of the Midwest's terminals could be daunting, especially for civilians. Some of the busiest ones in the nation were located in the region. Take the number of intercity trains. In June 1942 St. Louis Union Station led the list of the eighteen most active with 156, Kansas City Union Station was second with 133, Chicago Union Station was third with 124, and Cincinnati Union Terminal ranked fifth with 112. Tied for eighteenth place were Akron Union Station with 40 and Milwaukee Road Station in Minneapolis, also with 40. The volume of military traffic, both on regularly scheduled and troop trains, made for busy hubs and crowded coaches, sleepers, and diners. Railroad after railroad, including passenger-carrying interurbans, urged patrons to realize that wartime demands had altered traditional travel. In its December 1942 public timetable, the North Shore Line devoted a full page to "the WAR TRANSPORTATION . . . and YOU!" The copy said in part, "Naturally there are new problems to be met. With more and more people shifted to public transportation, equipment must be used to the utmost. At the same time the most rigid conservation of vital materials must be effected." The commentary added, "The North Shore Line, in addition to carrying a greatly increased number of war workers and an ever-growing host of tire and gasoline restricted travelers, also has important Military transportation responsibilities. It serves two of the nation's most important Army and Navy establishments—Fort Sheridan and Great Lakes Naval Training Station. In effect, this is the same as though several densely populated cities had suddenly been added to the many important ones the railroad already serves." The North Shore Line suggested when to purchase tickets and the best and worst times to travel. With its heavy patronage, riders were urged to board and leave trains as rapidly as possible.[49]

The traveling public understood that it must make adjustments. Diner opportunities became restricted. Multiple railroads limited service to breakfast and dinner, perhaps requiring the evening meal to take place as early as 4:00 p.m. Sleeping car space might be difficult or impossible to book, and toward the end of the war the Office of Defense

Transportation ordered railroads to end Pullman trips that were 450 miles or less. It also suspended trains that averaged less than 35 percent occupancy. Some riders had to stand for all or part of their journeys. "During the war our passenger trains were filled to overflowing," recalled a Santa Fe official. "Everyone, it seemed, was on the move, especially the servicemen. Their wives and children traipsed back and forth across the country trying to keep up with them. I saw many women with tiny babies stand in a vestibule, or sit on a suitcase, from Chicago to Los Angeles." A young schoolteacher who was riding on the Milwaukee Road from Marion (Cedar Rapids) to Coon Rapids, Iowa, a distance of 165 miles, recalled that she never found a coach seat, using her suitcase instead. While personally uncomfortable she knew that the "soldier boys" and the elderly trumped her needs. Travelers endured.[50]

No wartime train ride was "typical." There were dirty cars, late departures and arrivals, and impolite trainmen. After V-J Day thousands of discharged army, marine, and navy personnel flocked to the rails. At times it was chaos, especially when they were joined by nonmilitary travelers during the 1945 Christmas season. More than fifteen thousand people packed Chicago Union Station on December 21. The following day the NYC, which used the nearby La Salle Street Station, briefly suspended ticket sales for its eastbound trains. Military personnel and civilians probably remembered their wartime railroad experiences, and some (maybe many) resolved that they would never again take a train, or at least not in the foreseeable future. It was time to travel the highways and byways of America in automobiles.[51]

INDIAN SUMMER

Midwestern railroaders knew that they had contributed significantly to the national euphoria of V-E Day and V-J Day in May and August 1945. While travelers, especially those who had experienced troop movements by rail, may have wanted to avoid trains for an extended period, the industry expressed its optimism about its future, anticipating a prosperous peace. Notwithstanding the burdens of state and federal regulation (although with modest concessions having been provided by the Transportation Act of 1940), carriers entered what might be considered an

Indian summer. These years gave railroaders a false sense of well-being and proved rather short lasting, dating roughly from the close of World War II to the end of the Korean War. Railroads encountered the growing sting of modal competition. Most came from automobiles and trucks, which traveled over an expanding network of toll roads and superhighways, aided immensely by the Interstate Highway Act of 1956. Airlines with their faster and larger craft took their toll as well. Yet by the mid-1950s, air transport claimed only 26.1 percent of all intercity passenger travel, while railroads had 42.3 percent, although down from 53.1 percent at the end of the 1940s. Airline, barge, bus, and trucking companies were aided by having most of their infrastructure built and maintained by government, and each enjoyed lower tax burdens. Railroads encountered other problems, including management-labor relations caused by persistent inflation and work-rule issues.[52]

Why this initial rosy outlook among railroaders? There were numerous indicators that the postwar period would be a time of prosperity. There was a pent-up demand for consumer goods, scarce or unobtainable during the war. These pressures stimulated manufacturing, especially in the factory centers of the Midwest, as the country transitioned from "guns to butter," or what economists called "reconversion." And lumber and building materials were needed to respond to an acute housing shortage. Wartime savings, whether in bank accounts, in savings bonds, or stuffed in mattresses, meant that there was discretionary money to spend for new homes, automobiles, appliances, and everyday needs. This occurred even though war-era taxes had soared, and employers for the first time were required to withhold federal taxes from wages. The bugaboo of inflation continued. Also, for many residents of the region, there was the urge to travel and to do so in style. Perhaps it might be a trip to the summer resorts of the North Woods of Michigan, national parks in the West, or somewhere else, or simply to visit family or friends. Dinner in the diner could now be enjoyed at a leisurely pace, and menu items were plentiful. Jelly and jams, for example, reappeared, and coffee, which had been limited to a single cup at breakfast, could be consumed to one's desire.[53]

Just as the Zephyr and the M-10000 caught the public's imagination before the war, a host of new streamliners, designed for long-distance travel, appeared as the decade waned. One eye-opener was an industry first, introduced by the Burlington. This was the Vista-Dome car. The company placed the prototype "Silver Dome" on one of its northbound Twin Cities Zephyrs that departed from Union Station in Chicago on July 23, 1945. It allowed passengers to see in all directions around the train and offered an "engineer's eye view." In this case they could enjoy the scenery as tracks skirted portions of the upper Mississippi River. The Budd Company began producing domes for the Burlington; it received an order for forty more and soon found additional customers. This enthusiasm for quality streamliners was expressed by Harry Murphy, Burlington's pro-passenger president: "Take away the passenger train, and a railroad is nothing more than a truck company."[54]

Dome cars, whether gracing passenger, diner, parlor, or sleeping cars, helped spur leisure travel and combat airplane competition. Other railroads that operated in the Midwest acquired dome equipment, including the B&O, GN, Milwaukee Road, Northern Pacific, Santa Fe, UP–North Western, and Wabash. The latter road took pride in its new Blue Bird train set, which entered the competitive market between Chicago and St. Louis in February 1950. This $1.5 million streamliner offered three dome chair cars and a dome parlor-observation car for which the Pullman Company provided the staff. It appeared to be a shrewd investment. In "Trains That Pay," which appeared in the May 1952 issue of *Railway Age,* the Blue Bird was singled out as one of the country's leading moneymaking passenger trains.[55]

During the immediate post–World War II years, most Class I railroads that served Chicago, St. Louis, and other midwestern cities upgraded their principal passenger trains. The NYC stands out with its betterments. "If any railroad could have made passenger service profitable, certainly New York Central could have," opined historian Geoffrey Doughty. "The railroad spent millions of dollars on stations, equipment, property, labor, and advertising." The company began its hype in 1946: "The low-level passenger routes of the New York Central System, noted for comfort and ease of operation over the lowest altitudes and easiest grades between East and West, and always leaders in passenger transportation, are now receiving new sleeping cars and deluxe coaches the like of which never has been seen." Two years later it introduced the "Great

Steel Fleet" of diesel-powered and Budd-built named trains. "That is the supreme importance of the *New* in the New York Central," advertised the company. "This program of progress is reinforcing one of America's vital rail lines . . . the Great Steel Fleet that links East and West along the *Water Level Route*." Every major line had one or more of these smart trains. Midwesterners could take the James Whitcomb Riley between Chicago, Indianapolis, and Cincinnati; the Ohio State Limited between Cincinnati, Dayton, Columbus, and New York City; the Twilight Limited between Chicago and Detroit; and the Detroiter between the Motor City and New York City. Included in this lineup of "Now—World's Largest Fleet of Newly Equipped Trains" was the refurbished 20th Century Limited. Proclaimed the NYC, "*The* favorite train of famous people." No one questioned that this New York to Chicago limited was designed for the high-end clientele. Business executives with their expense accounts could afford its posh accommodations. The company also announced, "The 20th Century-Limited is known for three things—dependability of its schedule, the tasteful elegance of its appointments, and the variety of special services it offers to make your trip comfortable, convenient, and completely enjoyable." On September 17, 1948, its two train sets entered service between Grand Central Terminal and La Salle Street Station, making this trip in sixteen and a half hours. (The PRR's Broadway Limited, also upgraded in 1948, had a similar running time.) The NYC and other carriers might discover that the inauguration of their upgraded trains bolstered patronage on companion ones that had not received streamlined equipment.[56]

Even a small midwestern Class I road enhanced its core postwar passenger operations. The Chicago, Indianapolis & Louisville Railroad (the Monon), a 552-mile largely Indiana carrier, is the foremost example. In 1946 the company received new leadership when a talented railroader, John W. Barriger III, took the throttle as president. He immediately sought to improve this bankrupt, rather woebegone property. Betterments included revitalizing its mainline passenger service between Chicago and Louisville and Chicago and Indianapolis. With limited resources the company bought twenty-eight carbon-steel hospital cars that American Car & Foundry had built recently for the US Army. Refurbishing followed. Workers at the Monon's Lafayette shops converted this equipment into air-conditioned coaches, grill coaches, dining-parlor cars, dining-bar-lounge cars, and mail-baggage cars. Their attractive gray, white, and bright "Monon Royal Red" exterior paint scheme came at consultant Raymond Loewy's suggestion, as did their pleasing parlor-car interiors. The public liked these streamliners, and ridership initially spiked but soon declined. The Monon was no speedway, and automobile competition explained declining revenues.[57]

During the summers of 1948 and 1949, the optimism shown by railroads in the Midwest (and the nation, too) led to an exhibition extravaganza in Chicago. "The railroads, which usually talk to the public in conservative full-page ads and statistics," observed *Time* Magazine, "tried it with whoop-de-do and the can-can." What took place was the Chicago Railroad Fair, a "National Exhibition of Pageantry and Exhibits Depicting 100 Years of Railroad Progress." At the time it claimed the honor of being the largest public exposition ever mounted by a single industry.[58]

Where did the idea for "the Greatest Railroad Show" originate? Francis (Frank) Koval, publicity manager for the North Western, can be credited with the concept. He viewed the 1948 centennial of the first train in Chicago, which operated on North Western predecessor Galena & Chicago Union, as an opportunity for company self-promotion. The top administration officers, including President Roland (Bud) Williams, endorsed Koval's suggestion. Working closely with the *Chicago Tribune* and the Museum of Science and Industry, the North Western made plans and raised money.[59]

On July 20, 1948, the fair opened south of the Loop on a fifty-acre strip along Lake Michigan. Thirty-five railroads and the Pullman Company joined the North Western with displays and other attractions, including the "Wheels a-Rolling" pageant. Attendance exceeded expectations. More than 2.5 million visitors paid several million dollars to learn about how railroads revolutionized the Windy City and America and to see aspects of this modern way to move goods and people. The enthusiastic public response led to an encore the following year.[60]

While the evolution of the railroads was proudly displayed at the Chicago Railroad Fair, there was seemingly a hitch in the onward progress of the industry. This involved efforts in the 1950s to introduce futuristic trains. They were diesel-powered, lightweight, and low-center-of-gravity products, and two stand out in the Midwest. Although the Indian summer had largely passed, some railroad leaders still believed, as had Dr. Thomas Conway of C&LE fame, that a market existed for medium-distance, ultramodern rail service.

On January 30, 1956, the Rock Island placed in operation between Chicago and Peoria its exotic Jet Rocket (renamed the Peorian). Built by American Car & Foundry Company, this lightweight, low-center-of-gravity, and fuel-efficient three-car train that tilted on curves had an EMD 1,200-horsepower locomotive patterned after Talgo trains found on the Spanish National Railways. "It is our belief that with this train we will be able to re-educate the traveling public to the advantages of train travel getting them off jam-packed highways and into the worry-free relaxation of a train," explained company president Downing Jenks. This new train, however, quickly disappointed Jenks, the Rock Island, and the public. There were mechanical problems, including the braking system. Almost immediately passengers made numerous complaints. The train was noisy and rough-riding, seats were small, toilets cramped, and ceilings low. Riders quickly (and appropriately) named the Jet Rocket the "Jolting Jet." A novel closed-circuit television camera, mounted in the nose of the locomotive, hardly added to the enjoyment for lounge patrons. "[It showed] the repeated near-misses with pedestrians, school buses, gasoline trucks and gravel haulers at grade crossings," observed one writer, "[and] excitement quickly gave way to sheer terror." After several months the Peorian was replaced with its predecessor consists. After modifications this experimental train entered commuter service between Chicago and Joliet, Illinois, and made its last run on April 24, 1965. Due to high maintenance costs and lack of a buyer, it became scrap. Had it been worth its initial price tag of $788,000?[61]

The NYC likewise tried a futuristic train, promoted enthusiastically by board chairman Robert R. Young, who in June 1954 seized control of the company. It would run between the three largest cities in Ohio: Cleveland, Columbus, and Cincinnati. Company officials believed that such a train would bolster ridership along this corridor and reduce operating costs. Baldwin–Lima–Hamilton (Lima had been absorbed by Baldwin in 1951) produced the 1,000-horsepower diesel-hydraulic drive locomotive for Xplorer, renamed the Ohio Xplorer (the X connoting innovation). Pullman-Standard provided the nine short, lightweight articulated coaches with their low center of gravity and guided axles. The train, too, claimed high-speed capabilities. Although the NYC announced the debut of the Ohio Xplorer in late April 1956, it did not enter revenue service until May 27, 1956. As with the Rock Island's Peorian, passengers made multiple complaints, emphasizing its rough riding qualities. Crew members likewise grumbled. The train experienced annoying mechanical problems, including a transmission that sometimes overheated. Since engine and transmission components were German made, replacement parts were specialized and at times hard to find. The NYC dispatched the Ohio Xplorer for its final run on August 17, 1957, and the equipment soon left the property. The owner of the Pickens Railroad, an upstate South Carolina shortline, acquired the train set and briefly operated it on excursions over his eleven-mile road between Easley and Pickens. Later the Xplorer became a derelict artifact of the lightweight passenger train interlude, being scrapped in about 1970. Simply stated, lightweight trains proved a bust, and this midcentury dream died.[62]

A passenger train option that did not turn to dross was the Budd Rail Diesel Car—the RDC, often called the Budd Car. This new concept option for passenger carriers, which the Edward C. Budd Company manufactured between 1949 and 1962, offered that smart stainless-steel streamlined look, resembling at a glance a Burlington Vista-Dome car. (Unlike what some trackside observers thought, only the cooling system radiators were roof mounted.) The Budd Company designed this product for branch-line and commuter service. Its highly functional propulsion system was inspired by wartime knowledge gained from powering tanks with compact diesel engines. Budd installed these lightweight, self-propelled rail cars with two small under-the-floor 275-horsepower General Motors/Detroit Diesel engines. It offered four basic options: the RDC-1 with ninety seats; the RDC-2 baggage section with seventy-one seats; the RDC-3 with a Railway Post Office car, a baggage compartment, and forty-nine seats; and the RDC-4, a self-contained RPO-express car. Budd also built an RDC-9. This was a coach without controls. As *Trains* editor David P. Morgan opined correctly, "[The RDC] is more than a glorified doodlebug."[63]

A compelling demonstration of the quality of Budd-built RDCs came in May 1955 when the Washington, DC, chapter of the National Railway Historical Society arranged with the B&O for a Memorial Day weekend excursion aboard a trio of RDCs (one RDC-1 and two RDC-2s) between the nation's capital and Chicago, a distance of 768 miles. On the westbound trip, this consist made brief stops for refueling or crew changes at Cumberland, Maryland; Pittsburgh, Pennsylvania; New Castle Junction, Pennsylvania; Willard, Ohio; and Garrett, Indiana. It took only twelve and a half hours at an average speed of 61.5 miles per hour to reach the Windy City. Railroaders thought this an impressive run, considering that the route involved crossing the spine of the Appalachians at Allegheny Mountain, West Virginia, and through Pittsburgh, one of the most congested industrial and metropolitan centers in the country. The eastbound return run, which repeated details of the westbound journey, was equally stellar. These two trips showed that RDCs, even though designed for short-haul trips, could provide fast acceleration on heavy grades, stop smoothly, and ride comfortably on a long mainline assignment. And there were no equipment failures; they were "magnificently built machines."[64]

Although the Budd Company found its best market for RDCs from railroads in New England and the mid-Atlantic states (being most popular on the Boston & Maine), they appeared regularly in the Midwest. RDC-1s operated on the Chicago & Eastern Illinois, the Duluth, South Shore & Atlantic, the NYC, and North Western; RDC-2s on the Grand Trunk Western and the North Western; and RDC-3s on the Duluth, Missabe & Iron Range, the Duluth, Winnipeg & Pacific, the Grand Trunk Western, the Northern Pacific, and the NYC. The B&O, Minneapolis & St. Louis, NYC, and Rock Island also acquired RDC-4s. These cars were dispatched either in single units or in multiple hookups, especially when assigned to commuter service. Some roads, such as the North Western, used their RDCs for only a few years. But unlike the lightweight experimental trains, these rugged cars readily found buyers in the secondhand marketplace.[65]

A footnote to the Budd Car story involved an RDC-3 that became the star in an unusual experiment on the NYC. Employees at its Cleveland

Technical Center took an older RDC, which had operated previously in Michigan, and made major modifications, most remarkably the installation of two General Electric J-47 jet engines. The goal was to set a US speed record. The tests of M-497, officially the Pride of the Central, took place on July 23–24, 1966, on 24.34 miles of tangent track between Butler, Indiana, and Stryker, Ohio. On the first eastbound run, the car reached a speed of 140 miles per hour, but on the repositioned second one it recorded an impressive 183.85 miles per hour. President Alfred (Al) Perlman, who rode in the fireman's seat, was pleased. What happened that July may have boosted company morale but really did nothing else.[66]

NEW STATIONS

Two of the late-date great midwestern passenger facilities appeared in Ohio, coming in June 1930 with Union Terminal in Cleveland and March 1933 with Union Terminal in Cincinnati. Both were architecturally stunning, state-of-the-art facilities, and each had appropriate interior designs that told passengers where to buy tickets, wait, and board trains. The Cleveland Union Terminal, located in the lower portion of the fifty-two-story Terminal Tower on Public Square, was not a bona fide union station; the PRR continued to use its lakefront depot. What became Forest City's most familiar and enduring landmark took years to complete, starting with site excavation in 1924 and steel work two years later. The Queen City of Ohio had long lacked a union station, with multiple depots dotting its urban landscape. Beginning at the turn of the twentieth century, there had been repeated attempts to construct such a facility. In 1923 the impasse was broken when the Cincinnati Railroad Development Company came into being. Five years later the Cincinnati Union Terminal Company was established, and construction of what became a "Great Temple of Transportation" started on the eve of the Wall Street crash of 1929. When completed, the Cincinnati facility (unlike the one in Cleveland) featured a green park, terraced fountains, and a dual-roadway plaza. Yet it was not centrally located, being one and a half miles west of the city center.[67]

The Indian summer years saw two additional union stations in the region, also in Ohio. One was located in Toledo and the other in Akron.

In 1950 Central Union Terminal opened in Toledo, south of downtown, and was described by the *New York Times* as the "$5,000,000 Dream of 40 Years." It replaced the city's outmoded 1886 Union Depot, which a fire had severely damaged in 1930. The repaired structure disappointed residents, who considered it a community embarrassment. Civic wrath reached such a pitch that a local businessman erected a billboard that read, "DON'T JUDGE TOLEDO BY ITS UNION STATION." Although NYC officials thought it unwise to replace a passenger station as automobile and airline competition intensified, C&O board chairman Robert R. Young pressured the other railroads to build that long-sought replacement. Young held considerable power in the railroad world and lived up to his growing reputation as "the gadfly on the rails."[68]

During "Dedication Week," September 7–12, 1950, Toledoans cheered the "Palace of Glass," a large, architecturally modified art deco structure, featuring the extensive and creative use of glass materials. After all, Toledo was known as the Glass City. The station offered a practical four-story layout, with the third level housing the main waiting room, ticketing facilities, and a connecting covered walkway to multiple tracks reached by elevators and stairs. There was also a covered terminal entrance that bridged the frontage street to a public parking and green-space area (today's Martin Luther King Jr. Plaza). The ground floor housed baggage and US mail facilities, and the second floor featured a YMCA and bunk rooms for train crews. The top level provided office space for the NYC's Toledo Division personnel. When the station opened, four trunk roads used it: B&O, C&O (successor to the Pere Marquette), NYC, and Wabash. Until the demise of privately operated passenger service, the complex became a local showcase. Yet it apparently had an operational shortcoming. In the late 1950s, NYC President Al Perlman complained that the station was "built on a curve, thereby complicating coupling." He was more unhappy with the substantial property-tax hike that came with this replacement facility.[69]

The post–World War II Akron union station coincided with what took place in Toledo, but with greater complexities. Just as Toledo had an old union depot, so did Akron. Since 1891 the station had served the B&O and PRR, and in 1901 the Erie joined as a tenant. (Later the AC&Y had its own depot adjacent to North Howard Street.) The city's population explosion during the 1910s due to the rapid expansion of the rubber industry made that facility obsolete. Furthermore, the depot was situated on a curve, showed signs of age, and was poorly placed at East Market and Canal Streets outside the downtown commercial core. In the early 1920s, civic leaders sought a better one but failed. Although increased automobile use and the Great Depression lessened demands for this community improvement, the early wartime surge of travelers sparked a renewed drive for a replacement. Soon the New Union Depot Civic League, composed of businessmen who included rubber company executives, pressured local and state government officials and the three railroads for action. Success, of sorts, followed. In 1942 the Ohio Public Service Corporation agreed to the organization's request. But the three passenger carriers did not jointly create a union station. The Erie quickly announced that it would construct its own depot. Tired of fussing with the B&O and PRR, President Woodruff and his board concluded that a separate depot would be less costly. This small two-level box structure of midcentury-modern-style architecture with an Indiana limestone facade, located on South Broadway Street about five blocks from the existing station, opened in 1947. It was both a passenger station and offices for local operations. The station continued in use following the Erie merger with the Delaware, Lackawanna & Western in 1960, which created the Erie Lackawanna Railroad. The final passenger train, the Lake Cities, ended the depot's purpose in January 1970, and the vacated structure was later demolished. Still, the Rubber City got its Union Depot. It was much larger than its Erie counterpart but had a similar architectural style. The joint B&O-PRR depot opened on April 28, 1950, to the joy of Akronites. Area residents used it primarily to board the B&O trains to Chicago, Pittsburgh, and Washington, DC. Resembling the Toledo and Erie structures, the Akron Union Station had an enclosed concourse that extended over the tracks, which were reached by either an elevator or stairs. Also, the city's newly built Greyhound Bus Terminal on South Broadway Street had a connecting over-the-tracks walkway. After the last train, the B&O's the Capitol Limited, left the city on May 1, 1971, the structure later became the property of the University of Akron and presently houses the Lisle M. Buckingham Center for Continuing Education.[70]

"Indian summer" had passed for midwestern railroads when the Santa Fe replaced its Galesburg, Illinois, station in 1964 with this one-story midcentury-modern-style structure. Some area residents preferred the existing depot, but the Santa Fe wanted a practical, energy-efficient building. *(Author's collection)*

The construction of union stations in the four Ohio cities pleased passengers, civic boosters, and participating railroads. Other midwestern metropolitan centers continued to have pre-automobile-era structures that were largely obsolete by the Indian summer years. They could be found in such places as Chicago, Indianapolis, Milwaukee, St. Louis, and the Twin Cities. These facilities with their headhouses and train sheds were too big and inconveniently located in the midst of downtown traffic congestion, where parking spaces were inadequate or virtually nonexistent. The new structures found in the Buckeye State did not generally share these limitations. Furthermore, they were less expensive to heat, light, and maintain.

The small manufacturing, meatpacking, and trade city of Ottumwa, Iowa, location of the Burlington Railroad's Ottumwa Division on its Chicago-to-Denver mainline, took delight in a replacement station that opened in 1951. The railroad engaged the architectural firm of Holabird, Root & Burgee to design this state-of-the-art combination passenger and divisional office structure. This company-made photograph dates from May 8, 1951. *(Don Hofsommer collection)*

Throughout the Indian summer years, remodeled and replacement depots appeared throughout the Midwest. If passenger service had ended, the waiting-room section of a combination-style depot might be removed. Fires, windstorms, the rare train wreck, or simply old age necessitated replacements. Most were small, being adequate to handle a dwindling number of passengers and LCL freight, and contained an agent's office. These plans generally came from internal company designs. Professional architects were occasionally involved. These structures were commonly of cement blocks or perhaps prefabricated metal and often had air-conditioning units.[71]

Ottumwa, Iowa, became one place with an upscale version of a smaller station. This manufacturing and meatpacking city of approximately twenty-five thousand residents and a Burlington division point had a deteriorating passenger-office depot, and so in the 1940s discussions developed for a replacement. Rather than creating plans internally, the railroad engaged the Chicago architectural firm of Holabird, Root & Burgee (now Holabird & Root) to draw plans for an appropriate structure. A few years earlier, it had designed the Burlington, Iowa, station following a fire that had consumed that elderly building. The result in Ottumwa was a similar two-story modernist-style station, consisting of a flat roof, broad eaves, and a stone-clad exterior. The trackside level featured a large waiting room, a ticket desk, and a baggage section, and the second floor housed Ottumwa Division offices. The formal opening occurred in May 1951. Technically, this was a union station. For a short time, the Rock Island joined the Burlington, operating a daily motor train between Eldon, Iowa, located on its transcontinental Golden State Route, and Des Moines.[72]

CONTINUING DIESELIZATION

The diesel revolution helps explain the optimism of midwestern railroads during the Indian summer interlude. High usage during the war years had taken a toll mechanically on thousands of steam locomotives. "We have many worn out old steamers there in Decatur and Moberly," observed a Wabash employee in 1947. "It's time to get rid of most or all of them." Undeniably, replacements were badly needed. Moreover, less frequent shopping, range of operations, and pulling power were convincing selling points. Not to be ignored were the possibilities of labor savings. Take this example: if there were no steamers, there would be no need for water department employees who helped quench the thirst of the iron horses. It took little or no persuasion for most railroads to dieselize as rapidly as possible. "There was no reason for any fast smart talking diesel salesmen coming to headquarters," recalled a North Western official. "They didn't even need to have big expense accounts."[73]

Railroads had a wide range of choices for their specific power needs. By 1950 there were six major diesel builders, although EMD dominated with production plants in La Grange and Cleveland. What became the workhorse locomotive for numerous midwestern roads, large and small, appeared in October 1949 when EMD introduced its first General Purpose road-switcher—the GP-7 or "Geep." Soon demonstrator No. 100 performed well on the North Western, Milwaukee Road, and Soo Line. It had evolved quickly from the disappointing BL2s (designed for branch lines and local service) that the company had produced in 1948 and 1949. Of the fifty-eight BL2s built, most of these semistreamlined locomotives had gone to the C&O/Pere Marquette, Missouri Pacific, Monon, and Rock Island. Operators complained about numerous problems associated with these diesels. The BL-2 was "the diesel that didn't." A better albeit comparable replacement was the goal, and it would be the GP-7. In 1950 alone EMD built 459 of these new models. This versatile and economical hood-unit diesel could function as a switcher but could also work in freight and passenger service. (If assigned to passenger runs, the Geep required a boiler for train heating.) The GP-7 and later the GP-9 and GP-18 were aptly described as "handy all-around units." Reflected EMD chief engineer Max Ephraim Jr. in 1995, "Thus was the 'Geep,' like the mythical Phoenix, born from the ashes of its predecessor, the BL2, and it became the most popular locomotive ever built."[74]

Whether a Geep or some other diesel type, the triumph of diesel-electric technology—likely the biggest change in railroading since the air brake—resulted in an altered corridor landscape, as water tanks and coaling towers (a few too expensive to raze) came tumbling down. The process of dieselization contributed to a larger permanent decline in railroad employment than any other single development in industry history. Steam back shops, once staffed by scores of boilermakers and other skilled workers, became diesel repair facilities with fewer employees or were permanently closed. Still, those railroaders who worked on diesel maintenance needed multiple skills. There was that early exaggerated saying: "On a steam locomotive it took five minutes to find a problem and five hours to fix it, but on a diesel it took five hours to find the problem and five minutes to fix it."[75]

By 1960 the first generation of dieselization had mostly ended. This came about due in part to financing arrangements that commonly extended from fifteen to twenty years and mechanical obsolescence. There also existed the need for more powerful locomotives as longer and heavier freight trains became more common, although adding more units to the head end was an unpopular alternative. By the mid-1950s steam locomotives seemed exotic; the US had become the leader among large nations in dieselization. Roads like the C&O, IC, and PRR were slower to dieselize, being heavily dependent on the coal business. As the 1950s ended, a few steamers remained in "standby service"; they might be dispatched when there was a surge in traffic or when floodwaters inundated tracks. Take the Burlington. In 1963 its roster listed just seven steam locomotives. This factor in this wholesale technology replacement is frequently overlooked: the substantial financial gains that dieselization gave railroads had mostly run their course by the early to mid-1950s.[76]

"FEATHERBEDDING"

Railroad companies in the Midwest could have reaped greater savings from the post–World War II diesel revolution had it not been for "featherbedding." (This is a pejorative term and a dirty word among organized railroad labor.) What it means is unneeded and unproductive work. Wabash president Herman Pevler called it "the continuance of archaic working rules." When it came to diesels, were firemen really necessary? Had state full-crew laws become an expensive anachronism? Were small-town station agents earning their keep?

After World War II, a bitter fight erupted over the extent to which management could alter work rules. The greatest conflict involved the struggle to remove firemen from diesel locomotives. Earlier in the twentieth century, gasoline-powered motor trains lacked firemen, as did pioneer diesel switch engines. But that policy changed. When the Burlington and Union Pacific introduced their streamliners, they agreed to place a fireman in the cab. Why? The answer is twofold: diesels were rare, and the companies thought that passengers would feel safer if they knew that these technologically advanced fast trains were fully staffed.

But as the Indian summer waned, carriers notified the Brotherhood of Locomotive Firemen and Enginemen (BLFE) that firemen were at best optional. The Association of American Railroads, the industry's trade group, orchestrated a nationwide attack on the BLFE. One advertisement read, "*More* FIREMEN FEATHERBEDDING? . . . a threatened return to the horse and buggy era!" After a seven-year struggle between labor and management, the union eventually lost its hard-fought battle. It took the US Supreme Court in March 1963 to finally uphold the industry's right to alter work rules. The BLFE continued to fuss and to seek member protection. Ultimately diesel demonstrated that time-honored work rules could not survive the inroads of new technologies.[77]

Another set of work rules that midwestern rail managements fought were state-imposed full-crew laws. The most blatant one involved an Indiana statute that required freight trains operating within its borders to have a third brakeman if the consist had seventy or more cars. The law made sense when trainmen needed to scamper from car top to car top to set and release brakes, which was especially dangerous and even life-threatening during inclement weather. Hoosier State lawmakers did not repeal this law until 1972, notwithstanding opposition from the Brotherhood of Railroad Trainmen (BRT), the largest of the railroad brotherhoods.[78] Yet there was a protection clause. If a BRT trainman had been hired before that time, they were protected. This job security lasted into the early 1980s. Other states, including Ohio and Wisconsin, had statutes that made mandatory five crewmen on freight trains, and they remained in effect until the 1970s and 1980s. Deaths, retirements, and resignations also helped eliminate make-work.[79]

A glaring example of featherbedding could be found among small-town station agents. It would be the North Western that spearheaded the drive to remove employees who worked for only a few hours a day, some laboring for as little as an hour or less. What followed was another conflict between management and labor, specifically the North Western versus the Order of Railroad Telegraphers (ORT). The railroad proposed a central-agency concept for managing what had become mostly carload freight operations; passenger trains had largely disappeared from much of its eleven-thousand-mile system, and all had from its maze of low-traffic branch lines. A company representative explained that when these stations opened, "they served a farm economy geared to horse-drawn transportation. Today passenger and LCL traffic have virtually disappeared from one-man stations, but station forces have not been adjusted to modern requirements." The ORT was not satisfied with any more than a few closings. The reduction policy became a drawn-out affair. The union sought to block the company by employing provisions of the National Labor Railway Act. After exhausting its legal options and disregarding the responses of two US secretaries of labor and a presidential emergency board that recommended generous allowances for displaced agents, the ORT struck to North Western on August 30, 1962. But public unhappiness with the strikers and anger directed at them from thousands of Chicago-area commuters forced the union to accept binding arbitration. The result led to a resounding defeat for the ORT, being described as "a stunning setback for the telegraphers." Although the North Western (and other carriers) gained the right to decide the number of agent-operators, there were concessions to the ORT. It agreed to provide employees with ninety days' notice of discharges and to pay released employees 60 percent of their annual earnings for as long as five years. The North Western and other carriers frequently delayed depot closings to allow veteran agents, whose retirements were imminent, opportunities to work their final days, weeks, or months.[80]

"MERGER MADNESS"

Midwestern carriers generated impressive revenues resulting from the recent world war. This allowed them to emerge from Great Depression–era bankruptcies, retire or reduce their indebtedness, and pay stock dividends. Furthermore, earnings spiked with strong postwar consumer demands, especially for housing, automobiles, and other durable goods. Railroad executives also appreciated that dieselization contributed greatly to the positive side of their ledgers. Altering work rules offered still another way to bolster incomes, but that process was slow, and occasionally lengthy legal battles and strikes erupted. As modal competition increased from airlines, barges, pipelines, and trucks and oppressive regulation remained, there needed to be a way to prevent massive amounts of red ink. That response involved corporate mergers, although this was hardly a new concept. Mergers, acquisitions, and leases were part of railroad history. After all, the post–Civil War era had experienced massive "system building," a combination of new line construction, leases, and company consolidations. In the 1920s the Van Sweringen brothers had shown amazing success in constructing a railroad empire not through a series of mergers but by creating holding companies, including the enduring Alleghany Corporation.

During the 1930s and 1940s, the ICC approved only a limited number of mergers, in part because of the Great Depression and because carriers showed little interest in uniting. A notable exception occurred in 1947 when the Gulf, Mobile & Northern (a 1941 union between the Gulf, Mobile & Northern and the Mobile & Ohio) merged with the Chicago & Alton to form the Gulf, Mobile & Ohio Railroad (GM&O). This 1,180-mile road linked Mobile and New Orleans with East St. Louis, Chicago, and Kansas City.[81]

As the euphoria of the Indian summer vanished, industry attitudes about corporate marriages changed. Midwestern railroad executives took note of two that blazed the way. These involved the 4,785-mile Louisville & Nashville absorbing the 1,043-mile Nashville, Chattanooga & St. Louis and the 2,132-mile Norfolk & Western taking over the largely parallel 611-mile Virginian. The former was designed for retrenchment and economies. Its architects believed that line downgrades and abandonments and elimination of duplicate support facilities and personnel would produce the anticipated benefits. The process started in 1955, and the effective date for the merger became August 31, 1957. The latter union was intended to enhance earnings. The merger of these two profitable predominantly coal-carrying roads, which the ICC speedily endorsed, took place officially on December 1, 1959.[82]

The 1960s witnessed the start of a flurry of merger activities. Railroad executives, board members, bankers, and others considered consolidations. Some were planned discussions or failed proposals, but others became realities. The aggressive North Western, under the generalship of board chairman Ben Heineman, envisioned a massive midwestern rail system. It would ideally include his company, the Milwaukee Road, Rock Island, and others. While neither the Milwaukee Road nor the Rock Island entered the North Western orbit, it did acquire the M&StL

in 1960 and the Great Western eight years later and soon a pair of freight-generating former Iowa interurbans, Des Moines & Central Iowa and Fort Dodge, Des Moines & Southern. Heineman embraced this thinking: "Mergers can kill off unwanted and unneeded competition in overbuilt regions." Although significant parts of the M&StL remained, the North Western retired much of the Great Western. Yet it wanted to serve the Great Western's Roseport Industrial District near St. Paul and to gain access to the Kansas City gateway from a mainline connection at Marshalltown, Iowa. Later that trackage would be abandoned after the North Western purchased from the liquidating Rock Island its "Spine Line," a shorter and better-engineered route between Kansas City and the Twin Cities.[83]

About the time the North Western absorbed the M&StL, the 2,313-mile Erie Railroad joined ranks with the 940-mile Delaware, Lackawanna & Western. On October 17, 1960, these two properties made their debut as the Erie Lackawanna Railroad (EL). Since the mid-1950s serious talks about consolidation had been ongoing. The reasons were obvious. Both companies struggled financially due to high terminal costs in the New York City area, money-losing commuter operations in New Jersey, high rates of property taxation in New Jersey and New York, and the negative impact of superhighways, including toll roads in New York, Ohio, and Indiana. The monetary gains from dieselization, moreover, had been finite.[84]

After a shaky and discouraging start, the merged company showed modest promise. Most of all, the economies predicted by a respected consulting firm became reality. By 1963 savings amounted to about $21 million annually rather than the $13 million initially anticipated. But the management team in charge, which consisted primarily of "Erie men," performed poorly. That triggered a substantial Lackawanna brain drain, unfortunate because those who departed were talented railroaders. Two examples of the negative impact of Erie domination were failure to modernize an obsolete station service and not closing at least a half dozen terminals, including the one in Huntington, Indiana, actions that could have produced considerable savings.[85]

Management did change. In 1963 the board of directors decided that it must have stronger leadership and succeeded in bringing to Cleveland headquarters William "Bill" White "to clean house." He was an excellent choice, having served as president of the Lackawanna and the NYC and then chief executive officer of the Delaware & Hudson (D&H). White's "Lackawannization" boosted morale, increased efficiencies, and helped end red ink. Yet he could only do so much. White and his associates correctly concluded that the EL could not operate in perpetuity. Mega-mergers, which eventually produced Penn Central, CSX, and Norfolk Southern, were beginning to develop. Poorer roads like EL needed to find merger mates. While the company made modest yearly profits during White's tenure (he died suddenly in 1967), it was no moneymaker. "A small cold could easily turn into fatal pneumonia," opined an EL executive. Said one industry analyst with EL in mind, "Merging two relatively weak roads can result in a bigger weak road."[86]

The Norfolk & Western (N&W), the future Norfolk Southern, seemed to offer the best hope for financial security. As a condition of its merger with the Nickel Plate and lease of the Wabash in 1964, the ICC provided for inclusion of the EL in the expanded N&W. At EL's insistence, the ICC ordered N&W in June 1967 to include EL, D&H, and the Boston & Maine in its galaxy of subsidiaries. (The Boston & Maine later decided not to enter.) On March 27, 1968, the US Supreme Court upheld the ICC's position. There was rejoicing in Cleveland's Midland Building but none at N&W headquarters in Roanoke, Virginia. Five days later EL entered the N&W orbit. How would N&W run EL and D&H? Rather than absorbing both railroads, the N&W launched a holding company, Dereco, Inc., to protect itself in case of an EL or D&H collapse. Dereco, this wholly owned subsidiary of the N&W, took Erie Lackawanna Rail*road* and merged it into the Erie Lackawanna Rail*way* as part of the restructuring.[87]

The holding company strategy made sense. Although N&W transferred several talented railroad executives from Roanoke to Cleveland and their presence boosted employee morale, EL began to slip. By the early 1970s, it jokingly had become "Erie Lack-of-Money." Seemingly, the alignment of the celestial bodies was against the railroad. It sustained enormous physical damage and traffic disruptions caused by Hurricane Agnes in June 1972, especially in Pennsylvania; competitor Penn Central diverted traffic, not wishing to "short haul" itself, and full-crew state laws and restrictive union contracts likewise hurt the bottom line. As for the latter, President Gregory Maxwell said pointedly, "Labor was bleeding us dry." These factors did much to explain why the EL entered bankruptcy on June 26, 1972. The railroad remained under court protection until the coming of the Consolidated Railroad Corporation (Conrail) in 1976.[88]

While the saga of the EL probably caught public attention in such midwestern cities as Youngstown, Akron, Cleveland, Marion, Huntington, and perhaps Chicago, another merger and subsequent bankruptcy grabbed newspaper headlines and made radio and television news broadcasts throughout the region. This event was the debut of the monster 20,500-mile Penn Central Transportation Company (PC). Although its two principal components, NYC and PRR, had since 1962 received stockholder approval to unite, it took ICC a lengthy period before it granted its approval. "Nothing the ICC does occurs quickly," opined industry writer Fred W. Frailey. "The term 'bureaucracy' probably sprang from within its walls." "M-Day" for PC, which included the New Haven—"a hopeless invalid"—occurred on January 1, 1968. But this was not a marriage made in heaven. From the start the railroad bled money, stemming in part from poor premerger planning, a clash of corporate cultures, and a deteriorating physical plant. The inevitable happened; it declared bankruptcy on June 22, 1970, claiming the dubious distinction of being the largest business failure in American history to that point. The PC collapse sent shock waves throughout the financial community and its interregional service area. Could the company be reorganized successfully? Would its thousands of customers be adequately served or served at all?[89]

The national railroad picture changed dramatically with this PC bankruptcy. It produced a landmark piece of federal legislation, the Railroad Revitalization and Regulatory Reform Act of 1976—better known as the 4R Act. In addition to making funds available for the restructuring of the Northeast carriers, it created Conrail, a sprawling interregional and quasi-public railroad. This new company, which became an important midwestern fixture, appeared on "Conveyance Day," April 1, 1976.

The creation of Penn Central followed by Conrail proved the harbinger of additional megamergers. There had been other big unifications that affected the Midwest prior to the debut of Penn Central, including the C&O's control of the B&O in 1963 and Norfolk & Western's merger with the Nickel Plate and lease of the Wabash a year later. (In 1991 Wabash officially joined the mega-Norfolk Southern system.) Another monster union came after futile decades of trying. The Hill Lines (or the "Northerns") for decades had sought a legal marriage; it was an old dream, dating back to 1896. As the twentieth century began, this aspiration led to the launching of the Northern Securities Company. Unfortunately for its backers, the US Supreme Court in 1904 by a five-to-four vote squelched that endeavor three years after this holding company (or "trust") appeared. The Transportation Act of 1920, which called for the ICC to rationalize the national railroad network into nearly a score of strong systems, revived the hope for unification. The commission endorsed the union of Great Northern, Northern Pacific, and Spokane, Portland & Seattle (SP&S), but the Burlington was excluded. The Northerns would not accept such an omission, and so the proposal died. A merger of the Burlington, GN, and Northern Pacific did not materialize until formation of the 26,386-mile Burlington Northern Railroad (BN) on March 2, 1970, a process that began in 1961. (Included in the BN, which became longest railroad in North America, was the lease of the SP&S and the absorption of subsidiaries, Colorado & Southern, Fort Worth & Denver, Oregon Electric, and Oregon Trunk.) Seven years later the BN made a major and strategic acquisition, taking control of the 4,600-mile St. Louis–San Francisco (Frisco), which served a sizeable portion of Missouri and several Sunbelt states.[90]

With the Frisco joining the BN, St. Louis experienced the loss of one its long-standing corporate railroad headquarters, just as it had when N&W took control of the Wabash. Still the Gateway City claimed the home offices of the Missouri Pacific, a company that orchestrated its own mergers, becoming an 11,500-mile powerhouse by the 1980s. By 1976, it had added the Chicago & Eastern Illinois and Texas & Pacific into its realm along with several smaller non-midwestern roads.[91]

During this extensive wave of corporate marriages, attempts at new combinations of midwestern railroads also developed. One much-discussed failure involved the merger of the North Western and the Milwaukee Road into the Chicago, Milwaukee & North Western Transportation Company. In 1966 shareholders gave this proposal the green light, but the ICC after hearings in 1967 and 1968 took until April 1, 1970, to deny the application. A bankrupt and truncated Milwaukee Road (no longer with its Pacific Coast Extension) eventually became part of the Soo Line Railroad, itself an earlier union of the Minneapolis, St. Paul & Sault Ste. Marie; Duluth, South Shore & Atlantic; and Wisconsin Central.[92]

The complex midwestern merger story involved a spectacular regulatory fiasco, although strikingly different from the Penn Central. This blunder would alter the course of future railroad unifications. In the early 1960s, the financially strapped Rock Island sought a merger partner. After much discussion, it petitioned in 1964 to join the wealthy Union Pacific. UP was interested, mostly because it desired access over Rock Island rails to reach the Chicago and St. Louis gateways. Once in control, the UP planned to sell Rock Island trackage south of Kansas City to the Southern Pacific. That company coveted the Rock Island's Golden State Route between Kansas City and Tucumcari, New Mexico, where it historically interchanged with the Rock Island. This acquisition would provide the Southern Pacific with its own direct line between California and the Midwest, being more attractive than relying on its St. Louis-Southwestern (Cotton Belt) subsidiary for access to the region. In May 1966 hearings on the Rock Island and UP merger began in Chicago, but there would be no forthcoming decision by the ICC. It was not until 1973 that the case ended following 150,000 pages of testimony, exhibits, briefs, petitions, and replies. By the time of the examiner's final report, which approved the merger, the UP withdrew its offer—the Rock Island in its opinion had become a transportation slum. Rock Island management nevertheless had made a determined effort to save the road, but it lacked the resources to maintain its main arteries, motive power, and rolling stock. One wag called its locomotives and freight equipment a "rolling junkyard." The excessive length of time to close the case would haunt the ICC and became one of the nails in its not-so-distant coffin. The unreasonable delay also proved to be a fatal blow for the struggling Rock Island. In the mid-1970s the company entered bankruptcy protection. In 1980, however, the federal court ruled that a profitable reorganization was not possible, and the railroad should be liquidated. Dismemberment followed. Line abandonments took place, but most of the railroad remained in service, acquired by trunk roads and newly organized regional and shortline carriers. "The fact that the Rock Island was dissolved by a bankruptcy judge, but operates today under a bevy of different owners," commented Fred Frailey in 2011, "suggests it wasn't so redundant after all."[93]

The 1980s and 1990s became a time of forming more railroad behemoths. These unifications directly affected freight customers throughout the Midwest. In 1980 the Chessie System and SCL Industries united to create CSX Transportation Company. Its approximately twenty-one-thousand-route-mile system served twenty-three states, including Illinois, Indiana, Michigan, Ohio, and Wisconsin. Two years later N&W united with the Southern to create Norfolk Southern Corporation (NS). "It will make shipping by rail between the Midwest and the South much easier," explained the company. "For example, Norfolk Southern will open five new corridors in this area to facilitate the movement of goods between North and South and East and West. In addition, the unified rail system will blanket many key industrial areas of the country." Then in 1983 UP, which had scorned the Rock Island, scored triumphs when it acquired the Missouri Pacific and Western Pacific. Somewhat later the Omaha-based colossus gained ownership of the long-struggling but somewhat streamlined Missouri–Kansas–Texas. Its Kansas City–Texas core was the attraction. In 1995 the UP bought the North Western, gaining access to Chicago and a line to the Twin Cities together with several grain-carrying branches in Iowa. Another spectacular unification involved Burlington Northern and Santa Fe, which took effect at the end of 1996, twenty-five years after the debut of the BN. Unlike the UP–Rock Island unification filing, the launch of Burlington Northern Santa Fe (BNSF) went smoothly. "On February 7, 1995, shareholders of both Santa Fe and Burlington Northern approved the merger," noted Santa Fe and BNSF executive Robert Krebs. "The Interstate Commerce Commission had instituted a quick review process. On August 23 [it] approved our corporate marriage unanimously with only a few, very minor, conditions."[94]

Conrail also participated in corporate expansions. In time this quasi-public corporation, which grew out of the Penn Central debacle, became a vibrant property, having benefited from the 4R Act and the

1980 Staggers deregulation measure. The company eliminated excessive trackage, shed money-draining commuter operations, expanded intermodal traffic, and benefited from progressive management. In 1985 the federal lawmakers passed the Conrail Privatization Act, which authorized a public stock offering that would return the railroad to the private sector. And investors took advantage of this opportunity. A dramatic change took place in the mid-1990s when CSX announced that it planned to acquire the railroad. NS intervened and prevented the sale to its principal interregional rival. A compromise followed. In early 1997 NS and CSX acquired Conrail through a joint stock purchase. In July 1998 the Surface Transportation Board, recent successor to the ICC, approved the acquisition and restructuring of Conrail. CSX received 42 percent, acquiring much of the remaining former NYC, and NS took 58 percent and gained ownership of most of the surviving PRR routes. The final agreement also created a shared-assets subsidiary that provided terminal operations in Detroit, Newark, and Philadelphia.[95]

By the twenty-first century, Class Is had grown even larger. The Canadian National Railway (CN), which the Canadian government privatized in 1995, took control of the Illinois Central in 1998. This acquisition transformed the CN's focus from being an east–west Canadian carrier into being a north–south one. With the signing of the North American Free Trade Agreement (NAFTA) in 1994, which created a trilateral trading block, rail movements between Mexico, the US, and Canada became more important and profitable. CN continued to expand. In 2001 it acquired the regional Wisconsin Central, which provided more efficient connections between the Chicago gateway and the Canadian West, including its Pacific Ocean ports of Prince Rupert and Vancouver. Seven years later CN took possession of the strategic Elgin, Joliet & Eastern Railway, improving its traffic flow around the western side of the congested Chicago rail hubs.[96]

It came as no surprise that CN had its eyes on the smallest remaining Class I railroad in the US, the Kansas City–based Kansas City Southern (KCS). But it was not alone. Canadian Pacific (CP) likewise wanted this property. Its attractiveness centered on having won control of key commercial corridors to Veracruz and Lazero Cardenas, Mexico, through its subsidiary Kansas City Southern de Mexico (KCSdeM). (Founded in 1996, KCSdeM was a joint venture between KCS and Transportacion Ferroviaria Mexicana, but in 2005 KCS bought out its partner, giving it full ownership of KCSdeM.) A heated battle erupted between the two Canadian carriers for this acquisition prize. Other US railroads, multiple on-line communities, and related interests did not want either the CN or CP to win. Finally, on March 15, 2023, the Surface Transportation Board approved the $28 billion merger of the CP and KCS, creating Canadian Pacific Kansas City Limited (CPKC). Regulators, except for one member, liked that these two strong railroads served adjoining territories with little duplication of facilities, being a classic "end-to-end" union. The regulatory decision, which forged the biggest merger in two decades, meant that CPKC would be the only carrier directly serving the three countries of the North American trade zone. The merger created the continent's first "transnational railroad." Moreover, this could be the last major merger of what has become six Class I mega-freight railroads: BNSF, CN, CPKC, CSX, NS, and UP, although CPKC is the smallest with 20,000 miles of track (only 8,600 miles in the US).[97]

Remarkably, no transcontinental railroad under a single corporate structure emerged. "Really there was no need for a coast-to-coast railroad," explained veteran railroad official Kent Shoemaker in 2005, who had worked for B&O and Soo Line and was a founder in the early 1990s of the Twin Cities & Western and Red River Valley & Western Railroads. "There were financial and legal considerations, but inter-company agreements, including run-through trains, allowed seamless service. Of course, by the 1990s you had giant systems—take Union Pacific—that could handle traffic between the Pacific Northwest and Texas and Alabama." Shoemaker added perceptively, "The industry had reached a plateau of stability." The emergence of the CPKC will not likely alter the situation.[98]

During the industry upheavals of the immediate decades before Staggers deregulation, some midwestern railroads considered or actually sought extensive diversification by acquiring nonrailroad assets through newly launched holding companies. In one case such a corporate structure exited the railroad business altogether. In the mid-1960s North Western board chairman Ben Heineman concluded that a better way to increase shareholder value would come not from rail betterments or mergers but from investments outside the transportation sector. Profits for his railroad were limited at best; the industry seemed unable to alter labor contracts, control pricing, and manage other regulatory matters. "To put it simply," Heineman told the business press, "I've been discontented with the railroad industry and its long-range outlook under present circumstances, because its rate of returns is disgustingly inadequate."[99]

Those at the North Western, Illinois Central Gulf, Santa Fe, and additional companies believed that the advantages achievable from nonrailroad investments were considerable. If satellite enterprises generated profits, a stronger corporation would result. The railroad itself could also gain from the protection offered by contra-cyclical businesses. There would be attractive tax considerations as well, achieved by the nonrail concerns using the tax-credit carry-forwards of the parent railroad. If nationalization of the railroad industry occurred—there existed a widespread fear that it was a possibility—diversification offered financial protection.

For the North Western, nonrailroad businesses started in 1965. Using Norwest Corporation (later Northwest Industries), its first acquisition was Velsicol Chemical Corporation, based in Rosemont, Illinois. Three years later the Heineman organization emerged as a fully fledged conglomerate, taking control of additional businesses, although it failed in 1969 to capture Akron-based B. F. Goodrich Company. Soon thereafter Heineman and his associates decided that Northwest Industries and the railroad should part company. Heineman and North Western president Larry Provo hammered out an arrangement whereby the railroad would be sold to its employees. In October 1970, a few months after the Penn Central debacle, Northwest Industries entered into an agreement with an employee group to sell its rail assets for a modest sum and to have that successor company assume its debt. Northwest Industries would receive some cash and, more significantly, a large amount of tax credits that it could use to offset profits from its subsidiaries. The ICC endorsed this creative proposal, and on June 1, 1972, the North Western Employee Transportation Company, soon renamed the Chicago & North Western Transportation Company (C&NWTCo), emerged. Later the Provo management did well at the public trough, receiving substantial loans under the 4R Act that allowed it to bring about a rebirth of sorts, especially substantial upgrades to its mainline between Chicago and its major interchange, the UP connection at Fremont, Nebraska. The departure of Northwest Industries from the life of C&NWTCo was positive; the railroad no longer operated in the shadow of a growing holding company. Yet for some time, the carrier struggled.[100]

SHORTLINES AND REGIONALS

Mergers and megamergers together with bankruptcies and sell-offs in the Midwest led to a remarkable number of small-mileage shortline and larger regional railroads. (The latter was defined in the mid-1980s as having at least 350 route miles or substantial annual revenues making it a Class II rather than a Class III railroad.)[101] The Midwest, in fact, became the breeding ground for the modern formation of these regional rails. The shortline and regional rail phenomenon emerged because enlarged Class I roads wanted to focus operations on their core routes, often interregional corridors. They realized that they had the ability to handle heavy freight traffic and could court big shippers effectively. These mega roads also understood that they possessed unneeded trackage of all types, main and secondary lines but most of all low-density appendages. Class Is had options. Abandonments were an obvious response. The legal process to achieve such actions had become easier due to friendlier federal legislation, including the Northeast Rail Service Act. This measure, passed in 1981, enabled Conrail to abandon virtually any line at will. All of the eight states experienced a drastic reduction in mileage, but Iowa stands out. Its railroad network, which once ranked fourth nationally, shrank from 8,300 miles in 1960 to 3,825 miles in 2020. Michigan was not far behind with trackage reductions.[102]

Once rails were lifted, the public still might benefit from the original line. The modern rails-to-trails movement had a midwestern origin. May Theilgaard Watts, a naturalist at the Morton Arboretum in Lisle, Illinois, who had been inspired by her hiking experiences in England, proposed in a May 1963 letter to the editor in the *Chicago Tribune* a constructive use for abandoned rights-of-way. She suggested that the recently defunct Chicago, Aurora & Elgin interurban become a recreational path: "We

Thousands of miles of branch lines in the Midwest never received a renewed life as a shortline or as part of a new regional carrier. Such was the case of the North Western's thirty-eight-mile Bingham Lake to Currie, Minnesota, appendage. By the early 1960s, the track was in poor physical shape. Also revealed in this photograph is a grain-carrying truck; more shippers opted for this transportation alternative. Abandonment of the Currie branch soon followed. *(Author's collection)*

are human beings. We are able to walk upright on two feet. We need a footpath. Right now there is a chance for Chicago and its suburbs to have a footpath, a long one." Watts, who was well known among environmentalists and outdoor enthusiasts, spawned a grassroots crusade to convert sections of the weed- and brush-choked right-of-way located largely in Du Page County into what became the Illinois Prairie Path. In 1965 the formation of the Illinois Prairie Path Corporation, a landmark organization in the rails-to-trails phenomenon, led to the realization of Watts's proposal. Ultimately much of the right-of-way emerged as a sixty-one-mile network of mostly crushed-stone bike and walking trails between Maywood and Wheaton with spurs to Aurora, Batavia, Elgin, and Geneva.[103]

Illinois was hardly unique with the Prairie Path; all midwestern states have seen various rails-to-trails conversions. The longest one can be found in Missouri. The Katy Trail State Park stretches 240 miles between St. Charles and Henry Counties, mostly along the abandoned St. Louis trackage of the former Missouri–Kansas–Texas Railway. Rails-to-trails can also serve as "railbanking" or "trails-to-rails," allowing the return of railroad service. There have been modest efforts to restore rail lines, but they have been largely unsuccessful in the Midwest due mostly to local objections.[104]

Although the value of the rails-to-trails concept might appear to be obvious, not everyone has been enthusiastic or cooperative about having public paths. Some urban residents who lived along or near an abandoned rail line fretted about individuals using such corridors to gain access to their properties, perhaps committing criminal acts, causing excessive noise, or littering their immediate neighborhoods. Farmers might also object, wanting this land to expand their agricultural operations. In 1989, for example, the Iowa Natural Heritage Foundation, a nonprofit conservation organization, sought to preserve a section of the abandoned Great Western right-of-way near Marshalltown but found itself outbid by farmers who then plowed up the ground to grow corn and soybeans.[105]

While the divestiture of trackage by merged railroads led to scores of rails-to-trails projects, it also fostered extensive shortline creations. This process saved rail service for numerous communities, a development that pleased customers who depended on an alternative to motor transport. When an abandonment occurred, it could force the closure of a factory, paper mill, mine, or some other business. When trucks provided the sole transportation option, higher freight rates often resulted. Grain handling represents a good example of where elevator operators usually are forced to pay more for their outbound shipments.

Shortlines are hardly a recent concept. At the dawn of the Railway Age, all railroads lacked much length. Even with system building and new construction, especially during the 1880s, small roads remained. Their owners might be content to preserve the status quo, or the financial value of their properties was not great enough to attract the interest of larger carriers. These shortlines served varied customers, ranging from agricultural shippers to factories and mining companies. With growing competition from automobiles and trucks after World War I, together with better roads, and followed by the Great Depression, multiple shortline owners sought abandonment. But with the onrush of merger madness in the 1960s and as bankruptcies, reorganizations, and liquidations accelerated, the number of new, smaller roads exploded nationwide. The Midwest, though, can claim few if any functioning shortlines that date back to the nineteenth century; there is nothing comparable to the Strasburg Rail Road in Pennsylvania. This four-mile tourist and common carrier, which operates under a state charter granted in 1832, opened for business in 1851. Today its passenger operations attract thousands of visitors to Old Amish Country, and it serves a growing number of freight customers.[106]

Throughout the Midwest scores of shortlines have appeared since the 1970s. As a response to this national phenomenon, the ICC felt obliged to publish a booklet titled *So You Want to Start a Small Railroad: The ICC Small Railroad Application Procedures*. The formation of Conrail in 1976 contributed significantly to this surge when it liquidated hundreds of miles of trackage. Michigan became a leading midwestern example. "[Conrail] sparked a period of dramatic change in Michigan's Lower Peninsula, altering forever the state railroad map," observed *Trains* contributor Ron Cady in 1987. "Conrail radically restructured Penn Central's Michigan lines. New short lines have surfaced in the big railroad's wake." They were not always pieces of former Conrail trackage. Grand Trunk Western (GTW), for one, spun off mileage that led to the launching of several shortlines. "Much activity [for line sales] centered on Durand GTW's historic crossbands," observed company historian Don Hofsommer. During the late 1980s, the railroad lopped off about five hundred miles. The cash generated went largely to improving its core arteries.[107]

Taking advantage of opportunities provided by a restructured Conrail and other Class I carriers, these modern shortlines have had or continue to have various types of ownership. Often they trace their origins to startups sparked by individuals, outside speculators, or groups of on-line investors who lived in rail-dependent communities. Others owe their existence to public development authorities. In Michigan five shortlines have evolved from leasing portions of 665 miles of likely-to-be-abandoned trackage that the state acquired from their Class I owners. This Michigan intervention represents a textbook illustration of "lemon socialism," being reminiscent of British nationalization of its failing coal-mining industry in 1946 and of the troubled iron and steel makers three years later. Moreover, the public purchase of rail lines harkens back to public ownership that had occurred during the formative years of the Railway Age. In time, some financially attractive properties entered the orbit of national concerns, highlighted in the Midwest by holding firms Genesee & Wyoming Inc., Watco Companies, and Progressive Rail. Genesee & Wyoming of these three is the eight-hundred-pound gorilla, controlling approximately one hundred shortline and regional railroads in forty-two states.[108]

Shortlines in the Midwest and elsewhere have varied histories. They might endure or last only briefly. These roads exemplify the latter: Ahnapee & Western Railway (WI), Kewash Railroad (IA), Marquette & Huron Mountain Railway (MI), Muncie & Western Railroad (IN), Nobles Rock Railroad (MN), Northern Missouri Railroad (MO), Pioneer & Fayette Railroad (OH), and Prairie Central Railroad (IL).

Volatility is understandable, explained in part because those that entered the corporate graveyard were commonly poorly maintained cast-offs. The track structure may not have been strong enough to support heavier, modern freight rolling stock—286,000-pound covered hopper cars, for example. Funds to upgrade might not have been available, and so deteriorating track and weak bridges forced abandonment. Lack of capital might also mean that there was little or no money to operate—to pay bills in advance of revenue receipts. And the degree of business may never have developed as planned (or hoped for), being plagued by a dearth of originating traffic. *Railway Age* editor Gus Welty explained why this led to shortline failures: "Overly rosy traffic projections, based on too much enthusiasm and/or too little accurate data." Motive power, too, may have been of junk caliber, and money unattainable for major repairs or replacements. Management problems may have plagued these shortlines. Operating persons, even enthusiastic railfans, who were in charge, may have lacked marketing and other essential business skills.

Relationships with connecting Class I roads, especially if the failed shortlines had but a single interchange option, might not have been cooperative, creating operational and financial difficulties.[109]

Viable shortlines do more than provide their customers with connections to the national rail network. They are lauded for their friendly, reliable, and consistent service by showing greater responsiveness to shipper needs than the Class Is. They work with customers around their schedules whenever possible. This might involve picking up cars late at night for interchange with a regional or Class I road or making certain that customers receive their deliveries as soon as possible and spotted properly. They often act as an intermediary agent between customers and Class Is, since Class Is have remote and centralized managements without a strong marketing focus. Fortunately for shortline owners after Staggers, the ICC did not require labor protection when an established railroad sold a line to a new entrant. Although initially shortlines nationally nearly always had a nonunionized workforce, the situation has changed for many. Unions realized that shortlines and regionals were where employee growth was occurring, and so they stepped up their organizing efforts. Yet these railroads nearly always have agreements that preserve their own work rules, which commonly allow flexible job classifications. A worker might operate a locomotive, conduct mechanical chores, or repair track in the course of a month, a week, or maybe a day. Not to be overlooked is that Class I roads benefit by having shortline feeder traffic without the obligations of operating what their managements view as low-density and maintenance-draining appendages.[110]

The saga of two midwestern upstarts, one in Iowa and the other in Ohio, reveals how the former failed quickly whereas the latter survived and ultimately entered the orbit of a shortline and regional conglomerate. The failure was Central Iowa Railway. By 1970 the Rock Island, its owner, was experiencing a rapid decline, and hopes of a merger with UP had become bogged down in the ICC bureaucracy. During this time the Rock Island system had deteriorated to the point of decrepitude.

Part of the extensive Rock Island mileage in Iowa included the Montezuma branch. This seventy-mile line linked Iowa City, situated on its trans-state route, with Montezuma, the small Poweshiek County seat.

By the early 1970s, abandonment seemed likely for virtually all of this appendage. If freight service ended, it would adversely affect multiple on-line customers, who were overwhelmingly agribusinesses. A group of local boosters responded to this threat by deciding to acquire this endangered trackage. The cash-strapped Rock Island readily agreed to sell most of the line at a reasonable price. Like all other contemporary transportation concerns, the Rock Island also faced the economic challenges of stagflation, high interest rates, and the negative impact of the Arab oil embargo. Backers of the new railroad launched the Central Iowa Transportation Cooperative (renamed the Central Iowa Railway), headquartered in Kalona. It became the prototype of the new era of shortlines in the Hawkeye State. On February 2, 1974, operations began on the sixty-three miles between Hills, near Iowa City, and Montezuma, and its slow-moving freights served a dozen small communities, including Kalona, South English, Thornburg, and Wellman. Dangerous track conditions, inadequate financing, and limited traffic forced suspension of service in October 1974. Resuscitation efforts floundered, and in May 1978 the ICC approved abandonment. Liquidation followed: the sole locomotive was sold, rails lifted, and most of the right-of-way reverted to adjacent property owners.[111]

Unlike the fragile Central Iowa Railway, the Ohio Central Railroad (OCRR) did not falter and collapse. Approximately the same length as the short-lived Iowa shortline, the OCRR began service on April 16, 1988, between a connection near Brewster with the soon-to-be regional railroad Wheeling & Lake Erie, and the CSX and Ohio Southern Railroads at Zanesville, a distance of seventy-one miles. This road, spearheaded by Jerry Joe Jacobson, a US Air Force veteran, board-certified nurse anesthetist, and rail enthusiast, once had been part of the original Wheeling & Lake Erie and was later owned by the Nickel Plate, Norfolk & Western, and ultimately Norfolk Southern.

Differing from backers of the Central Iowa Railway, Jacobson had had considerable shortline railroad experience. He became involved with Ohi-Rail, a thirty-five-mile former NYC branch between Minerva and Hopedale, which the State of Ohio had purchased from Conrail in 1982. Two years later Jacobson took a controlling interest in this shortline. It came with two diesel locomotives, two full-time employees, and other as-needed workers. He also had involvement with the Youngstown & Austintown Railroad, a four-mile industrial road that the Mahoning Valley Economic Development Corporation had acquired from Conrail, and the thirty-two-mile Ohio Southern Railroad, which linked New Lexington with Zanesville.[112]

Headquartered in Sugar Creek, OCRR rapidly improved its physical plant and its customer base. The stated Jacobson motto was "Big enough to serve you, small enough to care." One effective way that the company increased traffic (and revenues) involved a lumber transload facility in Sugar Creek. Another way to bolster revenues (and Jacobson's pride and joy) involved steam-powered excursions that began in summer 1988 between Sugar Creek and Baltic, a distance of seven miles. The OCRR took advantage of its presence in Holmes County, situated in the heart of Ohio's Old Order Amish country and a thriving tourist destination. These four-times daily round trips allowed passengers to view Amish farms operated by horses and nonmotorized equipment. "Thousands of passengers and trackside observers made countless memories of those trips that have been preserved in written accounts, photographs, movies and video tapes." These excursions, which ended in 2003, did not operate on Sundays in deference to the religious beliefs of the local Amish population and Jacobson's wife, Laura.[113]

Jerry Jacobson found additional opportunities in the Buckeye State. In 1990 he took control of the former Panhandle (Pittsburgh, Cincinnati, Chicago & St. Louis) mainline of the PRR between Columbus and Mingo Junction (near Steubenville). These 145 miles became OCRR subsidiary Columbus & Ohio River Railroad. At its peak Jacobson controlled a shortline empire of 486 miles that included ten railroads in Ohio and Pennsylvania. His holdings offered good service, an enviable operating ratio, and a stable or growing traffic base. In 2008 he sold his Ohio Central Railroad System to Genesee & Wyoming, realizing a substantial personal profit. This allowed Jacobson and his wife to concentrate on their pet project, developing the Age of Steam Roundhouse Museum near Sugar Creek. In time this eighteen-stall brick structure housed an impressive collection of steam and vintage diesel locomotives, freight and passenger cars, and other artifacts. It quickly became a popular place for railroad enthusiasts and others interested in steam technology and transportation history.[114]

While Jacobson assembled a largely disconnected rail network, other individuals in the Midwest spearheaded nonfragmented regional roads. Edward Burkhardt, longtime executive with the North Western, and Thomas Power Jr., former financial officer with the Milwaukee Road, gained industry recognition for coleading a group of investors that purchased the 2,300-mile Lake States Transportation Division of the Soo Line Railroad in 1987. This Soo Line unit was short-lived and the least permanent of the latter-day regionals in the Midwest. The explanation largely involved two factors: failure to achieve flexible work-rule changes and the parent company's need for cash to reduce its debt, which had quadrupled as a result of its recent purchase of the truncated Milwaukee Road.[115]

The Burkhardt-Power-led regional became christened the Wisconsin Central Transportation Corporation Ltd. (Wisconsin Central), with lines concentrated in the Badger State but also extending into the Upper Peninsula of Michigan. In 1992 the firm added the Green Bay & Western and Fox River Valley Railroads, gaining several large shippers. The Wisconsin Central had become a 2,850-mile road. Above all, it developed a corporate culture that embraced customer service. Employees, including train crews, had authorization to make decisions that better served patrons. This meant that a "loose" or single car would be handled with dispatch. Business boomed. The Wisconsin Central, which sported hundreds of miles of welded rail and centralized traffic control and dispatched more than twenty daily trains, unfortunately experienced a nasty internal upheaval in 1999. Conflict between Burkhardt and Power centered over how the company was managed and structured. While Power wished to take this privately held company public, Burkhardt did not. This led to Burkhardt's forced resignation. Yet this talented railroader became involved in other railroad activities, including heading another newly launched regional, the Montreal, Maine & Atlantic Railway.[116]

Wisconsin Central itself would experience two major changes. In 2001 the Canadian National acquired the property, and in 2022 Watco

Companies purchased about nine hundred miles of this trackage. Wisconsin Central remains one of the nation's largest regional carriers.[117]

CHICAGO, CENTRAL & PACIFIC AND INDIANA RAIL ROAD

The Midwest claimed two sharply different regional railroad experiences. These involved the Chicago, Central & Pacific Railroad (CCP) and the Indiana Rail Road (INRD). In both cases the words of nineteenth-century essayist Ralph Waldo Emerson ring true: "An institution is the lengthened shadow of one man." If Emerson had lived in the region during the 1980s, he might have had the CCP and the INRD in mind. For the CCP the driving force would be John (Jack) Haley (1936–2011) and for the INRD Thomas (Tom) Hoback (1947–).

The future CCP became possible when the Illinois Central Gulf (ICG), the product of the merger between the 6,790-mile IC and the largely parallel 2,372-mile GM&O in 1972, decided to focus on its trackage between Chicago and Gulf of Mexico port terminals at New Orleans and Mobile. This was the time when Illinois Central Industries, the holding company that had controlled ICG since 1963, was actively diversifying into consumer and industrial businesses and became intent on selling much of its rail lines. Management's goal was to fashion a streamlined railroad that operated a core north–south system of approximately three thousand miles. It believed that a slimmed-down ICG, fed by regional spinoffs, could make money, and perhaps the remainder of the railroad would ultimately be profitably sold. In the words of IC executive Harry Bruce, this was a way to "focus on growth." In the mid- to late 1980s, ICG succeeded, liquidating a substantial part of its sprawling system and generating an estimated $450 million. By the close of the decade, it operated only 2,872 miles. No Class I pruned more trackage than this company. (In 1988 ICG changed its name back to Illinois Central.)[118]

A major sale took place west of Chicago. In late 1985 this portion of the former ICG flew the CCP banner. Specifically, this regional, which blazed the way for similar regional carriers, operated 798 miles. Its network of trackage extended west from the Chicago area to the Council

Bluffs/Omaha gateway and from Tara near Fort Dodge to Sioux City. Several branches were part of this newly launched company. One included a link from the main stem at Manchester, Iowa, to Cedar Rapids, the second-largest city in the Hawkeye State. The sale also involved acquisition of additional trackage near Cedar Rapids. CCP received the seven miles between Marion Junction and Marion, a segment of the former Milwaukee Road trans-Iowa line that ICG had acquired in the early 1980s. The CCP also controlled the feeder Cedar Valley Railroad, a former ICG branch from near Cedar Falls to outside Albert Lea, Minnesota.[119]

It was Jack Haley who single-handedly made the CCP. He grew up in a Union Pacific family in Valley, Nebraska. His father, grandfather, and great-grandfather were not white-collar workers in the nearby UP Omaha headquarters building; rather, they worked in train service. Early on the young Haley became fascinated with railroads. While in high school, he hired out as a section hand and brakeman with the UP during summers and school breaks, and he continued part-time railroading during his student years at the University of Nebraska. Following graduation Haley entered the US Air Force. During his twenty-year career as an officer and pilot, he received numerous assignments, including flying night-attack aircraft during the Vietnam War and serving aboard Air Force One. After retiring in 1978 with the rank of lieutenant colonel, Haley became involved in a real-estate partnership. He claimed to have put together some $65 million worth of commercial deals in the Lincoln, Omaha, and Washington, DC, areas. Haley also lectured on how to invest in real estate.[120]

The business interests of Jack Haley changed dramatically in the mid-1980s. He decided to buy a railroad. When asked why this abrupt career change, Haley, according to his daughter Kathy Haley Buhrman, said he "wanted to help change an industry in trouble because of obsolete work-rules and non-aggressive marketing." He also saw profitable opportunities made possible by the Staggers Act. In early 1984 Haley sent letters to seven Class I roads asking if they had any feeder lines for sale, learning nine months later that the ICG had available its Albert Lea branch. He quickly conducted his due diligence. Haley contacted a group of farmer-owned cooperatives in northern Iowa and southern Minnesota who fretted about their likely loss of rail service. "Jack was impressed with the shippers' enthusiasm," wrote his daughter. "They were not resigned to losing rail service. He liked its location in the heart of the grain belt. It was a good start-up road for him, with the possibility of expansion. He had found his railroad." Haley liquidated his real-estate assets and invested $720,000 of his own funds toward the purchase of this line. He borrowed the remainder from the Greyhound Leasing and Financial Corporation, amounting to approximately $2.5 million. A new midwestern shortline was aborning.[121]

Soon the 109-mile Cedar Valley Railroad (CVR) had its official launch. The date for dispatching its first train was September 22, 1984. The company gained trackage rights into both Albert Lea and Waterloo and owned an eight-mile appendage to Stacyville, Iowa. The road handled mostly outbound agricultural products and inbound traffic of fertilizer, feed, and lumber. The principal interchange for the CVR was in Waterloo with the ICG; the company established its headquarters in Osage, Iowa.[122]

Jack Haley went to work to ensure that CVR customers were served. This meant upgrading the badly neglected track structure where ten-mile-per-hour slow orders dominated and seeking new business, especially traffic lost to trucks. There was no question that Haley was a charismatic go-getter. While lacking experience in railroad management, Haley showed that he could succeed. Through his hands-on efforts, CVR carloadings rapidly increased. This traffic centered on shipments of corn, soybeans, oats, and wheat, and these crops constituted 80 percent of outbound movements. The company dispatched trains with blocks of thirty to sixty cars two or three times weekly to the ICG connection. The Haley road offered customers attractive rates by grouping their shipments, being cheaper than what competing truckers charged. This "Gathering Train Service," unusual among shortlines, worked well.[123]

While the public may have noticed increased freight movements on the CVR, they likely heard about, saw, or rode its dinner train, the Star Clipper. In a joint venture between Haley and Osage restauranteurs Walt and Randi Vaning, the first dinner train rolled slowly over CVR rails on May 5, 1985. Haley acquired two former North Western F-unit diesels and refurbished three ex–Lackawanna Railroad dining cars, one of which became the kitchen car, for what would be an average of a three-and-a-half-hour trip through the rural countryside along portions of the scenic Cedar River valley. The excursion usually covered fifty to sixty miles round trip. Depending on the day of week, the train, which offered "Elegant Dining on the Rails," departed on its evening runs from Osage, Waverly, and Cedar Falls, Iowa, as well as from Glenville and Lyle, Minnesota. For thirty-five dollars, diners received a four-course meal on white linen tablecloths complemented by crystal stemware, china, and candlelight. By November 1985 the Star Clipper had carried about twenty thousand passengers and had received extensive publicity, including national television and newspaper coverage. Contemporary dinner trains were rare, if not unique among shortlines. Haley demonstrated imagination.[124]

Jack Haley was not content with having only the Cedar Valley Railroad. Either he contacted ICG representatives or they contacted him about his interest in acquiring the historic yet deteriorating Iowa Division of the former IC. This was no showcase railroad; track in the greater Dubuque area was considered some of the worst in the Midwest. Furthermore, ICG had failed to provide proper management for this far-flung trackage. "The ICG was a puzzle to me," recalled Peter Rickershauser, who at the time served as district sales manager for Norfolk Southern. There were obvious managerial shortcomings: "[It had] the most demoralized, leaderless employees and absolutely brain-dead non-existent sales/marketing coverage. As far as serving customers, generating business, there was no commercial counterpart at ICG (they had a sales rep in Waterloo; western Iowa was covered by a loose cannon with a lot of personality problems/quirks out of Omaha)." Added Rickershauser, "Other railroads—most notably C&NW—were poaching business from ICG everywhere. [The North Western was] using carload offerings at joint points (Fort Dodge particularly), and intermodal elsewhere (Webster City–originated appliances moving TOFC over C&NW's Boone, IA ramp)."[125]

During the mid-1980s the ICG launched its gigantic garage sale; five major packages of lines would be sold, creating the regionals CCP;

Top and above, A somewhat worse-for-wear former Illinois Central EMD F-7 locomotive has become Cedar Valley Road No. 9363 and awaits in Osage, Iowa. A former Chicago & North Western F-unit is on the point of the Star Clipper dinner train in Waverly, Iowa. *(Sid Vaught and Wilbur St. Peters photographs, author's collection)*

Chicago, Missouri & Western; Gulf & Mississippi; MidSouth Rail; and Paducah & Louisville. Metropolitan Rail (Metra), a unit of Chicago's Regional Transportation Authority, acquired its forty-six-mile electric suburban property. If Haley took over the Iowa Division, he understood that he must slash operating costs, most of all ending or modifying existing union contracts. He knew the financial advantages of having smaller, flexible nonunion crews. Because of the Staggers Act, there had not been labor protection issues when he took over the Albert Lea branch. If Haley were to succeed with the ICG property, he required favorable work rules. Success would also necessitate strong, cooperative financial support, an expanded customer base, more interchange traffic, upgraded trackage, and other improvements.[126]

Before financing was completed and operations launched, Haley needed to iron out matters associated with obsolete train-crew work rules. He sought a favorable local contract, but one that would not have national ramifications. By talking to most of the approximately 550 ICG employees at dozens of informational meetings held across Illinois and Iowa, Haley made it clear that he was not asking them to become nonunion, yet they must adjust to the realities of modern rail transport. "He wanted them to earn a fair wage," explained his daughter, "and he was not proposing cuts in their wages, but he wanted to eliminate wasteful work rules that bled money out of railroad operations." Haley sought three-person train crews rather than having five and a pay scale based on hours worked and not mileage traveled. He envisioned a freight crew running from greater Chicago to Waterloo and another making the remaining mainline trip to Council Bluffs/Omaha. He also proposed profit-sharing and stock-purchase plans and expected "our employees to become the highest-paid railroad workers in the United States." Haley succeeded in his work-rule objectives. In the words of Thomas DuBois, international vice president of the United Transportation Union, who served as chief negotiator for the unions, "We regard this [agreement] as a break-through toward recapturing business that has been lost to barge lines and truckers. It gives a new look to the art of railroading." There would be neither firemen nor the sacrosanct "100-mile rule" that constituted a full day's travel. Once CCP was functioning, Haley estimated operating-crew savings at roughly 40 percent.[127]

Financing needed to be completed. Jack Haley required a major money commitment to finalize the purchase, approximately $75 million. Working with his attorney, Haley got the lion's share of the funding in the form of a twelve-year loan from General Electric Credit Corporation (later General Electric Capital). This New York firm also included $5 million in startup capital. Haley brought in a minority equity partner—the Cimmred Corporation, a unit of Midwest Energy (today's Midwest Resources Inc.). Haley seemed satisfied with these arrangements, optimistically expecting that the CCP would gross $75 million in its first year of operation. "If weighing the benefits and risks gave Jack pause for reflection," commented his daughter, "he had no doubt about his ability to fulfill his end of the [financial] agreements."[128]

With labor and financial matters resolved, the CCP prepared for its formal debut. Headquartered in downtown Waterloo with Jack Haley as board chairman and president and with motive power (ninety-eight former ICG road and switch engines), crews (577 mostly ex-ICG employees), and a reopened back shop in Waterloo, all was in readiness. Operations commenced on Christmas Eve 1985. On day one, CCP trains originated and terminated at the ICG's Markham classification yard in Markham, Illinois, a south Chicago suburb. In addition to its main stem, Sioux City line, and Cedar Rapids branch, the CCP held trackage rights not only to the Markham classification yard but also to Hawthorn Yards in Cicero (Chicago) and a Commonwealth Edison Company coal-fired power plant in Joliet. (This became the most profitable move for the railroad.) Modest expansion occurred a year later when CCP acquired twenty-five miles of a recently retired North Western branch line in Iowa that extended west of Carnarvon to Ida Grove. In December 1986 service began on that appendage. Even before this acquisition, the CCP had become the fourth-largest railroad in Iowa.[129]

What was the overall condition of Jack Haley's second railroad? John Rebensdorf, who served as the vice president for strategic planning at the UP, made these comments based on his high-railing trip over the mainline between Chicago and Council Bluffs shortly before Haley left the CCP: "As we went over the railroad I remember thinking to myself that this is the classic overbuilt Iowa line. On-line industry at the time appeared to be scarce, and some major shippers were in trouble." He

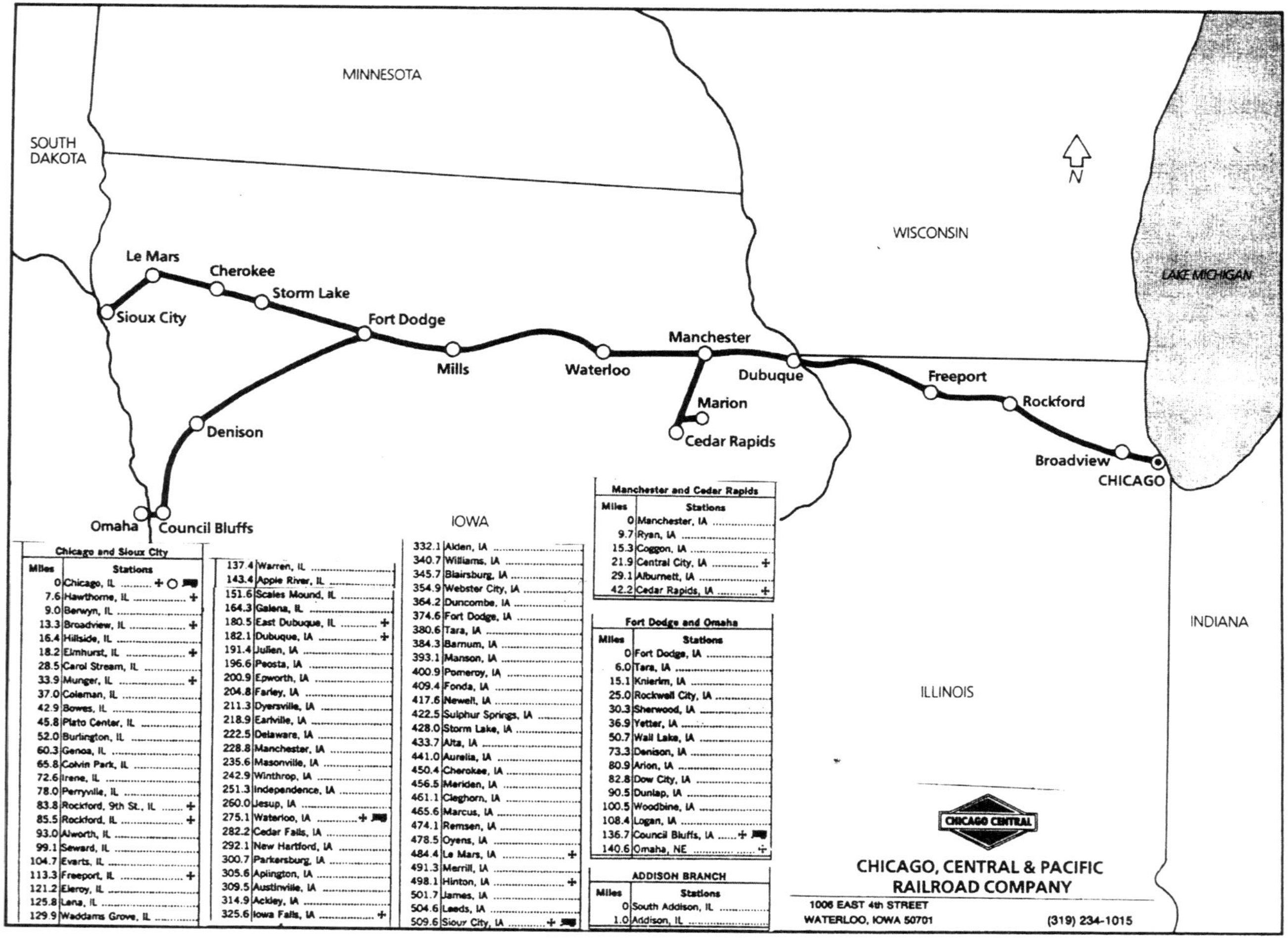

Chicago and Sioux City

Miles	Stations
0	Chicago, IL .... + ○
7.6	Hawthorne, IL .... +
9.0	Berwyn, IL ....
13.3	Broadview, IL .... +
16.4	Hillside, IL ....
18.2	Elmhurst, IL .... +
28.5	Carol Stream, IL ....
33.9	Munger, IL .... +
37.0	Coleman, IL ....
42.9	Bowes, IL ....
45.8	Plato Center, IL ....
52.0	Burlington, IL ....
60.3	Genoa, IL ....
65.8	Colvin Park, IL ....
72.6	Irene, IL ....
78.0	Perryville, IL ....
83.8	Rockford, 9th St., IL .... +
85.5	Rockford, IL .... +
93.0	Alworth, IL ....
99.1	Seward, IL ....
104.7	Evarts, IL ....
113.3	Freeport, IL .... +
121.2	Eleroy, IL ....
125.8	Lena, IL ....
129.9	Waddams Grove, IL ....
137.4	Warren, IL ....
143.4	Apple River, IL ....
151.6	Scales Mound, IL ....
164.3	Galena, IL ....
180.5	East Dubuque, IL .... +
182.1	Dubuque, IA .... +
191.4	Julien, IA ....
196.6	Peosta, IA ....
200.9	Epworth, IA ....
204.8	Farley, IA ....
211.3	Dyersville, IA ....
218.9	Earlville, IA ....
222.5	Delaware, IA ....
228.8	Manchester, IA ....
235.6	Masonville, IA ....
242.9	Winthrop, IA ....
251.3	Independence, IA ....
260.0	Jesup, IA ....
275.1	Waterloo, IA .... +
282.2	Cedar Falls, IA ....
292.1	New Hartford, IA ....
300.7	Parkersburg, IA ....
305.6	Aplington, IA ....
309.5	Austinville, IA ....
314.9	Ackley, IA ....
325.6	Iowa Falls, IA .... +
332.1	Alden, IA ....
340.7	Williams, IA ....
345.7	Blairsburg, IA ....
354.9	Webster City, IA ....
364.2	Duncombe, IA ....
374.6	Fort Dodge, IA ....
380.6	Tara, IA ....
384.3	Barnum, IA ....
393.1	Manson, IA ....
400.9	Pomeroy, IA ....
409.4	Fonda, IA ....
417.6	Newell, IA ....
422.5	Sulphur Springs, IA ....
428.0	Storm Lake, IA ....
433.7	Alta, IA ....
441.0	Aurelia, IA ....
450.4	Cherokee, IA ....
456.5	Meriden, IA ....
461.1	Cleghorn, IA ....
465.6	Marcus, IA ....
474.1	Remsen, IA ....
478.5	Oyens, IA ....
484.4	Le Mars, IA .... +
491.3	Merrill, IA ....
498.1	Hinton, IA .... +
501.7	James, IA ....
504.6	Leeds, IA ....
509.6	Sioux City, IA .... +

Manchester and Cedar Rapids

Miles	Stations
0	Manchester, IA ....
9.7	Ryan, IA ....
15.3	Coggon, IA ....
21.9	Central City, IA .... +
29.1	Alburnett, IA ....
42.2	Cedar Rapids, IA .... +

Fort Dodge and Omaha

Miles	Stations
0	Fort Dodge, IA ....
6.0	Tara, IA ....
15.1	Knierim, IA ....
25.0	Rockwell City, IA ....
30.3	Sherwood, IA ....
36.9	Yetter, IA ....
50.7	Wall Lake, IA ....
73.3	Denison, IA ....
80.9	Arion, IA ....
82.8	Dow City, IA ....
90.5	Dunlap, IA ....
100.5	Woodbine, IA ....
108.4	Logan, IA ....
136.7	Council Bluffs, IA .... +
140.6	Omaha, NE .... +

ADDISON BRANCH

Miles	Stations
0	South Addison, IL ....
1.0	Addison, IL ....

Facing, Jack Haley's Chicago, Central & Pacific Railroad is shown in this contemporary map of its lines in Illinois and Iowa. The company did not abandon any of this former Illinois Central Gulf trackage but instead added modest mileage in the Hawkeye State. *(Author's collection)*

continued, "A large portion of IC's revenue on the line came primarily from perishables and lumber from the UP in Council Bluffs and on-line packinghouse products, both of which were in steep decline by the time of Haley's arrival. The two [coal] trains per day each way from UP were mostly gone by that time. Also, like a lot of Iowa Lines, CCP was overbuilt for the volume of business it was then handling, with signaling in some places still in place for passenger trains."[130]

Haley and his marketing staff worked diligently at bolstering business. "How can we help you?" became the question posed to every customer or potential customer. The company added at the bottom of its stationery, "*Service is our only Business.*" One trade journal described this as "hungry marketing." Traffic increased. In recognition of its initial performance, *Modern Railroads,* an industry trade publication, gave CCP its 1987 Golden Freight Car award. The rationale for this honor centered on the company's grain rates, which diverted significant shipments from road to rail. Part of the overall traffic mix included TOFC traffic, and soon the railroad had an aggressive intermodal subsidiary. These hotshot intermodals, with their sixty-mile-per-hour limit, were dedicated trains that ran the length of the mainline. Still the CCP required continued growth, ideally more bridge traffic from the UP.[131]

It might appear that all was going well for CCP. The reports for 1986 revealed that the company moved over 110,000 cars, significantly more than when ICG operated the Iowa Division. Its operating ratio stood at a respectable 80 percent. But difficulties loomed. Haley realized that his company had to address multiple needs for track rehabilitation. The Sioux City line required immediate attention; slow orders plagued operations, often reducing speeds between Tara and Le Mars to ten miles per hour or less. There existed the threat that the Federal Railroad Administration would embargo the line. If that happened, traffic would be lost and customer goodwill damaged. Even though the CCP had received funding from the Iowa Department of Transportation, an additional $3 million was required to cover the costs for these critical track repairs. General Electric Credit Corporation (GECC), however, declined to provide financial support, insisting that the railroad must control expenses based on actual revenues. Soon a power struggle erupted between Haley and his principal investor.[132]

From Jack Haley's perspective, the ongoing negations did not go well. He considered GECC to be meddling in his railroad world and fretted that the financial issues could not be resolved. In summer 1987 matters came to a head. After a brief legal confrontation, Haley concluded that he had no future with the CCP; GECC, in his mind, had not operated in good faith concerning the loan. Perhaps he was correct. The GECC point of view was that Haley was incompetent, and expenditures were exceeding revenues. The railroad also wasted money on its expensive Waterloo headquarters, dispatched too many trains, and had an excessive number of employees. On September 1, 1987, Haley maneuvered the company into bankruptcy as an act of desperation. Eleven days later the CCP founder resigned after reaching a financial settlement with GECC, returned to Omaha, and reentered the commercial real-estate business. "I had the thing [CCP] wired right," commented Haley. "I just couldn't get enough electricity in it." Reflected Rebensdorf, "I think Haley had both an emotional and business attachment to the industry. Possibly the emotional attachment and the desire to run his own railroad somewhat blinded him to what appeared to be the relatively fragile railroad we observed in our trip over the CCP. I am not sure anyone could have saved CCP at the time." Nevertheless, Haley had made his mark as a regional railroad pioneer.[133]

Although Jack Haley appeared to have abandoned railroading, he had not. Haley retained the CVR, but this shortline remained in his control for only a few more years. In May 1991 the railroad abruptly shut down for financial reasons. Its customers, though, did not suffer. The ICC allowed the CCP to provide service, and in December 1992 the CCP took over the line through a newly launched subsidiary, Cedar River Railroad.[134]

The CCP did not die with the departure of Jack Haley. GECC decided to spend more on the property, investing enough to permit continued operations. Following debt restructuring the bankruptcy ended in October 1987. However, GECC did not remain involved. In time the railroad's senior management, led by two former executives from Burlington Northern, Lyle Reed and Donald Wood, assumed ownership. In 1996 the IC repurchased the railroad. It paid approximately $140 million plus assuming $18 million in debt—or about twice the 1985 sale price. IC operated the former CCP as a subsidiary until the CN acquired it two years later. Integration into IC's new parent began on July 1, 1999.[135]

While Jack Haley disappeared from the Midwest railroad scene, Tom Hoback, another regional founder, did not. His Indiana Rail Road prospered (not to be confused with the Indiana Railroad, a major interurban that served the Hoosier State between 1930 and 1942). Both men came from railroad families and loved trains. Hoback's father was a veteran Santa Fe employee, having served as relief operator and station agent before becoming a dispatcher and chief dispatcher in Illinois and Iowa.[136]

There existed striking differences between the founders of CCP and INRD. Hoback, who spent much of his early life in Fort Madison, Iowa, left the Midwest to earn a degree in transportation and economics at Golden Gate University in San Francisco. Unable to find a position with a railroad, he nevertheless launched a career in transportation. Initially he worked for Foremost-McKesson, a food and pharmaceutical distributor. As a traffic manager, he gained insights into the operations and outlooks of highway and rail transport firms. After two years Hoback resigned to join the Western Pacific Railroad. At this San Francisco–based road, he broadened his knowledge of the industry. Hoback started out as an economic analyst, learning what drove costs. These skills became valuable in understanding how to market railroad freight services.[137]

A major change in Hoback's professional career took place in 1977. Wishing for more interesting and challenging work than what he had encountered at Western Pacific, Hoback returned to the Midwest to take a management job with the upstart Erie Western Railway. This carrier, launched in September 1977 and headquartered in Huntington, Indiana, had once been the western section of the high-speed, double-tracked mainline of the EL. When EL joined Conrail, its new owner did not want the trackage between Marion, Ohio, and Hammond, Indiana, having other routes to reach Chicago. Led by Craig Burroughs, who headed Trans-Action Associates, based in Joliet, Illinois (and was a controversial figure in the shortline industry), the Erie Western's core stretched across the Hoosier State, being a well-built and maintained 158 miles. The eastern portion reached Wren, Ohio, near the Indiana state line. From there Erie Western held trackage rights over another ex-EL startup, Spencerville & Elgin Railroad, allowing entry into Lima, Ohio, twenty-eight miles to the east. Yet Erie Western seldom used this connection. Its western end was Hammond. At this rail hub, the Erie Western trains ran over the Chicago & Western Indiana to reach the Windy City. The Burroughs company also operated a twenty-seven-mile former PRR (née Grand Rapids & Indiana) branch between the Indiana county-seat towns of Decatur and Portland, "which had a large concentration of businesses that CR wrote off." But Erie Western could not afford to buy the ex-EL mainline and instead leased it from Erie Lackawanna Inc., the Cleveland-based liquidating estate.[138]

From its inception Erie Western was badly underfunded. It struggled notwithstanding subsidies from the Federal Railroad Administration and the State of Indiana. The railroad might have received greater financial support from Hoosier lawmakers had there not been heavy demands from other groups seeking to save and rehabilitate pieces of threatened trackage. Taxpayers could not afford these overwhelming monetary requests. (Incidentally, Burroughs had invested little in the Erie Western, totaling just $12,000.) Hoback, who served as vice president of marketing, sought to build up an intermodal business. Although he worked diligently at expanding its customer base, Erie Western failed to generate enough revenue-producing business. It collapsed on June 24, 1979.[139]

Proof of an inadequate traffic base on the Indiana section of the former EL mainline is demonstrated by what later happened. Several of the Erie Western executives, including Tom Hoback, knew that "Burroughs had to go." Hoback explained their course of action: "A couple of us were able to get our lead bank to call in his loan, which essentially bankrupted Craig, the sole shareholder, and he had no choice but to resign." The successor company, Chicago & Indiana Railroad (C&I), had

Top and above, These two photographs, both taken in 1978, show Erie Western power. Four Alco RS-3 locomotives head a string of covered hopper cars eastbound from the Griffith, Indiana, interchange. This rare image is probably a publicity photo. A less well-maintained Alco, No. 9363, crosses the Wabash River in Huntington, Indiana. *(Gary Clark photographs, Thomas Hoback collection)*

two goals: abandon trackage and sell off what could reasonably become a viable shortline. Hoback served as C&I president: "We put what had been the Erie Western out of its misery." As by design its history can be measured in months and not years. Soon most of the rail was lifted and assets sold. The remaining portion became the Tippecanoe Railroad and operated between Monterey and North Judson, Indiana. Its owner, Gordon Taiclit, was the business-savvy head of the Buckeye Feed and Supply Company in Monterey. This sixteen miles of trackage flew the Tippecanoe banner for a decade until it was sold in 1990 to Daniel Frick, who renamed the property JK Line, Inc.[140] Yet this grain-hauling segment had a finite lifespan; it folded in 2004. These events reflect what has happened to multiple failed midwestern shortlines; they left behind complicated corporate histories.[141]

Knowing the saga of Erie Western and its successor operators, Hoback realized that any initial shortline could be fragile; most or all upstarts faced uphill struggles to become profitable. In his words, "It took an extraordinary leap of faith for a customer to take a chance with a new short line railroad." As Erie Western sputtered, Hoback began to look for pieces of Class Is that he could acquire and grow. He did exhaustive research, and a branch of the Illinois Central Gulf attracted his attention. This was the 177-mile Effingham-to-Indianapolis line. Even though this interstate trackage suffered from deferred maintenance, especially between Bloomington and Bargersville, Indiana, and over time had lost considerable on-line traffic, it continued to serve a major electric generating plant in Indianapolis that required large shipments of coal. There was more to like. In addition to the substantial business created by the Indianapolis Power & Light (IP&L) facility, the line served three large grain elevators, a Marathon Oil refinery, several southern Indiana low-sulfur coal mines, and the bustling Indiana capital city. By the late 1970s, metropolitan Indianapolis had emerged as one of America's top ten distribution centers, benefiting from a strategic network of interstate highways: I-65, I-69, I-70, and I-74.[142]

When Jack Healy wanted to become a railroad owner, he found the ICG anxious to sell off trackage. Tom Hoback did not have a similar experience. His initial efforts to acquire the Indianapolis line, which took place a decade or so before Healy's acquisition of the CVR, went nowhere. Hoback and his business partners were stymied. Two reasons largely explain their bewilderment. ICG withdrew its earlier application for abandonment of the Indianapolis line, and IP&L wanted a Class I railroad to provide its coal transportation. Yet Hoback remained determined. Throughout his career, he repeatedly showed resolve and resourcefulness. In 1977 Hoback accepted employment with the ICG as director of coal marketing, a position that he would find beneficial in making the INRD successful.[143]

Hoback must have rejoiced when in 1981 he learned that the ICG planned to sell multiple lines. On the liquidation list was the 110 miles between Sullivan, Indiana, and Indianapolis.[144] If Hoback wanted to bid on that trackage, IC officials did not want him to be an employee. Hoback complied.[145]

There would be still another job for the future owner of the Indianapolis line. Hoback relocated to Tampa, Florida, where he joined the Tampa Electric Company (TECO). He had not left the transportation field, however. Hoback worked on modernizing TECO's coal traffic by focusing on its water transport operations. Still, he did not forsake his railroad dream. While in the Sunshine State, Hoback and his assembled financial backers negotiated with ICG for a sale. In that process they needed to defeat other active suitors. Success followed. In early 1986 the Hoback group closed a purchase agreement to acquire that Sullivan-to-Indianapolis segment. Harry Bruce, who represented ICG, had reached a mutual understanding with Hoback, a handshake that he honored. What next occurred was a hectic scramble to ensure that the $6 million dollar price tag could be paid. Hoback put virtually every dollar he had into meeting the sale price, going so far as to sell his house and borrow from his widowed mother.[146]

After March 17, 1986, Tom Hoback finally had a railroad; it turned out to be a bargain. In the following months and years, he oversaw employee hiring, motive power and freight car acquisitions, track maintenance and upgrades, and most importantly expansion of the customer base. Although the INRD eventually lost its largest customer when IP&L shuttered its coal-fired plant, replacements emerged. Through hard work, Hoback and his staff generated new traffic sources, ranging from coal operators to lumber-products distributors who used transload facilities in Indianapolis. Not to be overlooked was a cordial relationship with CSX, and this involved connecting traffic and financial investments in the railroad itself.[147]

By 1990 INRD was much more than the original Sullivan-to-Indianapolis line. Its connection with the IC was established farther west at Newton, Illinois, making for a 155-mile railroad. It also gained trackage rights over the Pekins–Evansville branch of the ICG between Newton and Browns, Illinois, adding another fifty-seven miles. INRD gained a similar arrangement over the former Nickel Plate line from Tipton, Indiana, into Indianapolis, a distance of forty miles. Yet that operation did not prove long lasting. Although the INRD in 1989 had won a hard-fought battle with ICG to acquire the remaining line to Effingham, it never exercised that option. The system map, though, was not set in stone. Changes followed. As the next decade began, the company also operated the popular Hoosierland Limited dinner train out of Indianapolis, but this was canceled after a brief period due to increased freight traffic.[148]

The 1990s saw the INRD strengthen. Its financial relationship with CSX grew. In 1994 the Jacksonville-headquartered giant granted the Hoback road a $2 million loan. Under the arrangement it could be converted to a 40 percent share of preferred INRD stock. As CSX became more closely involved, it appreciated the way the INRD functioned and gave it "extraordinary autonomy to manage its own affairs and operate the railroad the way it sees fit."[149]

With a stronger financial footing and creative management, INRD underwent major physical betterments, including rebuilding track and upgrading equipment. Between 1986 and 2015, the year Hoback retired, the railroad invested more than $225 million in internally generated revenues in infrastructure improvements, a remarkable amount for any regional railroad. In addition it used more than $20 million in public funding for grade crossing and bridge upgrades.[150]

What stands out involves innovations, such as the adoption of remote-control switching and single-person train crews. In 1996 the company launched a pilot remote-switching project, and it worked well. For one thing, it saved money for businesses that required several daily switches. More remarkable came the introduction in the late 1990s of

In this 2014 photograph, Thomas Hoback stands on a shining Indiana Rail Road Electro Motive Division 4,300-horsepower SD9043MAC locomotive. The occasion is the ribbon cutting to formally open the downtown Senate Avenue Intermodal Terminal in Indianapolis. In 2008 the railroad acquired ten of these SD9043MAC locomotives, and they became the backbone of its motive power fleet. As of 2023 they have since been largely replaced with ten former Norfolk Southern SD70Ms. *(Thomas Hoback collection)*

the one-person train crew. (INRD calls this individual a "train operator" rather than an engineer.) Hoback and his associates did extensive research into the possibility (and safety) of this radical way of operating freight trains. In cooperation with operating employees, who were an essential part of the discussions, it has endured. Hoback believes that the technology exists to have no one in the locomotive cab, but that has yet to occur.[151]

As the twenty-first century progresses, the INRD, now a CSX property, continues to stand out as a progressive carrier. Its lines, both those owned and where it has trackage and haulage rights,[152] include access to the Clearing Yard of the Belt Railway of Chicago. This critical connection, established in 2006, maximized the flow of inbound and outbound traffic and quickly doubled company revenues. As for the Louisville gateway, which was also reached in 2006 with trackage rights over the CSX (former Monon) and the Norfolk Southern, this arrangement into the South failed to continue, ending because of poor track and problems with the signaling system. CSX, for its part, could not justify the expense of repairs or of upgrading these signals. Subsequently, haulage rights began over the Louisville & Indiana Railroad, a shortline that emerged from Conrail, and lasted longer. INRD ultimately concluded that business was inadequate to justify serving the Louisville gateway. A standout operation, however, has been its Senate Avenue Intermodal Terminal in Indianapolis. INRD has doubled this business every five years—an astounding accomplishment. This assessment made by Peter Rickershauser rings true: "The industry was going through structural changes during this time frame. Hoback for one could see the future and what it would take to turn his viable-but-not-enough-business railroad into something profitable—not easy but doable." Tom Hoback can look back on what has evolved as a major accomplishment in the saga of midwestern regional railroads.[153]

Although the trackage of what was formally the CCP and the flourishing INRD can be considered largely enduring, the corporate railroad map of the Midwest in the twenty-first century remains in flux. One recently launched shortline suggests that more may appear, in addition to existing ones joining railroad holding companies. In 2016 a shortline with an awkward name, Belpre Industrial Parkersburg Railroad (BIP), made its debut. This forty-eight-mile pike operates over cast-off CSX trackage in Parkersburg, West Virginia, and southeastern Ohio. BIP consists of two component parts. At Belpre, situated opposite Parkersburg on the Ohio side of the Ohio River, is the junction for a short extension west to Porterfield and a much longer one to the north through Marietta to the Washington County, Ohio, hamlet of Relief. The shortline handles a variety of shipments, including aggregates, carbon black, coal, metals, and petrochemicals. Recently Isaac Miller, a contributor to *Railfan and Railroad*, concluded that "with near-constant operations, the large bridge over the Ohio, and street running [in Marietta], BIP packs a lot into a small area. The glory days of Parkersburg's railroads may be over, but BIP is at the forefront of a new era of customer-driven local service."[154]

AMTRAK

By 1960 railroads worried about their passenger train operations, an ailing and deficit-ridden sector of their business. Some Class I carriers in the Midwest had already become "freight service only," including the Ann Arbor, Chicago & Illinois Midland, Detroit & Mackinac, and Monon. Still, classy trains remained, particularly those operating west of Chicago. These included the Burlington's California Zephyr, Great Northern's Empire Builder, Northern Pacific's North Coast Limited, and Santa Fe's Super Chief. These companies were not planning to seek regulatory approval for their discontinuance, seeing them as having advertising value, boosting employee morale, and generating a cash flow. Travelers with discretionary money and leisure time viewed these luxury trains as "cruise liners," supporting the notion that "the going is half the fun." Throughout the region mainline local trains (perhaps mail trains with an attached coach or two) and those on branches could still be found. The latter were often of the mixed-train variety. They either had their schedules listed in public timetables and the *Official Guide of the Railways* or requested that passengers "consult agent," indicating that departure times varied. There were passenger train cutbacks during the 1960s on Midwest rails, and initially they tended to be gradual. But that trend accelerated toward the end of the decade. This was also true nationally. In 1960 fifty railroads operated passenger service over nearly ninety thousand route miles; a decade later the twenty-five remaining passenger roads ran over approximately forty-four thousand miles.

Why these retrenchments? In 1959 a widely cited article that appeared in *Trains*, "Who Shot the Passenger Train?," consumed the entire feature section. Editor David P. Morgan succinctly explained this troubling situation: "Passenger trains are regulated like a monopoly, manned under World War I–era labor contracts, surrounded by a public transportation plant now being enlarged again because of jets and the 'I' [Interstate] highway program." He could have included in his analysis that the US Post Office was abandoning trains in favor of airplanes and trucks. The department also expanded its network of highway post office buses ("hypos"), which it had introduced in the late 1940s.[155]

How would the industry manage its money-draining passenger sector? By the end of the 1960s, more trains had disappeared, and for a railroad's bottom line these takeoffs helped. Moreover, existing ones were commonly downgraded. The NYC and Santa Fe, for example, added coaches to their formerly all-Pullman trains. In some cases the overall state of these trains deteriorated—dirty cars and windows, broken toilets, and air-conditioning and heating failures. A *Wall Street Journal* reporter made these devastating comments about a family trip taken during July 1969 on Penn Central's Admiral from Chicago to New York City: "The train was dirty, to begin with, mother later complained. For want of a receptacle, trash was being piled on top of the drinking fountain which dispensed warm water only." He continued, "The ladies' room had a 'disgusting odor.' There was no dining car. The snack bar lacked electricity for making breakfast coffee. And the cooling system wasn't working in the mid-July heat." Such conditions did much to create a public feeling that railroad management had a "public-be-damned" attitude. Present-day executives were seemingly cut from the same piece of cloth as a William Vanderbilt. As Fred Frailey put it, "Railroad presidents stood somewhere between cemetery lot salesmen and carnival pitchmen in public esteem, and the common wisdom was that passenger trains weren't doing well because their owners didn't want them to."[156]

Railroad officials faced real challenges. While they knew that freight would always be their bread and butter, concern grew about the future of this traffic in the Midwest. Industries were leaving or dispersing to the

South and West. Travelers, though, did not grasp the industry's problems and did not understand that they were commonly being furnished a transportation service below cost. In 1969 Penn Central chairman Stuart Saunders said this about the Broadway Limited, his road's flagship New York City–to–Chicago train: "[It] was a solid Pullman Train. We offered every convenience passengers could possibly want. And in the last two years of operation, the average number of people using the train was 60. The crew numbered more than 70. We didn't have as many passengers as we had working on the train." Al Perlman of the NYC described the situation more succinctly: "Passenger trains are a stupid waste of money."[157]

The desperate straits of Penn Central and the growing deterioration of its physical plant triggered a passenger rail crisis. Its crumbling mainlines were plagued with numerous slow orders. In 1970 the company still dispatched passenger trains over about five thousand route miles, including long-distance runs between the East and the Midwest. If PC were to suspend operations, travelers who lived along its corridor lines would suffer. Other forces were at play. In 1967 the US Post Office decided to divert mail from passenger rail to air, truck, and piggyback freight except in the Northeast Corridor, thus depriving the head-end business that helped mitigate passenger fare declines. It had paid "retail" rates for haulage, and this financial loss became a leading reason for the death of much of the existing service. A year later the Railway Express Agency shut down its operations. By this time even healthy railroads faced crippling passenger deficits. The financial strain could no longer be tolerated.[158]

A solution emerged, and it involved federal intervention. There were those within railroad circles who worried that if Washington aided passenger service, this could be a step toward nationalization. A government subsidy, however, might satisfy all concerned parties. Senator Vance Harke, an Indiana Democrat who supported passenger rail, received considerable industry support for such an approach. That legislative alternative went nowhere after the election of Richard Nixon to the presidency in 1968. His administration adamantly opposed federal subsidies for intercity passenger operations. After much political maneuvering, the executive branch agreed to support what became the Rail Passenger Service Act of 1970. "From Nixon's point of view," observed transportation writer Don Phillips, "the Vietnam War was unpopular enough, and he didn't need to become the grinch that stole the passenger train." With little enthusiasm Nixon signed the legislative measure. The law created the quasi-public National Railroad Passenger Corporation, with its common stock acquired by the participating railroads that did not opt for tax credits and its preferred stock owned by the federal government. This entity became "Railpax"[159] but was soon renamed. Amtrak became the new moniker, a contraction of the words "America" and "track." It would be financially supported by ticket sales, federal loans and grants, and onetime charges from those railroads who were being relieved of their money-losing passenger operations. Nevertheless, Amtrak lacked adequate funding.[160]

On day one, May 1, 1971, Amtrak made most railroads "freight only." That morning the new government-sponsored system operated passenger trains over just twenty-three thousand miles on twenty railroads. Several companies did not join the national network: Denver & Rio Grande Western, Georgia Railroad (part of the Family Lines—Seaboard Coast Line, L&N, and Clinchfield), Rock Island, and Southern. The Chicago, South Shore & South Bend, the nation's last interurban, also refused to enter the Amtrak orbit. The only other Midwest carrier to opt out was "the Rock." Its reason differed from any of the others: it could not afford the entry price. This meant that it had to operate its two daily trains between Chicago and Rock Island and its four daily ones between Chicago and Peoria until March 1, 1973. At that time it could reconsider joining Amtrak. If the company did not, it would need to continue service until January 1, 1975, with no assurance that a discontinuance would follow. The Rock Island, which entered bankruptcy in March 1975, remained in the passenger business until December 31, 1978, assisted by fare hikes authorized by the Illinois Commerce Commission and grants from the Illinois Department of Transportation.[161]

Although the national intercity passenger train network was drastically reduced, the Midwest as a region did reasonably well with the dawning Amtrak era. Chicago remained the nation's passenger rail hub. Instead of using more than a single terminal in the Windy City, Amtrak trains arrived and departed from Union Station, Chicago's newest facility, having opened in 1925. This marked the city's first consolidated

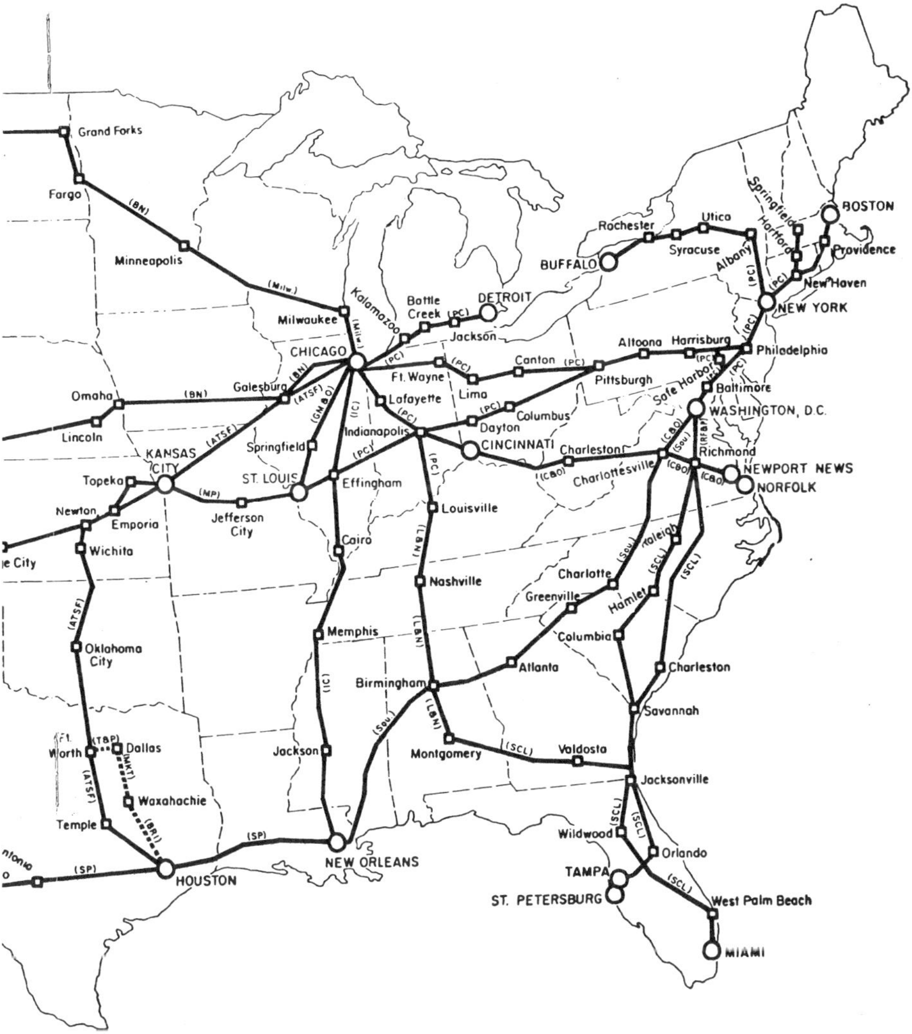

In the initial Amtrak public timetable, the system map shows how the eight midwestern states received continuing passenger service. Notably, such cities as Cleveland, Des Moines, Duluth, and Springfield, Missouri, lacked access to these trains. *(Author's collection)*

long-distance passenger terminal. Other stations either handled commuter trains or closed and were subsequently partially or totally demolished. From a historic preservation perspective, these were tragic losses. Grand Central Station stands out. This massive brick-and-brownstone structure with its 247-foot tower, 11,000-pound bell, magnificent leaded stained-glass windows, and marble fireplace in the general waiting room closed in 1969 after seventy-nine years of service. When it was razed in 1971, Chicago architect Harry Weese called this an act of "wanton destruction."[162]

Even though travelers would have fewer passenger train options in the Midwest and elsewhere, David Kendall, who chaired the National Railroad Passenger Corporation board, stated in the first public timetable that he believed in the future of long-distance rail travel: "We feel that this network of trains—which has been developed through months of intensive analysis—provides a solid base upon which to build and expand the scope and quality of intercity passenger service. This new system can and will succeed because it unified for the first time the operation and promotion of the nation's passenger service." Kendall closed with these thoughts: "The Board of Directors of Amtrak asks the support of the traveling public as this schedule is introduced and service improvements are implemented. On our part, we pledge our best efforts to providing the American people a modern, attractive rail service as rapidly as possible."[163]

Not everyone was as sanguine as David Kendall about the future of Amtrak. Some thought that the system would collapse, perhaps within a few years. Others wondered if even its skeleton network might undergo substantial cuts. There was the realization that Amtrak had inherited old equipment, and, in some cases (such as on the Penn Central), tracks could not sustain fast, reliable service. Although the quasi-public corporation bled money, it continued to function and attempted to serve public needs. Rather than wholesale contraction, new trains and routes appeared in the Midwest, including the Black Hawk between Chicago, Rockford, and Dubuque. Service began in February 1974 but ended in September 1981. Other changes occurred. There was an Amtrak victory of note. In 1976 it took ownership of the 456-mile Northeast Corridor, consisting of former Penn Central and New Haven trackage between

Washington, DC, New York, and Boston. The purchase also included PC's Philadelphia–Harrisburg and New Haven–Springfield lines as well as one between Michigan City, Indiana, and Kalamazoo, Michigan.[164] "We did not know if our fledgling creation would survive its first two years," wrote an early participant in the Amtrak saga in 1991. "Today Amtrak is still threatened from time-to-time, but it has taken on a life of its own." In 1998, however, a troubling piece of legislation occurred: the National Railroad Passenger Act. It required Amtrak to break even financially on its operations in five years. This was an impossibility, and fortunately Congress continued to provide financial assistance. Moreover, Amtrak has been helped considerably with state-supported operations. In the Midwest they have been ongoing in Illinois, Michigan, Missouri, and Wisconsin. Being underfunded nevertheless remains true in the twenty-first century. Amtrak is not going away, and there is hope for major betterments. The Biden administration's Infrastructure Act of 2022, supervised under the auspices of the Federal Railroad Administration, granted $22 billion over a five-year period to modernize the Amtrak rail network. Passenger service in the Midwest should benefit, expand, or at least stabilize. As in the past, Amtrak attempts to please multiple constituencies—mass transportation for the general population between big cities, an efficient conveyance for business travelers, a pleasurable experience for vacationers, and a lifeline for residents of smaller communities to connect with the outside world.[165]

BOXES

While most midwestern railroads (except the Rock Island) benefited from Amtrak's creation, they took greater satisfaction from expanding intermodal opportunities. TOFC had been accelerating in popularity since the mid-1950s and pleasing participants. It combined the flexibility and door-to-door pickup and delivery provided by a truck together with the cost-effectiveness of a rail-line haul. The modern TOFC came about due in part to the skills of Gene Ryan, who in 1952 launched the Rail-Trailer Company (subsequently Trailer-Train and renamed TTX in 1991). He responded to the alleged or real disadvantages of the piggyback concept. Ryan and others made improvements, including placing two

The Chicago Great Western, a piggyback pioneer, continued into the post–World War II era to offer this intermodal service. In May 1953, the year that the industry was taking note of the revenue possibilities of TOFC, four EMD F3s power such a consist headed toward the Twin Cities a few miles north of Oelwein, Iowa. *(Don Hofsommer photograph)*

trailers on each lengthened flatcar (often seventy-five feet), employing double instead of single jacks, and streamlining loading and unloading facilities. Trailers were initially moved on and off standard flatcars by means of ramps, circus-train style, but by the mid-1950s specialized gantry cranes and giant forklift trucks accelerated the process. Although profit margins were tight, carriers knew that they got little use from their massive fleets of boxcars. In the post–World War II years, a typical boxcar spent most of its time idle in a yard or on a siding, being in revenue service often for less than 10 percent of its life expectancy. Furthermore, as Curtis Buford, who headed Trailer Train Company in the early 1980s, explained, "A public emphasis on highway construction with public funds—this time the Interstate System—was one of the factors that stimulated railroad concern and prompted strong efforts by railroads to bring piggybacking into its own."[166]

In the 1960s the truck trailer had a new companion, the metal container or "box." The concept of transporting freight in this fashion had been introduced by steam and electric interurban railroads during World War I and immediately afterward but appeared on only a limited number of Class I roads. In 1931 the ICC gave a crushing blow to container operators, the result of complaints made by unhappy truckers and some competing carriers. This decision negated their preferred rate-making approach, known as the "Freight-All-Kinds" schedule. The cost of shipping an entire box before 1931 depended entirely on mileage variations, not the contents, which benefitted container customers.[167]

A new day for containerized freight did not arrive until the 1950s. Malcom McLean, a trucking executive from North Carolina and founder of Sea-Land, promoted the idea of separating the road wheels and chassis from truck trailers to allow freight to move seamlessly on and off trucks and ships. McLean converted an old oil tanker into what he called a "seagoing tractor." In the spring of 1956, his *Ideal X* with a load of fifty-eight of these modified truck trailers or containers sailed between the ports of New York and Houston, Texas. The container idea started to revolutionize ocean shipping, especially during the Vietnam War, and effectively erased distances. While the concept looked encouraging, railroads did not soon follow McLean's lead, due mostly to cost considerations. If intermodal operations received funding and technical assistance, they were earmarked for expansion of TOFC. But that would ultimately change.[168]

During the gestation or demonstration period of modern containerization, there came an interesting twist. It came about under the direction of Al Perlman, the dynamic head of the NYC. It was christened "Flexi-Van" and eliminated trailer wheels. A van or container, rather than a truck trailer (with wheels), was swung onto or off of a Flexi-Van custom-built, low-center-of-gravity aluminum car to an awaiting chassis (structural skeleton of a truck). The process consisted of a hydraulic turntable on the flatcar that received its power from electrical cables attached to the truck-tractor. The driver would spin the trailer into place by hand. The loading process was accomplished in reverse fashion. Once the Flexi-Van was moved from truck to flatcar, the train could move at higher speeds because of reduced wind resistance. There were additional advantages: the Flexi-Van system ended the need for intermodal terminals and mechanized cranes. This novel way of transporting LCL, US mail, and other goods began in 1958 and lasted for about a decade. Although it was deemed a success, NYC decided in 1964 to join Trailer-Train in order to have a source of TOFC cars, and two years later it expanded that operation. Several major midwestern terminals, including Chicago, had benefited from the Flexi-Vans, but better service came from the widely employed TOFC alternative.[169]

In the early 1970s, midwestern carriers began to provide container-on-flatcar (COFC) service. The North Western was a leader in this form of intermodal offering. In spring 1973 it began dispatching its "Falcon" TOFC and COFC intermodal service between Chicago and Fremont, Nebraska, and a seamless interchange with the UP. This traffic grew because of speed and dependability. "It's a simple philosophy of C&NW people," observed *Railway Age* in 1977. "You run as many trains as you need, you leave on time, you don't get in a Falcon's way out on the road, and you get in on time—or better."[170]

Major transportation deregulation measures, including the Staggers Act, energized the TOFC and COFC business. The ICC vacated its power to control railroad rates, except for a few commodities, and railroads could negotiate long-term contracts that set rates and terms of service. Also, trucks and railcars that had been required to return empty could now solicit cargoes for backhauls. These changes collectively proved to be a win-win for customers and railroads. As for the latter, carriers were able to reclaim market share from truckers in major long-haul traffic lanes, such as Chicago–New York and Chicago–Los Angeles. As a result, COFC boomed. "Modern freight shippers have taken to containerization with the same zeal other facets of American society are showing for computers," opined transportation specialist John White Jr. of the Smithsonian Institution in 2003.[171]

A dramatic change in how railroads hauled the metal box came in the 1980s. To increase capacity and revenues, roads embarked on double-stack operations. In March 1984 the UP and North Western forged the first transcontinental double-stack operation in conjunction with Conrail. Double-stack trains thus crossed the approximately nine-hundred-mile width of the Midwest. At the Port of Los Angeles, cranes transloaded these containers from ships onto lightweight low-to-the-ground flatcars known as "well cars." They reduced vertical clearance and lowered the center of gravity of a loaded car. This rolling stock allowed a train to carry twice as many containers with only a 30 percent increase in weight compared to conventual COFC trains. Part of the intermodal revolution led to the construction of large, mechanized inland terminals to transfer trailers and containers between highway and railroad. Burlington Northern (now BNSF), for example, built such an intermodal facility at its sprawling yard complex in the Chicago suburb of Cicero, Illinois.[172]

American railroads, with a few exceptions, did not embrace another new technology, the RoadRailer system. The concept is imaginative although not exactly original—the Bonner Rail Wagons of the Lake Shore Electric can be considered the prototype. The modern version likewise permits a trailer that can operate on both rails and roads. Specifically, a locomotive can pull these trailers without the use of flatcars by placing trailers on rails with an integrated set of railroad wheels. An air suspension system makes possible the transfer between these two modes of transportation.

The Midwest became the center of RoadRailer usage. The Chesapeake & Ohio first introduced this intermodal option in the mid-1950s to haul US mail over its Pere Marquette subsidiary. These "Railvans" were attached to the rear of passenger trains between Detroit, Grand Rapids, and Traverse City, Michigan, but this ended in 1967 when the Post Office Department cancelled its contract. The revival of the Railvan approach didn't appear until the 1980s. It would be Norfolk Southern that embraced what it called "RoadRailers." Its Triple Crown subsidiary, launched in 1986 and based in Fort Wayne, Indiana, focused heavily on door-to-door service to move auto parts between Detroit and Kansas City over the former Wabash speedway. General Motors became the principal customer, and at best NS developed only a niche market. The railroad, however, reduced its RoadRailer operations in 2015. Opined one intermodal analyst at the time, "Norfolk Southern's decision to scale back use of its RoadRailer trailer trains is a missed opportunity for the industry." Yet as railroad writer Brian Solomon observed, "RoadRailer trailers cannot be easily mixed into ordinary intermodal and freight consists in the same fashion as double-stack and other new types of intermodals." He added, "RoadRailer trailers have suffered from their inability to be coupled anyplace but at the end of consists. As a result, most freight railroads that have tried RoadRailer have tended to run the trailers in solid consists." He further noted, "Too often it is impractical to build traffic volumes with RoadRailers." After downsizing its RoadRailer service in 2015, NS continued to operate its Triple Crown RoadRailers between Detroit-area parts suppliers of Ford Motor Company and its assembly plant in Claycomo, Missouri (Kansas City). But by 2023 its remaining trailers had reached the point where they could not be economically maintained, and replacement costs were considered excessive. NS concluded that the better way to handle this service is to use intermodal trailers or containers.[173]

WEATHER

Inclement weather has always been the bane of railroaders. The industry has experienced its share of natural disasters, and the modern era is no exception. The continental-type climate of the Midwest is known for its extremes, hot, humid summers and cold, snowy winters. These conditions have produced heavy rains, floods, snows, and blizzards that have disrupted railroad service and increased maintenance and operating costs. The prolonged and paralyzing winter of 1935–1936 in the Midwest stands out as one of the worst on record, rivaling the "Long Winter" of 1880–1881 that for months stymied freight and passenger movements in much of the Upper Midwest, being especially severe in Minnesota.[174]

Specific happenings during the 1935–1936 winter were long remembered by everyone affected. January and February 1936 proved to be the most trying months with heavy snows, high winds, and record-setting low temperatures. The ugliest weather of that brutal season came in early and mid-February. Several events on the Great Western were representative. A motor train with fifteen passengers became hopelessly stuck near Melbourne, Iowa, and 150 shovelers labored for two days to free it. The bitter cold, which accompanied the snow, plunged overnight thermometers to thirty degrees or more below zero. In one occurrence subzero

During the hard winter of 1935–1936, railroaders in the Midwest battled snow and subzero temperatures. February 1936 was especially severe. A work gang attempts to extricate a trapped freight train near Gowrie, Iowa, on the Minneapolis & St. Louis. *(Don Hofsommer collection)*

temperatures "froze solidly" two carloads of hogs, something that no Great Western employee could ever recall happening. These unfortunate animals were aboard a side-tracked freight train in Clarion, Iowa. Even a touch of drama occurred: "The motor passenger train going east [from Stockton, Illinois] to Chicago on Saturday afternoon [February 3] bucked snow so forcibly that huge chunks of frozen snow broke the front windows of the train, exposing the motorman to the frosty breezes. A stop was made at Bryan [Illinois] to repair the windows, but they broke again before Chicago was reached." It was common for winds to drive snow into cuts recently cleared by rotary and wedge plows, flangers, and gangs of men and teenage boys, necessitating the removal process to begin again. Frigid readings continued until the end of the month. Freight shipments were at times impossible, especially critical when communities ran short of coal. This fuel was the nearly universal source of heat for homes, businesses, and factories. March weather fortunately produced less harsh conditions.[175]

The Great Western was hardly alone in battling Old Man Winter. The Milwaukee Division of the Milwaukee Road encountered serious snow removal challenges from mid-January to near the close of February. Only four times during a thirty-four-day period did the thermometer rise above the zero mark. When it did, blizzards or storms of near-blizzard intensity accompanied the "milder" weather. Division Superintendent J. H. Valentine, who helped direct snow removal, got little rest during mid-February. Early on the morning of the eighteenth, he learned that seventeen freight trains were stalled by deep snow at various locations. For the next fourteen hours, Valentine relentlessly cajoled every man on his division. His generalship worked. By the afternoon of February 20, all trains were free, and the Milwaukee Division was back in full operation. Finally, the worst of the winter of 1935–1936 was over for Valentine and his men.[176]

Challenging winters—snows, blizzards, ice storms—did not end with the record-setting events of 1935–1936. Severe weather continued to disrupt midwestern railroad operations. Although the blizzard that paralyzed parts of the Great Plains on New Year's Day 1949 and led to the dismissal of the Union Pacific president caused fewer problems east of the Missouri River, severe snowstorms in 1965 and 1977, for example, struck throughout much of the region. As with all snow events, service interruptions occurred. Railroaders had to endure. "*This* [winter] is the part of railroading I can do without!" remembered a Milwaukee Road trainman who worked in Illinois during the winter of 1977.[177]

River and stream flooding was different. These disruptions nearly always lasted longer than blizzards and heavy snows, and the dollar costs soared to greater levels. The midwestern floods of 1993 proved devastating. While there had been major high-water episodes in the twentieth century—in 1913, 1927, 1937, and 1949—what took place in 1993 became known among many of the region's railroads as *the* flood of the century.[178]

The epic floods of 1993 occurred largely in July, following three months of steady rains. These relentless storms, which at times produced cloudbursts, impacted virtually every railroad operating west from

In January 1977 Milwaukee Road employees labor to free a snow-bound train in Madison, Wisconsin. *(John Gruber photograph, © Center for Railroad Photography and Art)*

Chicago and St. Louis. They caused the worst damage in Illinois, Iowa, and Missouri and somewhat less in Minnesota and Wisconsin. Examples abound. In early July Santa Fe's Chicago–Kansas City mainline was inundated at Niota, Illinois, and nearby Fort Madison, Iowa; the "River Lines" radiating from St. Louis were submerged for weeks; Burlington Northern's mainline west of Ottumwa, Iowa, experienced washouts and water-covered rights-of-way; and Soo Line tracks in Davenport, Iowa, were under six to eight feet or more of muddy Mississippi River water for days. One dramatic event occurred on July 29 when the financially strapped regional Gateway Western Railway (former Chicago & Alton and GM&O trackage) lost a section of its 2,408-foot Missouri River bridge at Glasgow, Missouri, due to a surging flood crest. This resulted in the line being shut down for months. Then in August a barge struck and seriously damaged its Mississippi River bridge at Louisiana, Missouri. The president of the Association of American Railroads described the massive flooding as "one of the most devastating natural disasters to befall American transportation." No one suggested otherwise.[179]

Then came the snowmelt and rains in 2019. The flooding that resulted caused severe economic losses in nineteen states, with the Midwest being the hardest hit. These historic floods, which began in mid-March and lasted into early summer, covered, damaged, or wiped out large sections of main and branch-line tracks, rights-of-way, and bridges. Support facilities suffered as well. Take happenings along the Missouri River. On the Iowa and Missouri side of the "Big Muddy," the former Burlington trackage owned by BNSF experienced the worst effects, ending normal service between Kansas City, St. Joseph, and Council Bluffs for weeks. The Mississippi River also badly disrupted operations in sections of the Upper Mississippi Valley. In Burlington, Iowa, the BNSF and the shortline Burlington Junction Railway suffered when river waters remained outside their banks for 104 days, surpassing the 1993 record. "We've had another 100 year flood in just 26 years," exclaimed a local railroader.[180]

As with the disastrous flooding that befell the Midwest in 1993 and again in 2019, the Class Is and regionals encountered fewer detour options. A good illustration involved trackage between Chicago and Council Bluffs. Even before the 1990s, two historic routes had been largely abandoned. The better engineered and maintained trans-Illinois and Iowa line of the Milwaukee Road had much of its Hawkeye State track lifted in the 1980s. The Great Western had virtually all of its trans-Illinois and Iowa rails retired. By 2019 even more lines had disappeared. One example was the former 224-mile Wabash line between Brunswick, Missouri, and Council Bluffs; in fact, sixty-three miles in southwestern Iowa had become the Wabash Trace Nature Trail. As the result of widespread line abandonments, the railroad map of the region no longer resembled a plate of wet spaghetti.

Unlike in 1993, the internet in 2019 (which had been less advanced earlier) helped railroads cope with line disruptions. Carriers utilized their ability to create special websites that kept customers informed about conditions. In March BNSF launched one that had its track outage map and later its web page: www.bnsf.com/floodrecovery.

Not to be forgotten with weather calamities are the impacts they had on customers and railroads themselves. This is one of the indirect effects of weather, causing more or less revenue business and altering a railroad's bottom line. The massive floods of 1993 and 2019 wiped out or severely damaged the cash crops of thousands of farmers in the region. As heavy haulers of grain and ethanol, railroads felt the sting of significantly reduced amounts of corn and soybeans, meaning fewer car loadings. Yet some midwestern carriers benefited. Notably the Illinois Central captured traffic that had to be rerouted over its Illinois trackage.

"WHAT IS PAST IS PROLOGUE"

Bad weather is not the sole continuum in the story of railroading in the Midwest. When one compares the region's railroad map in the post–Civil War decades with the one that exists today, there are striking similarities. One hundred and fifty years ago, there was a mix of trunk lines, regional lines, and shortlines. Today much longer railroads dominate, but there exists a plethora of regional and shortline carriers. Of course, railroads have long lost their monopoly on land transportation; they are no longer all things to all people. Their total mileage has declined significantly as well. In the nineteenth century, there was no labor featherbedding. And as of the twenty-first century, that financially draining aspect of the workforce, which ran rampant after 1950 or so, has been mostly eliminated. Railroads furthermore have dropped some of their historic services, including LCL freight and passenger trains except for the quasi-public Amtrak. Yet they continue to be essential for moving commodities necessary for sustaining population and economic growth, whether it be TOFC, international and domestic COFC, bulk commodities, or general cargoes. There is no denying the inherent economy of steel wheels rolling over steel rails throughout the Midwest, the nation, and North America. Those carriers that serve the Midwest, with their total of 34,796 route miles, make a substantial contribution.[181]

EPILOGUE

HERITAGE

It is possible to experience what the Railway Age was once like in the Midwest. Over the past few decades, scores of locomotive and caboose displays, depot museums, tourist railroads, and historic sites have evolved. When it comes to present-day railroad museums and tourist excursions, California and Pennsylvania boast the greatest number—fifty-eight and forty, respectively. The eight midwestern states are also well represented. Illinois claims twenty-one, Indiana nine, Iowa ten, Michigan twenty-one, Minnesota fourteen, Missouri eighteen, Ohio twenty-four, and Wisconsin twenty. Several have achieved national prominence: the Boone & Scenic Valley Railroad and Museum in Boone, Iowa; the Fort Wayne Railroad Historical Society in Fort Wayne, Indiana; the Illinois Railroad Museum in Union (the largest in the nation); the National Museum of Transportation in St. Louis; the Mid-Continent Railway Museum in North Freedom, Wisconsin; the National Railroad Museum in Green Bay, Wisconsin; and the Steam Railroad Institute in Owosso, Michigan. The 250-acre Pullman National Historical Park Historic District in Chicago has a direct railroad focus. Another museum is in its developmental stage, the Railroad Heritage of Midwest America (RRHMA) in Silvis, Illinois. This organization owns the ninety-acre Silvis Shop complex with its ten miles of track. This facility, opened by the Chicago, Rock Island & Pacific Railroad in 1904, served that carrier until it shut down in 1980. Already the RRHMA has saved the last large erecting hall performing its original function. And it has made significant acquisitions, most notably the steam locomotive heritage fleet of the Union Pacific Railroad. More pieces of rolling stock are part of its holdings, and additional ones are slated to join its collection. In 2023, for example, Burlington Northern Santa Fe Railway donated a General Electric B40-8W diesel, formerly part of the Atchison, Topeka & Santa Fe's "Super Fleet" of GE locomotives that powered its hottest trains between Chicago and Los Angeles.[1]

While railroad museums display (and hopefully interpret) historical artifacts, tourist railroads—whether using steam or diesel locomotives that handle vintage or more modern passenger equipment—provide visitors with opportunities to view railroad corridors, including cuts and fills, bridges, trackside structures, and the like. What is dubbed "recreational railroading" can be enjoyed throughout the Midwest, extending from Ohio to Minnesota.[2]

Two tourist railroads, the Hocking Valley Scenic Railway (HVSR) and the North Shore Scenic Railroad (NSSR), are good representatives. Both are relatively short, employ steam and diesel locomotives, and offer a range of patron experiences. They are also structured as nonprofits 501(c)(3) designed for education and entertainment.

The older of the two is the Hocking Valley Scenic Railway. In the late 1960s, its backers conceived the idea of a tourist pike. Although they acquired a steam locomotive, their plans to operate it over a piece of southern Ohio trackage fizzled. Finally in 1972 the HVSR emerged. The location for what has become a successful operation was once part of the 320-mile largely coal-carrying Hocking Valley Railway, a Buckeye State carrier that connected Toledo, Columbus, Athens, and Pomeroy. Presently the HVSR owns a dozen miles of line between Nelsonville and Logan, where it connects with the Indiana & Ohio Railway, owned by shortline and regional conglomerate Genesee & Wyoming. According to *Trains* contributor Isaac Miller, "The railroad's childhood was difficult." A variety of rolling stock, including locomotives, came and went. Ultimately the HVSR achieved stability. It purchased a small steam switcher and in 2015 placed it in service. Several diesels also grace the roster.[3]

The attractions of a trip over the HVSR are diverse. The railroad advertises itself as "scenic," and it lives up to that name. Much of the right-of-way parallels the free-flowing Hocking River. With a train consist of vintage coaches and open-air cars, riders can enjoy this tributary of the Ohio River together with the surrounding Hocking Hills. They can view old brick kilns; a stone lock of the long-abandoned Hocking Canal, once a feeder to the Ohio & Erie Canal; and the onetime company town of Haydenville, a former coal-mining and brick- and ceramic-tile-making community. As with virtually all tourist railroads, the HVSR operates an array of trip offerings, including Dinner, Robbery, and Santa trains.[4]

The Duluth & North Shore Railroad (known as the North Shore Scenic Railroad), more than twice the length of the HVSR, provides patrons with spectacular scenery. This "Lakefront Line" follows the rugged Lake Superior shoreline for much of the distance between Duluth and Two Harbors. Constructed in the mid-1880s by the Duluth & Iron Range Railroad, the line later became the property of the Duluth, Missabe & Iron Range Railroad (DM&IR). Iron ore, pulpwood, and general merchandise traveled over this trackage, but in 1982 declining traffic led to the suspension of service. The track remained, and occasional trips were made under the auspices of the Lake Superior Railroad Museum (LSRM), located in Duluth's historic Union Station, built by the Northern Pacific in 1892. Eventually the DM&IR sought to retire the line. Museum and local civic leaders realized that it offered the promise of becoming a tourist attraction. Success followed. In 1986 the St. Louis and Lake County Regional Rail Authority orchestrated the purchase of this endangered trackage. Three years later it was marketed as the North Shore Scenic Railroad.[5]

Operations, which started in 1990, took time to stabilize. By 1996 the LSRM assumed control and expanded tourist activities. Over time the NSSR assembled a fleet of historic rolling stock. Included in its collection are a Budd RDC-1 car, a Great Northern EMD NW5 diesel, and a Duluth & Northeastern Consolidation-type 2-8-0 built in 1906. The principal tourist motive power is a former DM&IR EMD SD18 diesel. As is common with similar railroads, the NSSR dispatches a range of specialty trains. Popular ones include the Family Pizza Party Express, the Great Pumpkin Train, the Christmas City Express, and a dinner train. Each usually includes a dome car seating option.[6]

A person does not need to find a tourist line to have an enlightened midwestern railroad experience. Amtrak can provide an interesting and educational trip between a number of cities or even a shorter one between several station stops. Unlike the typical tourist pike, speeds are not limited to ten, twenty, or thirty miles per hour, offering a rider a better sense of those "limiteds" and streamliners of the past.

Persons interested in midwestern railroad heritage have additional options. There are multiple specialized historical societies that cover railroads in the region; as of 2023 there exist twenty-three such organizations. These are railroad specific and range from the smallest "fallen flag" companies—Illinois Traction Society, Chicago & Eastern Illinois Railroad Historical Society, and Monon Railroad Historical-Technical Society are examples—to sprawling former large carriers, represented by the Chicago & North Western Historical Society, New York Central System Historical Society, and Santa Fe Historical and Modeling Society. Nationally focused groups also provide opportunities to learn about the railroad history of the Midwest. The leading and oldest organization is the Railway & Locomotive Historical Society (R&LHS), founded in 1920. It publishes *Railroad History*, a scholarly semiannual journal. Not to be overlooked is the Center for Railroad Photography and Art in Madison, Wisconsin. Like the R&LHS, it has a professionally produced publication, the quarterly *Railroad Heritage*.[7]

A NEW ERA

An observant individual at trackside throughout the eight-state region can detect that the industry in recent years has changed appreciably. Noticeable is the absence of the caboose. This most individualistic piece of railroad rolling stock has virtually vanished.[8] In several ways the "little red caboose behind the train" of the children's song holds a historic connection to the Midwest. The region did not introduce this iconic piece of rolling stock for crew members—a conductor, brakemen, and perhaps a flagman—but over time its carriers made important improvements.

In 1863 the Chicago & North Western introduced the caboose cupola, allowing trainmen to observe the freight cars ahead. They could watch for shifting loads or other signs of trouble from their lookout seats. Much later the Akron, Canton & Youngstown introduced the bay window in the 1920s. Soon thereafter the Baltimore & Ohio and Milwaukee Road enthusiastically embraced this enhanced feature. The latter company's West Milwaukee Shops produced some three hundred welded-steel cabooses, featuring their eye-catching ribbed-side body style. Sadly for some traditionalists, the International Car Company in Kenton, Ohio, built the last commercially manufactured caboose in 1981.[9]

What killed off the caboose? The culprit was the end-of-train device (EOT or EOTD), pioneered by the Florida East Coast Railway in 1969. Its no-nonsense management demonstrated that this technology provided a safe alternative to the caboose. This portable apparatus, which is attached to the rear of a freight train, monitors air pressure in the air-brake system and train integrity and transmits this information by radio signal to the locomotive cab, where it is displayed. Then there were the financial savings. In 1987 the Association of American Railroads released a study indicating that the EOTD would cut expenses by fifty-seven cents per freight train mile. Not to be ignored was that the caboose was inherently unsafe for crew members, especially at high speeds. It could be a death trap. In one instance a Santa Fe conductor, who worked out of Shopton (Fort Madison), Iowa, recalled that when a brakeman was walking through the waycar (caboose on the Santa Fe), the train went into emergency braking, propelling his head through a glass window. He died instantly. Cabooses were always rough riding, and at the rear of a long train they acted like the end of a whip. For companies they were expensive to buy or build, haul, service, and repair. But perhaps not all railroaders welcomed their disappearance. As former *Trains* editor Kevin Keefe astutely observed, "The demise of the caboose was so symbolic of the cutbacks in crew size. Maybe a lot of them regretted seeing them go more than we realize. I'm thinking the railroads sure liked getting rid of them, but not so sure about all those thousands of brakemen who knew they were on the way out." It did not take long for carriers to sell, scrap, or otherwise dispose of their thousands of cabooses. A few have been retained for maintenance-of-way and yard assignments. If a train needs to back across grade crossing on a frequent basis, a crewman has a safe riding space to observe and direct highway traffic.[10]

For some time the once-ubiquitous railroad depot has largely disappeared. Most that remain active serve commuters in the greater Chicago area and are scattered along Amtrak lines. Some have been repurposed for storage of maintenance and signal equipment. So how do freight customers arrange for empty cars and pickups? If the Landus Agricultural Cooperative in Ralston, Iowa, situated on the former North Western Overland Route, needs cars and a movement, an office worker contacts the UP Service Center. And the railroad's traffic agent keeps in touch with Landus elevator personnel, whether by telephone, fax, or internet.[11]

There are new additions to locomotives and rolling stock that travel over midwestern rails. Class Is continue to modernize their locomotive fleets. Norfolk Southern (NS), for one, has a large number of AC-44C6Ms, Dash-9s upgraded to AC traction. Today's more powerful and fuel-efficient locomotives might be placed midtrain or at the end, a practice known as distributed power. They are designed to increase pulling power as train lengths and weights increase. The locomotives placed as distributed power or on the point might be from a "foreign" road on a run-through train. One popular piece of freight equipment is the stack car, built for transporting two intermodal containers with a low deck that allows double-stacking and is regularly used in two-car articulated form. Train watchers throughout the region encounter more of them as intermodal trains are a frequent part of freight movements. In fact, they constitute approximately half of all revenues generated by Class I roads. Unit trains also continue to ply the rails, carrying coal from low-sulfur mines in Indiana, Montana, and Wyoming to the dwindling number of regional coal-fired electric power plants, grain from midwestern elevators for domestic or export markets, fracking sand from the Upper Midwest to the oil patches in Texas and Oklahoma, and ethanol from Corn Belt processing plants for various destinations.

No matter the rolling stock (except locomotives and most passenger and commuter equipment), anyone watching a passing freight train repeatedly sees the handiwork of graffiti makers. The past chalk markings made by railroad workers or hobos have been replaced since the 1970s by spray paint. They run the gamut from sloppy gang-style tags to line drawings, stenciled imagery, and larger-than-life complex colored fields. Some observers may consider such designs beautiful, maybe rivaling the quality of the art made by Banksy, the British street artist. Others, probably the vast majority, are disgusted by what they see as unlawful disfigurations.

In recent decades much discussion has focused on the operation of high-speed intercity passenger trains. Although attention has centered on Amtrak's flagship Acela trains that operate up to 150 miles per hour on the Northeast Corridor, albeit for only about fifty miles of the nearly five-hundred-mile route between Washington, DC, New York, and Boston, the Midwest has not benefited from similar speeds. But there are hopeful signs. Ohio is illustrative. Efforts to connect the Cleveland–Columbus–Cincinnati corridor with high-speed trains have been on and off, including a failed attempt in the 1980s. Recently the Ohio Rail Development Commission has promoted fast trains in two corridors: Cleveland–Columbus–Dayton–Cincinnati and Cleveland–Toledo–Detroit. More realistically, there is an ongoing effort to expand Amtrak service in the state. The need is obvious. There is no direct air service between Ohio's "3-C" cities, and the connecting Interstate 71 is heavily traveled, including a section in greater Cincinnati that ranks as the sixth most congested in the nation. And Columbus is among the top fifty cities for highway delays. There also have been efforts to increase the flow of Amtrak service beyond the common limits of seventy-nine miles per hour. In 2023 the five daily trains between Chicago and St. Louis—Amtrak's Lincoln Service—were allowed to reach 110 miles per hour over this 284-mile route. This makes the scheduled time of a trip the same or shorter than driving on the largely parallel and frequently overcrowded Interstate 55. There is a catch. These trains are plagued with unpredictable freight train interference that disrupts on-time performance and reliability. In recent years there have been problems with mechanically unfit locomotives and cars, causing midroute breakdowns or late departures from Chicago or St. Louis. Furthermore, this Illinois speed project has resulted in massive cost overruns, best exemplified by its signaling

In recent years not all remnants of the Age of Steam have disappeared from trackside. In 1999 the coal tower on the former Chicago & North Western mainline through DeKalb, Illinois, remains, being too costly to remove. *(John Morris photograph, author's collection)*

system. The vender lacked prior railroad experience, and that contributed to extensive delays and high costs. These modest service improvements have come with a total investment of nearly $2 billion. Yet there is another midwestern high-speed Amtrak route: the roughly 250-mile line between Chicago and Detroit. Unlike the Chicago–St. Louis corridor, it has longer stretches of 110-mile-per-hour-authorized track. Since this trackage is mostly owned by Amtrak or the State of Michigan, this means minimal freight interference.[12]

A closer look at trackside reveals other changes. With the advent of light signals, the older semaphores with their distinctive moveable blades began to disappear and are no longer part of signaling systems on midwestern railroads. Also gone are the mechanically operated interlocking plants. Ridgely Tower in Springfield, Illinois, on the former Gulf, Mobile & Ohio (now UP) became the last of these manual facilities in the nation, closing in 2010. In recent years Class I carriers have placed detectors along their mainline tracks to identify mechanical problems with rolling stock and locomotives. For more effective detection, additional ones are being installed. Except on mostly branch lines and shortlines and on some regionals, jointed rails have largely vanished, being replaced by continuous welded ones. And a growing number of reinforced concrete ties rather than the once-universal hardwoods underlay them. Even ties made of steel and composite materials have appeared. There has been increased mechanization of maintenance-of-way equipment, such as continuous-action tampers and ballast cleaners. Manufacturers continue to make incremental improvements to these essential pieces of machinery. Onlookers might detect equipment designed to facilitate federally mandated Positive Train Control (PTC), a system devised to prevent train collisions, excess speeds, incursions into work zones, and switches set in the wrong position. PTC is a fixed signaling infrastructure that features coded track circuits and wireless transponders.[13]

Train watchers may recognize altered operating practices on Class I carriers. The most widely noted (and controversial) is Precision Scheduled Railroading (PSR). This concept was pioneered in 1993 on the Illinois Central by railroad executive Hunter Harrison. Later he employed the system in Canada and in 2017 on CSX shortly before his death. The concept, which other major carriers have copied, involves freight-car scheduling that emphasizes point-to-point moves on simplified routing networks. This results in trains running on fixed schedules, instead of being dispatched whenever a sufficient number of loaded cars are available. Longer trains frequently result, perhaps reaching ten thousand feet and fifteen thousand tons of mixed freight. Some have topped seventeen thousand feet. The end goal is greater efficiency, greater productivity, and lower operating costs, including fewer crews and less fuel consumption.

Fewer trains also mean a reduction in the carbon footprint. Critics of PSR abound, including politicians, safety experts, and train crews. They want shorter, more frequent trains. "They've gone from a mile and a quarter to 2 to 3 miles long," commented a Toledo-based NS locomotive engineer. "It can make the train difficult to handle, especially on curves and hills."[14]

There is no need for a trackside visit to learn that there is a remarkable absence from the Midwest—headquarters of Class I railroads. Although Chicago remains the rail hub of America, it is no longer home to major carriers—no more offices for these carriers that appeared in the *Official Railway Guide* of the immediate post–World War II period: Burlington; Chicago & Eastern Illinois; Chicago Great Western; Gulf, Mobile & Ohio; Illinois Central; Milwaukee Road; Monon; North Western; Rock Island; and Santa Fe. St. Louis has become devoid of these Class I–based roads: Cotton Belt, Frisco, Katy, Missouri Pacific, and Wabash. The Twin Cities have had their losses—namely, the Great Northern, Minneapolis & St. Louis, Northern Pacific, and Soo Line. Cleveland can't claim the Erie (and Erie Lackawanna), Nickel Plate, or Wheeling & Lake Erie, and Detroit has lost the Grand Trunk Western and Pere Marquette. In 2023 Kansas City lost the Kansas City Southern when it merged with the Canadian Pacific. The six remaining major roads are based in either Canada or elsewhere in the United States: BNSF–Fort Worth, Canadian Pacific Kansas City–Calgary, Canadian National–Montreal, CSX-Jacksonville, NS-Atlanta, and UP-Omaha. Will there be more corporate marriages and even fewer corporate headquarter cities? That's doubtful. It is also unlikely that any midwestern city will be honored again with a Class I carrier. Even a leading provider of railcars and related freight car management services, TTX Company, has abandoned the Midwest, relocating from Chicago to Charlotte, North Carolina. Those shortlines and independent regionals that operate in the Midwest commonly have their headquarters in local locations. The Iowa Interstate Railroad, which connects the Chicago and Omaha gateways over the former Rock Island mainline and also serves Peoria, is an example. Its operations center is housed in a modern office building in Cedar Rapids, Iowa. Its owner, Railroad Development Corporation, however, has its headquarters in Pittsburgh, Pennsylvania. In a similar development, megamergers have greatly reduced the number of interchange gateways throughout the region.

What will railroads in the Midwest be like in fifty or one hundred years? Although transportation experts, historians, and others are hardly clairvoyant, one can speculate. From a present-day perspective, it is apparent that railroads are more efficient and more environmentally friendly, especially for transporting large volumes of goods that move over long distances, positives that are not likely to change. In addition, containerization will continue to grow in importance. Railroads will take advantage of increasing modal shifts by partnering with third-party logistics companies that specialize in providing "first-mile/last-mile" deliveries. Advanced technologies, including artificial intelligence (AI), will surely be developed and employed. Already Norfolk Southern has installed a new generation of automated inspection portals, which are equipped with high-speed cameras that take hundreds of pictures of every passing locomotive and car to quickly spot safety defects. These images are then analyzed by AI software. There is the possibility that battery-powered autonomous freight cars might serve customers. If these are successful, will locomotives, engineers, and conductors vanish? Even if for unforeseen reasons railroads eventually disappear, the legacy of midwestern rails will remain.

NOTES

1. CREATION, 1835–1860

1. George W. Knepper, *Ohio and Its People* (Kent, OH: Kent State University Press, 1989), 112; James H. Madison, *The Indiana Way* (Bloomington: Indiana University Press, 1986), 59.

2. Rebecca Solnit, *Wanderlust: A History of Walking* (New York: Viking Penguin, 2000), 5–6.

3. Wylie J. Daniels, *The Village at the End of the Road: A Chapter in Early Indiana Railroad History* (Indianapolis: Indiana Historical Society, 1938), 13; G. Smith Stanton, *When the Wildwood Was in Flower* (New York: J. S. Ogilvie, 1910), 39; Philip D. Jordan, *The National Road* (Indianapolis: Bobbs-Merrill, 1948), 117–158; Karl Raitz, *The National Road* (Baltimore: Johns Hopkins University Press, 1996), 159–192.

4. William Willcox, ed., *The Papers of Benjamin Franklin*, vol. 19 (New Haven, CT: Yale University Press, 1976), 279.

5. Robert Payne, *The Canal Builders: The Story of Canal Engineers through the Ages* (New York: Macmillan, 1959), 10, 35–62.

6. Ronald E. Shaw, *Canals for a Nation: The Canal Era in the United States, 1790–1860* (Lexington: University Press of Kentucky, 1990), 128, 136; Lynn Metzger and Peg Bobel, eds., *Canal Fever: The Ohio & Erie Canal from Waterway to Canalway* (Kent, OH: Kent State University Press, 2009), 3–13.

7. Shaw, *Canals for a Nation*, 134–143; Ralph D. Gray, "The Canal Era in Indiana," in *Transportation and the Early Nation* (Indianapolis: Indiana Historical Society, 1982), 129; David J. Bodenhamer and Robert G. Barrows, eds., *The Encyclopedia of Indianapolis* (Bloomington: Indiana University Press, 1994), 190.

8. James W. Putnam, *The Illinois and Michigan Canal: A Study in Economic History* (Chicago: University of Chicago Press, 1918), 17–18.

9. Alice E. Smith, *The History of Wisconsin: From Exploration to Statehood*, vol. 1 (Madison: State Historical Society of Wisconsin, 1973), 436–463.

10. R. Max Gard and William H. Vodrey Jr., *The Sandy and Beaver Canal* (East Liverpool, OH: East Liverpool Historical Society, 1952), 170; Shaw, *Canals for a Nation*, 140–141.

11. It can be dangerous (and incorrect) to say any invention or event is the "first." The case can be made that the Hetton Colliery Railway in England was the

first all-steam railroad in the world. This occurred in 1822, three years prior to the opening of the Stockton & Darlington Railway. Unlike the Hetton Colliery Railway, the Stockton & Darlington was arguably the breakthrough railroad, having incorporated technical advances from other sources and operating with an advanced steam locomotive over a well-engineered line with wrought-iron rails.

12. William D. Middleton, George M. Smerk, and Robert Diehl, eds., *Encyclopedia of North American Railroads* (Bloomington: Indiana University Press, 2007), 1031–1033; John Debo Galloway, *The First Transcontinental Railroad: Central Pacific Union Pacific* (New York: Simmons-Boardman, 1950), 9. The *Niles Weekly Register* (Baltimore) for November 19, 1825, reported that the onlookers thought that Locomotion No. 1 might threaten their well-being:

> About this time the locomotive engine, or steam-horse, as it was more generally termed, gave "note of preparation" by some heavy aspiration, which seemed to excite astonishment and alarm among the "Jonny Raws," who had been led by curiosity to the spot, and who, when a portion of the steam was let off, fled in affright, accompanied by the old women and the young children who surrounded them, under the idea, we suppose, that some horrible explosion was about to take place; they afterwards, however, found courage sufficient to return to their posts, but only to fly again when the safety-valve was opened.

13. David Gwyn, *The Coming of the Railway: A New Global History, 1750–1850* (New Haven, CT: Yale University Press, 2023), 112; Stanton, *When the Wildwood Was in Flower*, 112.

14. H. Roger Grant, *The Louisville, Cincinnati & Charleston Rail Road: Dreams of Linking North and South* (Bloomington: Indiana University Press, 2014), 30–41; *Niles Weekly Register*, September 12, 1829.

15. Paul Trip, "The Detroit & Pontiac Railroad," *Railroad History* 168 (Spring 1993): 19.

16. During the earliest years of the Railway Age, companies often made "rail-road" two words rather than one.

17. William J. Petersen, "Railroads Come to Iowa," *Palimpsest* 41 (April 1960): 257.

18. Newspaper clipping, n.d., Norfolk Southern Archives, Atlanta, GA.

19. William C. Redfield, *A Sketch of the Geographical Rout of a Great Railway . . .*, 2nd ed. (New York: G. & C. & H. Carvill, 1830).

20. W. F. Bailey, *The Story of the First Transcontinental Railroad* (Pittsburgh: Pittsburgh Printing, 1906), 11–12.

21. Jack T. Johnson, "Plumbe's Railroad to the Moon," *Palimpsest* (1938): 92; John Plumbe Jr, *Sketches of Iowa and Wisconsin* (Iowa City: State Historical Society of Iowa, 1948), iv–vii.

22. David Haward Bain, *Empire Express: Building the First Transcontinental Railroad* (New York: Penguin Books, 1999), 31–46; Maury Klein, *Union Pacific: The Birth of a Railroad, 1862–1893* (Garden City, NY: Doubleday, 1987), 8–10.

23. Frank F. Hargrave, *A Pioneer Indiana Railroad: The Origins and Development of the Monon* (Indianapolis: William B. Burford, 1932), 49; Richard D. Stone, *The Interstate Commerce Commission and the Railroad Industry: A History of Regulatory Policy* (Westport, CT: Praeger, 1991), 2; Richard B. Morris, ed., *Encyclopedia of American History* (New York: Harper and Row, 1961), 193.

24. Willis F. Douglas Dunbar, *All Aboard! A History of Railroads in Michigan* (Grand Rapids, MI: William B. Eerdmans, 1969), 18–19.

25. Hargrave, *Pioneer Indiana Railroad*, 47.

26. William D. Edson, comp., *Railroad Names: A Directory of Common Carrier Railroads Operating in the United States, 1826–1982* (privately printed, 1984), 48.

27. H. Roger Grant, *The Railroad: The Life Story of a Technology* (Westport, CT: Greenwood, 2005), 2–3; Frederic L. Paxton, "The Railroads of the Old Northwest before the Civil War," *Transactions of the Wisconsin Academy of Sciences, Arts, and Letters, Part 1* 17 (October 1912): n.p.

28. Dunbar, *All Aboard!*, 20–21; Pierre Lacombe, "Stone Sleepers of Early 1800s American Railroads," *NRHS Bulletin* 85 (2022): 26–45; R. S. Kayler, "Ohio Railroads," *Ohio Archaeological and Historical Society Publications* 9 (1901): 190; Frederick C. Gamst, ed., *Early American Railroads: Franz Anton Ritter von Gerstner's Die innern Communicationen (1842–1843)* (Stanford, CA: Stanford University Press, 1997), 462–463.

29. Steam locomotives are commonly referred to by their classification in the Whyte system, devised in 1901 by Frederick Methvan Whyte, a mechanical engineer with the New York Central System. He used a three-number code consisting of pilot-truck wheels, drivers, and trailing-truck wheels to identify most steam locomotives. A 4-2-0 featured a four-wheel pilot, a single pair of drivers, and no trailing wheels. By the 1840s the more powerful (and widely popular) American Standard–type locomotive (4-4-0) appeared. It had one additional set of drivers.

30. Both of the Erie & Kalamazoo locomotives were built by Baldwin in 1837. Baldwin was also the major supplier of locomotives to the other earliest midwestern roads: one to the Madison & Indiana, three of the five to the Michigan Central, one to the Detroit & Pontiac, and one to the Northern Cross. All were built in 1837 or 1838. See Charles E. Fisher, "Von Gerstner and Our First Locomotives," *Bulletin of the Railway and Locomotive Historical Society* 62 (October 1943): 61–62.

31. Dunbar, *All Aboard!*, 22; Gamst, *Early American Railroads*, 463; *150 Years of Michigan's Railroad History* (Lansing: Michigan Department of Transportation, n.d.), 4. When the Cincinnati, Hamilton & Dayton Railroad opened in 1852, it offered only passenger service. At the end of its second year of operation, the company began to dispatch freight trains. William F. Gephart, *Transpiration and Industrial Development in the Middle West* (New York: Columbia University Press, 1909), 172.

32. Dunbar, *All Aboard!*, 31–56; Graydon M. Meints, *Railroads for Michigan* (East Lansing: Michigan State University Press, 2013), 32–33.

33. David E. Downen, "U.S. Railroad Lake Lines: Palace Steamers, Propellers, Package Freighters" (unpublished manuscript in possession of author), 17–46.

34. Prior to the early 1880s, except for a national narrow-gauge craze in the 1870s and early 1880s, gauge widths varied. The Ohio gauge of 4 feet 10 inches could be made compatible with standard gauge with some technical ingenuity. There were instances of "compromise gauge" measuring 4 feet 9.25 inches.

35. Paul F. Laning, "Frontier Railroads in Ohio's Great Lakes Region," *Inland Seas* 10 (1954): 182.

36. Gamst, *Early American Railroads*, 398; Paxton, "Railroads of the Old Northwest," n.p.; Kayler, "Ohio Railroads," 189.

37. Gephart, *Transportation and Industrial Development*, 161.

38. Gamst, *Early American Railroads*, 408–413; C. P. Leland, "The Ohio Railroad: That Famous Structure Built on Stilts," *Western Reserve Historical Society Tracts*, tract 81 (1892), 265–284; Gephart, *Transportation and Industrial Development*,

165–166. Promoters of the Ohio Railroad were not alone with the platform concept. In the early 1840s, the New-York & Erie Railroad, for one, constructed scores of miles of wooden pilings when it pushed westward through the Empire State's Southern Tier counties. In January 1840 an adviser to the company argued, "[A piled roadway] is not liable to rearrangement by frosts; it is not liable to be obstructed by snow; it is free from dangers of a graded road in consequence of the washing of the banks by floods and rains, and settling when set up in soft bottoms, there requiring constant expense to adjust the road and replace the earth materials." But untreated wood rotted rather quickly. H. Roger Grant, *Erie Lackawanna: Death of an American Railroad, 1938–1992* (Stanford, CA: Stanford University Press, 1994), 2–3.

39. George Rogers Taylor, *The Transportation Revolution, 1815–1860* (New York: Holt, Rinehart and Winston, 1951), 79; John F. Stover, *Iron Road to the West: American Railroads in the 1850s* (New York: Columbia University Press, 1978), 116, 138; *Railroad Record* 7 (January 1859): 475; Gephart, *Transportation and Industrial Development*, 168; *Cincinnati Gazette*, March 15, 1861.

40. Gamst, *Early American Railroads*, 439–442; Berry Robertson Sulgrove, *History of Indianapolis and Marion County* (Philadelphia: L. H. Everts, 1884), 135; Daniels, *Village at the End of the Road*, 17–39.

41. Richard S. Simons and Francis H. Parker, *Railroads of Indiana* (Bloomington: Indiana University Press, 1997), 10; Edson, *Railroad Names*, 67, 119.

42. Victory M. Bogle, "Railroad Building in Indiana, 1850–1855," *Indiana Magazine of History*, September 1962, 219, 220.

43. Stover, *Iron Road to the West*, 116; "Corporate History of the Wabash Railway Company: Compiled Pursuant to and in Accordance with Valuation Order No. 20, Interstate Commerce Commission, Dated May 13, 1915 (June 30, 1919)," 17–18.

44. *Exhibit of the Lake Erie, Wabash & St. Louis and Toledo and Illinois Railroad Companies, March 1, 1854* (New York: *Railroad Journal*, 1854), 4.

45. *History of Miami County, Indiana* (Chicago: Brant and Fuller, 1887), 289; *Biographical Record and Portrait Album of Tippecanoe County, Indiana* (Chicago: Lewis, 1888), 257.

46. *Report of the Toledo, Wabash and Western Railroad Company, Lately the Toledo and Illinois Railroad Co., and the Lake Erie, Wabash & St. Louis Railroad Company* (New York: George F. Nesbitt, 1857), 7–9.

47. *Report of the Toledo, Wabash and Western Railroad Company*, 5.

48. Jeffrey Darbee, *Indianapolis Union and Belt Railroads* (Bloomington: Indiana University Press, 2017), 53–63.

49. John H. Krenkel, *Illinois Internal Improvements, 1818–1848* (Cedar Rapids, IA: Torch, 1958), 9–10, 26–46; Putnam, *Illinois and Michigan Canal*, 21–22; Roy P. Basler, ed., *Collected Works of Abraham Lincoln* (New Brunswick, NJ: Rutgers University Press, 1953–1955), 1:5–6.

50. H. Roger Grant, *The North Western: A History of the Chicago & North Western Railway System* (DeKalb: Northern Illinois University Press, 1996), 5–6, 10; Simon Cordery, *The Iron Road in the Prairie State: The Story of Illinois Railroading* (Bloomington: Indiana University Press, 2016), 7.

51. William K. Akerman, *Early Illinois Railroads* (Chicago: Fergus, 1884), 17, 19; H. J. Stratton, "The Northern Cross Railroad," *Journal of the Illinois State Historical Society* 28 (July 1935): 10–15.

52. Cordery, *Iron Road in the Prairie State*, 10–11.

53. H. Roger Grant, *"Follow the Flag": A History of the Wabash Railroad Company*

(DeKalb: Northern Illinois University Press, 2004), 6–9; Cordery, *Iron Road in the Prairie State*, 6–11; Stratton, "Northern Cross Railroad," 13.

54. Grant, *North Western*, 6–13; *Chicago Daily Tribune*, December 13, 1852.

55. Paul Wallace Gates, *The Illinois Central and Its Colonization Work* (Cambridge, MA: Harvard University Press, 1934), 34–41. Eventually the Pioneer was saved from the scrap line, received star status at the post–World War II Chicago Railroad Fair, and was ultimately enshrined at the Chicago History Museum.

56. Dwight L. Agnew, "Beginnings of the Rock Island Lines," *Journal of the Illinois Historical Society* 45 (Winter 1953): 412; Henry W. Farnam, *Henry Farnam* (New Haven, CT: Morehouse and Taylor, 1889), 40–41. Illinois lawmakers were not the first to demand that an upstart railroad compensate a state-owned canal when it became a direct competitor. An Ohio law declared that a railroad must pay "such amounts annually as in the opinion of the Board of Public Works would be equivalent to one-half the tolls charged by the state at the time upon like property transported by canals during the season of navigation but for the existence of the railroad." The Cincinnati, Hamilton & Dayton Railroad, which competed with the Miami Canal, agreed and did so until this legal requirement ended. Gephart, *Transportation and Industrial Development*, 160–161.

57. Agnew, "Beginnings of the Rock Island Lines," 412–413; William Edward Hayes, *Iron Road to Empire: The History of 100 Years of the Progress and Achievements of the Rock Island Lines* (New York: Simmons-Boardman, 1953), 16–17.

58. H. Roger Grant, *A Mighty Fine Road: A History of the Chicago, Rock Island & Pacific Railroad Company* (Bloomington: Indiana University Press, 2020), 13–14.

59. Alvin F. Harlow, "Farnam Built the Rock Island," *Trains*, December 1948, 49; *American Railroad Journal* 10 (June 24, 1854): 398.

60. Grant, *Mighty Fine Road*, 22–28.

61. Richard C. Overton, *Burlington Route: A History of the Burlington Lines* (New York: Alfred A. Knopf, 1965), 3–14.

62. Overton, *Burlington Route*, 15–18.

63. Gene V. Glendinning, *The Chicago & Alton Railroad: The Only Way* (DeKalb: Northern Illinois University Press, 2002), 7, 21, 62.

64. Stover, *Iron Road to the West*, 108, 120, 135–139, 179, 218, 227; Glendinning, *Chicago & Alton Railroad*, 67.

65. Stover, *Iron Road to the West*, 116.

66. August Derleth, *The Milwaukee Road: Its First Hundred Years* (Iowa City: University of Iowa Press, 2002), 14.

67. Axel S. Lorenzsonn, *Steam and Cinders: The Advent of Railroads in Wisconsin, 1831–1861* (Madison: Wisconsin Historical Society Press, 2009), 52, 58.

68. Derleth, *Milwaukee Road*, 25.

69. Stover, *Iron Road to the West*, 151–152; W. H. Schmidt Jr., "The Singular Milwaukee—a Profile," *Railroad History* 136 (Spring 1977): 9; Lorenzsonn, *Steam and Cinders*, 96.

70. Stover, *Iron Road to the West*, 152.

71. Derleth, *Milwaukee Road*, 81–84.

72. Stover, *Iron Road to the West*, 153.

73. Richard C. Overton, *Milepost 100: The Story of the Development of the Burlington Lines, 1849–1949* (Chicago: Chicago, Burlington & Quincy Railroad, 1949), 19.

74. James Neal Primm, *Economic Policy in the Development of a Western State, 1820–1860* (Cambridge, MA: Harvard University Press, 1954), 105; *Western Journal of Agriculture, Manufactures* (September 1850): 384, quoted in John T. Gaertner, *The Great Rock Island Route: A History of the Chicago Rock Island & Pacific Railroad, Its Predecessor and Subsidiaries* (privately printed, 2022), 4.

75. Peter A. Hansen, Don L. Hofsommer, and Carlos Arnaldo Schwantes, *Crossroads of a Continent: Missouri Railroads, 1851–1921* (Bloomington: Indiana University Press, 2022), 39.

76. Overton, *Burlington Route*, 19–21, 54; Charles N. Glaab, *Kansas City and the Railroads: Community Policy in the Growth of a Regional Metropolis* (Madison: State Historical Society of Wisconsin, 1962), 40; *Poor's Manual of the Railroads of the United States* (New York, 1882), 788–789.

77. *St. Louis Globe*, January 5, 1847; John W. Million, *State Aid to Railways in Missouri* (Chicago: University of Chicago Press, 1896), 86.

78. James Neal Primm, *Lion of the Valley: St. Louis, Missouri, 1764–1980*, 3rd ed. (St. Louis: Missouri Historical Society Press, 1998), 209; H. Craig Miner, *The St. Louis–San Francisco Transcontinental Railroad: The Thirty-Fifth Parallel Project, 1853–1890* (Lawrence: University Press of Kansas, 1972), 25; Stover, *Iron Road to the West*, 157.

79. Paul W. Gates, "The Railroads of Missouri, 1850–1870," *Missouri Historical Review* 26 (January 1932): 136, 138.

80. H. Roger Grant, "The North Missouri: A St. Louis Railroad," *Railroad History* 213 (Fall–Winter 2015): 92.

81. Grant, "North Missouri," 93.

82. Grant, "North Missouri," 93–94.

83. Grant, "North Missouri," 94; *Fourth Annual Report of the Board of Directors to the Stockholders of the North Missouri Railroad* (St. Louis, MO: Drake, 1858), 3.

84. Grant, *Follow the Flag*, 32.

85. Grant, "North Missouri," 94–95; *American Railroad Journal* 40 (August 17, 1867): 773.

86. Gates, "Railroads of Missouri," 136.

87. Hansen, Hofsommer, and Schwantes, *Crossroads of a Continent*, 46–49, 68–70.

88. Grant, *Mighty Fine Road*, 17.

89. Grant, *Mighty Fine Road*, 17, 20–21.

90. Don L. Hofsommer, *Steel Trails of Hawkeye Land: Iowa's Railroad Experience* (Bloomington: Indiana University Press, 2005), 9; Donovan L. Hofsommer, "A Chronology of Iowa Railroads," *Railroad History* 132 (Spring 1975): 72.

91. Overton, *Burlington Route*, 57–61.

92. Grant, *North Western*, 17–19; W. H. Steward, comp., *Yesterday and Today: A History of the Chicago & North Western Railway* (Chicago: Chicago & North Western Railway, 1910), 40.

93. Hofsommer, *Steel Trails of Hawkeye Land*, 10.

94. Stover, *Iron Road to the West*, 116.

95. J. Fletcher Williams, *A History of the City of Saint Paul, and of the County of Ramsey, Minnesota* (St. Paul, MN: The Society, 1875), 303–306; Richard S. Prosser, *Rails to the North Star: A Minnesota Railroad Atlas* (Minneapolis: University of Minnesota Press, 2007), 5; Augustus J. Veenendaal Jr., *The Saint Paul & Pacific Railroad: An Empire in the Making, 1862–1879* (DeKalb: Northern Illinois University Press, 1999), 24, 26.

96. Veenendaal, *Saint Paul & Pacific Railroad*, 32; Don L. Hofsommer, *The Tootin' Louie: A History of the Minneapolis & St. Louis Railway* (Minneapolis: University of Minnesota Press, 2005), 4.

97. H. Roger Grant, *The Station Agent and the American Railroad Experience* (Bloomington: Indiana University Press, 2022), 27–31.

98. *Crawfordsville* (IN) *Review*, February 21, 1857.

99. Stover, *Iron Road to the West*, 188; Dunbar, *All Aboard!*, 222; Hargrave, *Pioneer Indiana Railroad*, 58.

100. Stover, *Iron Road to the West*, 203; Dunbar, *All Aboard!*, 215.

101. Grant, *Railroad*, 22–23; John H. White Jr., *The American Railroad Passenger Car*, pt. 1 (Baltimore: Johns Hopkins

University Press, 1978), 52–75; Hargrave, *Pioneer Indiana Railroad*, 147.

102. Gamst, *Early American Railroads*, 405.

103. Undated newspaper clipping from the *Summit Beacon* (Akron, OH), ca. 1859.

104. *Cleveland Herald*, October 7, 1850; *Summit Beacon*, ca. 1859.

105. J. L. Ringwalt, *Transportation Systems in the United States* (Philadelphia: Railway World, 1888), 151; Le Roy Barnett, *Railroads in Michigan: A Catalog of Company Publications, 1836–1980* (Marquette: Northern Michigan University Press, 1986), 161.

2. DEVELOPMENT, 1860–1890

1. John F. Stover, *The American Railroad*, 2nd ed. (Chicago: University of Chicago Press, 1997), 204–205; *The Chicago & North-Western Line* (Chicago: Chicago & North Western Railway, 1881), 2.

2. See George R. Taylor and Irene D. Neu, *The American Railroad Network, 1861–1890* (Cambridge, MA: Harvard University Press, 1956).

3. See Roger Pickenpaugh, *Rescue by Rail: Troop Transfer and the Civil War in the West, 1863* (Lincoln: University of Nebraska Press, 1998).

4. *A Chronology of American Railroads* (Washington, DC: Association of American Railroads, 1957), 7; William F. Gephart, *Transportation and Industrial Development in the Middle West* (New York: Columbia University Press, 1909), 184–185.

5. David Haward Bain, *The Old Iron Road: An Epic of Rails, Roads, and the Urge to Go West* (New York: Viking, 2004), 31; David Haward Bain, *Empire Express: Building the First Transcontinental Railroad* (New York: Penguin Putnam, 1999), 106–118.

6. Donovan L. Hofsommer, "A Chronology of Iowa Railroads," *Railroad History* 132 (Spring 1975): 73–74, 77.

7. Maury Klein, *The Life and Legend of Jay Gould* (Baltimore: Johns Hopkins University Press, 1986), 232; *Railway Age*, December 9, 1880, 633.

8. See Alvin F. Harlow, *The Road of the Century* (New York: Creative Age, 1947).

9. The complexities of the Pennsylvania Railroad in the Old Northwest are detailed in two works: George H. Burgess and Miles C. Kennedy, *Centennial History of the Pennsylvania Railroad Company, 1846–1946* (Philadelphia: Pennsylvania Railroad, 1949), 176–232, and Albert J. Churella, *The Pennsylvania Railroad: Building an Empire, 1846–1917* (Philadelphia: University of Pennsylvania Press, 2013), 241–344. Interview with Albert J. Churella, September 14, 2022. See also Marie Johnston, "The Building of the Grand Rapids and Indiana Railroad," *Indiana Magazine of History*, June 1945, 152–166.

10. Quoted in Craig Sanders, *Limiteds, Locals, and Expresses in Indiana, 1838–1971* (Bloomington: Indiana University Press, 2003), 5.

11. H. Roger Grant, *The North Western: A History of the Chicago & North Western Railway System* (DeKalb: Northern Illinois University Press, 1996), 25–33, 45–58, 62–67.

12. Grant, *North Western*, 69–81.

13. H. Roger Grant, *A Mighty Fine Road: A History of the Chicago, Rock Island & Pacific Railroad Company* (Bloomington: Indiana University Press, 2020), 34.

14. Grant, *Mighty Fine Road*, 59–61, 66–70.

15. H. Roger Grant, *The Corn Belt Route: A History of the Chicago Great Western Railroad Company* (DeKalb: Northern Illinois University Press, 1984), 4–5; *Railway World*, June 13, 1885; *St. Paul Globe*, August 13, 1885.

16. Grant, *Corn Belt Route*, 7–15.

17. Grant, *Corn Belt Route*, 21–27.

18. Taylor Hampton, *The Nickel Plate Road: The History of a Great Railroad* (Cleveland, OH: World Publishing, 1947), 23–48, 73, 150.

19. H. Roger Grant, Don L. Hofsommer, and Osmund Overby, *St. Louis Union Station: A Place for People, a Place for Trains* (St. Louis, MO: St. Louis Mercantile Library, 1994), 13–18.

20. Victor S. Clark, *History of Manufactures in the United States*, vol. 2, *1860–1893* (New York: McGraw-Hill, 1929), 73–75.

21. Grant, Hofsommer, and Overby, *St. Louis Union Station*, 12, 60–61.

22. Fred Ash, *Chicago Union Station* (Bloomington: Indiana University Press, 2018), 65–87; Ira J. Bach and Susan Wolfson, *A Guide to Chicago's Train Stations* (Athens: Ohio University Press, 1986), 43, 58; H. Roger Grant, "Depot: Economy and Style at Trackside," *Timeline* 1 (October 1984): 57.

23. John F. Stover, *History of the Illinois Central Railroad* (New York: Macmillan, 1975), 197–198; Everett Chamberlin, *Chicago and Its Suburbs* (Chicago: T. H. Hungerford, 1874), 458.

24. William D. Middleton, George M. Smerk, and Roberta L. Diehl, eds., *Encyclopedia of North American Railroads* (Bloomington: Indiana University Press, 2007), 456; John H. White Jr., *The American Railroad Passenger Car* (Baltimore: Johns Hopkins University Press, 1978), 21, 42–44, 438.

25. Chicago & Alton Railroad public timetable, March 1889.

26. H. Roger Grant, ed., *We Took the Train* (DeKalb: Northern Illinois University Press, 1990), 32–33.

27. Middleton, Smerk, and Diehl, *Encyclopedia of North American Railroads*, 827.

28. In "Pioneer and the Lincoln Funeral Train: How 'Honest Abe' Was Used to Create a Corporate Tall Tale," *Railroad History* 186 (Spring 2002): 88–100, Charles Long argues convincingly that the Pioneer had no association with the Lincoln funeral train on May 2, 1865. The famed car likely made a promotional trip over the Chicago & Alton later that month for a special showing in St. Louis.

29. Gene V. Glendinning, *The Chicago & Alton Railroad: The Only Way* (DeKalb: Northern Illinois University Press, 2002), 72–73; Stanley Buder, *Pullman: An Experiment in Industrial Order and Community Planning, 1880–1930* (New York: Oxford University Press, 1967); Liston Edgington Leyendecker, *Palace Car Prince: A Biography of George Mortimer Pullman* (Niwot: University Press of Colorado, 1992), 163–199.

30. H. Roger Grant, ed., "Detroit to Chicago in 1888," *Railroad History* 165 (Autumn 1991): 106–108.

31. Quoted in *Railway Passenger Travel, 1825–1880* (Scotia, NY: American Review, n.d.), n.p.

32. John H. White Jr., *The American Railroad Freight Car: From Wood-Car to the Coming of Steel* (Baltimore: Johns Hopkins University Press, 1993), 359, 367, 372, 375.

33. William J. Watt, *The Pennsylvania Railroad in Indiana* (Bloomington: Indiana University Press, 1999), 79.

34. Ian R. Bartky, "The Invention of Railroad Time," *Railroad History* 148 (Spring 1983), 14–15.

35. Technically, five zones were created on November 18, 1883. The northern portion of Maine set clocks on Atlantic Time. Carlton J. Corliss, "The Day of Two Noons," *Trains*, February 1942, 39.

36. See Ian R. Bartky, *Selling the True Time: Nineteenth-Century Timekeeping in America* (Stanford, CA: Stanford University Press, 2000).

37. J. H. Westbay, "The Standardization of the Track Gauges on American Railways," *Bulletin of the Railway and*

Locomotive Historical Society 34 (May 1934): 32.

38. George W. Hilton, *American Narrow Gauge Railroads* (Stanford, CA: Stanford University Press, 1990), 383–386; John H. White Jr., "The Narrow Gauge Fallacy," *Railroad History* 141 (Autumn 1979): 81; E. W. Mureen, "History of the Fulton County Narrow Gauge Railway: Spoon River 'Peavine,'" *Bulletin of the Railway and Locomotive Historical Society* 61A (August 1943): 8–35, 65–68, 72–76.

39. Solon Justus Buck, *The Granger Movement* (Cambridge, MA: Harvard University Press, 1913), 13–15.

40. A. B. Stickney, *The Railway Problem, with Many Illustrative Diagrams* (St. Paul, MN: D. D. Merrill, 1891), 24.

41. John Lauritz Larson, *Bonds of Enterprise: John Murray Forbes and Western Development in America's Railway Age* (Cambridge, MA: Harvard University Press, 1984), 152–155; George H. Miller, *Railroads and the Granger Laws* (Madison: University of Wisconsin Press, 1971), 17.

42. Edward W. Martin, *History of the Grange Movement, or The Farmer's War against Monopolies* (Chicago: National Publishing, 1874), 6.

43. Simon Cordery, *The Iron Road in the Prairie State* (Bloomington: Indiana University Press, 2016), 70; Miller, *Railroads and the Granger Laws*, 23, 82–96. See also Martin, *History of the Grange Movement*.

44. Robert T. Daland, "Enactment of the Potter Law," *Wisconsin Magazine of History* 33 (September 1949): 45–54; Charles Francis Adams Jr, "The Railroads and Granger Laws," *North American Review* 120 (April 1875): 406–408.

45. Mildred Throne, *Cyrus Clay Carpenter and Iowa Politics, 1854–1898* (Iowa City: State Historical Society of Iowa, 1974), 177–185.

46. D. Sven Nordin, *Rich Harvest: A History of the Grange, 1867–1900* (Jackson: University Press of Mississippi, 1974), 217; *Proceedings of the Iowa State Grange of the Patrons of Husbandry, 1873–1875*; *Ames* (IA) *Intelligencer*, January 7, 1886.

47. Martin Ridge, "Ignatius Donnelly and the Granger Movement in Minnesota," *Mississippi Valley Historical Review* 42 (March 1956): 693, 697, 701, 703; Ralph W. Hidy et al., *The Great Northern Railway: A History* (Boston: Harvard Business School Press, 1988), 26–27.

48. Munn v. Illinois, 94 U.S. 113 (1877); C. Peter Magrath, "The Case of the Unscrupulous Warehouseman," in *Quarrels That Have Shaped the Constitution*, ed. John A. Garraty (New York: Harper Perennial, 1987), 119–138. Technically *Munn v. Illinois* was not a railroad case but instead upheld the validity of government regulation of any business that was affected with the public interest.

49. Richard C. Overton, *Perkins/Budd: Railway Statesmen of the Burlington* (Westport, CT: Greenwood, 1983), 37–48; Russel B. Nye, *Midwestern Progressive Politics: A Historical Study of Its Origins and Development, 1870–1958* (East Lansing: Michigan State University Press, 1959), 48. See also Miller, *Railroads and the Granger Laws*, and Nordin, *Rich Harvest*.

50. Wabash, St. Louis & Pacific Railway Co. v. State of Illinois, 118 U.S. 557 (1886).

51. *Wabash*, 118 U.S. 557.

52. Ari Hoogenboom and Olive Hoogenboom, *A History of the ICC: From Panacea to Palliative* (New York: W. W. Norton, 1976), 8–17.

53. See Julius Grodinsky, *The Iowa Pool: A Study in Railroad Competition, 1870–1884* (Chicago: University of Chicago Press, 1950).

54. *Railroad Gazette*, November 12, 1880, June 23, 1882.

55. Walter Licht, *Working for the Railroad: The Organization of Work in the Nineteenth Century* (Princeton, NJ: Princeton

University Press, 1983), 240–242; H. Roger Grant, *The Station Agent and the American Railroad Experience* (Bloomington: Indiana University Press, 2022), 107–108. See also Archibold McIsaac, *The Order of Railroad Telegraphers: A Study in Trade Unionism and Collective Bargaining* (Princeton, NJ: Princeton University Press, 1931).

56. Paul Michel Taillon, *Good, Reliable, White Men: Railroad Brotherhoods, 1877–1917* (Urbana: University of Illinois Press, 2009), 39–57.

57. See Robert V. Bruce, *1877: Year of Violence* (Indianapolis: Bobbs-Merrill, 1959).

58. Klein, *Life and Legend of Jay Gould*, 362.

59. *The Official History of the Great Strike of 1886 on the Southwestern Railway System* (Jefferson City, MO: Tribune, 1886), 90–92; *Moberly* (MO) *Daily Monitor*, March 5, 1886; Klein, *Life and Legend of Jay Gould*, 361–362.

60. Richard C. Overton, *Burlington Route: A History of the Burlington Lines* (New York: Alfred A. Knopf, 1965), 206–211. See also Donald L. McMurry, *The Great Burlington Strike of 1888* (Cambridge, MA: Harvard University Press, 1955).

61. Richard J. Cook, *A Brief History of the Brotherhood of Locomotive Engineers* (Cleveland, OH: Brotherhood of Locomotive Engineers, 1977), 19–20.

62. Overton, *Burlington Route*, 213–214.

63. C. J. Colby, *Illustrated Centennial Sketches, Map, and Directory of Union County* (Creston, IA: printed by the author, 1876), 17–20; Shelton Stromquist, *A Generation of Boomers: The Pattern of Labor Conflict in Nineteenth-Century America* (Urbana: University of Illinois Press, 1987), 170–171.

64. Interview with D. Keith Lawson, October 18, 1980.

65. Peter A. Hansen, Don L. Hofsommer, and Carlos Arnaldo Schwantes, *Crossroads of a Continent, Missouri Railroads, 1851–1921* (Bloomington: Indiana University Press, 2022), 193–195.

66. Railroad Ys allowed noncrew personnel to become members, including railroad office, US postal, Pullman, and express company workers. See William Bender Wilson, *History of the Pennsylvania Railroad Department of the Young Men's Christian Association of Philadelphia* (Philadelphia: Stephen Greene, 1911), 91, 276.

67. John F. Moore, *The Story of the Railroad "Y"* (New York: Association Press, 1930); H. Roger Grant, ed., *Brownie the Boomer: The Life of Charles P. Brown, an American Railroader* (DeKalb: Northern Illinois University Press, 1991), 127.

68. See C. J. Wehmeyer, *History of the Railroad Y.M.C.A. in St. Louis* (St. Louis, MO: self-published, n.d.).

69. Typescript history of the Wabash Employee's Hospital Association, Wabash Memorial Hospital Association Archive, Decatur, IL (hereafter cited as WMHA Archive).

70. Mark Aldrich, "Train Wrecks to Typhoid Fever: The Development of Railroad Medicine Organization, 1850 to World War I," *Bulletin of the History of Medicine* 75 (2001): 257.

71. Ira M. Ruthow, "Railroad Surgery: A Forgotten Chapter in the History of American Surgery," *Archives of Surgery* 137 (May 2002): 624; Robert H. Wiebe, *The Search for Order, 1877–1920* (New York: Hill & Wang, 1967).

72. "California," *Harpers Monthly Magazine*, June 1872, 73; WMHA Archive; R. O. Woolsey, "The Modern Railway Hospital and Its Management," *Official Proceedings St. Louis Railway Club* 18 (August 8, 1913): 135.

73. "Dues," WMHA Archive.

74. *Moberly* (MO) *Monitor-Index and Evening Democrat*, April 6, 1997; Sister M. Clarella, O.S.F., to George Bruck,

September 18, 1965, Miami County Museum, Peru, IN.

75. Ron Goldfeder, "The Cleverest Thing of Its Kind in the World," *Railroad History* 228 (Spring–Summer 2023): 14–36.

76. Robin W. Winks, *Frederick Billings: A Life* (New York: Oxford University Press, 1991), 252–264.

77. See Carlos Schwantes, *Railroad Signatures across the Pacific Northwest* (Seattle: University of Washington Press, 1993).

78. Charles A. Burnham, "The Ashtabula Horror," in *Bliss and Tragedy: The Ashtabula Railway Bridge Accident of 1876 and the Loss of P.P. Bliss*, ed. Thomas E. Corts (Birmingham, AL: Sherman Oak Books, 2003), 91–111; *New York Times*, August 12, 1887; Wesley S. Griswold, *Train Wreck!* (Brattleboro, VT: 1969), 55–65, 87–97.

79. *Cleveland Daily Leader*, May 8, 1865; *Cincinnati Enquirer*, May 8 and 9, 1865.

80. T. J. Stiles, *Jesse James: Last Rebel of the Civil War* (New York: Alfred A. Knopf, 2002), 230–234; William A. Settle Jr., *Jesse James Was His Name* (Columbia: University of Missouri Press, 1966), 48.

81. H. Roger Grant, *The Station Agent and the American Railroad Experience* (Bloomington: Indiana University Press, 2022), 26, 112–115.

82. H. Roger Grant, *Ohio on the Move: Transportation in the Buckeye State* (Athens: Ohio University Press, 2000), 112.

3. MATURITY, 1890–1930

1. Charles Hoffman, "The Depression of the Nineties," *Journal of Economic History* 16 (June 1956): 137–164. See also Jack Kelly, *Blood on the Tracks: The Edge of Anarchy* (New York: St. Martin's, 2019), especially p. 58.

2. See Liston E. Leyendecker, *Palace Car Prince: A Biography of George Mortimer Pullman* (Niwot: University Press of Colorado, 1992); and Stanley Buder, *Pullman: An Experiment in Industrial Order and Community Planning, 1880–1930* (New York: Oxford University Press, 1967).

3. Ray Ginger, *The Bending Cross: A Biography of Eugene Victor Debs* (New Brunswick, NJ: Rutgers University Press, 1949), 111–114.

4. Leyendecker, *Palace Car Prince*, 221–223; Michael P. Malone, *James J. Hill: Empire Builder of the Northwest* (Norman: University of Oklahoma Press, 1966), 154–156; Nick Salvatore, *Eugene V. Debs: Citizen and Socialist* (Urbana: University of Illinois Press, 1982), 125–129; Ralph W. Hidy et al., *The Great Northern Railway: A History* (Boston: Harvard Business School Press, 1988), 14; Kelly, *Blood on the Tracks*, 20–21, 25.

5. John F. Stover, *History of the Illinois Central Railroad* (New York: Macmillan, 1975), 222–223.

6. Edward Chase Kirkland, *Industry Comes of Age: Business, Labor and Public Policy, 1860–1897* (New York: Holt, Rinehart and Winston, 1961), 368–369.

7. William Jennings Bryan, *The First Battle: A Story of the Campaign of 1896* (Chicago: W. B. Conkey, 1896); Jeffrey G. Mora, "William Jennings Bryan and the 1896 Campaign," *Railroad History* 199 (Fall–Winter 2008): 72–80. The Bryan campaign travel itinerary for his 1896 presidential bid was complex and involved multiple railroads. The first leg was centered in Illinois and Missouri and included traveling over the Illinois Central (IC), Baltimore & Ohio Southwestern (B&OSW), Missouri Pacific (MOP), and Chicago, Burlington & Quincy (Burlington). The second tour included stops along the Chicago, Rock Island & Pacific (Rock Island) and Burlington in Iowa and Illinois and the Pennsylvania (PRR), Lake Shore & Michigan Southern (LS&MS), Big Four, Toledo & Ohio Central, and Chicago & North Western (North Western) in Indiana, Ohio, and Wisconsin. The

next and longest trip, which covered 12,837 miles, involved the MOP and Wabash in Missouri; Baltimore & Ohio (B&O), Ohio Central Lines, Chesapeake & Ohio, B&OSW, Cincinnati, Hamilton & Dayton, Cincinnati & Muskingum Valley, Northern Ohio, Pittsburg & Western, LS&MS, PRR, and Cleveland, Lorain & Wheeling in Ohio; Burlington, Cedar Rapids & Northern, Milwaukee Road, and North Western in Iowa; Great Northern and Northern Pacific in Minnesota; Duluth, South Shore & Atlantic, North Western, Grand Rapids & Indiana, Cincinnati, Wabash & Michigan, Detroit, Lansing & Northern, Detroit, Grand Haven & Milwaukee, Flint & Pere Marquette, Chicago & Grand Trunk, and Michigan Central in Michigan; the PRR, Panhandle, Lake Erie & Western, Nickel Plate, Toledo, St. Louis & Kansas City, Louisville, New Albany & Chicago, Big Four, and Wabash in Indiana; and Big Four, Wabash, IC, North Western, Rock Island, Burlington, and Chicago & Alton in Illinois. The final and shortest trip was limited to Burlington lines in his adopted home state of Nebraska.

8. Richard B. Morris, ed., *Encyclopedia of American History* (New York: Harper and Row, 1961), 264–265.

9. John F. Stover, *American Railroads* (Chicago: University of Chicago Press, 1961), 165.

10. George H. Burgess and Miles C. Kennedy, *Centennial History of the Pennsylvania Railroad Company, 1846–1946* (Philadelphia: Pennsylvania Railroad Company, 1949), 538–540.

11. Ford R. Bryan, *Beyond the Model T: The Other Ventures of Henry Ford*, rev. ed. (Detroit: Wayne State University Press, 1997), 59–67; David R. P. Guay, "Ford's Railroad at the Rouge: Once One of the World's Biggest Industrial Railroads," *Railroad History* 218 (Spring–Summer 2018): 30–33, 57. Multiple industrial roads developed throughout the Midwest. A representative one is the Manufacturers Railway Company in St. Louis. Although the immediate area had three other major switching roads—namely, the Alton & Southern, Illinois Terminal, and Terminal Railroad Association of St. Louis—Manufacturers, which initially served the Anheuser-Bush Brewing Company, added additional customers and trackage following its creation in the late nineteenth century. See *The Manufacturers Railway Company* (St. Louis, MO: Terminal Railroad Association of St. Louis Historical and Technical Society, 2019).

12. Stover, *History of the Illinois Central*, 296–297.

13. Richard C. Overton, *Burlington Route: A History of the Burlington Lines* (New York: Alfred A. Knopf, 1965), 337–338.

14. George W. Hilton and John F. Due, *The Electric Interurban Railways in America* (Stanford, CA: Stanford University Press, 1960), 255, 275, 287, 335, 35, 357, 359, 365–369.

15. William D. Middleton, *The Interurban Era* (Milwaukee, WI: Kalmbach, 1961), 418–420.

16. See H. Roger Grant, *Sunset Cluster: Shortline Railroad Saga* (Bloomington: Indiana University Press, 2023); H. Roger Grant, "Atlantic Northern & Southern: An Iowa Twilight Railroad," *Annals of Iowa* 81 (Fall 2022): 303–338.

17. H. Roger Grant, *Twilight Rails: The Final Era of Railroad Building in the Midwest* (Minneapolis: University of Minnesota Press, 2010), 21–47.

18. Grant, *Twilight Rails*, 21–47.

19. Hilton and Due, *Electric Interurban Railways*, 287–289.

20. Grant, *Twilight Rails*, 69–73.

21. Grant, *Twilight Rails*, 74–91.

22. Grant, *Twilight Rails*, 94–96.

23. Graydon M. Meints, *Michigan Railroads and Railroad Companies* (East

Lansing: Michigan State University Press, 1992), 129.

24. Overton, *Burlington Route*, 244–245.

25. For the early personal and business life of the Vans, see Ian S. Haberman, *The Van Sweringens of Cleveland: The Biography of an Empire* (Cleveland: Western Reserve Historical Society, 1979), 4–17.

26. Richard Saunders Jr., *Merging Lines: American Railroads, 1900–1970* (DeKalb: Northern Illinois University Press, 2001), 50.

27. Saunders, *Merging Lines*, 53.

28. Herbert H. Harwood, *Invisible Giants: The Empires of Cleveland's Van Sweringen Brothers* (Bloomington: Indiana University Press, 2003).

29. Saunders, *Merging Lines*, 53.

30. "Memorandum on the Van Sweringens Railroads," n.d., 1–6, John W. Barriger III papers, John W. Barriger III National Railroad Library, St. Louis, MO (hereafter cited as Barriger papers).

31. "Memorandum of the Van Sweringen Railroads," 1–6, Barriger papers.

32. Herbert H. Harwood Jr., "Oris Paxton Van Sweringen [and] Mantis James Van Sweringen," in *Railroads in the Age of Regulation, 1900–1980*, ed. Keith L. Bryant Jr. (New York: Facts-on-File, 1988), 456.

33. Harwood, "Oris Paxton Van Sweringen," 456; Haberman, *Van Sweringens of Cleveland*, 105–120.

34. Marver H. Bernstein, *Regulating Business by Independent Commission* (Princeton, NJ: Princeton University Press, 1955), 264–265.

35. Michael Kammen, *Mystic Chords of Memory: The Transformation of Tradition in American Culture* (New York: Alfred A. Knopf, 1991), 48. See also Albro Martin, *Enterprise Denied: Origins of the Decline of American Railroads, 1897–1917* (New York: Columbia University Press, 1971).

36. Martin, *Enterprise Denied*, 113–115.

37. George M. Smerk, "The Elkins Act, the Hepburn Act, and the Mann-Elkins Act," in *Encyclopedia of North American Railroads*, ed. William D. Middleton, George M. Smerk, and Roberts L. Diehl (Bloomington: Indiana University Press, 2007), 924–927.

38. "Important Developments in the Transportation Field," *Railway World*, June 1913, 439.

39. Winthrop M. Daniels, *American Railroads: Four Phases of Their History* (Princeton, NJ: Princeton University Press, 1932), 84–86; *New York Times*, September 1, 1916.

40. K. Austin Kerr, *American Railroad Policies, 1914–1920: Rates, Wages, and Efficiency* (Pittsburgh: University of Pittsburgh Press, 1986), 13–16.

41. Maury Klein, *Union Pacific: The Rebirth, 1894–1969* (New York: Doubleday, 1989), 218.

42. Burgess and Kennedy, *Centennial History*, 561; *Erie Railroad: Showing Changes from 1901 to 1914, Inclusive* (n.d., n.p.); James H. Madison, *The Indiana Way: A State History* (Bloomington: Indiana University Press and Indiana Historical Society, 1990), 221.

43. Aaron Austin Godfrey, *Government Operations of the Railroads, 1918–1920* (Austin, TX: San Felipe, 1974).

44. See Kerr, *American Railroad Policies*.

45. Walker D. Hines, *War History of the American Railroads* (New Haven, CT: Yale University Press, 1928), 11–21; Kerr, *American Railroad Policies*, 44–49.

46. Hines, *War History of American Railroads*, 256–264; K. Austin Kerr, "Decision for Federal Control: Wilson, McAdoo and the Railroads, 1917," *Journal of American History* 3 (December 1967): 550–560.

47. Slason Thompson, *A Short History of American Railways* (Chicago: Bureau of Railway News and Statistics, 1925); James Lane, "USRA Freight Cars: An Experiment in Standardization," *Railroad History* 128 (Spring 1973): 28, 372; Eugene L.

Huddleston, *Uncle Sam's Locomotives: The USRA and the Nation's Railroads* (Bloomington: Indiana University Press, 2002), 1–3.

48. Stover, *American Railroads*, 178; interview with Milton G. McInnes, June 5, 1989.

49. *Thirty-Ninth Annual Report of the Chicago, Rock Island and Pacific Railway Company*, 7; William Edward Hayes, *Iron Road to Empire: The History of 100 Years of Progress and Achievement of the Rock Island Lines* (New York: Simmons-Boardman, 1953), 201–202.

50. Glenn E. Plumb, "What the Plumb Plan Means," *Forum* 62 (September 1919): 358–369; H. Roger Grant, "The Prince Plan: A Largely Forgotten Proposal for Railroad Consolidation," *Railroad History* 117 (Fall–Winter, 2017): 10–11.

51. Ari Hoogenboom and Olive Hoogenboom, *A History of the ICC: From Panacea to Palliative* (New York: W. W. Norton, 1976), 94–105; Sidney L. Miller et al. *Rates of Return: Class I Line-Haul Railways of the United States, 1921–1948* (Pittsburgh: University of Pittsburgh Press, 1950).

52. H. Roger Grant, *The North Western: A History of the Chicago & North Western Railway System* (DeKalb: Northern Illinois University Press, 1996), 145; Karl A. Borntrager, *Keeping the Railroad Running: Fifty Years on the New York Central* (New York: Hastings House, 1974), 218.

53. H. Roger Grant, *The Corn Belt Route: A History of the Chicago Great Western Railroad Company* (DeKalb: Northern Illinois University Press, 1984), 77–78.

54. Kevin P. Keefe, *Twelve Twenty-Five: The Life and Times of a Steam Locomotive* (East Lansing: Michigan State University Press, 2016), 10–11, 19.

55. Richard J. Cook, *Super Power Steam Locomotives* (San Marino, CA: Golden West Books, 1966), 7.

56. Cook, *Super Power Steam Locomotives*, 61.

57. John A. Rehor and Philip T. Horning, *The Berkshire Era: A Pictorial Review of the Nickel Plate Road, 1934–1958* (Rocky River, OH: privately printed, 1967), 9; Cook, *Super Power Steam Locomotives*, 34–35.

58. William L. Withuhn, *American Steam Locomotives: Design and Development, 1880–1960* (Bloomington: Indiana University Press, 2019), 373–378.

59. Donald Duke and Edmund Keilty, *RDC: The Budd Rail Diesel Car* (San Marino, CA: Golden West Books, 1990), 20–21.

60. "Gasolene Cars for Interurban Service," *Street Railway Journal* 22 (September 19, 1903): 584.

61. John H. White Jr., *The American Railroad Passenger Car* (Baltimore: Johns Hopkins University Press, 1978), 595.

62. Duke and Keilty, *RDC*, 22–25; White, *American Railroad Passenger Car*, 522, 594–596.

63. As a footnote to McKeen's common design, a different feature marked the Ann Arbor's five-car fleet: arch windows rather than the trademark portholes were used.

64. Duke and Keilty, *RDC*, 224–225; Hilton and Due, *Electric Interurban Railways*, 24, 38; Edmund Keilty, *The Short Line Doodlebug: Galloping Geese and Other Railcritters* (Glendale, CA: Interurban, 1988), 75, 81, 105–106.

65. White, *American Railroad Passenger Car*, 596; Charles H. Stats, "The Short Life of Chicago Great Western's Blue Bird of 1929," *North Western Lines*, no. 1 (2022): 18–31; Grant, *Corn Belt Route*, 94.

66. William D. Middleton, "The Strange, Successful Story of the Railroad That Was Once Named for a Race Horse," *Trains*, June 1959, 16–18; "Before Ford: The V-8 Locomotive of 1913," 21–22; Steve Glischinski, "MN&S: Unique and Colorful

Well beyond Its Size," *Classic Trains*, Summer 2005, 16–19.

67. Grant, *Twilight Rails*, 209, 212–213; Joseph A. Galloway and James J. Buckley, *The St. Joseph Valley Railway* (Chicago: Electric Railway Historical Society, 1955), 18–19, 24, 35.

68. Wallace W. Abbey, *The Diesel That Did It: General Motors' FT Locomotive* (Bloomington: Indiana University Press, 2022), 54.

69. David H. Hamley, "Ingersoll-Rand: Catalyst of Dieselization," *Trains*, December 1970, 24–31. Debate exists about what was the "first" diesel-electric locomotive. The case has been made that America's original dedicated freight diesel locomotive came from the Baldwin Locomotive Company, having been introduced on June 25, 1925. Yet it failed to be a workable prototype, largely because of its prime mover. And soon it was scrapped. Abbey, *Diesel That Did It*, 54–57.

70. John H. White Jr., *The American Railroad Freight Car: From the Wood-Car Era to the Coming of Steel* (Baltimore: Johns Hopkins University Press, 1993), 583, 587–590.

71. *New York Times*, July 28, 1897.

72. White, *American Railroad Freight Car*, 596.

73. H. Roger Grant, *The Railroad: The Life Story of a Technology* (Westport, CT. Greenwood, 2005), 21.

74. White, *American Railroad Freight Car*, 510.

75. Grant, *Railroad*, 59–60.

76. A. N. Williams, *Air Brakes and Railway Signals: Proud Creations of George Westinghouse's Brilliant Genius* (New York: Newcomen Society in North America, 1949), 7–11; White, *American Railroad Passenger Car*, 522; Overton, *Burlington Route*, 200.

77. George J. Belchick, "Westinghouse Air Brake Co.," in *Encyclopedia of North American Railroads*, eds. William D. Middleton, George M. Smerk, and Roberta L. Diehl (Bloomington: Indiana University Press, 2007), 1097–1098; "Brakes," in Middleton, Smerk, and Diehl, *Encyclopedia of North America*, 843–844.

78. Grant, *Railroad*, 62.

79. David Hudson, Marvin Bergman, and Loren Horton, *The Biographical Dictionary of Iowa* (Iowa City: University of Iowa Press, 2008), 92; Charles Clark, "The Railroad Safety Movement in the United States, 1869–1893" (PhD diss., University of Illinois, 1966), 283–290; "Mr. Coffin's Great Reforms," *Annals of Iowa* 5 (January 1903): 562.

80. Grant, *Railroad*, 63.

81. H. Roger Grant, *The Station Agent and the American Railroad Experience* (Bloomington: Indiana University Press, 2022), 113.

82. James B. Latimer, *Railway Signaling in Theory and Practice* (Chicago: Mackenzie-Klink, 1909), 354; "The Railroads' Nervous System: Telephone Supplanting the Telegraph as Means of Vital Communication," *Great Western Magazine* 5 (October 1926): 10.

83. *Electric Railway Journal* (January 29, 1921): 220; *Electric Railway Journal* (November 26, 1921): 949; Hilton and Due, *Electric Interurban Railways*, 134.

84. *Report of the Mechanical Advisory Committee to the Federal Coordinator of Transportation*, December 27, 1935.

85. *Railway Age*, November 7, 1917, 427; "Uniform Containerization of Freight: Early Steps in the Evolution of an Idea," *Business History Review* 43 (January 1969): 84; Mac Levinson, *The Box: How the Shipping Container Made the World Smaller and the World Economy Bigger* (Princeton, NJ: Princeton University Press, 2006), 29–30; *Railway Age*, August 6, 1920, 219–222; *Railway Age*, December 10, 1920, 1012.

86. William D. Middleton, *North Shore: America's Fastest Interurban* (San Marino, CA: Golden West Books, 1964), 93–95; William D. Middleton, *South Shore: The Last Interurban*, 2nd rev. ed. (Bloomington: Indiana University Press, 1999), 142.

87. Joseph Brinker, "Making Freight Trains Do More Work," *Popular Science Monthly* 95 (September 1919): 20; Herbert H. Harwood Jr. and Robert S. Korach, *The Lake Shore Electric Railway Story* (Bloomington: Indiana University Press, 2000), 122–123, 261–263; Lake Shore Electric Railway public timetable, February 22, 1931.

88. *Sixty-Fourth Annual Report of the Chicago and North Western Railway Company* (Chicago: Chicago & North Western Railway, 1924), 7.

89. William L. Withuhn, ed., *Rails across America: A History of Railroads in North America* (London: Smithmark, 1993), 113.

90. "Rainbow Run" got its name early in the twentieth century because of the color scheme used by the Chicago & Alton on its Alton Limited (red), Illinois Central on its Daylight Special (green), and Wabash on its Banner Blue Limited (blue). Arthur D. Dubin, *Some Classic Trains* (Milwaukee, WI: Kalmbach, 1964), 152.

91. Wabash ink blotter, 1926, in possession of author.

92. *Highway Magazine*, January 1929, 18; Burgess and Kennedy, *Centennial History*, 603.

93. Pennsylvania Railroad, Transcontinental Air Transport Inc, Atchison, Topeka & Santa Fe public timetable, July 7, 1929.

94. Burgess and Kennedy, *Centennial History*, 604. In the late 1920s, TAT was not the sole carrier to offer transcontinental air-rail service. Shortly before it began operations, Universal Aviation Corporation (UAC) opened a sixty-seven-hour service between New York City and Los Angeles. The Southwestern Limited, a deluxe New York Central (NYC) train, transported passengers from Grand Central Terminal in New York to Union Station in St. Louis. Next, a UAC plane carried them to Garden City, Kansas, and a connection with the Santa Fe for California. In August 1929 NYC again served as the link between New York City and St. Louis. A Southwest Air Fast Express flew passengers to Sweetwater, Texas, where they boarded a Texas & Pacific Railway train for El Paso, and from there a Standard Airlines plane completed the journey to Los Angeles. See R. E. G. Davis, *Airlines of the United States since 1914* (London: Putnam, 1972), 112–113.

95. Grant, *Corn Belt Route*, 97–98. As of fall 1933, the North Western continued its late-1920s arrangement with Kohler Aviation Corporation of providing daily rail connections between the Twin Cities and Milwaukee, allowing passengers to fly to Detroit via the Michigan cities of Muskegon, Grand Rapids, and Lansing. *The Official Aviation Guide* (Chicago: Official Aviation Guide Company, 1933), 19. Earlier the company had operated a short-lived air-rail service between Chicago, St. Paul, and Rapid City, South Dakota. Beginning on May 2, 1929, passengers used an overnight North Western train to St. Paul and then flew on Rapid Air Lines to Rapid City. The return was air during daytime and rail by night. Grant, *North Western*, 148.

96. The Southwestern also sold excursion tickets to a fifty-mile sightseeing flight over greater Cleveland in a Ford Tri-Motor aircraft. Apparently, this was a poor revenue producer.

97. "Railways' Newest Passenger Rival," *Railway Age*, March 17, 1928, 616; Jeffrey R. Brashares, *The Southwestern Lines* (Cleveland: Interurban Memories, 1982), 76; Hilton and Due, *Electric Interurban Railways*, 336.

98. Bryant A. Long and William J. Dennis, *Mail by Rail: The Story of the Postal Transportation Service* (New York: Simmons-Boardman, 1951), 114; Overton, *Burlington Route*, 75.

99. Clark C. Carr, *The Railway Mail Service: Its Origins and Development* (Chicago: A. C. McClung, 1909), 13–16; Long and Dennis, *Mail by Rail*, 110; "R.P.O.—Four Score and Four," *North Western Newsletter* 3 (July–August 1948). A debate exists among postal historians about what was the "first" Railway Post Office. It has been argued that the run over the Hannibal & St. Joseph in 1862 "constituted the first experimental railway post office because [William Davis] was the first to open, officially, brass-locked sacks and take out mail in transit to be advanced past a distributing post office." Long and Dennis, *Mail by Rail*, 114.

100. David P. Morgan, *Fast Mail: The First 75 Years* (Chicago: Chicago, Burlington & Quincy Railroad, 1959), 11–12, 19, 21.

101. Wallace O. Yoder, "An Evaluation of the Express Business in the United States as Conducted by the Railway Express Agency, Incorporated" (PhD diss., Indiana University, 1953); Klink Garrett and Toby Smith, *Ten Turtles to Tucumcari: A Personal History of the Railway Express Agency* (Albuquerque: University of New Mexico Press, 2003), 21–24; Alvin F. Harlow, *Old Waybills: The Romance of the Express Companies* (New York: D. Appleton-Centry, 1934), 476–477, 480–483.

102. Dennis S. Nordin and Roy V. Scott, *From Prairie Farmer to Entrepreneur: The Transformation of Midwestern Agriculture* (Bloomington: Indiana University Press, 2005), 33–34.

103. H. Roger Grant, *Railroads and the American People* (Bloomington: Indiana University Press, 2012), 143–144.

104. Mark Aldrich, *Death Rode the Rails: American Railroad Accidents and Safety, 1828–1965* (Baltimore: Johns Hopkins University Press, 2006), 15–18.

105. Although Ralph Richards led the "safety first" movement on steam railroads, he had a contemporary counterpart who worked in the interurban industry. This individual was E. F. Schneider, general manager of the Cleveland, Southwestern & Columbus Railway, one of the Buckeye State's major electric railroads. In 1912 he distributed approximately fifty thousand ink blotters with the words "Motto: Safety First" to schoolchildren in on-line communities. "Blotters for School Distribution," *Electric Traction*, November 1912, 1080.

106. Aldrich, *Death Rode the Rails*, 189; Edward L. Tinker, "Ralph C. Richards," *American Magazine*, December 1913, 44–45.

107. "The Industrial Toll of Death and Chicago & North-Western Railway's Exemplary 'Safety First' System," *Chicago Commerce*, April 11, 1913, 12; W. T. Gale, "Safety on the Chicago & North Western," *American Engineer* 87 (March 1913): 137–141.

108. *Daily Huronite* (Huron, SD), January 24, 1914; Robert E. Woodruff, *The Making of a Railroad Officer* (New York: Simmons-Boardman, 1925), 189.

109. Benjamin Sidney Michael Schwantes, *The Train and the Telegraph: A Revisionist History* (Baltimore: John Hopkins University Press, 2019), 128–132; Aldrich, *Death Rode the Rails*, 185.

110. William D. Middleton, *Landmarks on the Iron Road: Two Centuries of North American Railroad Engineering* (Bloomington: Indiana University Press, 1999).

111. Chicago Transit and Railfan, accessed January 26, 2023, http://www.chicagorailfan.com/elevate.

112. White, *American Railroad Freight Car*, 84, 86.

113. Manual block and automatic block signal data compiled from ICC reports;

Gary W. Dolzall, "The Case for C&EI," *Trains*, January 1990, 38.

114. Janet Greenstein Potter, *Great American Railroad Stations* (New York: John Wiley and Sons, 1996), 294, 310, 320, 337, 357, 364, 389, 408; "Cincinnati's New Union Terminal Now in Service," *Railway Age*, April 22, 1933, 575–590; Peter Wilson, "Cincinnati Union Terminal: Alive Again," *Trains*, May 1992, 41–43.

4. MODERN ERA, 1930–PRESENT

1. Frederick Lewis Allen, *Since Yesterday: The Nineteen-Thirties in America* (New York: Harper and Brothers, 1939), 17–20; David M. Kennedy, *Freedom from Fear: The American People in Depression and War, 1929–1945* (New York: Oxford University Press, 1999), 34–38; Christopher Knowlton, *Bubble in the Sun: The Florida Boom of the 1920s and How It Brought on the Great Depression* (New York: Simon and Schuster, 2020), 296–297.

2. Daniel A. Schiffman, "Shattered Rails: Ruined Credit: Financial Fragility and Railroad Operations in the Great Depression," *Journal of Economic History* 63 (September 2003): 802–825; John F. Stover, *History of the Illinois Central Railroad* (New York: Macmillan, 1975), 315.

3. *Historical Statistics of the United States, Colonial Times to 1957* (Washington, DC: US Department of Commerce, 1960), 456–458.

4. Roger Biles, *A New Deal for the American People* (DeKalb: Northern Illinois University Press, 1991), 23–24.

5. William D. Middleton, George M. Smerk, and Roberta L. Diehl, eds., *Encyclopedia of North American Railroads* (Bloomington: Indiana University Press, 2007), 929–930; John Will Chapman, *Railroad Mergers* (New York: Simmons-Boardman, 1934), 113–122; W. H. S. Stevens, "Railroad Reorganizations under the Bankruptcy Act," *Journal of Business of the University of Chicago* 15 (July 1942): 205–224.

6. Richard C. Overton, *Burlington Route: A History of the Burlington Lines* (New York: Alfred A. Knopf, 1965), 394–395.

7. Overton, *Burlington Route*, 396; *Rocky Mountain News* (Denver, CO), May 27, 1934.

8. Overton, *Burlington Route*, 396–397; *New York Times*, May 27, 1934; "First Month of Zephyr Brings Traffic Increase," *Railway Age*, December 22, 1934, 837; Richard C. Overton, *The First Ninety Years: An Historical Sketch of the Burlington Railroad, 1850–1940* (Chicago: Chicago, Burlington & Quincy Railroad, 1940), 36. The public excitement generated by the record-smashing trip of the Zephyr prompted RKO Pictures to rush into production a feature-length movie, *The Silver Streak*. This melodramatic thriller premiered in December 1934 at a theater in Galesburg, Illinois, a Burlington division point and major junction.

9. William van der Sluys, "The Lightweight Passenger Car with Special Reference to Pullman," *Railroad History* 143 (Autumn 1981): 49, 54; Maury Klein, *Union Pacific: The Rebirth, 1894–1969* (New York: Doubleday, 1989), 299–301. When a model of the future M-10000 was shown at the Century of Progress exposition in Chicago in 1933, transportation writer T. J. Maloney remarked, "It was called a 'rail-plane' but looks like a land fish." He made these additional comments: "Headed for tomorrow—the new 110-mile-an-hour Union Pacific passenger train—is now under construction. It hugs the rails, the bottom being but 9.5 inches over the rails and the top 11 feet above." T. J. Maloney, "Tomorrow's Transportation," *Review of Reviews and World's Work* (October 1933): 20.

10. Jim Scribbins, *The Hiawatha Story* (Milwaukee, WI: Kalmbach, 1970), 13.

11. "North Western '400' High-Speed Train," *Railway Mechanical Engineer* 109

(February 1935): 52–54; *Chicago Daily News*, December 25, 1935; Jim Scribbins, *The 400 Story* (Park Forrest, IL: PTJ, 1982), 10.

12. Scribbins, *400 Story*, 17–24; A. C. Kalmbach, "Saga of the '400,'" *Trains*, November 1941, 4.

13. The Chicago to Twin Cities passenger corridor was among the most competitive in the nation. Before practical long-distance automobile travel, other railroads provided through trains, including the Great Western, M&StL-IC, Rock Island, and Wisconsin Central. The successor to the Wisconsin Central, the Soo Line, remained in competition until after World War II.

14. Scribbins, *400 Story*, 39; Kalmbach, "Saga of the '400,'" 4–5.

15. Overton, *Burlington Route*, 398.

16. On January 1, 1941, Electro Motive Company became the Electro-Motive Division of General Motors.

17. *Heritage from the Gods: Burlington's New 7 Car Twin Zephyrs* (Chicago: Chicago, Burlington & Quincy Railroad, 1936), 2.

18. Kalmbach, "Saga of the '400,'" 4.

19. H. Roger Grant, *A Mighty Fine Road: A History of the Chicago, Rock Island & Pacific Railroad Company* (Bloomington: Indiana University Press, 2020), 175.

20. Lucius Beebe, *The Twentieth Century Limited* (Berkeley, CA: Howell-North, 1962); Arthur D. Dubin, *Some Classic Trains* (Milwaukee, WI: Kalmbach, 1964), 91.

21. Don Heimburger, "A Bus on Steel Wheels," *Trains*, May 1971, 26–28.

22. "Streamliner on the WI&M," *White Pine Route Quarterly* 23 (February 2022): 4, 6; Tony Reevy, *The Railroad Photography of Phil Hastings* (Bloomington: Indiana University Press, 2023), 152, 166.

23. Wallace W. Abbey, *The Diesel That Did It: General Motors' FT Locomotive* (Bloomington: Indiana University Press, 2022), 3, 94, 119; Brian Solomon, *EMD F-Unit Locomotives* (North Branch, MN: Specialty, 2005), 7.

24. Abbey, *Diesel That Did It*, 96.

25. Louis A. Marre, *Diesel Locomotives: The First 50 Years—a Guide to Diesels Built before 1972* (Waukesha, WI: Kalmbach, 1995), 361, 368, 396, 415.

26. *Historical Statistics of the United States*, 462; William R. Childs, *Trucking and the Public Interest: The Emergence of Federal Regulation, 1914–1940* (Knoxville: University of Tennessee Press, 1985), 35.

27. Charles H. Burgess and Miles C. Kennedy, *Centennial History of the Pennsylvania Railroad Company, 1846–1946* (Philadelphia: Pennsylvania Railroad Company, 1949), 601.

28. H. Roger Grant, "Chicago Great Western Railroad: Piggyback Pioneer," *Trains*, January 1986, 31–34; John S. Gallagher Jr., "Even Highway Trailers Are Going by Rail," *Trains and Travel*, August 1952, 24–27; Thomas Hoback to author, July 22, 2023.

29. John A. Jakle and Keith A. Sculle, *Supplanting America's Railroads: The Early Auto Age, 1900–1940* (Knoxville: University of Tennessee Press, 2017), 159–191; Ralph W. Hidy et al., *The Great Northern Railway: A History* (Boston: Harvard Business School Press, 1988), 177–178; Ralph Budd, "Discuss Rail-Highway Co-ordination," *Railway Age*, April 24, 1926, 1138; Overton, *Burlington Route*, 531–532.

30. Missouri Southern Railroad Company–Missouri Southern Transportation Company, Co-ordinated Service timetables, effective January 19, 1930; H. Roger Grant, "Missouri Southern: History of a Shortline," *Bulletin of the Railway and Locomotive Historical Society* 123 (October 1970): 48.

31. H. Roger Grant, *Ohio on the Move: Transportation in the Buckeye State* (Athens: Ohio University Press, 2000), 127.

32. George W. Hilton and John F. Due, *The Electric Interurban Railways in America* (Stanford, CA: Stanford University Press, 1960), 84; William D. Middleton, "Electric Railway Freight," *Railroad History* 151 (Autumn 1984): 34–35.

33. Hilton and Due, *Electric Interurban Railways*, 80–81.

34. Hilton and Due, *Electric Interurban Railways*, 266; *Deshler* (OH) *Flag*, July 3, 1930; Cincinnati & Lake Erie Railroad timetables, effective October 12, 1930.

35. Jack Keenan, *Cincinnati & Lake Erie Railroad: Ohio's Great Interurban System* (San Marino, CA: Golden West Books, 1974), 59–77, 204–205; William D. Middleton, *Traction Classics: The Interurbans Extra Fast and Extra Fare* (San Marino, CA: Golden West Books, 1985), 303–304.

36. Hilton and Due, *Electric Interurban Railways*, 266; Dubin, *Some Classic Trains*, 350.

37. Hilton and Due, *Electric Interurban Railways*, 82–83; Middleton, *Traction Classics*, 425; Paul H. Stringham, *Illinois Terminal: The Electric Years* (Glendale, CA: Interurban, 1989), 50–51.

38. John D. Horachek, "The Receiver Was an Optimist," *Trains*, October 1982, 34–45; Chicago, North Shore & Milwaukee Railroad timetables, February 9, 1941; William D. Middleton, *North Shore: America's Fastest Interurban* (San Marino, CA: Golden West Books, 1964).

39. Dale Jenkins, *The Illinois Terminal011 Railroad: The Road of Personalized Services* (Hart, MO: White River Productions, 1995), 116–117, 184–187, 190, 196, 206, 235; Illinois Terminal Railroad Company timetables, September 30, 1951; Hilton and Due, *Electric Interurban Railways*, 349.

40. Hilton and Due, *Electric Interurban Railways*, 335–338; Middleton, Smerk, and Diehl, *Encyclopedia of North American Railroads*, 237–238.

41. Robert E. Woodruff, "I Worked for the Erie" (unpublished manuscript, ca. 1954, in possession of author).

42. Interview with Charles C. Shannon, October 1, 1988; H. Roger Grant, *"Follow the Flag": A History of the Wabash Railroad Company* (DeKalb: Northern Illinois University Press, 2004), 186.

43. Preston Cook, "Production and Promotion: U.S. Locomotive Builders in World War II," *Railroad History* 202 (Spring–Summer 2010): 27.

44. Interview with Dan Knight, September 17, 1979.

45. "Right-of-Way," 16 mm film produced by the Office of War Information, 1943, National Archives, Washington, DC.

46. *Historical Statistics of the United States*, 430–431.

47. John Grover, "Highballing Oil to the East," *Erie Railroad Magazine*, October 1942, 8, 29.

48. John F. Stover, *History of the Baltimore and Ohio Railroad* (West Lafayette, IN: Purdue University Press, 1987), 305.

49. Joseph P. Schwieterman, "Midwest Metamorphosis: The Decline, Fall, and Sometimes Revival of a Region's Passenger Service," *Railroad History* 198 (Spring–Summer 2008): 50; Chicago, North Shore & Milwaukee Railroad timetables, December 1, 1942.

50. Claude Moore Fuess, *Joseph B. Eastman: Servant of the People* (New York: Columbia University Press, 1952), 270–296; H. Roger Grant, "War and Peace, Duty and Rebirth," in "Trains of the 1940s: Railroading's Decade of Trial and Triumph," ed. Robert S. McGonigal, special issue, *Classic Trains*, no. 15 (2014), 12; Middleton, Smerk, and Diehl, *Encyclopedia of North American Railroads*, 1124; interview with Mildred Middleton, July 4, 1999.

51. *New York Times*, December 22, 1945; interview with Charles C. Shannon, October 1, 1988.

52. Margaret Walsh, *Making Connections: The Long-Distance Bus Industry in the USA* (Farnham, Surrey, UK: Ashgate, 2000), 28.

53. Oscar Theordore Barck Jr. and Nelson Manfred Blake, *Since 1900: A History of the United States in Our Times*, 5th ed. (New York: Macmillan, 1974), 526–527.

54. Overton, *Burlington Route*, 495–496; Fred W. Frailey, *Twilight of the Great Trains* (Bloomington: Indiana University Press, 2010), 104.

55. Grant, *Follow the Flag*, 198–200.

56. Geoffrey H. Doughty, *New York Central's Great Steel Fleet, 1948–1967* (Lynchburg, VA: TLC, 1999), 4–5, 116; *Centennial of the Michigan Central Railroad—1846–1946*, 4, New York, New York Central, 1946; Dubin, *Some Classic Trains*, 72.

57. H. Roger Grant, *John W. Barriger III: Railroad Legend* (Bloomington: Indiana University Press, 2018), 92–95.

58. Clipping from *Chicago Tribune*, n.d., in possession of author.

59. H. Roger Grant, *The North Western: A History of the Chicago & North Western Railway System* (DeKalb: Northern Illinois University Press, 1996), 177.

60. Curtis L. Katz, "The Last Great Railroad Show," *Trains*, August 1998, 58–67; Grant, *North Western*, 178.

61. Grant, *Mighty Fine Road*, 212, 214.

62. Karl A. Borntrager, *Keeping the Railroads Running: Fifty Years on the New York Central* (New York: Hastings House, 1974), 200–201; Gary W. Dolzall and Stephen F. Dolzall, *Diesels from Eddystone: The Story of Baldwin Diesel Locomotives* (Milwaukee, WI: Kalmbach Books, 1984), 67–69. In a reflective letter, "High Lights on the New York Central History, 1952–1968," Karl Borntrager wrote in part, "The year of 1957 was even worse and at the end of that year, the Central was in the red and omitted its dividend. In January 1958, Mr. Young committed suicide. His train 'X' had proven a failure and he too had been unable to live up to his self styled title as 'A doctor of sick railroads.'" Karl A. Borntrager to Robert Sobel, March 17, 1978, copy in possession of E. Ray Lichty.

63. David P. Morgan, "Expected," *Trains*, October 1955, n.p.

64. John E. Long, "The Great RDC Race," *Trains*, October 1955, 11–23.

65. Donald Duke and Edmund Keilty, *RDC: The Budd Rail Diesel Car* (San Marino, CA: Golden West Books, 1990), 251–270. Interestingly, the M&StL made some immediate alternations to its two RDC-4s. Shop workers cut two additional windows in each side of the baggage compartment and added seats for seventeen passengers. The railroad, which purchased these RDC-4s in 1957, resold them to the C&O a year later.

66. "The Rolling Lab That Reached 183.85 MPH," *Trains*, October 1966, 16.

67. David D. Van Tassel and John J. Grabowski, eds., *The Encyclopedia of Cleveland History* (Bloomington: Indiana University Press, 1987), 279; Carl W. Condit, "Cincinnati Passenger Stations before 1930," *Railroad History* 132 (Spring 1975): 5–32.

68. Borntrager, *Keeping the Railroads Running*, 147.

69. Kirk F. Hise and Edward J. Pulhuj, *Images of Rail: Toledo Railroads* (Charleston, SC: Arcadia, 2005), 60–61; David P. Morgan, "Trains Talks to Talent," *Trains*, June 1957, 18.

70. Mark J. Camp, *Images of Rail: Railroad Depots of Northeast Ohio* (Charleston, SC: Arcadia, 2007), 27, 47; *Akron* (OH) *Beacon Journal*, August 23, 1946; October 22, 1946; July 16, 1947; April 28, 1950.

71. H. Roger Grant and Charles W. Bohi, *The Country Railroad Station in America* (Boulder, CO: Pruitt, 1978), 13, 171–173.

72. *Des Moines* (IA) *Register*, May 27, 1951.

73. Interview with Charles C. Shannon, October 1, 1988.

74. Max Ephraim Jr., "The Beloved Geep," *Trains*, June 1995, 44–47; Brian Solomon, *EMD Locomotives* (St. Paul, MN: Voyageur, 2006), 68.

75. Interview with Charles C. Shannon, October 1, 1988.

76. Overton, *Burlington Route*, 561.

77. Ian Gray, "Toward a Bright and Shiny Future: Railroad Public Relations in an Era of Transition," *Railroad History* 215 (Fall–Winter 2016): 64, 66–68.

78. In 1969 the Cleveland-based Brotherhood of Railroad Trainmen merged with three other unions—the Brotherhood of Locomotive Firemen and Enginemen, Order of Railway Conductors, and Switchmen's Union of North America—to form the United Transportation Union (UTU). This amalgamated labor union remained in Cleveland before relocating to suburban Lakewood, Ohio. In 2014 the UTU became part of the International Association of Sheet Metal, Air, Rail and Transportation Workers (SMART). The transportation unit established its headquarters in North Olmsted, Ohio, another Cleveland suburb.

79. Interview with James A. Zito, May 4, 1994.

80. H. Roger Grant, *The Station Agent and the American Railroad Experience* (Bloomington: Indiana University Press, 2022), 149–155; 1957 *Annual Report, Chicago and North Western Railway Company* (Chicago: Chicago & North Western Railway, 1958), 12.

81. Richard Saunders Jr., *Merging Lines: American Railroads, 1900–1970* (DeKalb: Northern Illinois University Press, 2001), 132–134.

82. Gus Welty, ed., *Era of the Giants: The New Railroad Merger Movement* (Omaha, NE: Simmons-Boardman, 1982), 85–86.

83. Grant, *North Western*, 210–211, 231.

84. H. Roger Grant, *Erie Lackawanna: Death of an American Railroad, 1938–1992* (Stanford, CA: Stanford University Press, 1994), 75–100.

85. Grant, *Erie Lackawanna*, 101–122.

86. Grant, *Erie Lackawanna*, 123–154.

87. Grant, *Erie Lackawanna*, 155–177; interview with Gregory W. Maxwell, June 12, 1989.

88. Grant, *Erie Lackawanna*, 178–209.

89. Fred W. Frailey, *Seldom Willing: A Novel of Railroading* (privately printed, 2023), 65.

90. David P. Morgan, "Farewell, CB&Q, GN, NP, and SP&S; Hello, BN," *Trains*, June 1970, 25–28.

91. H. Craig Miner, *The Rebirth of the Missouri Pacific, 1956–1983* (College Station: Texas A&M University Press, 1983), 28–30, 58–80, 86–111.

92. Welty, *Era of the Giants*, 87, 92.

93. Grant, *Mighty Fine Road*, 221–232, 245–247, 267–283.

94. "Norfolk and Western and Southern Get Together to Make a Little History," *Trains*, September 1982, 19A–19B.

95. Richard Saunders Jr., *Main Lines: Rebirth of the North American Railroads, 1970–2002* (DeKalb: Northern Illinois University Press, 2003), 340–345.

96. Saunders, *Main Lines*, 282, 337–340; *Chicago Tribune*, March 10, 2009.

97. *Kansas City* (MO) *Star*, March 15, 2023; *New York Times*, March 15, 2023; *Wall Street Journal*, March 15, 2023; Bill Stephens, "Canadian Pacific, Kansas City Southern Unite," *Trains*, June 2023, 4–5.

98. Interview with Kent Shoemaker, November 4, 2005.

99. Joseph Poindexter, "The Return of Ben W. Heineman," *Dun's Review* 99 (March 1972): 33–34, 36–37, 39.

100. Grant, *North Western*, 215–217; "Is It Endsville for the Railroads," *Forbes*, October 15, 1969, 196; interview with James A. Zito, May 4, 1994.

101. Thomas Hoback, founder of the Indiana Rail Road, made this comment about the definition of a regional railroad: "To use a football metaphor, the goal posts keep moving when it comes to defining what a regional railroad is." Continued Hoback, "There was a $25 million threshold and length of more than 350 miles, that defined a regional railroad, but I think the revenue number has been increased over time to $50 million. At last count there were between 15–20 regional railroads [nationally] including the likes of INRD [Indiana Railroad], IAIS [Iowa Interstate] and Lake States. Obviously holding companies are not included, but some of their individual properties are if they meet the criteria." Thomas Hoback to author, March 21, 2023.

102. The percentage of rail lines abandoned between 1916 and 2010 in the eight midwestern states is staggering: Iowa, 60.8; Michigan, 59.1; Wisconsin, 56; Missouri, 51.4; Minnesota, 50.6; Illinois, 44.8; Indiana, 42.8; and Ohio, 41.9. The data for the latter three states suggest that their east–west lines produced a somewhat lower percentage of line retirements.

103. *Chicago Tribune*, September 30, 1963; June 3, 2018; Peter Harnik, *From Rails to Trails: The Making of America's Active Transportation Network* (Lincoln: University of Nebraska Press, 2021), 49–51.

104. Thomas Hoback to author, March 30, 2023. A rare example of "Trails-to-Rails" took place in Centre County, Pennsylvania. In 2012 the R. J. Corman Railroad Group received permission from the Surface Transportation Board to rebuild twenty miles of a railbanked line to serve new industries. In 1990 Conrail had ceased operating over the trackage, and ten miles subsequently became the Snow Shoe Rails to Trails.

105. Dan Cupper, "Rails-to-Trails: History Underfoot," *Trains*, May 1991, 26.

106. Dan Cupper, "The Strasburg Rail Road You Don't Know," *Trains*, October 2023, 14–21.

107. *So You Want to Start a Small Railroad: ICC Small Railroad Application Procedures* (Washington, DC: Interstate Commerce Commission, 1985); Ron Cady, "Michigan Metamorphosis," *Trains*, October 1987, 26; Don L. Hofsommer, *Grand Trunk Corporation: Canadian National Railways in the United States, 1971–1992* (East Lansing: Michigan State University Press, 1995), 152–153.

108. *150 Years of Michigan's Railroad History* (Lansing: Michigan Department of Transportation, n.d.), 32–34.

109. Gus Welty, "Regional Railroad Planner's Guide," *Railway Age*, May 1989, 81; John F. Due, "New Railroad Companies Formed to Take Over Abandoned or Spun-Off Lines," *Transportation Journal* 24 (Fall 1984): 30–50.

110. Thomas Hoback to author, July 22, 2022.

111. Edward A. Lewis, *American Shortline Railway Guide*, 3rd ed. (Milwaukee, WI: Kalmbach Books, 1986), 229; Don L. Hofsommer, *Steel Trails of Hawkeyeland: Iowa's Railroad Experience* (Bloomington: Indiana University Press, 2005), 238.

112. *Akron* (OH) *Railroad Club Newsletter*, September 2017.

113. *Akron* (OH) *Railroad Club Newsletter*, September 2017.

114. Interview with Jerry Jacobson, December 2, 1994; John P. Hankey, "Newest Roundhouse in the Land," *Trains*, March 2010, 54.

115. Otto P. Dobnick, "The Wisconsin Central Story," *Trains*, September 1990, 35, 38.

116. Interview with Edward Burkhardt, October 23, 2013. After leaving the Wisconsin Central, Ed Burkhardt launched Rail World LLC, a railroad consulting, investment, and management firm. His connection with the Montreal, Maine & Atlantic Railway ended following that company's bankruptcy, triggered by the disastrous July 6, 2013, explosion of a train carrying crude petroleum in the center of Lac-Megantic, Quebec. This event killed forty-seven residents and destroyed multiple businesses and residences. Yet Burkhardt did not leave railroading. His Rail World operates Baltic Rail, a container-hauling railroad in Estonia; Rail Polska in Poland; and San Luis Central, a shortline in Colorado.

117. Dobnick, "Wisconsin Central Story," 32, 34; Steve Glischinski, "Ed Burkhardt and the All-American Regional Railroad," *Classic Trains*, Summer 2023, 64–65.

118. John F. Stover, *American Railroads* (Chicago: University of Chicago Press, 1961), 240, 247; Saunders, *Main Lines*, 282–285, 288.

119. Philip R. Hastings, "Jack Haley and His Chicago Central Crew," *Trains*, August 1986, 22.

120. Kathy Haley Buhrman, *Hear the Whistle: The Story of Jack Haley, American Entrepreneur and Railroad Pioneer* (Lincoln, NE: Steinauer, 2020), 11–66; *Des Moines Sunday Register*, June 2, 1985.

121. Hastings, "Jack Haley," 20; Buhrman, *Hear the Whistle*, 67; *Des Moines Sunday Register*, June 2, 1985.

122. Hofsommer, *Steel Trains of Hawkeyeland*, 259; Edward A. Lewis, *American Shortline Railway Guide*, 4th ed. (Milwaukee, WI: Kalmbach Books, 1991), 51.

123. Buhrman, *Hear the Whistle*, 2, 102–105.

124. Buhrman, *Hear the Whistle*, 108–109; *Des Moines Sunday Register*, May 20, 1985; Minneapolis *Star Tribune*, November 24, 1985; *Chicago Tribune*, February 23, 1986.

125. Peter Rickershauser to author, June 19, 2023 (hereafter cited as Rickershauser letter).

126. Steve Glischinski, "Seared, Burned, but Now Cooking: After a Flashy Start and Tumult, Chicago Central Is Quietly Successful," *Trains*, July 1992, 37–38.

127. Buhrman, *Hear the Whistle*, 120–127, 151; *Chicago Tribune*, February 11, 1986.

128. Gary Slutsker, "Working on the Railroads," *Forbes*, March 24, 1986, 128; Buhrman, *Hear the Whistle*, 118–120.

129. Buhrman, *Hear the Whistle*, 129, 144–145; Kent L. Peacock to Ray Jones, April 30, 1987, in possession of author; Hofsommer, *Steel Trains of Hawkeyeland*, 259. Although Chicago, Central & Pacific Railroad Company became the name selected, a more descriptive one was seriously considered: Chicago & Midwestern Railroad. Why the rejection? The name and reporting marks (CMW) were believed to be too close to those of the Chicago & North Western Railway (CNW). Railroad historian Richard Saunders thought the Chicago, Central & Pacific got stuck with a "corny name," and perhaps so.

130. John Rebensdorf to author, June 7, 2023.

131. Buhrman, *Hear the Whistle*, 142–144, 148; "Chicago Central & Pacific Grain Gathering Service," *Modern Railroads* 42 (June 1987): 20; Rickershauser letter; Glischinski, "Seared, Burned, but Now Cooking," 34–35.

132. Buhrman, *Hear the Whistle*, 158–159, 17.

133. Saunders, *Main Lines*, 286; John Rebensdorf to author, June 7, 2023. Jack Haley encountered income tax difficulties with the Internal Revenue Service. An ICG attorney was asked to assist in an investigation, remembering that Haley had allegedly fled to Brazil. Ultimately,

though, he spent his final days in the United States and lived freely.

134. Buhrman, *Hear the Whistle*, 167, 193; *Wall Street Journal*, September 18, 1987.

135. Glischinski, "Seared, Burned, but Now Cooking," 34–35; Michael W. Blaszak, "Illinois Central Wants to Rewrite Its Iowa History," *Trains*, April 1996, 16–18. The future of what was once Jack Haley's Cedar Valley Railroad appears dim. This trackage, which is owned and operated by Canadian National, remains in place between Waterloo, Iowa, and Glenville, Minnesota, where it joins the former Rock Island, now the Spine Line of the Union Pacific to Albert Lea, Minnesota. The track is out of service between Myrtle, Minnesota, and Glenville. Since CN has raised grain rates and is not supplying cars for these shipments, the only industry that is active is an ethanol plant at Mona, Iowa, and a feed mill at St. Ansgar, Iowa. Dan Sabin to author, August 19, 2023.

136. Grant, *Station Agent*, 128, 130–136.

137. Interview with Thomas Hoback, May 27, 2023 (hereafter cited as Hoback interview).

138. Grant, *Erie Lackawanna*, 212; Lewis, *American Shortline Railway Guide*, 3rd ed., 230; John T. Eagan Jr., *Erie Western in Color* (Scotch Plains, NJ: Morning Sun Books, 2016), 4, 25, 38; Joseph P. Schwieterman, *When the Railroad Leaves Town: American Communities in the Age of Rail Line Abandonment—Eastern United States* (Kirksville, MO: Truman State University Press, 2001), 76; Thomas Hoback to author, May 16, 2023.

139. Christopher Rund, Fred W. Frailey, and Eric Powell, *The Indiana Rail Road Company: America's New Regional Railroad*, rev. and expanded ed. (Bloomington: Indiana University Press, 2012), 42–44.

140. The owner of the J-K Line renamed the Tippecanoe Railroad after his two daughters, Jordyn and Katie, likely unique in the history of midwestern railroads.

141. Grant, *Erie Lackawanna*, 212; Hoback interview; Thomas Hoback to author, May 28, 2023; Lewis, *American Shortline Railway Guide*, 3rd ed., 230; Edward A. Lewis, *American Shortline Railway Guide*, 5th ed. (Greenberg Publishing, 1996), 163; Richard S. Simmons and Francis H. Parker, *Railroads of Indiana* (Bloom-ington: Indiana University Press, 1997), 185.

142. Rund, Frailey, and Powell, *Indiana Rail Road Company*, 44–46, 121.

143. Rund, Frailey, and Powell, *Indiana Rail Road Company*, 46–47.

144. ICG wished to retain the sixty-seven miles between Effingham and Sullivan because of the Marathon Oil facility and other on-line customers. The railroad had made a recent upgrade between Effingham and near Newton, Illinois, a distance of about twenty-five miles, to serve a coal-fired power plant.

145. Rund, Frailey, and Powell, *Indiana Rail Road Company*, 48.

146. Rund, Frailey, and Powell, *Indiana Rail Road Company*, 51–53, 55.

147. Hoback interview.

148. Lewis, *American Shortline Railway Guide*, 4th ed., 122; Rund, Frailey, and Powell, *Indiana Rail Road Company*, 139. The INRD dinner train did not endure. Increased traffic on the Indianapolis to Bargerville section led the company to sell this successful operation to investors, who relocated it to central Florida.

149. Rund, Frailey, and Powell, *Indiana Rail Road Company*, 137–138.

150. Hoback interview.

151. Thomas Hoback to author, July 3, 2023.

152. Trackage rights allow a railroad to operate over another company's line with its own motive power and crews. A haulage agreement is similar to trackage rights,

but the railroad that owns the line operates the power for the train that is being moved.

153. Hoback interview; Rickershauser letter.

154. Isaac Miller, "From B&O to BIP: Successful New Short Line in Southeast Ohio," *Railfan and Railroad* 42 (May 2023): 64–67.

155. David P. Morgan, "Who Shot the Passenger Train?," *Trains*, April 1959, 33.

156. *Wall Street Journal*, September 3, 1969; Frailey, *Twilight of the Great Trains*, 5.

157. Statement of Stuart Saunders before Surface Transportation Subcommittee, Senate Commerce Committee, 91st Congress, 1st Session, September 23, 1969, 184; Frailey, *Twilight of the Great Trains*, 171.

158. Frailey, *Twilight of the Great Trains*, 9.

159. The original working moniker, Railpax, might easily be corrupted. According to Amtrak official Arthur Lloyd, Railpax could become "Rail*pox*." Amtrak was less likely to be dubbed "Anthrax."

160. Geoffrey H. Doughty, Jeffery T. Darbee, and Eugene E. Harmon, *Amtrak, America's Railroad: Transportation's Orphan and Its Struggle for Survival* (Bloomington: Indiana University Press, 2021), 59–62; Frank N. Wilner, *Amtrak: Past, Present, Future* (Omaha, NE: Simmons-Boardman Books, 2012), 19, 26–27.

161. Grant, *Mighty Fine Road*, 239.

162. *Chicago Tribune*, April 30, 1969; David Garrard Lowe, *Lost Chicago* (Chicago: University of Chicago Press, 2010), 49.

163. Amtrak public timetable, May 1, 1971.

164. Eventually, the Michigan Department of Transportation acquired ownership of the line between Kalamazoo, Ann Arbor, and Dearborn. CSX or Norfolk Southern owned connecting trackage into Chicago and Detroit.

165. Bruce Goldberg, *Amtrak: The First Decade* (Silver Spring, MD: Alan Books, 1981), 88; Kevin M. McKinney, "At the Dawn of Amtrak," 51 (June 1991): 41; Doughty and Harmon, *Amtrak, America's Railroad*, 200–207. The Black Hawk was not the only Amtrak train in the Midwest to come and go during the 1970s and the early years of the twenty-first century. Six more are of note. There were two Chicago commuter trains, Indiana Connection and Calumet. The former operated from October 1979 to January 1986 and the latter from October 1979 to May 1991. The Kentucky Cardinal, an extension of the Hoosier State, began running between Indianapolis and Jeffersonville, Indiana (later extended to Louisville), in December 1999 but ended in July 2003. The Lake County Limited was short lived, being in service from Chicago to Janesville, Wisconsin, only from April 2000 to September 2001. Another train that did not last long was the Prairie Marksman connecting Chicago with Peoria. Its operation dated from August 1980 to October 1981. A non-Chicago commuter train was the Michigan Executive connecting Jackson, Michigan, with Detroit from January 1975 to January 1984. Finally, the River Cities represented expanded St. Louis service, linking the City of New Orleans at Centralia, Illinois, with St. Louis and Kansas City. It served this route from April 1984 to September 1994.

166. Middleton, Smerk, and Diehl, *Encyclopedia of North American Railroads*, 550, 552.

167. H. Roger Grant, *Visionary Railroader: Jervis Langdon, Jr. and the Transportation Revolution* (Bloomington: Indiana University Press, 2008), 98–99; David J. De Boer, *Piggyback and Containers: A History of Rail Intermodal on America's Steel Highways* (San Marino, CA: Golden West Books, 1992), 15.

168. Marc Levinson, *The Box: How the Shipping Container Made the World Smaller and the World Economy Bigger* (Princeton,

NJ: Princeton University Press, 2006), 51–53.

169. De Boer, *Piggyback and Containers*, 63–65; Brian Solomon, *Intermodal Railroading* (St. Paul, MN: Voyageur, 2007), 62–63.

170. "With Service Improved, C&NW's Falcons Are Bagging Bigger Game," *Railway Age*, May 30, 1977, 16–20.

171. Robert E. Gallamore, "Regulation and Innovation: Lessons from the American Railroad Industry," in *Essays in Transportation Economics and Policy*, ed. Jose A. Gomez-Ibanez, William B. Tye, and Clifford Winston (Washington, DC: Brookings Institution Press, 1999), 515–516; Richard D. Stone, *The Interstate Commerce Commission and the Railroad Industry: A History of Regulatory Policy* (Westport, CT: Praeger, 1991), 137; John H. White Jr., *On the Right Track: Some Historic Cincinnati Railroads* (Cincinnati, OH: Cincinnati Railroad Club, 2003), 37.

172. De Boer, *Piggyback and Containers*, 83–97.

173. Solomon, *Intermodal Railroading*, 145–155; "RoadRailer's Final Days?," *Railfan and Railroad* 42 (September 2023): 10–11.

174. See Cindy Wilson, *The Beautiful Snow: The Ingalls Family, the Railroads, and the Hard Winter of 1880–81* (St. Paul, MN: Beaver's Pond Press, 2020).

175. H. Roger Grant, *The Corn Belt Route: A History of the Chicago Great Western Railroad Company* (DeKalb: Northern Illinois University Press, 1984), 122–123.

176. Joseph C. O'Hearn, "The Winter of '36," *Trains*, December 1944, 20–26.

177. Jerry Pyfer, "The Part of Railroading I Could Do Without," *Trains*, December 1992, 54.

178. It would be wrong to suggest that earlier in the twentieth century the Midwest did not experience catastrophic flooding events. The worst one occurred during the later part of March 1913 and was centered in Indiana and Ohio. Between March 23 and March 27, more than eleven inches of rain fell at Richmond, Indiana. Similar amounts drenched large portions of the Buckeye State, including Akron, Columbus, and Dayton. The PRR bore the brunt of this weather disaster.

179. "Washout! Railroads Battle the Floods of '93," *Trains*, September 1993, 14–23; Stanley A. Changnon, *Railroads and Weather: From Fogs to Floods and Heat to Hurricanes, the Impacts of Weather and Climate on American Railroading* (Boston: American Meteorological Society, 2006), 34.

180. *New York Times*, March 18, March 19, September 11, 2019.

181. As of 2020 route railroad mileage for the eight midwestern states was as follows: Illinois, 6,883; Indiana, 4,041; Iowa, 3,828; Michigan, 3,465; Minnesota, 4,233; Missouri, 3,762; Ohio 5,330; and Wisconsin, 3,254.

EPILOGUE

1. Kevin P. Keefe, "The Promise of Silvis," *Classic Trains*, Fall 2023, 16–17; "Ride This Train!," *Trains*, May 2022, R2–R21; "BNSF Donates B40-8W to Silvis," *Railfan and Railroad* 42 (August 2023): 7.

2. Even before tourist railroads sprang up in the Midwest, determined railfans in the post–World War II years found opportunities to ride on several shortline carriers. Rail transportation journalist and editor J. David Ingles found three such roads in the region: Illinois Midland in Newark, Illinois; Louisville, New Albany & Corydon in Corydon, Indiana; and East Jordan & Southern in East Jordan, Michigan. See J. David Ingles, "Before There Were Tourist Lines," *Classic Trains*, Fall 2000, 46–49.

3. Isaac Miller, "50+ Years on Track: The Hocking Valley Scenic Railway Marks

a Half-Century on a Historic Ohio Route," *Trains*, May 2023, 19, 21–22.

4. Miller, "50+ Years on Track," 22–23.

5. Steve Glischinski, "North Shore Scenic Returns RDC to Missabe Line," *Trains*, December 1991, 34–36, 38.

6. Interview with Ed Robinson, October 27, 2023.

7. "Railroad Historical Society Directory," *Railfan and Railroad* 42 (May 2023): 68–70.

8. Railroaders in the Midwest and nationwide frequently called the caboose by other names. On the Burlington they were "waycars," on the Pennsylvania "cabins," and on some carriers and by some trainmen they might be "brain boxes," "buggies," "monkey buggies," "cabs," "crummies," "doghouses," or "vans."

9. William Benning Stewart, "The End," *Trains*, August 1990, 30, 33.

10. William D. Middleton, George M. Smerk, and Robert L. Diehl, eds., *Encyclopedia of North American Railroads* (Bloomington: Indiana University Press, 2007), 1060; John H. Armstrong, *The Railroad: What It Is, What It Does* (Omaha, NE: Simmons-Boardman Books, 1998), 112; Thomas Hoback to author, July 22, 2023; Kevin Keefe to author, August 22, 2023.

11. James Rueber to author, February 13, 2023.

12. *Akron* (OH) *Railroad Club Bulletin*, July–August, 2023, 5; Thomas Hoback to author, July 22, 2023; David Lassen and Bob Johnson, "Chicago–St. Louis Amtrak Trains Begin 110-mph Operation," *Trains*, September 2023, 8.

13. Interview with Thomas Hoback, May 27, 2023.

14. *Brass Switchkey Railnews*, May 14, 2023

INDEX

Page numbers in italics refer to illustrations.

H. ROGER GRANT was Kathryn and Calhoun Lemon Professor of History at Clemson University. He was author of more than thirty books, including *Sunset Cluster: A Shortline Railroad Saga*, *The Station Agent and the American Railroad Experience*, *A Mighty Fine Road: A History of the Chicago, Rock Island & Pacific Railroad Company*, and *Railroads and the American People*.

FOR INDIANA UNIVERSITY PRESS

TONY BREWER Artist and Book Designer

GARY DUNHAM Acquisitions Editor and Director

ANNA FRANCIS Assistant Acquisitions Editor

ANNA GARNAI Production Coordinator

KATIE HUGGINS Production Manager

ALYSSA LUCAS Marketing and Publicity Manager

DAVID MILLER Lead Project Manager/Editor

DAN PYLE Online Publishing Manager

JENNIFER WITZKE Senior Artist and Book Designer